BATTLE OF BRITAIN 1940

To all who lost their lives during the 'Finest Hour'

BATTLE OF BRITAIN 1940

THE FINEST HOUR'S HUMAN COST

Dilip Sarkar MBE FRHistS

AIR WORLD

AIR WORLD

BATTLE OF BRITAIN 1940
The Finest Hour's Human Cost

First published in Great Britain in 2020 and reprinted in 2025 by
Air World
An imprint of
Pen & Sword Books Ltd
Yorkshire – Philadelphia

ISBN 978 1 52679 796 4

A CIP catalogue record for this book is available from the British Library.

Typeset by SJmagic DESIGN SERVICES, India.

Printed and bound in the UK by CPI Group (UK) Ltd.

The Publisher's authorised representative in the EU for product safety is Authorised Rep Compliance Ltd., Ground Floor, 71 Lower Baggot Street, Dublin D02 P593, Ireland.
www.arccompliance.com

For a complete list of Pen & Sword titles please contact

PEN & SWORD BOOKS LIMITED
George House, Units 12 & 13, Beevor Street, Off Pontefract Road,
Barnsley, South Yorkshire, S71 1HN, England
E-mail: enquiries@pen-and-sword.co.uk
Website: www.pen-and-sword.co.uk

or

PEN AND SWORD BOOKS
1950 Lawrence Rd, Havertown, PA 19083, USA
E-mail: uspen-and-sword@casematepublishers.com
Website: www.penandswordbooks.com

Contents

Foreword

As a small boy, I was fascinated by stories of the Battle of Britain, with models of Spitfires and Hurricanes hanging from my bedroom ceiling, daily engaged once more in defending our nation from invasion. How could I have ever imagined that many years later I would have the immense privilege of counting members of Churchill's 'Few' as friends. As an RAF Chaplain I had long been involved with Battle of Britain events, but nothing could surpass being with 'The Few' at Memorial Day at Caple Le Fern, or Battle of Britain Sunday at Westminster Abbey.

Now those models on my ceiling had become real men, real heroes, claiming to be ordinary men and yet having done extraordinary things. It is all too easy to think of the 'great names' whose stories are recounted, but as Dilip Sarkar so skilfully reminds us in this book the Battle was fought and won by more than just those featured in the headlines.

In my growing relationship with 'The Few', (as Chaplain to the Battle of Britain Fighter Association) I learned so much from these 'ordinary' men who counted themselves not as heroes but as having simply done their duty. However, I also learned of the 'Human Cost' amongst those we call 'The Few' – hence why I am delighted that this book deals with this difficult and challenging theme.

To those of the Few who survived, the heroes of the Battle were those whose names are inscribed in *The Battle of Britain Roll of Honour* - which until recently those august survivors escorted in to the Abbey on Battle of Britain Sunday. Now, their successors, todays fighter pilots, represent them as they parade the Roll of Honour - a book of names, which is an aid to remembrance, but behind every name is an ever-increasing circle of those who are part of the Human Cost of such a Battle. Parents, wives, children, friends, colleagues all pay the cost when someone they love dies in conflict, and they do not forget. Neither should we.

This book helps us to do exactly that, by going behind the names, giving these men back their story. Dilip Sarkar's meticulous research puts both the ordinariness and extra-ordinariness of these men centre stage. He captures something of their personalities, their skill, and sense of duty and this helps us remember 'The Few' as they were. History is not just about events. It is also about people - and people are my business - and this is a book about people.

For anyone who is interested in the Battle of Britain, it is a 'must read' for it goes beyond the strategy and those wonderful aircraft to reveal the 'Human Cost'.

It is a book that is long overdue, and I am grateful for the opportunity in writing this foreword to once again say 'Thank you' to those we call the 'Few' and '*who by their valour and sacrifice did nobly save their day and generation'*.

The Venerable Ray J Pentland CB
Honorary Chaplain to The Battle of Britain Fighter Association

Group Captain Patrick Tootal OBE DL RAF (Ret'd)
Honorary Secretary
Battle of Britain Fighter Association
Battle of Britain Memorial Trust

The Venerable Ray Pentland and the author at Wing Commander JFD 'Tim' Elkington's Memorial Service, 11 May 2019.

FOREWORD

Group Captain Patrick Tootal with the author and Martin Mace of Frontline Books/ Pen & Sword, at the opening of Nicolson House in Southampton, commemorating Flight Lieutenant James Brindley Nicolson VC, on 19 October 2018.

Group Captain Patrick Tootal OBE DL, a former Hercules pilot now Honorary Secretary of the BoBFA and BoBMT - whose father was sadly a wartime pilot killed on operations with Bomber Command (Patrick Tootal).

Prologue

The time will come when thou shalt lift thine eyes
To watch a long-drawn battle in the skies;
While aged peasants, too amazed for words,
Stare at the flying fleets of wondrous birds.
England, so long the mistress of the sea,
Where wind and waves confess her sovereignty;
Her ancient triumphs yet on high shall bear
And reign, the sovereign of the conquered air.

The remarkable thing about that verse is that the English poet Thomas Gray wrote it in 1737 (*Luna Habitabillas*), 166 years before the Wright brothers made the world's first powered flight.

Eleven years after Orville and Wilbur first flew, a German airship dropped the first bomb on England – from which point on, warfare would never be the same again. To aircraft over-flying conventional ground and sea-borne forces, the actual front line was not a restriction; the reach of air power was limited only by an aircraft's range. Consequently, civilians on the Home Front found themselves very much in the line of fire, and no longer could Britain rely upon being an island for defence. Gray's, then, was quite some prophecy, one which became a traumatic reality for the British people in 1940.

On 1 September 1939, Nazi Germany invaded Poland, subsequently ignoring an ultimatum issued by Britain and France to withdraw. Two days later, Britain and France declared war on Hitler's Germany. Geographically, however, the western powers were not positioned to provide practical military support, and, inevitably, Poland was both first to fight and fall. There then followed a lull in which little happened. The Soviets finally overwhelmed the Finns, U-Boats continued attacking Britain's North Atlantic shipping, but elsewhere the 'Phoney War' persisted. With the exception of the Czechs and Poles, by early 1940 few people had so far unduly suffered from the conflict.

Britain's wartime leader, Winston Churchill, who mobilised the English language and, amongst others, coined the phrase 'Finest Hour' in his speech of 18 June 1940.

In early April, Hitler attacked Denmark and Norway, drawing Anglo-French forces into a hopeless campaign in inhospitable terrain. A month later came the long-expected attack on Holland, Belgium, Luxembourg and France, Germany taking the Allies completely by surprise with *Blitzkrieg* tactics. Indeed, this remains one of the most unanticipated and shocking victories in history. On that fateful day, 10 May 1940, Winston Churchill succeeded Neville Chamberlain as Britain's Prime Minister – and lost no time pointing out to the House of Commons that all he could offer at that perilous and uncertain time was 'blood, tears, toil and sweat'.

On the continent, highly mobile *Panzer* divisions negotiated the supposedly impassable Ardennes, outflanking the Maginot Line, paralysing the Allied command system and cutting off the British Expeditionary Force in a pocket around Dunkirk. The *Luftwaffe* enjoyed complete aerial superiority over the battlefield, making this lightning advance to the Channel ports possible. While the subsequent evacuation of over 330,000 Allied troops from the flat beaches around that French port was propagandised as a glorious victory, in reality the Fall of France was catastrophic. On 10 June, Italy's Mussolini declared war on the Allies, extending the conflict to the Mediterranean and North Africa. When France asked for an armistice shortly afterwards, Hitler hoped that Britain would do likewise. On 4 June, however, Winston Churchill had made Britain's stance clear:-

'Even though large tracts of Europe and many old and famous states have fallen, or may fall into the grip of the Gestapo and all the odious apparatus of Nazi rule, we shall not flag or fail. We shall go on to the end. We shall fight in France. We shall fight on the seas and oceans, we shall fight with growing confidence and growing strength in the air. We shall fight on the beaches, we shall fight on the landing-grounds, we shall fight in the fields and in the streets, we shall fight in the hills, we shall never surrender.'

Although it has been convincingly argued that Britain stood on the shoulders of its Empire and Commonwealth, in military terms Britain really was alone – and only its shores, not those of Commonwealth or Empire nations, were within range of German bombers and threatened by invasion. America, still smarting from casualties suffered during the still recent First World War, although largely sympathetic, steadfastly pursued its policy of Isolationism from events in Europe. Given Hitler's breathtaking military success to date, there was little beyond Churchill's stirring rhetoric to suggest that David would beat Goliath in the battle ahead.

An iconic image of the 'Finest Hour': St Paul's during the *Blitz*.

After the Fall of France, described by Churchill as 'a colossal defeat', there was a further lull, while Hitler made plans and regrouped. The *Führer* now considered an unanticipated opportunity: a seaborne invasion of southern England. Hitler's infamous Directive Number 16 stated his aims: -

'As England, despite her hopeless military situation, still shows no sign of willingness to come to terms, I have decided to prepare, and if necessary to carry out, a landing operation against her. The aim of this operation is to eliminate the English motherland as a base from which war against Germany can be continued and, if necessary, to occupy completely.'

Thirteen divisions of the German army, each some 19,000 strong, moved to the Channel coast as the vanguard of a landing force comprising thirty-nine divisions. Plans were made to disembark 125,000 men in Kent and Sussex during the first three days of the proposed invasion,

After his unprecedented victory on the continent, Hitler was presented with the unexpected opportunity to invade Britain – and issued orders for this on 16 July 1940. Deputy *Führer* and *Luftwaffe* chief *Reichsmarschall* Hermann Göring, tasked with achieving aerial superiority, was sublimely confident, expecting Britain to last only 'two or three weeks'.

On 20 August 1940, Churchill immortalised the aircrew of Fighter Command by describing them as the 'Few'. Pictured here are Pilot Officers David Crook DFC (left) and Geoffrey Gaunt of 609 'West Riding' Squadron; Crook was reported missing in 1944, Gaunt was killed in action on 'Battle of Britain Day'.

codenamed Operation *Seelöwe* (Sealion). To transport this force across the *Kanal*, the German navy assembled a makeshift invasion fleet of 170 large transport vessels, 1,500 barges, and several hundred tugs, trawlers, motor boats and fishing smacks. As the *Kriegsmarine* was hopelessly inferior to the Royal Navy in warships of every category, the German service chiefs agreed that the operation could only succeed if the *Luftwaffe* controlled the skies before the invasion fleet set sail. Reichsmarschall Hermann Göring was supremely confident: 'My *Luftwaffe* is invincible… And so now we turn to England. How long will this one last – two or three weeks?'

On 18 June 1940, Churchill again stirred the British people: -

'What General Weygand called the Battle of France is over. I expect that the Battle of Britain is about to begin. Upon this battle depends the survival of Christian civilisation. Upon it depends our own British life, and the long continuity of our institutions and our Empire. The whole fury and might of the enemy must very soon be turned on us. Hitler knows that he will have to break us in this island or lose the war. If we can stand up to him,

Group Captain Sir Douglas Bader was always quick to emphasise that the Battle of Britain was not won by a handful of 'aces' but by 'kids of nineteen or twenty'.

all Europe may be free and the life of the world may move forward into broad, sunlit uplands. But if we fail, then the whole world, including the United States, including all that we have known and cared for, will sink into the abyss of a new Dark Age, made more sinister, and perhaps more protracted, by the lights of perverted science. Let us therefore brace ourselves to our duties, and so bear ourselves that if the British Empire and its Commonwealth last for a thousand years, men will still say, "This was their finest hour"'.

Thus, the phrase 'Finest Hour' was coined – and so the rest of 1940, that most tempestuous year, would prove to be.

Officially, the Battle of Britain is considered to have begun on 10 July 1940, concluding sixteen weeks later on 31 October – by which date the *Luftwaffe* had failed to destroy Fighter Command and achieve aerial supremacy. Indeed, on 17 September, Hitler had postponed *Seelöwe* 'indefinitely'. Moreover, on 27 September, Hitler ordered that preparations be made for the invasion of Russia. Eastward expansion had always been Hitler's real war aim. Indeed from Hitler's perspective, continuing to pursue the prospect of invading Britain at this time was pointless, because as a small island Britain had not the natural resources or living space required by his Nazi empire. Alone, without essential American military support, Britain appeared hardly to be in a position to continue any significant resistance in the long term, so could be left, isolated, without undue risk, while Russia, the infinitely greater prize, was conquered. Britain could be dealt with later. This would prove to be a fatal error.

Although 31 October 1940 represents the Battle of Britain's official conclusion, German bombers continued pounding Britain by night until May 1941, and fighters of both sides clashed until the weather finally brought the 'season' to a close in February 1941. Because of Fighter Command, however, Britain remained in the war. This crucial British victory, unexpected across the Atlantic, marked a new level of American commitment and closer support of the war effort.

On 22 June 1941, Hitler invaded Russia; on 7 December 1941 the Japanese made a devastating, surprise air attack on the American Pacific fleet at Pearl Harbor. That night Churchill wrote of how he had been 'saturated and satiated with emotion and sensation, I went to bed and slept the sleep of the saved and thankful'. On 11 December 1941, Hitler, already fighting on two fronts, sealed the fate of Nazi Germany: he declared war on the United States of America. Ultimately, America poured men and materiel into Britain, from where, on 6 June 1944, the Allies eventually launched the liberation of enemy-occupied Europe. With the Russians investing Berlin, on 30 April 1945 Adolf Hitler committed suicide in his underground bunker. On 8 May, Germany surrendered unconditionally. In the Far East, the war against Japan continued until the Emperor surrendered – by which time the United States had avenged the ignominy of Pearl Harbor by dropping atomic bombs on Hiroshima and Nagasaki.

Without Fighter Command's victory in the Battle of Britain however, this Total Victory would not have been possible.

Nearly 3,000 aircrew of Fighter Command were combatants during the Battle of Britain. Of them, 544 lost their lives during the Battle; 791 more would perish before the war was won. On 20 August 1940, Churchill immortalised the aircrew concerned, who were still fighting this decisive battle: -

'Never was so much owed by so many to so Few'.

Later, Group Captain Sir Douglas Bader emphasised that the Battle had not been won by a handful of 'aces': -

'The Battle of Britain was won not by Malan, Stanford-Tuck and me, who got all the accolades. It was won by kids of nineteen or twenty, who maybe shot down nothing, or just one, before being killed themselves. They were the blokes who really won the Battle of Britain, make no mistake there. They were determined, by going off to fight and being prepared to die if necessary.'

Indeed Lord Dowding, Fighter Command's chief during the Battle of Britain, wrote in 1969: -

'I do not think that one should consider what happened in the battle in terms of individuals and personalities. It is more fitting to think of us as a team – men and women, aircrews and groundcrews, and operations and staff at all levels – in which everyone played an integral part. But for all the warmth of my feeling for those with whom I was associated in the fighting of the battle, I think that we should remember, with a very special esteem, those who did the actual fighting: the aircrews.'

Lord Dowding was surely right. While the pilots, navigators and gunners did do the fighting and deserve a special place in history, we must not forget that behind them was a great supporting infrastructure of ground staff, including aircraft engineers, armourers and numerous others, in addition to members of the Women's Auxiliary Air Force who performed various duties such as Operations Room work and nursing. These essential personnel were bombed, machine-gunned, and also suffered casualties. Moreover, the initial phase of the Battle of Britain was fought over the 'Coal Scuttle Brigade', merchant ships carrying coal to Southampton. A number of ships were sunk or damaged, and many seamen lost their lives. Not widely known is that a substantial number of these unfortunate sailors were from India, China and Hong Kong. Furthermore, owing to the reach of air power, many civilians also died during our 'Finest Hour' – some while toiling in vulnerable factories to produce Spitfires and other crucial weapons. When we think of the Battle of Britain, then, we should not just think in terms of the 'Few', but of the entire 'Home Team', which collectively made victory possible or stood fast against the threat of invasion. This book is a tribute all of those who gave their lives – and those left behind to endure the agony of their loss.

As time marches on, research into individual casualties becomes increasingly difficult. This, for example, is the grave at St Botolph's, Farnborough, Warwickshire, of Pilot Officer Peter King, an only son, a Spitfire pilot killed in action during the Battle of Britain, no living relatives of whom could be found.

Each chapter in this book concerns an individual, which can be read as a stand-alone account, or, preferably, as part of the whole. Traditionally, historians' focus has been on official documents and survivors' accounts. This book is different. My personal motivation has always been researching and sharing the stories of casualties, giving the dead, if you will, a voice. These stories are not widely known, most here being told in full for the first time. Such research as this is becoming increasingly difficult the further in time we become distanced from events. Rarely, for example, is it possible today to talk to someone who actually knew the casualty in his lifetime. Instead, if lucky, the liaison is with their family's second or even third generations, who are reliant for information upon whatever their ancestors have left behind and preserved. In rare cases this comprises an unseen treasure-trove of rich material; in most, the sources are fragmentary, incomplete and often minimal. Sadly, all too often, such as with Pilot Officer Peter King, a Spitfire pilot killed in action with 66 Squadron, it proves impossible to trace any living relatives. In some cases, no photograph of the casualty can be found, meaning that the likeness of an individual, having made the 'ultimate sacrifice', has been lost to history. That, perhaps, emphasises the sadness of it all, when, at no small human cost, Britain emerged triumphant from the 'Finest Hour', 'the sovereign of the conquered air'.

Author's Note & Glossary

The aviation-minded reader will notice that I have referred to German *Messerschmitt* fighters by the abbreviation 'Me' (not 'Bf', which is more technically correct), or simply by their numeric designation, such as '109' or '110'. This not only reads better but is authentic: during the Battle of Britain, Keith Lawrence, a New Zealander, flew Spitfires and once said to me, 'To us they were just "Me's", "109s" or "110s", simple, never "Bf".'

Regarding photographs, certain images for this book were supplied by the families involved and enthusiast friends. The remainder are from my own archive, collated over more than thirty years.

In another attempt to preserve accuracy, I have also used the original German wherever possible regarding terms associated with the *Luftwaffe*, such as: -

Adlerangriff	'Attack of the Eagles'
Adlertag	'Eagle Day'
Eichenlaub	The Oak Leaves, essentially being a bar to the *Ritterkreuz*.
Erprobungsgruppe	Experimental group, in the case of *Erprobungsgruppe* 210, a skilled precision bombing unit.
Experte	A fighter 'ace'. Ace status, on both sides, was achieved by destroying five enemy aircraft.
Freie hunt	A fighter sweep.
Gefechstand	Operations headquarters.
Geschwader	The whole group, usually of three gruppen.
Geschwaderkommodore	The group leader.
Gruppe	A wing, usually of three squadrons.
Gruppenkeil	A wedge formation of bombers, usually made up of vics of three.

Gruppenkommandeur	The wing commander.
Jagdbomber (‘*Jabo*’)	Fighter-bomber.
Jagdflieger	Fighter pilot.
Jagdgeschwader	Fighter group, abbreviated JG.
Jagdwaffe	The fighter force.
Jäger	Hunter, in this context a fighter pilot or aircraft.
Kampfflieger	Bomber aircrew.
Kampfgeschwader	Bomber group, abbreviated KG.
Kanal	English Channel.
Katchmarek	Wingman.
Lehrgeschwader	Literally a training group, but actually a precision bombing unit, abbreviated LG.
Luftflotte	Air Fleet.
Oberkannone	Literally the ‘Top Gun’, or leading fighter ace.
Oberkommando der Wehrmacht (OKW)	The German armed forces high command.
Ritterkreuz	The Knight’s Cross of the Iron Cross.
Rotte	A pair of fighters, comprising leader and wingman, into which the *Schwarm* broke once battle was joined.
Rottenführer	Leader of a fighting pair.
Schwarm	A section of four fighters.
Schwarmführer	Section leader.
Stab	Staff
Stabschwarm	Staff flight.
Staffel	A squadron.
Staffelkapitän	The squadron leader.
Störflug	Harrassing attacks, usually by lone Ju 88s.
Stuka	The Ju 87 dive-bomber.
Sturkampfgeschwader	Dive-bomber group, abbreviated StG.
Vermisst	Missing.
Zerstörer	Literally ‘destroyer’, the term used for the Me 110.
Zerstörergeschwader	Destroyer group, abbreviated ZG.

Each *geschwader* generally comprised three *gruppen*, each of three *staffeln*. Each *gruppe* is designated by Roman numerals, i.e. III/JG 26 refers to the third *gruppe* of Fighter Group (abbreviated ‘JG’) 26. *Staffeln* are identified by numbers, so 7/JG 26 is the 7th *staffel* and belongs to III/JG 26.

Rank comparisons may also be useful: -

Gefreiter	Private 1st Class
Unteroffizier	Corporal, no aircrew equivalent in Fighter Command.
Feldwebel	Sergeant
Oberfeldwebel	Flight Sergeant
Leutnant	Pilot Officer
Oberleutnant	Flight Lieutenant
Hauptmann	Squadron Leader
Major	Wing Commander
Oberst	Group Captain

RAF Abbreviations: -

AAF	Auxiliary Air Force
AASF	Advance Air Striking Force
A&AEE	Aeroplane & Armament Experimental Establishment
AFC	Air Force Cross
AFDU	Air Fighting Development Unit
AI	Airborne Interception radar
AOC	Air Officer Commanding
AOC-in-C	Air Officer Commanding-in-Chief
ATA	Air Transport Auxiliary
ATS	Armament Training School
BEF	British Expeditionary Force
CAS	Chief of the Air Staff
CFS	Central Flying School
CGS	Central Gunnery School
CO	Commanding Officer
DES	Direct Entry Scheme
DFC	Distinguished Flying Cross
DFM	Distinguished Flying Medal
DSO	Distinguished Service Order
E/A	Enemy Aircraft
EFTS	Elementary Flying Training School
FAA	Fleet Air Arm
FIU	Fighter Interception Unit
FTS	Flying Training School
ITW	Initial Training Wing

LAC	Leading Aircraftman
MRAF	Marshal of the Royal Air Force
MSFU	Merchant Ship Fighter Unit
NCO	Non-Commissioned Officer
ORB	Operations Record Book
OTC	Officer Training Corps
OTU	Operational Training Unit
PDC	Personnel Distribution Centre
RAFVR	Royal Air Force Volunteer Reserve
RFS	Reserve Flying School
RN	Royal Navy
RNAS	Royal Navy Air Service
SASO	Senior Air Staff Officer
SOO	Senior Operations Officer
SSC	Short Service Commission
UAS	University Air Squadron
U/S	Unserviceable

Chapter One

Sergeant Patrick Sherlock Hayes

65 'East India' Squadron
Missing in Action: 7 July 1940

Patrick Sherlock Hayes was born on 17 March 1916, the son of Robert, a civil servant, and Agnes Clara Patricia Hayes, in Leamington Spa, Warwickshire. Later, the family moved to Beckenham in Kent, and in September 1930 Patrick became a boarder at King's College, a private school in Taunton, Somerset. In March 1932, he left King's College to train with the Midland Bank in London, the air-minded youngster joining the Bank's Flying Club. Patrick had grown up in the shadow of the First World War, Europe's first, shocking, head-on collision with industrial warfare, and the prospect of another war with Germany was never far away. Far from the First having been the 'War to end all wars', as it was hoped, ironically the subsequent Paris Peace Settlement of 1919 laid the foundations for an even greater global conflagration. For some fit, intelligent and well-educated young men of the period, however, the prospect of another war also provided an unanticipated but immensely exciting opportunity: to become an RAF pilot and fly.

The provision of that opportunity had not been without difficulty. Historically, the responsibility for British military aviation had been shared by the army-controlled Royal Flying Corps (RFC) and the Royal Navy Air Service (RNAS). In spite of loud protests by both the Admiralty and War Office, the Royal Air Force (RAF) was born on 1 April 1918. By the Armistice, the junior service was the largest air force in the world and enjoyed technical superiority, with a strength of 22,000 aircraft and 188 operational squadrons. After the Paris Peace Conference, however, the world was understandably eager to disarm, and Britain lost no time in reducing the size of all three services. By the end of 1919, the RAF had been stripped to just 371 aircraft of all types and a mere twelve squadrons, such statistics hardly justifying the air force's status as an independent service. But the RAF's first Chief of the Air Staff (CAS) Air Chief Marshal (ACM) Sir Hugh Trenchard, believed strongly that a powerful air force could deter a potential aggressor – the strength of his convictions fortunately allied to an equally robust personality.

Patrick Hayes was a keen photographer, taking some remarkable snapshots of his time on 65 Squadron at Hornchurch, before and during the early war period – including this pre-war 65 Squadron Hawker Demon. (Michel Taylor)

On 11 December 1919, Trenchard's proposal concerning every detail of how his service should be developed was delivered to Parliament as a White Paper. The memorandum was entirely comprehensive, covering all aspects necessary to create an effective modern air force. According to Derek Wood and Derek Dempster, Trenchard's plan proved to be 'a model for most air forces of the world and stand the test of time'.

Fortunate for the RAF though Trenchard's appointment and intervention was, it was actually not good news for Britain's fighter force. Trenchard was a committed 'Bomber Baron'. Many influential people in both the services and in civilian life believed in the so-called 'knock-out blow' – which could only be delivered to an enemy by bombers. Indeed, such was the bomber's perceived power, Trenchard considered it unnecessary 'for an air force, in order to defeat the enemy nation, to defeat its armed forces first. Air power can dispense with that immediate step, can pass over the enemy navies and armies, and penetrate air defences and attack direct the centre of production, transportation and communication from which the enemy war effort is maintained. It is on the destruction of enemy industries and, above all, in the lowering of morale of enemy nationals

Sergeant Patrick Hayes, 65 Squadron. (Michael Taylor)

caused by bombing that the ultimate victory lies.' In 1932, Stanley Baldwin, then Prime Minister, emphasised the fear of bombing: 'I think it is as well for the man in the street to realise that there is no power on earth that can save him from being bombed. Whatever people may tell him, the bomber will always get through. The only defence is offence, which means that you have to kill more women and children more quickly than the enemy if you want to save yourselves.' What precious little spending there was on British air power between the wars, certainly until 1935, was overwhelmingly, therefore, focussed on the bomber force. This is unsurprising, considering Trenchard's view in 1921 that the aeroplane was 'a shockingly bad weapon for defence' and that the use of fighters was 'only necessary to keep up the morale of your own people'. Trenchard's doctrine revolved almost entirely around offensive operations. Defence was sidelined with the absolute bare minimum of resources.

Sergeant Peter Morfill, who later became an 'ace' with 501 Squadron, decorated with the DFM. He survived the war and died in 2004. (Michael Taylor)

Although reduced to a shadow of its former self in the immediate wake of the First World War, it was always intended that Trenchard's RAF could easily be expanded, should that ever prove necessary. The first half of the 1930s saw Britain and other nations 'hell-bent', according to Sir Maurice Dean, 'for collective security and prepared to accept incalculable risks in that cause'. In 1932, Britain abandoned what was a miniscule rearmament programme. A year later, Adolf Hitler and the Nazis came to power in Germany. Essentially Hitler's main aims were to overthrow the hated 1919 Treaty of Versailles, which severely restricted Germany's armed forces, and achieve 'living space' for the German people by territorial expansion, waging a racial war. The *Führer* immediately set about contravening both the military restrictions and what were seen in Germany as territorial injustices, rebuilding the *Wehrmacht* in the process. In 1934 Britain revisited rearmament, but given the restricted spending involved, Dean charged that 'even now Britain was not taking its problems seriously'. It was not just a reluctance to rearm that had contributed to this sorry scenario, however.

According to Angus Calder in his expansive *The People's War*, the 1930s were 'the best of times, the worst of times'. In 1929, the world had been plunged into an economic crisis when the Wall Street stock market infamously crashed, the resulting fiscal chaos directly affecting the next decade. The celebrated British novelist and broadcaster J.B. Priestley famously made his celebrated *English Journey* in 1934, finding 'three Englands': the old and traditional, green and pleasant land; that of Victorian industrialisation; and finally a new, American inspired, revived, England of 'motor coaches, wireless, hiking, factory girls looking like actresses' and belonging 'far more to the age itself than to this particular island'. Prosperity was largely confined to the 'New Britain' of the area south of a line between the rivers Severn and Humber. North of that line was the demoralized and declining 'nineteenth-century Britain'. The countryside too was hard-hit by the depression. In 1932, unemployment stood at 2,750,000. The British government between the wars, therefore, had serious social issues at home to deal with. Against this calamitous backdrop Nazi Germany busied itself with re-armament, while Churchill later wrote that so far as British military spending was concerned the years 1931-35 were those of 'the locust'.

'Locusts' or not, in November 1934 Stanley Baldwin told the House of Commons that Britain would 'in no conditions... accept any position of inferiority with regard to what Air Force may be raised in Germany in the future'. According to Dean, though, 'the plan of air re-armament adopted was quite inadequate to fulfil the pledge, and was indeed little more than a façade'. The simple truth was that neither the government nor British people were yet ready to pay the price required for aerial parity with

65 Squadron's groundcrew dismantling a crashed Spitfire, the circumstances of which are unknown. (Michael Taylor)

Nazi Germany. Moreover, the price would now be paid for Trenchard's offensive doctrine. In the mid-1930s the Air Staff still believed in a strict numerical ratio of fighters to bombers. This was, however, meaningless, because, again as Dean wrote, 'the requirements of defence' should be 'determined by the area to be defended and the nature of the probable attack'. The size of the bomber force, of course, was dictated by quite different factors. In sum, the complete lack of substantial re-armament and deficiencies in doctrinal thinking were caused by three things: financial constraints, the indifference of or opposition by politicians, and Trenchard's offensive thinking. Information received in Britain during 1935, however, confirmed that although Germany was unlikely to be ready for war until 1939, Hitler's preparations towards that end were so substantial that the threat could no longer be ignored. So, albeit tentatively, Britain at last began to rearm.

On 25 February 1936, Expansion Scheme 'F' was approved by the Treasury: 124 squadrons (1,736 aircraft of all types) by April 1937. Intelligence suggested that Germany's target was 2,000 front-line aircraft. Light bombers were dropped from the RAF programme, prioritising instead bombers with increased range and performance.

Another unrecorded mishap to a 65 Squadron Spitfire Mk IA. (Michael Taylor)

A trio of 65 Squadron make a low pass over Hornchurch. (Michael Taylor)

The previous expansion plan, Scheme 'C' of 1935, proposed 800 bombers to 420 fighters. While Scheme 'F' increased the number of bombers to 1,000, it maintained the existing fighter strength. Significantly, though, Scheme 'F' led directly to the formation, in April 1937, of the RAF Volunteer Reserve (RAFVR), which planned to recruit and train a total of 8,100 pilots, observers and wireless operators (air gunner) by the end of 1938. From the regular service 4,000 more pilots and 1,264 observers were required in the years 1936-39. Things had at last started moving in the right direction.

Trenchard's original concept had included another initiative aimed at providing a trained reserve for use in an emergency: the Auxiliary Air Force (AAF). Based on a County Association similar to the Territorial Army (TA), the AAF (much more of which later) comprised locally raised units, part-time in nature, and thereby unsuitable to train the numbers of aircrew which would soon be needed. The RAFVR, therefore, although part-time, was not based upon County Associations but on centres of population, particularly those of industrial areas. Flying training was provided at weekends by civilian flying firms, contracted to the Air Ministry, at aerodromes associated with town centres at which reservists, still holding down their full-time jobs, studied ground subjects during weekday evenings. Reservists were also expected to attend a two-week annual camp at an RAF aerodrome. Whereas the AAF was a social *corps d'élite*, many of its pilots being wealthy young

Spitfire K9910, FZ-N, being recovered following Sergeant Hayes's landing accident on 9 May 1939. (Michael Taylor)

men who had the means to fly their own aircraft privately for pleasure, the RAFVR, however, was based upon a 'Citizen Volunteer' principle intended to have a wide, popular, appeal – importantly with a common mode of entry and a commissioning scheme based upon merit, not social class. By the end of 1937, there were 845 reservists learning to fly with the nineteen civilian flying schools involved.

On 9 May 1937, Patrick Hayes, a clerk with the Midland Bank, answered the call, joining the RAFVR in London, grasping an unprecedented opportunity to become a pilot at His Majesty's expense.

Unfortunately detail in Patrick's RAF Service Record is sparse, as is so often the case. Where he undertook *ab initio* flying training is not documented, although he attended mandatory annual summer training camps at Redhill in 1937 and 1938, and we know that on 1 May 1939 he had been allocated to 65 'East India' Squadron at Hornchurch. This was a regular RAF unit, re-formed in 1934, as the press reported on 2 September: 'One of the most famous of the RAF war squadrons, afterwards disbanded, is being re-formed at Hornchurch aerodrome, near London. This is 65 Squadron, formed in August 1916 and which, equipped with Sopwith Camel biplanes, went to France in October 1917. It will now have two-seater Demons. The greatest air battle in which 65 Squadron was engaged occurred on 3 April 1918. While flying over the German lines in company with another RAF squadron it was attacked by an equal number of German scouting planes. Five enemy machines were destroyed, the remainder retreating over their own lines. The thirty British aeroplanes engaged returned safely.'

In July 1936, 65 Squadron exchanged its Demons for Gloster Gauntlets, re-equipping with Gladiators in July 1937. On 23 October, the 65 Squadron Operations Record Book (ORB) reported: 'Visit of German Air Mission to No 65 Squadron, *General der Flieger* Milch, Secretary of State for Air, *Generalleutnant* Stumpff, Chief of Air Staff, *Generalmajor* Ernest Udet, Director of Technical Equipment RLM, and Major Polte, accompanied by the AOC Fighter Command and the AOC 11 (F) Group and also the German Air Attaché.' *Generaloberst* Hans-Jürgen Stumpff, as he later became, would in due course command *Luftflotte* 5 during the forthcoming Battle of Britain – and together with his colleagues was no doubt delighted to see the RAF still biplane-equipped in 1937, whereas the *Luftwaffe* was already completely re-equipping its fighter arm with the new, modern, Me 109 monoplane fighter. Indeed, it would be some time later, on 21 March 1939, that 65 Squadron swapped its obsolete Gladiators for the new Supermarine Spitfire, this process completed by 19 April. The following day, 65 Squadron participated in Empire Air Day, with their fellow Hornchurch Spitfire squadrons, 54 and 74. While RAF Fighter Command was now achieving some kind of parity with the Germans, the *Luftwaffe* had a unique advantage: its *Kondor Legion* had fought in the Spanish Civil War, for Franco, in the mid-1930s, there gaining combat experience driving the development of sound, modern, tactics and weapons. While the RAF impressed the public with displays of close formation flying on Empire Air Days, having actually been to war would soon prove an immeasurable advantage to the Germans.

In September 1938, Adolf Hitler went to the brink over the Sudetenland, an area of largely German-speakers ceded to the new state of Czechoslovakia after the First World War. Hitler demanded that the Sudetenland was returned to the *Reich*, which it was, by Britain and France, against the Czechs' wishes, who were not even party to negotiations. The British Prime Minister, Neville Chamberlain, returned from Munich, brandishing his piece of paper guaranteeing 'Peace in our time', bearing the *Führer*'s signature as a solemn promise that there would be no war between Britain and Germany.

In March 1939 Germany absorbed what was left of Czechoslovakia into its Nazi empire. That month, Britain promised to support Poland in the event of any German aggression. On 1 May, Patrick Hayes left his Midland Bank job for good and joined 65 Squadron at Hornchurch on a full-time basis. What a contrast – from desk to Spitfire cockpit!

A few days later, Sergeant Hayes had a mishap, as the *Daily Express* reported on 9 May 1939: *Reserve pilot lands 365 mph plane on one wheel*. According to the newspaper's 'Air Reporter', Sergeant Hayes was 'Skimming above the ground at 80 mph to land at Hornchurch (Essex) yesterday, a 1,000 horse-power Spitfire fighter hit a tradesman's van in Southend-road beside the airfield. RAF men saw the back door of the van ripped off. But instead of crashing the 365 mph plane roared into the air again, with one leg of its undercarriage broken and hanging useless. Here is the rest of the story, from two points of view: -

1. The man in the plane. Pilot-Sergeant Hayes of the RAF Volunteer Reserve – who was flying a Spitfire for only the second time – heard this radio call from the ground as his plane zoomed upwards: 'One leg of your undercarriage is broken. Circle near the field until your petrol is nearly exhausted. Then land as slowly as you can.' A Spitfire pilot cannot see underneath his wings, so an officer on the airfield had rushed to the radio transmitter to warn him about his landing gear. He was told to use up his petrol because to land a one-legged plane with full tanks meant risking fire if the machine should crash. As Hayes droned round for an hour and a half, waiting for his tricky landing, he saw hundreds of RAF men and civilians watching him. He saw fire engines and an ambulance move out to be near the spot where he would come down. They were not needed. While the watchers held their breath, Hayes flattened out his damaged plane and touched its good wheel down. The machine settled with a jerk. Then he calmly unfastened his safety belt while RAF men crowded round cheering.

2. The men (and boy) with the van. Two men and a boy were with the grocery van that the Spitfire hit. – John Bush and James Farraway, both of North Road, South Ockenden, Essex, and fourteen-year-old Douglas Gaskin, from Grays, Essex. Farraway said 'I saw the plane coming straight at us, and I threw myself down on the ground. Bush dashed round the side of the van. Then came the crash as the back of the van was torn off. When I looked up, the plane was high in the air again. Douglas, our van boy, never turned a hair.'

Misjudged his approach though he had, Sergeant Hayes had certainly salvaged the situation by landing with minimal damage to His Majesty's aircraft, no loss of life – providing good copy for the tabloids. At this time, pilots were converted on squadrons to the types of aircraft they would fly operationally, and it was with this process that Sergeant Hayes was now engaged, clocking up flying hours on the Spitfire. Meanwhile the situation in eastern Europe was simmering away all that summer, soon to boil over.

On 23 August, the Nazi-Soviet Non-Aggression Pact was signed, allying the two powers and essentially giving Hitler a mandate to invade Poland. Clearly, war with Germany was now as imminent as it was unavoidable, so on 24 August thousands of British reservists were called up. On 1 September 1939, Germany finally invaded Poland, ending years of tension and uncertainty. That day, mothers, children and the disabled were officially evacuated from London and other major cities, thousands of people pouring through mainline stations into rural areas. At dusk, the blackout began. The Second World War had begun.

On 2 September 1939, the 65 Squadron ORB recorded that 'As a result of Germany having resorted to force in her effort to regain Danzig and

K9910 under tow back to dispersal. (Michael Taylor)

occupy the Polish Corridor, mobilisation was declared in Great Britain.' At 1100 hrs on 3 September 1939, Britain declared war on Germany, France following suit at 1700 hrs. On that momentous day, Sergeant P.S. Hayes was one of three non-commissioned officer (NCO) pilots in Flight Lieutenant G.A.W. 'Sammy' Saunders' 'B' Flight (amongst whose officers were two future fighter aces and wing leaders, namely Robert Stanford Tuck and Brian Fabris Kingcome). Patrick's parents were also doing their 'bit', his father enrolling as an air raid warden (ARP), his mother as a Red Cross nurse. And now started the so-called 'Phoney War', as Germany finished off Poland, and Lord Gort's British Expeditionary Force (BEF) went over to France, bolstering the border of France with neutral Belgium. Despite false alarms and other panics, and even the infamous 'Battle of Barking Creek' in which Spitfire pilots mistakenly shot down and killed a Hurricane pilot, no 'knockout-blow', fortunately, materialised. In truth, no-one really knew what to expect, although the fate of Guernica in Spain and Poland's Warsaw gave clear clues.

Understandably, the inexperienced and untried defences were a bit nervous to start with, 65 Squadron typically flying many patrols responding to reports of incoming enemy aircraft, which inevitably transpired to either be friendlies or erroneous. On 6 September 1939, both flights were subjected to anti-aircraft fire while over Sheerness, although Flight Lieutenant Saunders was fortunately uninjured when his Spitfire was twice hit by shrapnel. In October, the squadron left Hornchurch for Northolt, to the north-west of London, remaining there throughout that first winter of war. 65 Squadron's records, not uncommonly, are incomplete, so what flights Patrick made beyond his 'prang' at Hornchurch and until 1 February 1940, is unknown. On that day, between 1500 and 1530 hrs, in company with Flying Officer Kingcome and Sergeant Morfill, Sergeant Hayes patrolled from Northolt, but no aircraft were seen and the Section was ordered to land. On 28 March, 65 Squadron returned to Hornchurch. On 1 April, Sergeant Hayes was up again, between 1225 and 1315 hrs, in Spitfire K9912, patrolling a convoy. Squadron records then state that for the remainder of that month there was 'nothing to report', so whatever other activity Patrick was involved in is unknown.

At this juncture, let us examine the structure and operation of an RAF fighter squadron. Commanded by a squadron leader, a squadron consisted of twelve operational aircraft and pilots (plus reserves), divided into two flights, 'A' and 'B', each led by a flight lieutenant. The flights were sub-divided into two colour-coded sections of three aircraft: typically, red and

Another early Mk IA. (Michael Taylor)

yellow for 'A' flight, blue and green for 'B'. Each pilot had a number, from one to three, one indicating the section leader. Blue One, therefore, was the section leader of 'B' flight's Blue Section. Each squadron was identified by its own code letters, painted in large, grey, letters on the fuselage, forward of the national roundel. Individual aircraft were given their own unique identification letter, A – K for 'A' flight, and L – Z for 'B'. 'QV-K', therefore, would be a Spitfire of 19 Squadron's 'A' Flight. Every squadron also had a codename: 'Maida Blue 1', for example, being the leader of 152 Squadron's 'B' Flight's Blue Section.

During the forthcoming summer of 1940, if the weather was fine, the chances were that battle would be joined, the time and place, of course, dictated by the enemy. This could come both unexpectedly and suddenly – maybe in the middle of a game of chess or cards, or lighting a cigarette. The telephone became the pilots' master, its ring often heralding violent aerial action. The operational centre of a squadron was 'dispersal', usually a wooded hut in which was situated an orderly clerk and the all-important telephone, in addition to twelve beds on which the pilots rested between sorties. Outside, the aircraft were dispersed as a precaution against bombing, always facing the airfield's centre, so that the pilot could take off with the minimum of delay. During the daytime, pilots usually left their cumbersome parachutes on top of the port wing, straps hanging down below the leading edge and ready to be donned quickly. Leather flying helmets, radio lead plugged in, were left in the cockpit. There was no cockpit heating, so pilots wore thick socks to insulate against cold at high altitude, and leather flying boots (although some preferred shoes, for a better feel of the controls). Flying over the sea dictated that the pilot must also wear a bulbous, orally inflated, life preserver, painted yellow and known, for obvious reasons, as a 'Mae West'. In action, the pilot's head was covered by his flying helmet, his face by a canvas mask providing a radio-telephony microphone and delivering oxygen, his eyes by goggles. Hands were protected by leather gauntlets. Sometimes fighter pilots wore flying overalls, but often flew in uniform trousers and tunics – rarely in the bulky sheepskin Irvin flying jacket. The brightly coloured fighter pilot's silk scarf was not a pose, but very necessary: buttoned up, stiff, uniform shirt collars caused chafing as the pilot constantly searched the sky, all around, above and below, and neck ties had been known to shrink in saltwater. Baling out into the sea was risky, Air Sea Rescue facilities being in their infancy. Clearly, this was an uncertain and highly dangerous business.

Abruptly on 10 May 1940 the great storm finally broke: Hitler invaded Belgium, Holland, Luxembourg and France. Two days later Liege fell, and *panzers* crossed the Meuse at Dinant and Sedan. Hitherto, in the naïve hope of remaining neutral, the Belgians had refused Lord Gort's BEF permission to fortify their border with Germany. Now the Belgian King called for help, the BEF pivoting forward from its prepared defences on the Belgian-French border. The British advanced for sixty miles over unfamiliar ground, expecting to meet the German *Schwerpunkt* – point of main effort – anticipating the enemy following the same route as in the First World War. It did not. Holland was certainly attacked – the Dutch Air Force being wiped out on the first day – but the main enemy thrust was cleverly disguised. As Allied eyes were firmly focussed on the Belgian-Dutch border, *Panzergruppe* von Kleist achieved the supposedly impossible and successfully negotiated the Ardennes, much further south. German armour then poured out of the forest, bypassing the Maginot Line, rendering its concrete forts useless. The *panzers* then punched upwards, towards the Channel coast. Ten days later the Germans had reached Laon, Cambrai, Arras, Amiens and even Abbeville. Indeed, Erwin Rommel's 7th *Panzer* covered ground so quickly that it became known as the 'Ghost Division'. The effect on the Allies was virtual paralysis, so shocking was the assault, unprecedented in speed and fury. Civilians in Britain were equally shocked – not least after the bombing of Rotterdam on 14 May reportedly caused 30,000 civilian fatalities (although post-war estimates put the death toll at nearer 3,000). Hard on the heels of Guernica and Warsaw, Rotterdam's fate was terrifying news indeed.

The British Advanced Air Striking Force (AASF) had flown to France on 2 September 1939. Fairey Battle light-bombers went first, followed by Blenheims and Hurricanes – but no Spitfires. And Air Chief Marshal Dowding only spared Hurricanes for two reasons: firstly, due to political pressure, he had no choice but to support the French by providing a certain number of his precious fighters; secondly, that being so, he wisely decided only to send Hurricanes, which he knew were inferior to the Spitfire. Moreover, there were precious few Spitfires available in any case – certainly insufficient to send to France, thereby weakening Britain's defences for – as Dowding would later see it – no good purpose. On 10 May 1940 though, there were six squadrons of Hurricanes in France. One week later the equivalent of six more had crossed the Channel, and another four were operating from bases on the south-east coast of England, hopping over the Channel on a daily basis but returning to England – if they could – at the end of each day. Losses in France rapidly stacked up. The Air Ministry acted as though these casualties were a complete surprise. Dowding's sharp riposte was 'What do you expect? When you get into a war you have to lose things, including precious aircraft. That's exactly what I've been warning you about!' His fears regarding the wastage of fighters were now being realised. The crux of the problem was that the more fighters Dowding sent to France, the further he weakened Britain's defences. Already Dowding had insisted that the minimum strength required to guarantee Britain's safety

65 Squadron dispersal, summer 1939, 65 Squadron's code now being 'YT'. (Michael Taylor)

was fifty-two squadrons, and yet soon he was arguing a case to retain just thirty-six. Although Churchill later wrote that Dowding agreed with him the figure of twenty-five, the latter dismissed this statement as 'absurd'. With the French constantly clamouring for more fighters, and putting Churchill's War Cabinet under increasing pressure, things came to a head on May 15.

On that day, Dowding joined Air Chief Marshal Sir Cyril Newall, the CAS, at a Cabinet meeting. Both men spoke out against sending more fighters across the Channel. These could not, however, be entirely denied as elements of the BEF were poised to attack enemy communications near Brussels. Dowding was dissatisfied and later commented that 'There had already been serious casualties in France, and they alone had been worrying me a very great deal. I had to know how much longer the drain was going on, and I had to ask for a figure at which they would shut the stable door and say no more squadrons would be sent to France.' Unable to request an interview with the Cabinet every time a new demand for fighters was received, on 16 May Dowding sat and composed the strongest case he could to prevent further fighters being drained away in a battle already lost. The following is extracted from that letter, which Robert Wright described as 'one of the most important documents of the early part of the Second World War': -

'I must therefore request that as a matter of paramount urgency the Air Ministry will consider and decide what level of strength is to be left to the Fighter Command for the defence of this country, and will assure me that when this level has been reached not one fighter will be sent across the Channel however urgent and insistent appeals for help may be.

'I believe that, if an adequate fighter force is kept in this country, if the fleets remain in being, and if the Home Forces are suitably organized to resist invasion, we should be able to carry on the war single-handed for some time, if not indefinitely. But, if the Home Defence force is drained away in desperate attempts to remedy the situation in France, defeat in France will involve the final, complete and irremediable defeat of this country.'

On the very day that Dowding began his stance to stem the flow of British fighters to France, the Air Ministry required that a further eight half-squadrons be sent across the Channel. Worse, Churchill himself then flew to France, subsequently requesting a further six squadrons and a night attack by heavy bombers. This was ridiculous. Taking aside the problem of fighter strength, Britain had no heavy bombers at that time.

As Orange argued, 'This was the payoff for years of talk and little action.' By 19 May the situation on the continent had deteriorated further still. On that day the War Office and Admiralty began facing the possibility of evacuating the BEF from France, and Churchill finally saw sense. The Prime Minister's decision was recorded in a minute: 'No more squadrons of fighters will leave the country whatever the need of France.' By the following day, only three of Dowding's squadrons remained in France. He considered that this 'converted a desperate into a serious situation', or, as Wright put it, Fighter Command's chief was now 'able to mend some fences'. The importance to the defence of Britain of this change in policy cannot be overlooked.

As a Spitfire squadron, then, 65 Squadron was not sent to France, being preserved for the defence of Britain which Dowding knew, given the disaster on the Continent, lay ahead. However, on 17 May 1940, Sergeant Hayes flew in Green Section with Flying Officer Kingcome and Pilot Officer Grant over Flushing via Ostend. The ORB describes the action: -

'Offensive patrol over Flushing consisting of four sections led by Red Section – Squadron Leader Cooke; Yellow Section – Flight Lieutenant Olive; Blue Section – Flight Lieutenant Saunders; Green Section – Flying Officer Kingcome. Left Hornchurch and followed a course to Ostend and there up coast, arriving over objective approximately 0755 hrs. One enemy plane (Ju 88) was seen by Red Section and Flying Officer Welford was ordered to attack. Attacking from astern, Flying Officer Welford brought the aircraft down, causing it to crash on the beach below. The Squadron saw no other machines. The coastline was followed at heights between 9,000 – 11,000 feet, but no movements of any description could be seen. All our aircraft returned safely after a patrol lasting two hours. Flying Officer Welford had bullet holes in his wings. Formation adopted three sections in vic line astern, with one section astern and above.'

Welford's victim was a Ju 88A of *Stab*/III/KG30 on anti-shipping sortie over Flushing and which crash-landed on the beach at Renesse, Schouwen Island. Strangely, *Oberleutnant* Wagner and crew remained missing.

On 22 May 1940, Sergeant Hayes was again patrolling with Green Section over the French coast, between 1335 and 1515 hrs: -

'Squadron led by Squadron Leader Cooke patrolled Calais – Boulogne, Blue Section, led by Flight Lieutenant Saunders, attacked Ju 88,

A Spitfire Mk IA taxis for take-off at Hornchurch. (Michael Taylor)

Pilot Officer Smart killing the air gunner. The starboard engine was put out of action, and machine was last seen entering a cloud emitting black smoke.'

The following morning, Patrick flew on another Squadron patrol, led by Squadron Leader Cooke: -

'Fired at by destroyers of the Royal Navy on way home, some shots being uncomfortably near.'

And another patrol that lunchtime: 'Reported SW Calais being shelled but did not encounter any enemy aircraft.' An uneventful evening patrol of Calais concluded the day's flying for 65 Squadron.

On 24 May, Sergeant Hayes flew two more uneventful patrols over the French coast. Between 0420 and 0620 hrs on 26 May he was aloft again, in Green Section, this time led by Flying Officer George Victor Proudman, an SSC officer, from Woking: -

'Squadron of twelve machines led by Squadron Leader Cooke, Red Section, patrolled off Calais at 16,000 feet and encountered four vics of twenty Me 110s. Dogfights began in which Squadron Leader Cooke silenced the starboard engine of one Me 110. Pilot Officer Nicholas silenced the port engine of a 110. Both enemy aircraft then dived steeply away and it is impossible that they got very far. The leader of Green Section – Flying Officer Proudman – engaged an Me 110 causing it to crash in flames, and Pilot Officer Grant in the same action also got in a burst of 1126 rounds which caused the 110 to crash in flames. The other four members of the Section engaged Me 110s and using an average of 1,000 rounds of ammunition they made the enemy aircraft retire by escaping in the clouds, but it is very unlikely that they got far. Diving out of the dogfight, Flight Lieutenant Saunders and Sergeant Kilner – both of Blue Section – engaged a single Ju 88 and immediately attacked it. Flight Lieutenant Saunders fired three bursts of two seconds each, round the port and starboard engines. Sergeant Kilner then fired a further three bursts which caused the Ju 88 to dive steeply, both engines smoking; it was seen later to pull out of the dive but it is not thought that it could have got very far. One of our aircraft failed to return, this was Flying Officer Welford and it was later discovered that he was shot down by Anti-Aircraft guns. He attempted to jump out but his parachute did not open in time. He was last seen by other members of the Squadron going into six Me 10s and breaking them up, causing three to dive away very steeply as he had expended all his ammunition and was returning in order to rearm when he was hit by the AA fire.'

Although no combat report exists, we do know from surviving cine-gun camera footage that Sergeant Hayes fired his guns in anger for the first time on that dawn patrol, at an Me 110, although no result was claimed.

Flying Officer Welford's early loss was unfortunate, considering his experience and promise as a fighter pilot; his body was later washed up on the Kentish coast and buried at Minster (Thanet) Cemetery.

By now it was already clear that the Battle of France was lost. John Terraine made clear the importance of fighters to German air operations during this campaign, arguing that a powerful Allied fighter force could have prevented the Germans achieving aerial supremacy over the battlefield, making possible their devastating results on the ground. The fact was, though, that the Allies did not have 'a powerful fighter force'. On paper, for example, although the French fielded 790 operational fighters, the reality was that nineteen out of the twenty-six French fighter squadrons were equipped with the woefully obsolete *Morane-Aulnier* 406 – which was no match for the Me 109. Only Hurricane pilots had a suitable machine to take on the German aircraft – but those few Hurricanes were insufficient to stem the tide. The German fighters – over 1,200 of them, but above all the Me 109s – ruled the sky, and in doing so they achieved, for the first time against a major enemy, the saturation of a battle area by air power – and that is actually what won the Battle of France for Germany. The complete air superiority enjoyed by the *Luftwaffe* empowered the *Stukas* to perform, the *panzers* to roam at will. This was an achievement above all of the fighter arm, in particular the *Messerschmitt* 109. This was no coincidence – the Germans had learned so much in Spain. The outcome in France also confirmed how flawed British aerial doctrine was between the wars, and how wrong Trenchard had been regarding the value of fighters.

By 26 May the BEF was in danger of envelopment. There was therefore no alternative but the unthinkable: the BEF was ordered to retire upon and then evacuate from the flat beaches around Dunkirk. From then on, the whole nature of air operations over northern France changed. The RAF now had to provide a protective umbrella for the retreating BEF in addition to covering the actual evacuation in due course. It was now that Dowding committed his precious Spitfire force to battle over the French coast.

It was a busy day for 65 Squadron, which clashed with Me 109s on a later patrol, although Sergeant Hayes did not himself fly again on 26 May until 1600 hrs, when he took off for a patrol with Flight Lieutenant Saunders only to be recalled ten minutes later owing to bad weather.

The *Luftwaffe*'s focus now became preventing the evacuation. The contest, however, would be far from one-sided; according to *The* Luftwaffe *War Diaries*: -

'The *Luftwaffe* was having to operate at an ever-increasing distance from most of its bases. The *Stukas* of VIII Air Corps were now based on airfields east of St Quentin, but even from there the Channel coast – Boulogne, Calais, Dunkirk – represented the limits of their range… Two weeks of gruelling operations had sapped much of the *Luftwaffe*'s strength. Many of the bomber *gruppen* could only put some fifteen aircraft out of thirty into the air. But they went in, raining down bombs on the quays and sheds of Dunkirk harbour. Around noon on the 26th the great oil tanks on the western edge of the town went up in flames. In a precision raid *Stukas* destroyed the lock gates leading to the inner harbour. Bombs tore up the tracks of the marshalling yard; ships were set on fire; a freighter sank slowly to the bed of the battered harbour basin.'

The problem for Fighter Command was that Dunkirk lay fifty miles from 11 Group's closest airfield at Manston. This flight was over the sea, and contact would be over the French coastline. The inherent dangers were obvious and hardly conducive to preserving the Spitfire force. Providing continuous fighter patrols from dawn to dusk was impossible, as this would have required every single one of Dowding's precious fighters – leaving Britain itself vulnerable to attack. Another hugely significant factor in the fighting over Dunkirk would be that the British fighters were unassisted by radar. The 'System' only provided a radar network for the defence of Britain, its stations incapable of gathering data from as far away as Dunkirk and beyond. This is why Dowding knew that the battle ahead would be so exhausting for his pilots: as they could not predict or have early warning of an enemy attack it would be necessary to fly as many standing patrols as possible. Even so, Dowding knew that given the size of the force he was able to make available – sixteen squadrons – there would be times, howsoever brief, that cover would be unavailable. The man entrusted with Fighter Command's contribution to this endeavour – Operation Dynamo – was the commander of 11 Group: Air Vice-Marshal Keith Park. For what Park and his pilots now had to do, there was no precedent.

On 27 May, 65 Squadron, including Sergeant Hayes, patrolled between 0645 and 0840 hrs: -

'The Squadron of eleven machines, led by Squadron Leader Cooke, patrolled Calais. Very few enemy aircraft were seen but on return two Do 17s were sighted. Squadron Leader Cooke and Flight Sergeant McPherson attacked from astern and though they emptied their guns into the machine it did not, at that time, appear badly damaged for it made off into the clouds, though evidently experiencing a little trouble. Later, however, this machine was confirmed by Pilot Officer Deere of 54 Squadron, who had earlier been shot down and was on the beach at Calais at the time. In this sortie, Flying Officer Proudman also sighted a Do 17 and managed to get in a burst of very long duration and it was seen to make for the clouds with smoke pouring from its engines, and it is very improbable that it ever reached its aerodrome. Flying Officer Proudman was wounded in the left leg, the bullet entering from the rear and then going through the rudder bar, then entering his leg and finally finished in his parachute.'

Although not mentioned by the ORB, Sergeant Hayes also attacked a Do 17, at 0745 hrs, at 7,000 feet, north of Dunkirk: -

'On the above patrol I was Green Three when we sighted twelve Do 17 bombers about 2,000 feet below us. I attacked one of a formation of three from astern with no apparent effect. I broke away and attacked another enemy aircraft with Green Two, firing about a nine second burst from 400 to 300 yards. The enemy aircraft had dropped back from the formation and white smoke was seen coming from the port engine.'

Above and below: FZ-P airborne from Hornchurch, summer 1939. (Michel Taylor)

Green Two, Pilot Officer Stan Grant, reported that: -

'I was Number Two in Green Section when we sighted twelve Do 17s in four vics of three. I attacked number two of one section from astern, firing bursts totalling about eight seconds with no apparent effect. I broke away and attacked number two of another section from below with a burst of four seconds, which silenced the lower rear gun. I broke away to the right and keeping the same level as enemy aircraft came in again and fired the remaining ammunition in an astern attack, by which time the enemy aircraft had dropped back from his formation considerably, with smoke coming from his engine.'

Green Two and Three were awarded an equal share of the Do 17 jointly attacked, which was considered a 'probable'. Like many other Spitfire pilots fighting over the French coast, Patrick Hayes had opened his account.

Between 1300 and 1435 hrs, 65 Squadron was back over the French coast again, Sergeant Hayes once more included in the 'B' Flight formation:-

'The Squadron, led by Squadron Leader Cooke, patrolled Calais – Dunkirk, encountering *Messerschmitts* and eighteen mixed bombers in formations and sections. In the general dogfight that ensued, Flight Sergeant Phillips sent one Do 17 crashing. Blue Section, led by Flight Lieutenant Saunders, saw a further one go down in flames. Red Section, led by Squadron Leader Cooke, saw two Do 215s descend in flames and Sergeant Franklin on his way home shot down a further Ju 88. In addition, two Do 215s and two Me 110s were engaged but managed to escape into clouds with smoke pouring from their engines.'

By 28 May, 54 and 65 Squadrons had been reinforced at Hornchurch by Duxford's 19 Squadron, which led the Hornchurch contingent across the Channel for an uneventful dawn sweep over Calais and Boulogne. The 65 Squadron ORB later reported that: -

'At 0900 hrs, the same formation with the addition of one more machine once more patrolled the Calais area, this time with more success. Squadron Leader Cooke, in coming out of a cloud-base sighted nine Do 17s. Opening up to full boost he caught them up and attacked one of them. Very heavy cross-fire was encountered but the enemy aircraft attacked had stopped firing. Five of our own aircraft arrived and a dogfight ensued, in which one of our aircraft was hit and forced down. This turned out to be Pilot Officer Smart, who had been hit in the glycol tank. He managed to land safely on the beach and after burning his machine eventually got back to England uninjured two days later. In the meantime, Squadron Leader Cooke once more attacked he original Do 17, from below, and saw it dive steeply away. It was later confirmed by the French that this machine had crashed. Flight Sergeant Franklin and Sergeant Kilner of Blue Section, flying in line astern, attacked another Do 17 and succeeded in getting in a six second burst and three long bursts successively. This enemy aircraft was seen to crash on the beach and was confirmed by the French.'

Sergeant Hayes had flown a number of patrols covering the Dunkirk evacuation, meeting the enemy for the first time, but reduced to just eight Spitfires, that sortie on 28 May was 'the end of the "Blitzkrieg" for next day the Squadron was sent to Kirton-in-Lindsey, their place being taken by 222 Squadron from the same place, in order that the pilots should have a rest and the damage done to their machines repaired.' During these few days of heavy fighting, 65 Squadron's combat claims amounted to nineteen confirmed destroyed with fourteen more 'probables', offset against Flying Officer Welford killed and three aircraft destroyed.

While 65 Squadron rested and refitted, the desperate evacuation continued. By 3 June 1940, it was all over. The Fall of France itself was, without question, an unmitigated disaster of immeasurable proportions. The BEF had left behind 68,000 men including 40,000 prisoners of war, and all its armour and artillery. A total of 200 ships had been sunk during the operation – which began hoping to evacuate up to 45,000 troops. The total actually rescued was some 340,000. The Dunkirk evacuation, therefore, can only be considered a victory within the wider context of what was an absolutely catastrophic defeat. Importantly, the Spitfire, although at this time technically inferior to the Me 109 in certain key respects, had performed well, its pilots, having hitherto chased lone German bombers around England, now had invaluable first-hand experience of fighter combat.

The campaigns fought thus far had proved that an air force with superiority and possessed of the initiative could give powerful and decisive support to rapid armoured thrusts – by preparing the way ahead with concentrated bombing, and then protecting the flanks of friendly forces from enemy counter-attack. The effectiveness of airborne troops, either conveyed by glider or parachute – providing aerial superiority had already been achieved – had also been proven. Over Dunkirk the Spitfire had earned the enemy's respect. Even so, this was only a foretaste of effective fighter opposition, the implications of which *Reichsmarschall* Göring, supremely confident, failed to recognise. His *Luftwaffe* now had bases in Northern France, vastly extending the range of its bombers and, most importantly, putting even London within range of the Me 109. That changed everything. The tacticians who had written Fighter Command's Air Fighting Manual could never have predicted Hitler's unprecedented advance to the Channel coast, making this possible. Göring, however, did not necessarily support the proposal for a seaborne invasion of southern England. Rightly he recognised that 'the planned operation can only be considered under conditions of absolute air superiority'. He believed that a landing under fire was unnecessary because the war against Britain had 'already taken on a victorious course'. The essential condition was destruction of the RAF. As Group Captain Peter Townsend wrote, 'Without air defences Britain would be impotent… Invasion would then be unnecessary.' This, then, was the task that Göring set to: annihilation of Fighter Command. After the Fall of France, therefore, the *Luftwaffe* prepared for a new assault.

At a time when the British should have been enjoying their annual summer holidays, at such south-east Victorian coastal resorts as Brighton, Eastbourne and Hove they braced themselves for a German seaborne invasion. At London's railway stations lists appeared of hundreds of coastal locations that could no longer be visited for 'holiday, recreation or pleasure'. Large tracts of the coastline became 'Defence Areas', entry forbidden to those without special permits. Sea-front hotels were requisitioned, beaches were criss-crossed by barbed wire, and machine guns sprouted from pillboxes everywhere. A curfew was imposed. The great British novelist and broadcaster J.B. Priestley visited Margate and wrote that 'The few signs of life only made the place seem more unreal and spectral.' The British were in no mood, perhaps, for holidays.

In less than a year, the map of democratic Europe had been redrawn. The process had provided graphic and terrifying examples of destruction wrought by aerial bombing. The fear of the bomber that had gathered in intensity throughout the 1930s was confirmed. Having read with horror of the fate of Guernica, Warsaw and Rotterdam, the British people now braced themselves. Hitler had swept aside all challengers and now stood just twenty-two miles from Britain. There was no doubt as to what lay ahead. Churchill's speeches made that clear enough. The *Luftwaffe* appeared supreme, the undefeated master of the skies over Spain, Poland, Norway, Denmark, Holland, Belgium, Luxembourg and even France. It seemed just a question of 'when', not 'if' Germany would deliver that long awaited 'knock-out blow'. But Britain's attitude was not defeatist. It was defiant. There was no question of capitulation.

Immediately after Dunkirk, the British Prime Minister, Winston Churchill, made the future clear to the House of Commons: -

'We shall go on to the end, we shall fight on in France, we shall fight on the seas and the oceans, we shall fight with growing confidence and growing strength in the air, we shall defend our island, whatever the cost may be, we shall fight on the beaches, we shall fight on the landing grounds, we shall fight in the fields and in the streets, we shall fight in the hills; we shall never surrender.'

Whatever lay ahead, the vast majority of Britons had no doubt that the war against Germany should continue – no matter how hopeless that appeared at that time.

Nonetheless, after such intensive fighting there now followed a lull, during which the enemy largely probed British nocturnal defences, causing slight damage but significant nuisance, disrupting both sleep and production. Air Chief Marshal Dowding explained that 'After the evacuation from Dunkirk, the pressure on Fighter Command became less intense, but it by no means disappeared... and the Battle of Britain followed on with no appreciable opportunity to rest and reform the units which had borne the brunt of the fighting.'

Little wonder, then, that 65 Squadron's respite at Kirton was short-lived: against the foregoing backdrop, on 5 June 1940, two days after Dynamo concluded, the squadron returned to Hornchurch. With a lull in the day-fighting, the squadron was still able to receive replacement pilots and provide more training and operational experience. The sorties on which Sergeant Hayes flew are listed below, against a dramatic backdrop: -

9 June 1940: 2100 – 2205 hrs, patrol of Rochford and Canterbury. No E/A seen, poor viz.

On 18 June, the Prime Minister roused the nation: -

'The Battle of France is over. I expect that the Battle of Britain is about to begin... The whole fury and might of the enemy must very soon be turned on us. Hitler knows that he will have to break us in this island or lose the war. If we can stand up to him, all Europe may be free and the life of the world may move forward into broad sunlit uplands. But if we fail, then the whole world, including the United States, including all that we have known and cared for, will sink into the abyss of a new Dark Age made more sinister, and perhaps more protracted by the lights of perverted science. Let us therefore brace ourselves to our duties, and so bear ourselves that if the British Empire and its Commonwealth last a thousand years, men will still say "*This* was their Finest Hour".'

20 June 1940: 1900 – 1940 hrs, patrol – X Raid, turned out to be a friendly fighter. On this sortie, Patrick was joined by a Pilot Officer Norman James Brisbane, a 22-year-old SSC pilot from Enfield, who had first flown with 65 Squadron on a convoy patrol five days previously. Over the next few days, Brisbane would participate in a number of uneventful patrols, increasing his hours on Spitfires.

21 June 1940: 2000 – 2115 hrs, patrol. Recce over Northern France, no E/A but Flight Sergeant McPherson slightly damaged in oil tank by heavy AA fire over Calais.

A line-up of 65 Squadron Spitfires, starter-trollies plugged in and ready to go. (Michael Taylor)

On 22 June 1940, France finally surrendered.

Britain fought on. Professor Richard Overy rightly dismisses as a myth that Britain was 'alone', emphasising that this disregards the 'vital and substantial support of Canada, South Africa, Australia, New Zealand, India and the colonial empire'. Nonetheless, none of those nations actually stood within sight of Dunkirk's blazing oil tanks or, indeed, were within range of German bombers. And that is the point, one which the socialist historian Angus Calder completely missed when arguing that the Battle of Britain in its entirety is nothing more than a 'myth'. That the British people did not falter or fail in facing the prospect of the devastating air attacks feared for so long is not a myth. That they were prepared to weather the storm and preserve their chosen way of life and territory is demonstrable fact. To save them, the people now increasingly looked to the young pilots of Fighter Command.

27 June 1940: 1030 – 1140 hrs, offensive patrol, Calais – Boulogne, no E/A or 'even AA were encountered'.

1 July 1940: 1950 2115 hrs, Offensive patrol followed by 12 other Spitfires of two squadrons, E/A 'failed to rise to the bait and no interception made'.

Things were about to take a turn, meaning that Fighter Command would not have to prowl over France looking for trouble – the trouble was coming to find them. During the late afternoon of 1 July, the *Luftwaffe* began attacking

Britain in daylight. These initial raids were made against Wick in Scotland, and various ports on the north-east coast, sixteen bombs being dropped killing nineteen people. Significantly, on this date, the *Oberkommando der Wehrmacht* (OKW), the German High Command, ordered all three services to begin preliminary planning for the seaborne invasion of southern England. This opportunity was, of course, completely unexpected, because nobody could have predicted the overwhelmingly successful campaign against the west to date. Although the OKW lacked experience and, in truth, the resources necessary to mount such a huge undertaking, with the British army having left behind a large proportion of heavy weapons in France, Hitler certainly considered the invasion of Britain a distinct possibility. The *Führer* recognised that such an operation could only be achieved with complete aerial supremacy – and inquired of Göring when this might be expected.

The following day was a quiet one for 65 Squadron, but not for Fighter Command as a whole, twenty-eight squadrons of which, during the hours of daylight, flew 120 patrols representing 570 sorties, destroying just five enemy aircraft which had probed the defences. On 4 July, things distinctively changed, although again this was a quiet day for 65. On that day, two major attacks were made, the first against shipping and naval installations at Portland, the second raid on a convoy comprising nine ships steaming through the Dover Strait. Fighting erupted over both targets. The Portland raid, however, caught 10 Group wrong-footed, and was long-gone by the time Air Vice-Marshal Brand's fighters arrived on the scene. Over the Dover Straits, 79 Squadron's Hurricanes, up from Hawkinge, intercepted two *staffeln* of Do 17s, escorted by some thirty Me 109s – losing a pilot killed. That evening, 32 Squadron's Hurricanes were scrambled from Biggin Hill to patrol over Dungeness, but were vectored too late onto Raid 20 – comprising three *staffeln* of Me 109s on a *Freie Hunt*. Within seconds, two Hurricanes were destroyed, although both pilots were safe, and Pilot Officer Rupert Smythe claimed two of the enemy destroyed. These high-flying fighter sweeps would prove lethal in the months ahead, the German fighters incoming just below the stratosphere, the advantage of height and sun providing many opportunities to execute the perfect ambush, or 'bounce', on the RAF fighters below.

As the 65 Squadron ORB noted, 5 July 1940 was 'a bit livelier' compared to the squadron's post-Dunkirk experience to date. At 0535 hrs, Flying Officer Proudman led off five 'B' Flight Spitfires, including Sergeant Hayes and the new Pilot Officer Brisbane, to patrol Dover.

Having been given several vectors by the Controller, Proudman, Blue One, sighted an He 111, leading his section in line astern to execute a textbook No 1 Attack. At 200 yards, Blue One opened fire before breaking away, succeeded in doing likewise, in turn, by Blue Two, Sergeant Kilner, and Blue Three, Pilot Officer Hart. Flying Officer Proudman then made a further attack, the enemy bomber turning towards land, losing height, before alighting in the sea and sinking immediately. The crew of this He 111H-2 of 8/KG1 were all captured.

6 July, according to 65 Squadron, was 'back to normal' and another quiet day generally.

7 July began with RAF fighters destroying several German reconnaissance bombers over the Channel. At mid-morning, German fighters swept over the south coast between Bognor and Dover. Further east, 54 Squadron's 'B' Flight was scrambled from Manston to investigate an X-Raid, finding a lone He 111, but before the Spitfire pilots could attack, they were bounced by Me 109s; two Spitfires subsequently force-landed near Deal, another back at base. The enemy reconnaissance aircraft were closely watching a convoy steaming east, making for the Thames Estuary. Naturally, the Germans aimed to attack where the ships were most vulnerable: the Dover Strait. By early evening, the convoy was off Folkestone, hoping to negotiate the Strait, ever under watchful German eyes, after dark. Above, 11 Group fielded a constant protective umbrella of at least nine fighters, flying 215 sorties between noon and 2000 hrs. The enemy had other ideas however: at 1930 hrs, forty-five Do 17s of I and II/KG2 took off from their bases around Arras, heading for the convoy. In response, 64 Squadron was scrambled from Kenley, and at 2015 hrs, Flight Lieutenant 'Sammy' Saunders led off 65 Squadron's 'B' Flight – Pilot Officer Hart and Sergeant Franklin joining him in Blue Section, while Flying Officer Proudman, Pilot Officer Brisbane and Sergeant Hayes made up Green Section. Before the Spitfires arrived, bombs fell on the convoy, one ship being sunk and three others damaged. By the time 65 Squadron appeared over the Strait, Me 109s were sweeping over Kent and Sussex to counter such a threat to the bombers. The scenario had disaster written all over it.

Flight Lieutenant Saunders: -

'I was leading Blue Section… Green Section was in line astern of me. We were patrolling between Folkestone and Dungeness at approximately 10,000 feet. Green One reported to me that he had seen some aircraft and I told him to lead his Section in their direction and I would follow.

Green One turned fairly steeply and dived through some clouds. I followed and after coming out of clouds could not locate Green Section as there was another cloud layer below. I was then told by Blue Two that there were aircraft diving on us from behind, I turned sharply and saw five Me 109s who immediately opened fire. Blue Section then broke formation and I found myself behind and above an Me 109, he half-rolled and dived steeply for the sea. I followed and in the dive was attacked by another Me 109 and was forced to break away slightly. I then saw the first Me 109 flying towards France, just on top of the water. I chased him and when within range (3-400 yards) gave three long bursts. After the third burst he hit the sea and was skidding on top of the water, throwing up a lot of spray. At that moment I was again attacked by a second Me 109 and had to break away in a steep turn and discovered that I had practically no ammunition left. By now I was ¾ of the way across the Channel so I headed back to England. The second Me 109 followed and started to attack from above and behind, and opened fire well out of range. I did two steep turns and again headed for England and was not followed again.'

Flight Sergeant Franklin: -

'At 2020 hrs… I was Blue Two and sighted five Me 109s attacking us from the rear. I informed Blue One and the Section broke up and manoeuvred to attack enemy aircraft. I pursued one enemy aircraft nearly to Calais, fired a short burst and enemy aircraft crashed into sea. Returning to the English coast I sighted several Me 109s protecting bombers. They were roughly in two vics of three and four respectively. I climbed above and attacked several times four to five aircraft. One machine was hit in the engine and pulled away towards France through clouds. I followed, firing at intervals and finally saw the machine make a forced descent in sea about ten miles from the English coast. The enemy aircraft sank.

'Returning towards land, I saw what I thought to be another "Me 109" and attacked it but recognised it to be a Hurricane. I looked for markings and saw none. I examined aircraft closely and the only markings visible were a red "dope" centre (not identification red) and a dark blue outer circle on wings. No marking on fuselage visible. I was doubtful and returned to base without firing.'

The Commanding Officer of 79 Squadron, Squadron Leader John Joslin, a Canadian, had been shot down by a Spitfire, baling out of his Hurricane at 20,000 feet. His section, comprising Pilot Officers Don 'Dimsy' Stones DFC and Tom Parker, had been attacked from above and behind, Stones and Parker turning in to their attackers whom they recognised as Spitfires. Certain sources suggest that this was 65 Squadron's 'B' Flight, but the circumstances do not in fact match: Saunders and Franklyn clearly state that they were attacked first by the enemy aircraft they engaged, not the other way around, as the 79 Squadron pilots describe. Whatever happened, Squadron Leader Joslin was killed, his parachute having failed to open.

As the battle over the convoy continued, the pilots of 65 Squadron's Blue Section returned safely to Hornchurch between 2100 and 2115 hrs.

Of Green Section, there was nothing ever heard of again. Flying Officer Proudman, Pilot Officer Brisbane and Sergeant Hayes just disappeared, the squadron diarist scribing their simple epitaph: 'It is tough luck losing three of our boys like this but such is war.'

But what had happened to Green Section?

On 19 July, Squadron Leader Cooke reported on the action to the Station Commander at Hornchurch, concluding that on Blue Section's '… return they kept a look-out for them. R/T also failed to elicit any reply. Green Section were therefore not seen since the beginning of the engagement and no news is available in spite of considerable enquiries.' All three pilots were posted 'missing'. Three days later, Station Commander reported to the Air Ministry that after Flying Officer Proudman had been ordered by Flight Lieutenant Saunders to lead the way for the close engagement of the raiders, '… in the ensuing fight no contact was made with Green Section…

The same Spitfire receiving attention from the essential groundcrew. (Michael Taylor)

It appears probably that the Section was surprised in or below clouds and engaged by superior numbers of the enemy. Flying Officer Proudman had considerable experience and was a very excellent fighter pilot. The loss of this officer and the other two pilots with him is deeply regretted.'

On 2 January 1941, the Air Ministry, in anticipation of officially presuming the death of the three pilots, wrote to their next-of-kin, enquiring as to whether they had received any news. Mr Hayes, who had regularly communicated with the Red Cross in case information was received that Patrick was a prisoner, replied in the negative. Death officially presumed for legal purposes was one thing, the emotional lack of closure for families of the missing quite another. As late as 23 October 1945, after the war in Europe was over, Flying Officer George Proudman's uncle, the Reverend A.J. Proudman of St Mary's, Evesham, Worcestershire, wrote to the Air Ministry requesting an investigation into his nephew's disappearance. The response, dated 17 November, confirmed that the operational conditions involved coupled with the 'complete absence of news, can only point to the conclusion that the aircraft came down in the sea and that your nephew lost his life'.

German records are incomplete, but we can ascertain that the following *jagdfliegern* claimed Spitfires destroyed over the Channel that evening: -

Leutnant Hermann Segatz	5/JG51	SW Dover.
Leutnant Hermann Striebel	5/JG51	South of Hastings.
Leutnant Herbert Huppertz	6/JG51	NW Dungeness.
Oberfeldwebel Fritz Beek	6/JG51	East of Dungeness.
Unteroffizier Eduard Hemmerling	6/JG51	NW Folkestone.

It is highly likely that certain of these enemy pilots, from what was the only German fighter group in the Pas-de-Calais at this time, surprised and shot down Green Section, the pilots of which crashed into the Channel. All three are remembered on the Air Forces' Memorial on Cooper's Hill, Runnymede, dedicated to more than 20,000 airmen and women of the Commonwealth air forces lost on operations flying from bases in the United Kingdom and North and Western Europe, and who have no known grave.

The afternoon following Green Section's disappearance, 65 Squadron was again in action over Dover, engaging elements of JG 51 once more on a *Freie Hunt*. Flight Sergeant Franklin saw an Me 109 'stalking' a Spitfire below him, attacked and hit the German, observing an undercarriage leg drop and an explosion in the 109's cockpit, a few seconds after which the damaged fighter crashed into the sea. Squadron Leader Henry Sawyer, attached to 65 as supernumerary, gaining experience before succeeding Squadron Leader Desmond Cooke in command, was attacked by a *schwarm* of Me 109s, one of which he hit before making good his escape. Squadron Leader Cooke led his section into cloud, but upon emerging the CO was nowhere to be seen. Like Pilot Officer Proudman, Pilot Officer Brisbane and Sergeant Hayes, the 33-year-old apparently disappeared. 65 Squadron's popular CO was in fact shot down by *Oberleutnant* Josef Föző of 4/JG51, his name also included on the Runnymede Memorial.

Two days after Patrick was reported missing, his doting grandmother, Clara Chapman, travelled by bus from Beckenham to Hornchurch in an effort to discover news of her beloved grandson. The journey was one she had made before, after Patrick had 'buzzed' his grandparents' home at low level, to the annoyance of neighbours who complained. On that occasion Grandma had hastened to Hornchurch to warn the young Spitfire pilot of the impending trouble, but this time her journey was more earnest and, indeed, fruitless. Not only was there no news of Patrick, but 65 Squadron was in a depressed state after losing four pilots in two days. As the ORB recorded, it was 'certainly shaky losing the CO in this way'. These losses confirm just how lethal an adversary the Me 109 and its combat-hardened pilots were, and the extent and inherent dangers of fighting over the Channel at this time.

In 1942, the Air Ministry decided to compile a list of aircrew who had perished during the Battle of Britain, so that their names could be included on a national memorial. It was decided that, for official purposes, the Battle of Britain was fought between 10 July and 31 October 1940. It is difficult to understand, however, why those dates were chosen. After the Fall of France and Operation Dynamo, as we have seen, the new phase in daylight air operations against Britain, the emphasis and tempo of which was dictated by the *Luftwaffe*, began on 2 July 1940 – on which the OKW also first issued orders concerning a proposed seaborne invasion of southern England. Between then and 9 July inclusive, Fighter Command reacted to over a dozen raids of up to fifty enemy aircraft – in the process losing sixteen fighters destroyed with three more damaged, and, much more importantly, thirteen pilots killed and three more wounded. Little wonder then that the survivors of this fighting, those who were wounded and either returned to operations after 31 October 1940, or perhaps not at all, and the families of those thirteen pilots – including Flying Officer Proudman, Pilot Officer

The Runnymede Memorial to missing British and Commonwealth airmen – where Sergeant Patrick Sherlock Hayes is commemorated.

Brisbane and Sergeant Hayes – were, and in some cases remain, vexed at being denied the coveted Battle of Britain Bar to the 1939-45 Star.

In his 'Despatch' on the Battle of Britain, published in the *London Gazette* on 11 September 1946, Lord Dowding, as he became, suggested that 'The Battle may be said to have started when the Germans disposed of the French resistance in the summer of 1940 and turned their attention to this country… It is difficult to fix the exact date on which the "Battle of Britain" can be said to have begun… There are grounds for choosing the date of 8 August, on which was made the first attack in force against laid objectives in this country, as the beginning of the Battle.' Nonetheless, 10 July 1940 was chosen by the Air Ministry, apparently arbitrarily considering the fighting throughout the previous week, which was no different to that on 10 July. Arguably equally arbitrary was the closing date of 31 October 1940. The decisive day of the battle was 15 September; Hitler postponed his invasion plans, Operation *Seelöwe*, indefinitely on 17 September; the daylight contest was really won on 30 September, by which time the German bomber force could no longer sustain such heavy losses by daylight and so switched to night-bombing; so why not any of those dates? Indeed, nothing changed on 31 October 1940. There was no distinct end to the fighting, the opposing fighter forces continuing to clash over the Channel and south-east England until the weather of February 1941 brought an end to it. Then, the *Nachtangriff*, the *Blitz* on British cities was in full swing, reaching its terrible zenith on the night of 11 May 1941. The following month, on 22 June 1941, Hitler invaded the Soviet Union – and that, in fact, is the date German historians argue with conviction that the Battle of Britain finally concluded.

Be all that as it may, three days before the Battle of Britain *officially* began, 24-year-old Sergeant Patrick Hayes perished in action over the Channel in defence of our 'Sceptred Isle'. He had flown Spitfires since May 1939, so had some experience, including participation in Operation Dynamo, during which he fired his guns in anger, making at least one combat claim. Flight Lieutenant Kazek Budzik, a Pole who flew Spitfires from after the Battle of Britain until the war in Europe ended, once told me that 'Flying and fighting in a Spitfire were two very different things. In combat, everything happened so fast, there was just so much going on, all around, and then – nothing, an empty sky. Pilots who could fly *and* shoot really were exceptional, especially if early on in their careers.'

With perhaps surprising modesty and humility, that legendary fighter pilot and leader Group Captain Sir Douglas Bader once explained that 'You must remember that a lot of these chaps were very young and actually had little experience. The Battle of Britain was won not by Malan, Stanford-Tuck and myself, who got all the accolades, it was won by kids of nineteen or twenty, who maybe shot down either nothing or just one before being killed themselves. They were the blokes who won the Battle of Britain, make no mistake there, by being determined, by going off to fight and being prepared to die if necessary, that's the point.'

Another of the Few, Peter Hutton Fox, a 19-year-old Hurricane pilot in the Battle of Britain, once described himself to me as an 'also ran'. It was the 'also rans', however, who made up the majority, and were up there, as Sir Douglas said, doing their duty, sacrificing their lives in Britain's defence.

Sadly, there were many of them – professionals, amateurs and reservists like Sergeant Hayes – who gave lives during our 'Finest Hour', whether between the Battle of Britain's official dates or during the wider definition of those desperate days; none must be forgotten.

Chapter Two

Pilot Officer Jack Royston Hamar DFC

151 Squadron

Killed on Active Service: 24 July 1940

Jack Royston Hamar was born on 21 December 1914 at Knighton in Radnorshire, the eldest son of Arthur Thomas Hamar and his wife Sarah Anne. The family owned and ran a long-standing wholesale and retail grocery and provisions business, William Hamar & Son, supplying customers and village shops within a thirty-mile radius of rural Knighton. Until the First World War, transport was largely horse-drawn, but after the army took all but one of the family's horses, Model 'T' Ford motor vans were used – although these could not compete with horses to reach certain remote places in these Welsh hills, especially in winter. This, of course, was a now long bygone age, which, Fred, Jack's younger brother, remembered as 'simple days, days of bone-setters and wise women'.

Within this rural idyll, Jack first attended Knighton Primary School before becoming a pupil at the John Beddoes Grammar School in Presteigne. By this time he was already addicted to speed, largely on account of his grandfather's influence who was a great horseman, always owning the fastest horse in town, and before the First World War, Jack's father and three uncles were motorcycle enthusiasts, collectively known as the 'Mad Hamars'. Indeed, a pillion passenger of Uncle Alfred's recalled having been 'left sitting on thin air after he made a sudden take-off!' An entrepreneur, Alfred also ran three cinemas, in Knighton, Presteigne and Rhayader, travelling around them in his Model 'T'.

Later, Alfred became a pilot in the RFC, serving in France. After one home leave, he returned to the continent with his mother's fur coat, so cold were the open cockpits of the biplanes in service at that time. Returning from a successful bombing raid on 8 April 1917, with two other 55 Squadron machines, Lieutenant Hamar and his observer, Lieutenant J.A. Myburgh, were jumped by thirty enemy fighters. Hamar's was the only aircraft to escape, albeit severely damaged and both occupants fatally wounded. Alfred somehow returned to base, only losing consciousness when landing, suffering further injury in the resulting crash. At 1550 hrs that afternoon, Alfred died in the New Zealand Stationary Hospital. Lieutenant Myburgh, a 19-year-old South African, expired two days later, after imparting important information gleaned during that last, fatal, reconnaissance flight. Both officers were buried at St Pierre Cemetery, Amiens.

Pilot Officer Jack Hamar of 151 Squadron, home on leave in Knighton, Radnorshire, with his bright red Morgan.

It would not be the only loss suffered by the Hamars owing to aerial warfare. Another of Jack and Fred's uncles, Richard Clarence Hamar, had emigrated to Canada before the First World War, joining up after Alfred's death and also becoming a pilot. During training on 4 June 1918, his aircraft collided with another machine and crashed. Cadet Hamar was killed, aged 23, and was buried at Beamsville, Canada.

After leaving school, during the 1930s, Jack worked in the family business, expanding the animal and poultry feed department. In pursuance of his need for speed, young Jack progressed from an Ariel 250 cc motorcycle to an Ariel Red Hunter, which he rode successfully on a number of hill climbing competitions. After motorcycles came fast sports cars, first a three-wheeler Morgan, then an Aero Minx, and finally an MG. With his uncles' background, it was no surprise to Fred when his elder brother joined the RAFVR on 16 May 1938, learning to fly with the Civilian Flying School at Yatesbury in Wiltshire. On 17 June he received his licence to fly 'private flying machines', covering 'all types of landplanes', reporting to No 1 RAF Depot Uxbridge on 9 July, when commissioned as a pilot officer in the Reserve of Air Force Officers. After 'square bashing' it was back to flying, completing service flying training at the Central Flying School. Afterwards, Jack took an SSC and joined the 12 Group Pool of pilots, awaiting an operational posting.

This requires some explanation. Originally, Trenchard's vision for his new independent air force was that all pilots would be officers.

Pilot Officer Hamar shortly after arriving on 151 Squadron, pictured with a Hawker Fury biplane fighter.

At that time, the qualification for a commission was attendance at a public school, a Certificate 'A' from their school's Officer Training Corps, a good school report and an application counter-signed by any colonel. These were 'Permanent Commissions' (PC), which is to say that an officer served for the duration of his working life. The ability to fly, however, is a skill over and above, literally, the traditional officer function of leading men into battle. Aircrew are, therefore, a breed apart, an élite group by virtue of that ability to fly and dangers associated with that activity. It was soon clear that the fee-paying RAF College Cranwell, where Trenchard's officers were trained, would be unable to provide the numbers of pilots required – especially in time of emergency. 'Boom', as the CAS was known, therefore did two things. Firstly, contrary to his initial ruling that all pilots would be officers, in 1921 Trenchard agreed that a small number of serving NCOs could become pilots,

Right: Pilot Officer Hamar and friend at home in Knighton.

Below: Pilot Officer Hamar at North Weald with a Mk I Hurricane – note the fixed-pitch airscrew.

flying for five years before resuming their original trades while eligible for recall in the event of war. The initiative was both popular and economic. Secondly, Trenchard inaugurated what was a revolutionary idea: the SSC. Recognising that PCs led to a 'dead man's shoes syndrome', and understanding that flying was a young man's activity, suitably qualified and able men could now take a commission for just four years active service, followed by six on the reserve. Consequently, the SSC substantially increased pilot numbers and also expanded the trained reserve. The SSC also gave young men an unprecedented opportunity for flying and adventure, without having to commit a lifetime to the service. So Jack Hamar now found himself an SSC officer, awaiting a posting to an operational unit, which soon came through: on 4 March 1939, Pilot Officer JR Hamar reported for duty with 151 Squadron, a regular RAF fighter squadron based at North Weald in Essex.

In August 1936, 151 Squadron had been formed at North Weald from a flight of 56 Squadron's Gauntlet biplanes. In November 1938, the squadron was re-equipped with the new eight-gun Hawker Hurricane Mk Is, with which type 141 was equipped when Jack arrived four months later. Previously, the most modern fighter type Jack had flown was the Demon biplane, so his conversion to the Hurricane monoplane took place on 151 Squadron, which was how things were done pre-war. Having successfully passed into Hurricane flight, after the Second World War was declared on 3 September 1939, Jack crashed in a Magister communications aircraft at Debden on 11 February 1940. While landing, the aircraft had stalled, alighting heavily, smashing the undercarriage and airscrew; fortunately the pilot was unhurt.

By this time, in anticipation of Hitler attacking the west, Lord Gort's British Expeditionary Force was on the continent, supported by the Advanced Air Striking Force. When the German invasion came, on 10 May 1940, chaos reigned; 151 Squadron's CO, Squadron Leader (later Air Commodore) E.M. 'Teddy' Donaldson, remembered that 'The Low Countries refused to allow British troops in before the Germans broke through France. Then the French bolted, including their air force. I have never seen so many people running so fast anywhere, so long as it was west. The British 'Tommies' were marvellous, however, and fought their way to the sand dunes of Dunkirk. I was in command of No 151 Squadron, and our Hurricanes were sent to reinforce the AASF, flying from Manston to France on a daily basis.

'In some respects, the Germans were grossly over confident in the air, and so didn't have it all their own way. But every day we had damaged

Above left and above right: Jack modelling flying clothing, circa 1939, North Weald.

Hurricanes and no ground crews to mend them, dictating that we had to return to Manston every evening. In any event, our airfields in France were being heavily bombed, so had we stayed, although pilots could have got off the airfield to sleep, our aircraft would have taken a beating. No 151 Squadron would fly up to seven sorties a day, against overwhelming odds, and on one occasion even stayed on patrol after expending our ammunition so as to prevent the *Luftwaffe* attacking defenceless British troops on the ground.'

At 0830 hrs on 17 May 1940, Pilot Officer Hamar was amongst Donaldson's pilots landing at Abbeville, near the Somme estuary. At 1000 hrs, 151 Squadron took off on an offensive patrol of the Lille/Valenciennes areas. An hour later, two *Stukas* were sighted at 12,000 feet, a considerable distance to the south-east. Ordering Blue and Yellow Sections to provide top cover, Donaldson and Red Section gave chase. Twenty *Stukas* of III/StG51 were found, the whole Squadron participating in the interception over Valenciennes, which occurred at low altitude. Six *Stukas* were subsequently destroyed, including one of 9/StG51, by Pilot Officer Hamar. Squadron Leader Donaldson recalled that 'It was fairly easy as the Germans were grossly over-confident.' Jack's first brush with the *Luftwaffe*, however, could easily have been his last: upon landing, he counted ten bullet holes in his Hurricane. Donaldson recalled, 'We had no option but to return to Manston that night, as we had several damaged Hurricanes and no ground crews to mend them. Next day we were back to France and continued every day, because our airfields in France were heavily bombed. While pilots could get away to sleep off the airfield, the Hurricanes would take a terrific beating on the ground.'

At 2 pm on 18 May, 151 Squadron flew to Vitry, and were again in action at 1530 hrs. The 151 Squadron ORB documents that 'A colossal dogfight took place above the aerodrome in which about twenty Me 109s came out of the sun and attacked a squadron of Hurricanes taking over escort duties.' At 1845 hrs, 151 scrambled from Vitry to intercept several 109s seen over the aerodrome; three miles north-west of Vitry, Pilot Officer Hamar caught an Me 110: -

'I climbed to 7,000 feet and attacked two Me 110s, succeeding in getting onto the tail of one enemy aircraft (E/A). I opened fire at 300 yards with

Pilot Officer Hamar with another early Hurricane.

a burst of five seconds. While closing in I noticed tracer passing over my head, from behind, and looking around discovered the other E/A on my tail. I immediately half-rolled away and noticed two Hurricanes chasing another E/A, which was diving to ground level. I followed down after the Hurricanes, and, as they broke away, I continued the chase, hedge-hopping, but did not seem to gain on the E/A. I got within 500 yards and put in a five second burst. I saw my tracer entering both wings, but did not observe any damage. As my windscreen was by this time covered in oil from my own airscrew, making sighting impossible, I broke away and returned to Vitry.'

On 22 May, having returned to Manston, three sections of 151 Squadron escorted Ensign transport aircraft to Merville. On the return journey, twenty-four *Stukas* were seen dive-bombing St Omer. Donaldson's pilots attacked, their resulting 'bag' being four confirmed destroyed and two unconfirmed. Pilot Officer Hamar was again successful: -

'The leader ordered Red Section to attack and we dived towards the *Junkers* 87s. I lost sight of my leader and circled to select a target. I closed on one which was diving, but failed to attack before the E/A dropped its bombs onto a village. As the E/A pulled up, I attacked, giving a five second burst at 200 yards, which killed the rear gunner.

151 Squadron at the outbreak of war, Pilot Officer Jack Hamar front row, extreme left.

I closed to 100 yards and after a seven second burst the E/A turned on its side with smoke pouring from its engine. It went into a steep dive and crashed in a field. I attacked another E/A at which I fired a short burst from 200 yards, after which I experienced no further fire from the rear. I closed to 100 yards and opened fire, which tore off the side of the fuselage and top of port wing. I was forced to break away without observing what happened to this E/A because I ran into another five Ju 87s. I did not see any further E/A crash but saw a parachute descending. Having turned the petrol supply onto the gravity tank, and having fifteen rounds per gun remaining, I returned to base.'

One of Jack's targets was possibly a Ju 87B of 4/StG77, which crash-landed back at Rocroi, having been badly shot up by a Hurricane during an attack on a crossroads east of St Omer.

On 25 May, Jack was in action again: -

'While flying as Red Two with Yellow and Blue Section carrying out a general sweep in the Calais – Boulogne district, a Ju 88 suddenly appeared out of the clouds, passing slightly across and above our formation. The leader ordered a No 1 Attack. The E/A dived for sea-level and after Red One, Squadron Leader Donaldson, broke away, I attacked… I used full throttle and gradually closed, opening fire at 300 yards. The slipstream effect was noticed and keeping the sights dead on, I fired two long bursts, finishing at fifty yards, using all of my ammunition. I then broke away. During the attack, I noticed three large pieces drop from the port side of the E/A, which may have been a bomb. No other damage was noticed.'

The following day, the decision was reluctantly made for Lord Gort's BEF, now in danger of envelopment, to retreat to and evacuate from the flat beaches of Dunkirk. The unthinkable had happened: the battle of France was lost, in no small part owing to German aerial superiority, demonstrating the crucial importance of air power in the conflict ahead.

Three days later, 151 Squadron escorted a formation of Defiants on patrol, when a fierce combat took place with Me 109s; a Ju 88, believed to be a decoy, was destroyed by Squadron Leader Donaldson and Pilot Officer Hamar, as the latter reported: -

'While flying as Red Two on a high escort patrol over Dunkirk, a Ju 88 was seen flying approximately due east at 7,000 feet. The leader ordered Red

Section into line astern and delivered a No 1 Fighter Attack. The leader also ordered Yellow One to take over and remain above on guard. As I followed the leader into attack, I also saw a large formation of Me 109s high above. As the leader broke away, I saw white smoke pouring from the E/A's port engine, and it started flying crab-like. Thinking that this may be a ruse, I decided to attack again, aiming at the port engine. I opened fire at approximately 150 yards and continued the burst until about twenty yards. Large pieces of the port engine were seen to drop off. I did not experience any fire from the rear of E/A, which neither executed any evasive actions other than a fast dive towards cloud, nearly on its side. I then re-joined Red One.'

The Ju 88 was that of *Oberleutnant* Alfred von Oelhaven, *Staffelkapitän* of 6/LG1, who crash-landed his damaged bomber on Nieuport beach at 0830 hrs. Von Oelhaven and *Feldwebel* W. Notzke were captured unhurt, but *Oberfeldwebel* F. Stobbe and *Flieger* S. Tessmann were both killed.

By 3 June 1940, the Dunkirk evacuation was as complete as the resounding defeat suffered by the western Allies.

151 Squadron pilots snatch some sleep during the Battle of France, Jack Hamar in black flying overalls.

Squadron Leader 'Teddy' Donaldson: -

'During the Battle of France and Operation DYNAMO, the air operation covering the Dunkirk evacuation, 151 Squadron flew as many as seven sorties a day against overwhelming odds. At Dunkirk we even stayed on patrol after running out of ammunition to complete a one-hour patrol. This hindered the *Luftwaffe* from attacking the defenceless troops on the ground. When we finally returned to North Weald, we were involved in escorting RAF bombers attacking German communications and the thousands of invasion barges massing along the Pas-de-Calais beaches, rivers and canals. Most, if not all, of the Hurricane squadrons which had operated from French airfields had by this time been rested, except 151. Basil Embry, a man without fear, was commanding a bomber squadron in those days and always asked for 151 as escort because we always stayed close.

'One of the pilots we lost at Dunkirk was Flight Lieutenant Allen Ives, a friend of Jack Hamar's. He was partially trained as a doctor, so I gave my permission for him to remain on the beaches to help treat badly wounded soldiers. He put up a marvellous show before getting on a boat. This was sunk and "Ivy" was swimming in the water when shot through the head by a German soldier lying on the deck of an E-Boat. An eye-witness account of the incident was given to me by another 151 Squadron pilot, a New Zealander, also shot down over Dunkirk.

'After the fall of France and the Dunkirk evacuation, the *Luftwaffe* switched their attacks to British shipping in the English Channel, then our radar stations and airfields, in order to achieve aerial superiority, thus enabling Operation *Seelöwe*, the proposed invasion of southern England, to take place. Of course, it was our job to stop them. Altogether, I flew 303 sorties, missing only one; Victor Beamish, the North Weald Station Commander, wanted me for something important, although I was able to get back to the airfield and greet the Squadron on its return.

'Our Group Commander, Air Vice-Marshal Keith Park, told me at the time that he was sorry to have to work the Squadron so hard, thus giving us more than our fair share of the harder jobs. However, he explained that as 151 was battle hardened, he could rely upon us to do our duty.'

After the Fall of France and completion of the Dunkirk evacuation, the battered units of the AASF were absorbed back into the defence of Britain, as squadrons were reorganised and replenished. Now presented with an

Squadron Leader 'Teddy' Donaldson, third from left, in conversation with North Weald's popular station commander, Wing Commander Beamish; Pilot Officer Hamar fourth from right.

unexpected opportunity to invade Britain, with supreme confidence the as-yet-undefeated *Luftwaffe* made good losses and deployed its forces for the battle ahead. *Luftflotte* 5 moved up to bases in Norway and Denmark, while eleven bomber groups moved to operate from new bases in France and Belgium. Command and communications networks were rapidly established to coordinate the assault on Britain, which would largely be undertaken by *Luftlotten* 2 and 3, based around the Pas-de-Calais and Cherbourg. At first the enemy was comparatively cautious, probing British defences and focussing upon Channel-bound shipping bring supplies to the besieged island. On 9 July, one day before the Battle of Britain officially began, 151 Squadron was involved in a bitter combat twenty miles east of Margate with a formation of some 100 He 111s, Me 109s and 110s. Pilot Officer Hamar reported: -

'At 1430 hrs, "A" Flight of 151 Squadron was ordered to patrol a large convoy about five miles off the coast, just north of the Thames Estuary. I was flying as Red Two in the formation. At 1540 hrs a large number of E/A in several waves were sighted flying NW at about 10,000 feet.

It was impossible to attack the first wave, consisting of He 111 bombers, because of the large number of escorting fighters, which were very near us. Red One, therefore, ordered line astern and attacked the nearest formation of fighters, which consisted of twelve Me 110s. No 1 Fighter Attack was used, and after Red One had broken away and attacked the rear Me 110, I closed to 150 yards and gave it a five second burst. I saw my bullets tearing into the fuselage and wings of the E/A, which staggered badly. I then had to break away quickly as the air seemed full of enemy aircraft.

'I then saw bombs exploding near the convoy which I approached at full throttle. I chased a section of three E/As away from northern end of the convoy but failed to get into a position to open fire. I then continued to patrol the convoy for about fifteen minutes as the air had by this time cleared of E/A. No ships in the convoy had been hit, so I returned to base as my fuel was running low.'

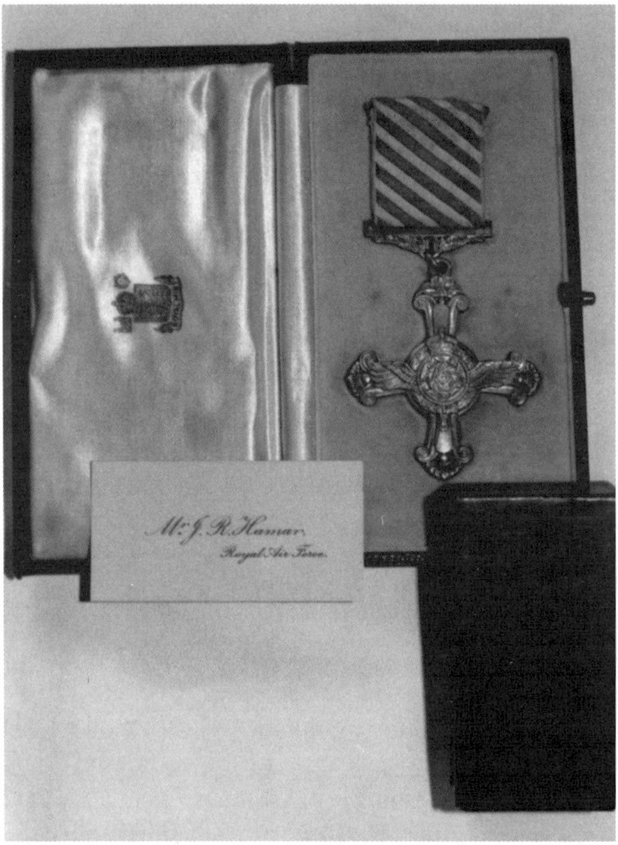

Jack Hamar's DFC, still in case of issue.

A Midshipman Wightman later reported seeing an enemy aircraft dive into the sea, which was that claimed by Pilot Officer Hamar and shared with Wing Commander Beamish and Flying Officer Foster – an Me 110 of III/ZG26, which crashed into the Thames Estuary; both crew members remain *vermisst*.

14 July was a day of poor weather, helping protect Channel convoys, but the *Stukas* of IV/LG1, escorted by thirty Me 109s of JG3, attacked a convoy off Eastbourne that afternoon. In response, the Hurricanes of 151 and 615 Squadrons scrambled to intercept, together with the Spitfires of 610 Squadron. Pilot Officer Hamar reported: -

'At 1500 hrs the Squadron was ordered off from Rochford to intercept E/As south of Dover. At approximately 1520 hrs, when the Squadron was almost over Dover, a bunch of Me 109s were sighted about 5,000 feet above our formation. I was flying Red Two in the formation. As it looked as though the E/A were about to attack us, the leader ordered our defensive line astern tactics. As we turned sharply to port, two Me 109s were seen diving to attack the last aircraft in our formation. Milna Leader (Squadron Leader Donaldson) attacked the leading Me 109 and I attacked the second. I turned inside the E/A, which had pulled up into a steep left-hand climbing turn. I closed rapidly and opened fire at about 250 yards with a 45° deflection shot. The E/A seemed to falter and straightened out into a dive. I placed myself dead astern at about fifty yards. I opened fire, closing to almost no distance. I saw a large explosion just in front of the pilot and a large amount of white smoke poured from the E/A, which was by this time climbing steeply. I was then forced to break away quickly owing to fire from the rear, and lost sight of the E/A and therefore did not see it crash. This action was seen by Flying Officer Forster.'

White smoke meant that the aircraft's coolant system had been hit, so the Me 109 Jack hit may have been a machine of 8/JG3 which force-landed at Wissant, on the coast near Calais, at 1511 hrs.

The following day there was cause for 151 Squadron to celebrate: a signal was received at North Weald to the effect that Pilot Officer Hamar had been awarded the DFC. The Air Ministry's recommendation for the award, approved by King George VI, read, 'Since December, this officer has participated in all operations and most of the patrol flights undertaken by his Squadron. He has shown coolness and courage of a high order and has personally destroyed six enemy aircraft.' It was a well-deserved and early honour.

Squadron Leader Teddy Donaldson: -

'Jack Hamar was my Number Two. A leader has to navigate as we as coordinate and lead attacks. He can only do this if he has a good Number Two, whom he can completely rely on. A CO then knows that no-one can creep up behind him as long as his Number Two is in place. I always knew that Jack would be there. If he were shot down, I knew that the last thing he would do would be to tell me on the radio that he had "had it". Looking after me was an extremely hazardous task. Jack did it loyally and even managed to shoot down six and a half enemy aircraft. The half was for a German bomber which we shared; I had damaged it but it may have returned to its base, so Jack blew it out of the sky in flames. I made nine forced landings in total but was never shot down with Jack Hamar my Number Two.

'From mid-July, we slept the night in dugouts on the airfield at North Weald. There were eight pilots on camp beds at the beginning. By 24 July, only Jack and I were left. On the previous night, Jack had sat on my bed and said "Sir, I think you and I will come through this. We have been to hell and back together and are still alive.

'I said, "For God's sake don't say that, it's bad luck!"'

On 24 July 1940, the enemy maintained the pressure with isolated reconnaissance and nuisance sorties, in addition to a heavy attack on a convoy in the Thames Estuary during which the escorting Me 109s came off second best when attacked by three Spitfire squadrons, losing six of their number. During the afternoon, a lone raider crossed the Sussex coast, flying blind in thick cloud, and was subsequently reported over an area of a thousand square miles when fleetingly glimpsed by the Observer Corps. Sections of RAF fighters were scrambled, but no contact was made. At 1516 hrs, an aircraft, with wheels down, appeared about to land at Brooklands airfield – but this was actually a clever ruse by the pilot of a Do 17 which dropped sixteen fifty-kilo bombs.

Squadron Leader Teddy Donaldson: -

'That day the weather was appalling. I got an urgent telephone call from the AOC. He said "The weather is bloody awful, but I have an unidentified aircraft circling Felixstowe at 10,000 feet and I don't like it. As the weather is so bad I must ask you, not order you, if you can go after him."

'I turned to my Red Two, Pilot Officer Jack Hamar, and said "What about it?" Jack replied, as I knew he would, "Let's get the bastard!"

'Air Vice-Marshal Park said "Thanks a lot", so off we went.

'Visibility was down to about a quarter of a mile. The danger at North Weald was the international radio masts, which went up several hundred feet, and while the controllers could get pilots back to the field, to avoid the masts you had to see them in time.

'No sooner were we airborne with wheels up than Group identified the bogey as friendly. We turned around and, flying slowly at 120 mph and only some sixty feet above the ground, I waited for North Weald to reappear, which it did in a few minutes. I ordered Jack to break. To my horror he broke upwards and commenced an upward roll. In a Hurricane it was impossible to carry out such a manoeuvre at that low speed. As I saw him start his right-handed roll, I screamed "Don't, *don't*!" down the R/T – but it was too late. Jack stalled and hit the deck upside down.

Pilot Officer Hamar's impressive memorial at Knighton Cemetery. (Donna Davies)

'I was on the ground and beside him within seconds. Jack had had his hood open to improve visibility in the awful weather conditions, which had caused massive head injuries. I was devastated.'

Pilot Officer Hamar had crashed at 1400 hrs, in Hurricane P3316. His loss was a completely unnecessary waste of a young life, devastating family and friends, who that fateful day celebrated the news of Jack's DFC; within an hour of his letter arriving, informing his family of the award, Jack's parents received the telegram notifying them of their eldest son's death.

On 28 July, Pilot Officer Hamar was given an impressive military funeral at Knighton Cemetery, receiving over a hundred floral tributes. Indicating the young fighter pilot's popularity, the firing party from North Weald attended at their own request.

On 4 September, Jack's father received a letter from Buckingham Palace: -

'I have the honour to inform you that your attendance is requested at Buckingham Palace at 10.30 o'clock a.m. on Tuesday 17 September next, in order that you, as next of kin, may receive from the King the decoration of the late Pilot Officer Jack R. Hamar, which he would have received personally, had he survived.'

At the investiture, Lord Clarendon, the Lord Chamberlain, was at the King's side, calling out the names of the heroes and then their relatives who were to step forward and receive decorations. Mrs Hamar proudly accepted her late son's DFC, returning with it to Knighton, a world away from London at the Battle of Britain's height. Naturally, the family was extremely proud of Jack's achievements, but, as his brother Fred told me many years later, 'I don't think as a family we ever really got over it.'

Clearly Air Commodore Donaldson never got over the death of his friend either. After a distinguished career in the service, Teddy became the air correspondent for the *Daily Telegraph* until retiring in 1979. He died in 1992, and was buried at Tangmere, his regard for his wingman and friend as strong then as on that fateful day at North Weald in 1940. As Teddy said, 'Jack and I were extremely close; I loved the fellow.'

Chapter Three

Pilot Officer Charles Alec Bird

4 Ferry Pilots' Pool
Killed in Action: 25 July 1940

Charles Alec Bird – commonly called 'Alec' – was born at Horsforth, near Leeds, on 1 March 1917, and as a young boy was inspired by stories of his father, a decorated observer in the RFC during the First World War. Alec wanted so much to fly that he undertook private flying lessons at Yeadon without his parents' knowledge, who were somewhat less keen on the idea. Having attended Leeds Modern School and Leeds Technical College, in October 1938, Alec took an SSC, becoming a service pilot. On 2 September 1939 – the last day of peace – Pilot Officer Bird married Miss Marjorie Wilmshurst of Colton. In anticipation of the imminent outbreak of war, however, the 22-year-old pilot was recalled to duty early the following, fateful, morning and posted to 2 Ferry Pilots' Pool at Filton.

Within a few days, Lord Gort's BEF was on the continent, supported by the AASF. At Filton, Pilot Officer Bird joined the 4 Continental Ferry Flight, ferrying Blenheims and Hurricanes to squadrons in France. After the *Blitzkrieg* against the west began, on 18 May 1940, Alec ferried a Hurricane to Glisy, but after landing the French airfield was attacked by He 111s. Taking off immediately, Pilot Officer Bird intercepted the enemy bombers, setting the port engine of one ablaze. Without oxygen, however, he was forced to discontinue the combat at 22,000 feet, his aircraft hit three times by return fire. His target, an He 111H-2 of 6/KG1, crash-landed at Le Cateau, its crew unhurt. Soon afterwards, he was posted to 4 Ferry Pilots' Pool, firstly operating from Cardiff before moving to Kemble, the home of 5 Maintenance Unit (MU), near Cirencester. This is further evidence of the lack of foresight regarding the allocation of pilots to fighter squadrons. Pilot Officer Bird had considerable experience on the Hurricane – and even had a combat success – so considering fighter squadrons' need for replacement pilots of experience, it is difficult to understand why he was not posted to one – especially when, as we will see, pilots fresh from operational training with but a handful of hours on type were posted straight to squadrons in

Left: Pilot Officer Alec Bird.

Below: Flight Lieutenant P.P. Hanks DFC, who withdrew his claim for the Ju 88's destruction upon hearing of Pilot Officer Bird's previous and clearly decisive intervention.

the combat zone. A far wiser policy, surely, would have been to screen replacements, sending, wherever possible, new pilots of little experience to squadrons out of the main battle area, or to roles such as ferrying, enabling them to accumulate more experience, while pilots like Alec took their place in the front line. Be that as it may, it was with 4 Ferry Pilots' Pool that Pilot Officer Bird remained.

Marjorie Bird had followed her husband, the couple taking a house at 29 London Road, Cirencester. On 24 July 1940, the Birds were shopping in Cheltenham when Alec spotted a poem called *Wings* in a magazine; adapting the last verse, he gave it to Marjorie, saying 'When I am killed, put that on my gravestone and take me back to Yorkshire.' The following day, Alec drove down the driveway of their home, off to the airfield, but stopped and came back to his wife: 'I don't want to leave you today, somehow,' he said. Nonetheless, premonition of death or not, duty called and Pilot Officer Bird was soon at Kemble, preparing for the day ahead.

A Ju 88 crew of 5/KG51 based at Paris-Orly airfield was also making warlike preparations that morning, briefed to carry out a *Störflug* to attack the Gloster Aircraft Factory at Hucclecote in Gloucestershire. These were harassing attacks made by lone enemy aircraft, usually the Ju 88, relying on its excellent performance and heavy armament to get out of trouble, and slipping in and out of cloud to reach and safely return from targets. The crew concerned comprised the pilot, *Unteroffizier* Friedel Dörner, the pilot, a 25-year-old from Gruiten in the Rhineland, *Unteroffizier* Wilhem Hugelschäfer, the navigator and observer, aged 23 from Kleinlangheim, *Unteroffizier* Walter Theiner, the flight engineer, aged 26 from Breslau, and *Gefreiter* Gottfried Treue, the wireless operator, aged 19, from Bielefeld. Before lunch, Dörner took off, Hugelschäfer later recalling that the crew were in high spirits, singing aloud as their bomber headed for action. Passing over the Isle of Wight at 18,500 feet, he also remembers the weather was fine, unsuited, in fact, to the nature of their solo mission owing to the distinct lack of cloud. East of their target, the Ju 88 turned to pass directly over the Gloster Aircraft Factory. Hugelschäfer was concerned that the aircraft could so clearly be seen, and unsurprised when Theiner suddenly shouted the warning '*Achtung! Jäger*!'

As Hugelschäfer had correctly anticipated, the Ju 88's unwelcome presence had not gone unnoticed by the defenders. Lying sprawled out on the airfield at Kemble, enjoying the sunshine, Pilot Officer E.W. 'Bertie' Wootten heard the unmistakable sound of the 88's unsynchronised engines passing overhead. Kemble's response was to immediately scramble two Hurricanes, flown by Pilot Officers Richard Manlove and Alec Bird. Climbing northwards to 12,000 feet, the pair turned south, Alec's aircraft, P3271, fitted with the superior Rotol Constant Speed propeller, overhauling Manlove's. As Pilot Officer Bird closed in and Theiner shouted his warning, Hugelschäfer, the aircraft's captain, jettisoned the bombs as Dörner turned SSW, racing for the far-off coast and home. Anti-aircraft fire then burst between the two Hurricanes, Manlove, slightly behind, watching his comrade close in for a stern attack on the Ju 88, level with the bomber at 18,000 feet. As the bombs were jettisoned, Dörner changed course abruptly and dived for the nearest patch of thin cloud. No sooner had he done so than Hugelschäfer felt 'A severe jolt in the back'. While converging from the port side, Manlove saw Bird 'close right in and deliver his attack from very close quarters before turning away upwards and to port'. At the top of the break, Manlove watched Bird's Hurricane suddenly go into a spin.

Alone, Pilot Officer Manlove then opened fire from long-range, some 500 – 600 yards, at which point the Ju 88's starboard engine broke up and a parachute left the aircraft. Inside the bomber was chaos. At 12,500 feet, Dörner lost control, ordering the crew to bale out. Manlove had followed the bomber's downward spiral, observing Pilot Officer Bird's Hurricane still spinning but down to only 500 feet. Then he saw 'a flock of Spitfires arriving', which orbited the burning Hurricane. Reluctantly accepting that Alec Bird's fate was sealed, Manlove returned to Kemble.

The 'Spitfires' were from nearby 5 OTU at Aston Down, and actually Flight Lieutenant Peter Prosser Hanks DFC in Spitfire P9501, and a pupil in a Hurricane. The pair were engaged on dogfight practice when informed by the Duty Controller of the Ju 88's presence. Hanks, who was already an ace, having scored eight confirmed victories during the Battle of France while flying Hurricanes with 1 Squadron, remembered in 1985: -

'When I first saw the Ju 88, he was well above me, being chased by a Hurricane, presumably Bird's. I went after them, leaving my pupil a long way behind. When the 88 entered cloud, Bird's Hurricane was about 800 yards astern of it and followed the bomber into the cloud. I was still about a thousand feet below. I carried on below cloud in the general direction of the Ju 88, which after only a short while broke cloud about a thousand yards ahead of me. It looked to be flying quite normally and I saw no damage or pieces falling off. I closed with it and started firing. I must admit to having been surprised to have received no return fire, and almost immediately the crew began baling out.'

Above: From left: *Unteroffizier* Wilhelm Hügelschäfer, *Gefreiter* Gottfried Treue, and *Unteroffizier* Friedel Dörner.

Right: Local boys Arthur and Colin Winstone with *Unteroffizier* Hügelschäfer's flying boot.

At 2.15 pm, Albert Stephens had the shock of his life while hedge-cutting when the Ju 88 crashed into Bidcombe Bottom, between Oakridge and France Lynch, near Stroud. High above, the close proximity of the newly arrived British fighters, as he descended by parachute, was perturbing for Hugelschäfer, and the descent seemed to take forever. Suddenly the ground was rushing up towards the young German, who landed heavily in a cornfield: -

'After only a short time, I saw some people, land workers carrying scythes and pitchforks, hurrying towards me. At the same time, a car carrying some policemen also arrived. They spoke to me but I could not understand the language. They put me in a car and drove to a nearby airfield.'

Gefreiter Gottfried Treue had landed in the Cotswold garden of a Mrs le Bailley: -

'For a moment, I thought that the airman would strike the holly tree but he missed it and landed on the lawn, striking his mouth on the sundial.'

Mrs le Bailley, together with her maid, 19-year-old Mavis Young, and her brother Ray, the gardener's 'boy', approached the enemy airman.

The wrecked Ju 88 cockpit at Oakridge.

Above and below: The Oakridge Ju 88 crash site – then and now. (latter Will Matley)

Propping the shaken Treue against a tree, Mavis handed the German a whisky. With Teutonic manners, the wireless operator, also 19, clicked his heels together, said 'Thank you', and kissed the blushing maid's hand. Mrs le Bailley's neighbour, the local schoolmaster Mr Watson, then took charge and called the police.

At nearby Miserden, the church bells rang in alarm, mobilising the Local Defence Volunteers – otherwise known as the 'Home Guard' – who arrested

Unteroffizier Dörner, who had landed on top of a house. Captain Guise, the unit's CO, reported that the German 'seemed very frightened. I think the Germans must have told their people that we ill-treat or kill our prisoners, but he cheered up when we gave him a cigarette.' Guise then went on to take Hugelschäfer into custody, who continues the story: -

'Upon arrival at the airfield I was taken to a barracks and inside were two of my crew, Dörner and Treue. A nurse gave us some tea and gave me an old gym shoe to replace the flying boot I'd lost. We sat for a few hours but it was difficult for us to converse. In the evening a lorry came to take us away. It was a frightening moment – we were led to the lorry along an aisle of soldiers with fixed bayonets.

'We spent that night in a prison, in single cells. We were in some sort of basement and on the ground was an old, dirty mattress and a single blanket. The window was covered by an iron plate with small holes in it. In the iron door there was a peep-hole through which a guard peered every hour or so. Next morning, we were taken to London by train, guarded by armed soldiers. I was placed alone in a room at a building in Hyde Park and remained there for about a week. Throughout, I was handled in a very correct manner. Eventually I was taken to a prisoner of war camp at Oldham where I remained until January 1941, when I shipped out to Canada, returning to England in the spring of 1946, remaining there until repatriation in 1947.'

Unteroffizier Theiner was not so lucky. Hit by machine-gun bullets during Pilot Officer Bird's attack, he was thrown out of the Ju 88 as the Hurricane smashed into it. Several hours later his body was discovered by the Brimscombe Home Guard, who had formed a line to comb the hills after previous attempts had failed to locate the fourth airman. Ten yards into Oldhills Wood, Theiner was found hanging head-down from a tree, his parachute unopened. With great chivalry not uncommon during this early war period, he was subsequently buried with full military honours at Brimscombe Church (later being reinterred at the *Soldatenfriedhoff* at Cannock Chase).

Pilot Officer Bird's Hurricane crashed at Bournes Green, Oakridge, on the Bisley Road. Soon a posse of special constables arrived on the scene, finding the fighter burnt out and the pilot's remains being removed by a Mr P. Handy of Painswick. What, though, had caused the crash?

Unteroffizier Hugelschäfer, an experienced combat flyer, remained convinced to the day he died that his aircraft had been deliberately

Right: The funeral, with full military honours, of 26-year-old *Unteroffizier* Walter Theiner at Brimscombe Church, Gloucestershire.

Below: Pilot Officer Bird's grave at St John the Baptist Churchyard, Adel, Yorkshire, where he has more recently been joined by his widow 'Marjie', who did actually re-marry. (Glenn Gelder)

rammed by Bird. Certainly, in the opinion of Pilot Officer Manlove, 'there is no doubt that the aircraft (Ju 88) was destroyed by Pilot Officer Bird', although his combat report does not provide an explanation for Alec going into a spin, or mention seeing his Hurricane collide with the Ju 88. Upon hearing of Pilot Officer Bird's involvement and fate, Flight Lieutenant Hanks retracted his claim for the raider's destruction. Whatever happened that day war came abruptly to the peaceful Cotswolds, the destruction of Hugleschäfer's aircraft was accredited to Pilot Officer Bird.

The story of Pilot Officer Bird, who made the ultimate sacrifice between the officially defined dates of the Battle of Britain, raises an important point: although he gave his life in action against the enemy, Alec Bird's name will not be found amongst those of the fabled Few. Nor will that of Flight Lieutenant Peter Prosser Hanks or Pilot Officer Richard Manlove. Why? Simply because neither served with one of the seventy-one fighter squadrons and appended units accredited by officialdom as having fought the Battle of Britain. When considering that a pilot with one of those units could quality for the coveted Battle of Britain Bar to the 1939-45 Star simply through having flown one uneventful operational patrol of whatever duration, between 10 July and 31 October 1940, this does seem rather unfair. Perhaps more appropriately the Air Ministry could have considered aircrew for inclusion from non-accredited units on a case-by-case basis, the criteria being that they actually saw action in the defence of England during the sixteen weeks in question. Not to do so seems exceptionally harsh in the case of those like Pilot Officer Bird who gave their lives – and he was not alone.

Some may wonder why it is important, all these years later, whether a pilot's name appears amongst the Few – or not? Well it is, the reason being that while the history of the Few continues to be well documented and their deeds 'remember'd', those not appearing on that all-important list are in danger of sliding into anonymity and obscurity – and, at the going down of the sun, as we commemorate the Battle of Britain, so must we spare a thought for and remember the Pilot Officer Birds too.

Finally, Marjorie did take Alec home to Yorkshire, where he was buried at Adel (St John the Baptist) Churchyard on 29 July 1940. On his headstone was inscribed the poem he had found and adapted only five days before: -

He has wings, for as the plane dived deep,
His spirit, free within the realms of space,
On newfound wings, flew with a swifter sweep,
Fearless and laughing, to the Throne of Grace.

Chapter Four

Subedar

Indian Merchant Navy
Died of Wounds: 11 August 1940

As an island nation, historically the British have been seafarers, a strong navy defending the country, trade routes and its interests abroad. Indeed, for a century, until 1914, Britannia's ruling of the waves went unchallenged, and by then Britain enjoyed the benefits of imports from its huge Empire, covering 24% of the world's land-mass, and upon which, it was said, 'the sun never set'. During the Second World War, Britain became heavily reliant upon American aid, which, of course, had to be transported by sea, a perilous undertaking, beset by surprise attacks from German submarines in their infamous 'Wolf Packs'; the Battle of the Atlantic's story is rightly well-known. Wartime convoys to and from Russia, in freezing conditions, were equally hazardous and are well-documented. Less so is the story of the small convoys over which the early part of the Battle of Britain was fought, the so-called 'Coal Scuttle Brigade' which bravely steamed between Southend and Southampton, through the Dover Strait, in full view of the ever-watchful Germans just a few miles away. Throughout the summer of 1940, this modest sea route became the most ferociously contested in the world.

After the Fall of France, the English Channel was deserted – all except for the black dust-encrusted colliers. To industrial Britain, coal was essential, firing as it did the power stations, furnaces and railways. According to some estimates, the weekly requirement was for a staggering 40,000 tons. This, however, Britain did not have to import, being rich in coalfields itself, but the miners' yield in Wales and the north-east still had to be transported to London and the south coast port of Southampton. The only practical means was by sea, to which there was no alternative. From the north-east, the colliers travelled south down the east coast, to Southend, the Thames Estuary and London's docks. East-bound convoys would assemble at Glasgow, making their way south down the west coast, meeting ships from South Wales, chugging across the Bristol Channel, around Land's End, and east to Southampton.

A *Stuka* prepares to dive-bomb a British freighter in the Channel.

There was limited U-boat activity in the comparatively shallow Channel – the greatest threat was from the air and shelling by German batteries around Calais. E-Boats, fast surface raiders armed with torpedoes, were another threat. Minefields were another danger. Naturally, convoys were afforded protection by the Royal Navy (RN), usually in the shape of two destroyers and half-a-dozen armed trawlers. There was, inevitably, a lack of preparedness however. No major exercise training in convoy cooperation and protection had been held before the war, the small number of convoy passage exercises were inclined more towards the RN practising operation of its primitive submarine-detecting radar. There were no specialist aircraft available and nor was air integrated into any formal convoy management plan. As it happened, keeping the 'Coal Scuttle Brigade' steaming through the Channel became about much more than just the vital coal the tramps carried – and those aboard the colliers doubtless wished that more thought had been given to their protection.

On the Channel coast, *Oberst* Theo Osterkampf's JG51 Me 109 pilots were anxious to set about England. As we have seen, in real terms the Battle of Britain arguably began on 2 July 1940, on which date the first Channel convoy was attacked. For the Germans, the priority was now the destruction of British fighters, the objective being aerial supremacy for the seaborne invasion of Britain that Hitler now considered a realistic proposition. First, though, the RAF fighters had to be drawn into battle, and with that foremost in mind, shipping was attacked. On that first day, the SS *Aeneas* was lost with twenty-one souls, while others were killed and injured on the damaged SS *Baron Ruthven*. By close of play on 4 July, five more ships had been sunk by bombing, two by mines, another by an E-boat, and fourteen more damaged by aerial attacks – sufficient to cause the Prime Minister to inquire of the Admiralty what arrangements were being made by the RN and RAF to protect the convoys. In response to this aerial bombardment, the Admiralty closed the Channel to all shipping except the 'Coal Scuttle Brigade'. The RAF fighters, consistent with Dowding's policy of carefully shepherding and preserving his limited resources, were not committed to battle *en masse* over the Channel; indeed they never were, no matter what inducement the enemy prioritised. Instead, the RAF fighters intercepted by flight and individual squadron, more often than not meeting much larger enemy formations comprising both bombers and fighters.

Over the days ahead, more colliers would be sunk or damaged. The worst day, 'Black Thursday', came on 25 July, when five ships were sunk and five merchantmen plus two destroyers damaged by bombing. Clearly things needed to change, especially because Göring openly boasted that his *Luftwaffe* had already achieved aerial superiority over the English Channel.

A convoy under aerial attack in the Dover Strait.

Getting the Coal Scuttle Brigade through became a matter of national pride. The scene was set for the Battle of Convoy 'CW9' (Coal West 9), codenamed Peewit. Twenty colliers sailed from the Medway on the evening of 7 August, intending to pass through the narrow Dover Strait under cover of darkness. The German Freya radar, however, detected the convoy, which was promptly attacked by E-boats before a full-blown air assault was incoming by day. By the time Peewit, or what was left of it, reached its destination at Swanage, six ships had been sunk and another fifteen damaged. In their defence, the RAF had lost thirteen Hurricanes and a Spitfire, with thirteen pilots killed. It was an intense battle (covered elsewhere in this book) and the crescendo of the Battle of Britain's first phase, the focus of which now shifted to inland targets.

Between 2 July and 8 August 1940 inclusive, at least 227 merchant seamen lost their lives in the English Channel, the youngest of their number being several 16-year-olds, the oldest 66. Many were not British, but foreign nationals – a significant number non-white. For example, ten sailors lost with the SS *Aeneas* on 2 July were from Hong Kong. Indians made up the largest number of non-British personnel, either serving with sea-going lines or the Indian Merchant Navy (IMF). On 29 July, of the thirteen killed when the SS *Clan Monroe* went down, twelve were Indians of the IMF. Likewise, on 2 August, eight more IMF sailors were lost with the SS *City of Brisbane*, another dying a few days later. Interestingly, all of these Indian sailors who lost their lives aboard these two ships appear to have been Muslims from pre-partitioned India. Although no figures are available for 1940, in his article 'Merchant seamen during the war', published in 1946, Sir William Elderton tells us that in 1938 there were 192,375 employed on British merchant ships, of whom 131,885 were British, 9,790 foreigners, mainly Europeans, and 50,700 Indians and Chinese. By 1938, 27% of seamen engaged on foreign-voyages were Chinese or Indian, with a further 5% including Arabs, West Africans and West Indians domiciled in British ports. It was these men who crewed the 'Coal Scuttle Brigade' and merchant ships bringing essential supplies to the besieged island.

On 2 August, the Ellerman Line-owned and Liverpool-registered British merchantman SS *City of Brisbane* was bound from Port Pirie, Australia, to London carrying lead, flour, tinned fruit and other foodstuffs, when it was attacked and badly damaged by German bombers. Beached on the southern end of Long Sand in the Thames Estuary, the battered hulk burned for three days before breaking in half and sinking. Eight Indians were killed, all of whom remain missing and are remembered on the Chittagong Memorial, which commemorated the 400 sailors of the Indian Navy and 6,000 of the IMF lost at sea during the Second World War. One man, fatally wounded, was brought ashore, only to die on 11 August 1940. All that is known of the 36-year-old Muslim is that his name was, simply, Subedar, the son of Sheikh Modee and husband of Tahera Bibi. Buried at Brookwood in the Mohammedan section, his story and likeness are now lost to history – and this contribution by Chinese and Indian sailors is, to be sure, 'hidden history', into which research is required.

The sailors from the Commonwealth who lost their lives in both world wars number 50,700 – some of those during the Channel convoy battles of July and August 1940. Of that number, 35,800 have no known grave. Those of the Merchant Navy and Fishing Fleet with no grave but the sea are commemorated on the Tower Hill Memorial, near the Tower of London. As we remember and reflect upon the cost of our 'Finest Hour', these men, from all four corners of the world, should be remembered too.

The grave of Subedar at Brookwood. (Kev Barnes)

Chapter Five

Flying Officer Richard Stephen Demetriadi

Killed in Action: 11 August 1940

&

Flight Lieutenant William Henry Rhodes-Moorhouse DFC

Killed in Action: 6 September 1940

601 'County of London' Squadron

In 1945 Evelyn Waugh published *Brideshead Revisited: The Sacred and Profane Memories of Captain Charles Ryder*, which became an international bestseller. Harking back to the 'golden age' between the wars, this most nostalgic and reflective of all Waugh's novels relates Ryder's close association with the Flytes and their rapidly disappearing, privileged, world. Waugh's tale, set mainly in the 1920s and '30s, provides a window on an enviable lifestyle which ordinary folk could only dream of. In truth, the inspiration and model for Waugh's doomed Marchmains were actually the Lygons of Madresfield Court, an ancient country house in the shadow of Worcestershire's imposing Malvern Hills, where the novelist spent much time before the war. In the churchyard adjacent to the Court's grounds (still a private house) can be found buried generations of this aristocratic dynasty, amongst them one Richard Michael Bernard Rowley, wherein lies another tale – one of many connecting high society and the 'Brideshead' world with the Battle of Britain.

Rowley was an Old Etonian who went up to Oxford where he joined the University Air Squadron and learned to fly before becoming a member of 601 'County of London' Squadron of the AAF in 1937. Commissioned in 1938, the following year Rowley married Lady Sibell Lygon, a one-time on-off lover of the Canadian-born press magnate Max, Lord Beaverbrook. Within weeks of the wedding however, there was a scandal: Rowley admitted bigamy, having previously married a German woman in 1938,

Above left: The grave of 601 Squadron's Michael Rowley at the churchyard adjacent to Madresfield Court in Worcestershire: the 'Real Brideshead'.

Above right: Willie Rhodes-Moorhouse learned to fly aged 17 while still at Eton, and is pictured here with his aviatrix mother, the remarkable Linda, with the DH Moth at Heston in 1931. (W.B. Rhodes-Moorhouse VC Charitable Trust)

after a drunken Mexican lunch! Eventually, the first marriage was dissolved, but having flown with 601 during the Battle of France, and 145 Squadron during the Battle of Britain, Rowley developed a brain tumour, leading to him being invalided out of the service in 1941. Nursed by Lady Sibell until the end, Flight Lieutenant Rowley died in Oxford on 19 September 1952. Laid to rest at Madresfield, on his headstone is proudly etched a winged sword – the crest of 601 Squadron, better known as the 'Millionaires' Mob'.

The AAF was created in 1924, Trenchard adopting the army's well-trodden territorial principle. Locally-raised squadrons of part-time airmen, who flew at weekends and attended an annual summer camp at an RAF station, represented an essential trained reserve, there to be mobilised in time of emergency. This was unlike the RAFVR, created in 1936, which was based upon 'Citizen Volunteers' and around main centres of population. These reservists were not formed into units but represented another trained reserve ready to be called to full-time service and deployed as replacements throughout the RAF (including the AAF). By 1930 the AAF represented five per cent of the service's strength, and was demonstrably a *corps d'élite*, the circumstances and attitude of which was perfectly explained by a distinguished auxiliary, namely Group Captain Sir Hugh 'Cocky' Dundas: -

'In all the history of arms there can seldom have been a body of men more confident and pleased with themselves than the pilots of the AAF. We wore a big brass "A" on the lapels of our tunics and no amount of official pressure during the war would persuade us to remove them. The regulars insisted that the "A" stood for "Amateur Airmen", or even "Argue and Answer Back". To us they were the symbols of our membership of a very special club. The pilots of the AAF were lawyers and farmers, stockbrokers and journalists; they were landowners and artisans, serious-minded accountants and unrepentant playboys. They had two things in common: a passion for flying and a determination to prove that anything the regulars could do the auxiliaries could do better.'

By 1939, there were twenty auxiliary squadrons. In this elite, in which socio-economic status was everything, all pilots were officers. Many of these young men were of independent means, who even owned their own aeroplanes and flew for pleasure. James Edgar 'Johnnie' Johnson, on the other hand, was a policeman's son from Melton Mowbray: -

'I was a member of the local territorial yeomanry but rather fancied flying a Spitfire in preference to riding a bloody great horse. So, I went along for an interview for the AAF and the senior officer present, noting that I was from Leicestershire, said "With whom do you hunt, Johnson?"
I said "Hunt, Sir?"
He said "Yes, Johnson, hunt; foxes. With whom do you hunt?"
I said, "Well, Sir, I don't hunt, I shoot, pheasants and such on the wing with a 12-bore".
He said, "Thank-you, Johnson, that will be all".
I simply didn't have the right social background so that was that.'

Johnson, of course, went on to join the RAFVR and become the RAF's top-scoring fighter pilot and fighter leader *par excellence* of the Second World War. It is important, however, to understand a little of Britain's socio-economic history between the wars, to appreciate the AAF in context.

In the First World War's wake, Britain experienced privations caused by the Great Depression. Widespread unemployment emphasized the disparity, for example, in the distribution of wealth. Indeed, Mowat described the 1930s

Above: Willie enjoyed a privileged lifestyle, seen here in his element as a champion skier. (Tessa Haughton)

Right: The society beauty Amalia Demetriadi. (Tessa Haughton)

as 'gloomy', the 'devil's decade'. A 'golden age' to Waugh it may well have been – but only for a select few. According to Branson and Heinemann, in 1937, 35.7% of the population earned under £2 10s per week; 37.8% earned between £2 10s and £4; 21.3% earned £4 to £10, but only 5.2% earned over £10. The lowest wage earners represented 4,318,000 families, while the top earnings concerned just 635,500. Although social class was not decided solely upon income, these figures nonetheless bring into sharp focus the inequality between classes. Mowat concluded that there were actually 'several Englands' between the wars and that 'their differences had never been so sharply drawn'. In 1933, the novelist and broadcaster J.B. Priestly made his *English Journey*, finding 'four Englands; that of the southern counties and guide books, the industrial north with many silent furnaces, the prosperous Home Counties and the England of the dole'. The distribution of wealth, therefore, was not simply a matter of class but also one of geography.

It is also important to understand a little of education in Britain between the wars. The social pyramid's elite 5.2% sent their children to independent

Above left: Willie and Amalia Rhodes-Moorhouse on their wedding day.

Above right: Willie Rhodes-Moorhouse serving with 601 Squadron of the Auxiliary Air Force before the Second World War. (W.B. Rhodes-Moorhouse VC Charitable Trust)

fee-paying schools known as 'public schools'. The top three such schools were Eton, Harrow and Winchester, all of which were notably located in southern England. The annual fees at these schools was in excess of £240 per annum – a sum clearly beyond the means of all but the wealthiest of families and exceeding the annual income of a great many in Britain at that time. These public schools were considered training grounds for the nation's future leaders and its 'captains of industry'. Indeed, 68% of Conservative MPs between 1920 and 1940 were educated at public schools, 27.5% at Eton. Of 271 civil servants earning over £1,000 per annum in 1939, 190 came from public schools, as did fifty-six of sixty-two bishops and thirty-three of sixty-seven High Court judges. Public school influence also dominated the business sector: in 1940, the three major banks had 103 directors, eighty-six of them from public schools. Indeed, in 1931, it was estimated that of 691 holders of high office in the church, state and industry, 76% were educated at public schools. It was also the public schools who provided officers for the armed forces, and Trenchard's initial vision was that all his pilots would be officers; they certainly were in the pre-war AAF – and 601 Squadron was the elite of the elite.

Considering the back-story to the AAF, it should come as no surprise to the reader that the origins of 601 'County of London' Squadron were in London's most exclusive gentleman's club: White's, at 37 St James Street, Mayfair, members of which were drawn from royalty, the aristocracy and high society. Interestingly, Waugh was a member, as of course was 601's founder, Lord Edward Arthur 'Ned' Grosvenor, son of the first Duke of Westminster, an Old Etonian, adventurer and passionate aviator. Indeed, Grosvenor had bought two of the first commercially produced aeroplanes made by the pioneering Frenchman Louis Blériot, learning to fly at Brooklands before putting himself and his machines at the country's disposal for the First World War. During the conflict, 'Ned' learned about military aviation, afterwards promoting civilian aviation. Grosvenor believed that in addition to the regular air force, the country also required a part-time, essentially civilian, reserve, seizing the chance, when news filtered through of Trenchard's intention to create the AAF, to host a dinner at White's and propose the foundation of 601 Squadron.

Grosvenor then recruited his like-minded and high-born friends to form a unit of trained pilots, under his command, presenting this to the Air Staff on a plate. Initially, five squadrons were formally raised, 601 'County of London' Squadron's formation as a bomber unit being announced on 14 October 1925. Based at Northolt, equipped with Avro 504s, summer camps were held at Lympne. There, on Romney Marsh, the two landowners adjacent to the airport, namely the actor Noel Coward and none other than the Under Secretary of State for Air, Sir Philip Sassoon, opened their homes to Grosvenor's officers. Sassoon's generous hospitality at his Porte Lympne mansion was such that 601's annual training camp became known as the 'Summer Outing of White's Club'! While this sets the scene, there is more: the eccentric and autocratic Grosvenor was, bizarrely considering his background, a former member of the French Foreign Legion – for which reason 601 became known as the 'Legion', its members 'Legionnaires'. A silver figure of a legionnaire brandishing a rifle in one hand and a sword held high in the other gave rise to the squadron's famous badge: the winged sword. Sadly, Grosvenor died prematurely in 1929, and was succeeded in command of 601 Squadron by that great friend of the 'Millionaire's Mob', Sir Phillip Sassoon.

A potential new recruit for 601 Squadron was one William Henry Rhodes-Moorhouse.

'Willie' was born in Brompton Square, London, on 4 March 1914, the only son of William Barnard Rhodes-Moorhouse and his wife Linda Beatrice (née Morrit). This was not what could be described by any standards as an 'ordinary' family. During the nineteenth century, Willie's great-grandfather, William Barnard Rhodes, had been amongst the first Englishmen to arrive and make a fortune from farming and other businesses in New Zealand, his huge estate of £750,000 being inherited by his adopted daughter Mary Ann, who married Edward Moorhouse, a New Zealander; the couple settled in England where their four children were raised. Having attended Harrow, William Barnard Rhodes-Moorhouse went up to Cambridge, but was much more interested in engineering and speed than academia. Consequently, he left Trinity College in 1909, becoming an airman and even produced his own aircraft. 1911 saw William winning air speed records in America, and in 1912 he made the first flight across the Channel with three passengers – including his new and equally adventurous wife Linda.

The following year, the family purchased Parnham, near Beaminster, according to Linda, 'a very beautiful Elizabethan house in Dorset… a large and splendid example…' A year later, Willie was born. That was good. Not so good was that on 28 July 1914 the First World War erupted. Volunteering for the RFC, William was soon at the front in France, flying BE2s with 2 Squadron at Merville. By 26 April 1915 he was a lieutenant and set off on a hazardous mission to drop a 100lb bomb on the important railway centre at Courtrai. This Lieutenant Rhodes-Moorhouse did, from

Right: Springett and Richard Demetriadi enjoying summer holiday between the wars. (Tessa Haughton)

Below: The Demetriadi children during happier times: Springett, Amalia and Richard. (Tessa Haughton)

just 300 feet, attracting intense machine-gun and small arms fire, wounding him, while shrapnel from his exploding bomb damaged his aeroplane. Badly injured, instead of making a forced landing and receiving life-saving medical attention from the Germans, Rhodes-Moorhouse pressed on towards base, attracting further fire. With grievous wounds, he eventually crash-landed having safely achieved Allied lines, making a perfect landing, and insisting on making out his report, imparting valuable intelligence, before being hospitalised. The following day, William died of his wounds, aged 27. At his own request, William's remains were returned to Parnham where they were buried with full military honours. For his 'signal act of valour' Lieutenant William Barnard Rhodes-Moorhouse was awarded the VC – the first airman ever to be so recognised. Before expiring, the VC wrote his first and only letter to his baby son Willie, expressing a desire that he would become an engineer and maintain his inherited station in life as a landowner, with responsibilities, and a gentleman. There can be little doubt that his intrepid and heroic father's example defined young Willie's life.

Willie grew up at Parnham, the family seat shared with his grandparents and aunt, Anne, and her children – to whom Willie, with his 'love for adventure became their idol'. As he grew up, Linda noted her son's mannerisms inherited from Will, father and son sharing the 'same mercurial gaiety… quick reactions in a crisis… courage… and love of speed and danger'. With good looks, charisma and a family fortune, as his mother said, Willie had 'the world at his feet'. Enviable holidays were largely divided between skiing abroad in winter, and spending the summer at the family's Cornwall cottage. Willie was, unsurprisingly, a natural skier, rapidly becoming an expert and winning the Kandahar Ski Club's coveted 'Gold K'. After taking up ski-jumping, though, the youngster hit a tree while hurtling through a wood at Megève in France, bursting a lung. Willie recovered, but then came a life-changing moment when Parnham was, for a variety of domestic reasons, sold,

Flying Officer Richard Demetriadi, 601 Squadron, while flying Blenheims. (Tessa Haughton)

Another dynamic and dashing personality on 601 Squadron was Roger Bushell – later to be shot down over Dunkirk while commanding 92 Squadron, and ultimately amongst fifty prisoners of war murdered by the *Gestapo* following their recapture after the 'Great Escape'. (Tessa Haughton)

the family returning to live in London. Concurrently Willie moved up from his preparatory school to Eton. It was now that aviation took hold of the boy.

During a Swiss skiing holiday, Willie had become friends with a Harrovian, Gordon 'Mouse' Cleaver, another young skier of repute, whose mother, Adelaide, owned her own Percival Mew Gull aircraft. One trip in the little plane and Willie was as intoxicated with flight as his late, august, father. Sale of a stamp collection bought a DH Moth for Willie, who learned to fly at Heston, where he took to the new activity with 'apparently no effort', Linda recalled. In 1931, aged 17, Willie rowed for Eton and – remarkably – achieved his pilot's licence, becoming known as the 'Flying Etonian'. Mrs Rhodes-Moorhouse and Willie subsequently enjoyed many airborne adventures together, flying around the UK during the school holidays, and even further afield, to France and Germany. When Willie returned to Eton, Linda learned to fly at Heston herself, successfully taking her 'ticket' in 1931. Upon leaving school, Willie set off on an international hunting expedition with a fellow Old Etonian and a professional explorer, but while he was away, Linda accidentally destroyed their beloved Moth in a crash, fortunately surviving herself relatively unscathed. Then Linda was off to the US at the invitation of Lord and Lady Howard de Walden, acting as their daughter's chaperone. Upon return, plans were made to visit New Zealand, the origin of the family's wealth, to which end a twin-engined De Havilland Rapide was purchased. The trip would never happen: Willie had fallen in love. As Linda explained: 'The object of his affections was a lovely young woman… her name Amalia, but instead of being called by this beautiful name always answered to "Muggins".' According to one newspaper report, Amalia was 'a woman with beauty, brains and wealth. Her beauty is Grecian, and some of her wealth too…' Amalia was the daughter of Sir Stephen Demetriadi, whose parents were Greek, a wealthy man from 'cotton, jute and other Indian commodities'.

Sir Stephen's parents, Constantine Demetriadi and Amalia Thalassinos, were certainly Greek, but their son was born on 7 March 1880 in Lancashire, and educated at Marlborough. He became a highly respected civil servant, author of two well-received books on government office and reform. During the First World War, Sir Stephen was Director of Naval and Military War Pensions, later serving as first Chairman then President of the London Chamber of Commerce. Having married Gulielma Bates, Sir Stephen's eldest son, Springett Stephen, was born in 1914, Amalia Gulielma in 1915, and Richard Stephen in Chelsea on 14 August 1918. The Demetriadis made their home in Sussex, overlooked by the county's highest point, the Ditchling Beacon. Both boys would attend Eton, while, in due course, "Muggins" was presented at Court as a debutante, enjoying two seasons on the high society party circuit. Amalia and Willie had much in common, from skiing to greyhounds, and a shared, intimate familiarity with a privileged lifestyle – a perfect match. On 15 September 1936, Amalia and Willie married, simply and without fuss, at Marylebone Registry Office. Afterwards they honeymooned in America before continuing their idyllic existence. The only cloud was Willie having been selected for the British Winter Olympic team that season, but unable to compete owing to an accident on the ramp. Still, there were worse places to convalesce than St Moritz, where Willie and Amalia were in good company.

Amongst those enjoying the international rivalry of what remained a comparatively young sport was one Flight Lieutenant Roger Bushell – a practising barrister, gifted sportsman and a dynamic member of 601 Squadron. There can be little doubt that Bushell became an influence. Willie, of course, was an obvious recruit for 601 Squadron, which he joined on 28 July 1937, when commissioned into the AAF as a pilot officer. By then 601 was based at Hendon flying the Hawker Demon biplane light-bomber. 601 shared the field with 600 'City of London' Squadron of the AAF,

Right: The raid on Borkum as imagined by a war artist.

Below: Flight Lieutenant Willie Rhodes-Moorhouse with his wife Amalia and mother Linda, 3 September 1940, attending the investiture at Buckingham Palace for Willie's DFC – three days later he was shot down and killed in action over Kent.

the two founding units inevitably setting the tone and standard for subsequent auxiliary squadrons to emulate. According to Group Captain Dundas, at Hendon could be found 'a group of enthusiasts, well laced with young men of great wealth, giving every moment of their spare time to the squadrons, many of them affecting an approach to their training as to appear almost frivolous, yet achieving a standard of efficiency in the air which surpassed many regular squadrons'. The flying and camaraderie of 601 Squadron suited Willie perfectly. Understandably, the dashing, intrepid and accomplished Willie was idolised by Amalia's younger brother, Richard, who, as an Old Etonian from a prominent family and the brother-in-law of Pilot Officer Rhodes-Moorhouse, son of the first air VC, also had the necessary credentials, therefore, to join the 'Millionaires' Mob'. Richard was just a boy, while Willie, just four years older, was an accomplished man of the world, a married man, someone to look up to and emulate. After Eton, Richard was attached to the Royal estate at Sandringham and in 1938 also became a 'Legionnaire'. On 25 July 1938, 19-year-old Richard was commissioned as a pilot officer into 601 Squadron, learning to fly the Demon part-time. With nepotism underpinning admission to this most exclusive club, in 601 Squadron young Richard found many compatriots, including 'Mouse' Cleaver, Willie's schoolfriend whose mother's aeroplane had provided Willie's first air experience. For sure, Richard found 601 to be virtually an extended family – which was exactly the idea – with which to share the adventure of military aviation with his idolised brother-in-law.

Sir Stephen Demetriadi, accompanied by Amalia and Linda, made his own enquiries after his son-in-law was reported missing, discovering a Hurricane crash site which he paid private contractors to recover. This was confirmed to be the aircraft and the remains of Willie Rhodes-Moorhouse, realising the family's worst fears. (Tessa Haughton)

In November, the squadron re-equipped with the single-seater

Willie Rhodes-Moorhouse's ashes were buried adjacent to his VC-winning father's remains at Parnham. (W.B. Rhodes-Moorhouse VC Charitable Trust)

Gloster Gauntlet and became a fighter squadron. This was, of course, two months after the crisis over Czechoslovakia, after which, in spite of Hitler's guarantees, it was patently obvious that war with Germany was inevitable. While between the wars the emphasis of air power doctrine and consequently rearmament was on the bomber force, Fighter Command's chief, Air Chief Marshal Dowding, forcibly disagreed, believing that the cornerstone of defence was not the 'knockout blow' on an enemy delivered by bombers, but 'fear of the fighter'. With war now looming, efforts were at last stepped up to increase the fighter forces available to Dowding for the inevitable battle ahead. The Gauntlet biplane however was no match for the lethal Me 109 monoplane fighter. Fortunately, by then the Hawker Hurricane and Supermarine Spitfire had entered the arena, although it would take time for Fighter Command to re-equip and convert its squadrons to the new, modern, types. 601 Squadron, however, was not to be amongst those receiving the Hurricane and Spitfire: in January 1939 the 'Millionaires' Mob' exchanged its Gauntlets for the fighter version of the Bristol Blenheim – a twin-engined monoplane with a crew of three, originally intended as a light-bomber.

The Blenheim Mk IF was developed as a long-range daytime fighter, with a pack of four forward-firing Browning machine guns fitted beneath the fuselage.

The machine also boasted a wing-mounted Browning and a dorsal turret with gunner and two more machine guns. The aircraft's top speed, however, was 266 mph, insufficient to overhaul German bombers (for example, the Ju 88's top speed was 292 mph), and, again, this ponderous twin-engined aircraft was in no way comparable to the Me 109. The other problem was that 601 Squadron's pilots now had to convert from singles to twins. To this the squadron applied itself enthusiastically, a colour movie in the family's possession showing a beaming young Richard and friends with their Blenheims at various locations. Training on the new type peaked at the 1939 summer camp, held at Ford, soon after which, on 25 August 1939, 601 Squadron was mobilised and called to full-time service, its pilots making their way to Hendon from all points of the compass. By then, Grosvenor's successor as CO, Sir Philip Sassoon, who had been Under Secretary of State for Air when the AAF was formed, had also died a young man, aged 50, in June 1939 – meaning that neither of 601 Squadron's primary architects lived to see the 'Legion' in action.

On 2 September 1939, the day before war broke out, 601 Squadron moved from Hendon to Biggin Hill. On the fateful Sunday of Mr Chamberlain's broadcast, twelve 601 Squadron pilots were scrambled to intercept an 'intruder'– which transpired to be nothing more threatening than a distant refrigerator motor. Upon return to base, the glass-nosed Blenheims were mistaken for enemy bombers and fired at by the Station's defences, although fortunately none were hit. Nonetheless, the Second World War was now a reality, the future for all young men, regardless of rank and status, now extremely uncertain.

Of Richard Demetriadi, Group Captain Dundas remembered that he was the 'youngest member of the Squadron, who had not been fully trained when the war started, but had pleaded so earnestly to stay with the Squadron, and was so popular with the other officers, that he was surreptitiously awarded his wings and allowed to stay'. This is clear evidence of the auxiliary attitude and disdainful treatment of the service's rules and regulations, and ability to circumvent the system with impunity.

With war declared, things would never be the same again. In 1939 Willie had bought Mortham, a Peel tower, a fortified house in the borders of County Durham, on his maternal uncle's Rokeby estate. Linda oversaw restoration of this historic property, transforming it into a family home. The project was enthusiastically and capably delivered by David Hodges, husband of Linda's niece Silvia Ryle, one of Willie's cousins with whom he shared childhood at Parnham. Mortham was a long way from London however, so Linda, unable to bear being away from the main events, volunteered for

Having been reported missing during a huge air battle of Portland on 11 August 1940, on 15 September Flying Officer Richard Demetriadi's body washed up on the French coast. He was buried at Cayeux. (via Kev Barnes)

the Auxiliary Fire Service as a driver in the capital. Amalia went to live with her father at the Hut, his house atop the Downs at Streat. So, while Mortham's people became swept up in events beyond their control, the house remained steadfast, standing guard, as it had for centuries. Sadly, it would never become the family home envisaged when Willie purchased it.

Back at Biggin Hill, Flying Officer Rhodes-Moorhouse, as he now was, found himself responsible for ensuring the squadron's officers had sufficient petrol for their private transports. To overcome the privations and inconvenience of rationing, the solution was obvious: Willie simply bought the civilian garage located on the road running through the base, the route having been closed for security reasons. The ongoing supply of fuel was assured by virtue of fellow Legionnaire Loel Guinness just happening to be a director of a Shell subsidiary. When the road was reopened,

Willie even managed to sell the garage for a profit. It was all great fun, the war, or so it seemed, as Tom Moulson wrote in the squadron history: 'The Legionnaires sat around the Biggin Hill crew room drinking beer and playing backgammon, or on the airfield grass, eating splendid lunches delivered by Fortnum and Mason. Only occasionally did they remember that they were at war.' Given the geography involved, although Britain and France declared war on Nazi Germany following Hitler's invasion of Poland, in practical terms it was impossible to provide military support. Consequently, this was now the 'Phoney War', with little happening in the west – the lull before the storm. For Fighter Command, while the AASF went to the continent in support of the BEF, home-based squadrons intercepted the odd German reconnaissance or nuisance raider, provided protection for convoys, and trained hard, in 601's case flying all kinds of training sorties including searchlight cooperation and night-flying, it having already been appreciated that the Blenheim was obsolete as a day-fighter.

Nonetheless, there was excitement for 601 on 27 November: three aircraft each of 'A' and 'B' Flights, including Flying Officer Rhodes-Moorhouse who flew in the section commanded by Flight Lieutenant Max Aitkin, son of Lord Beaverbrook, were ordered to Northolt. There the auxiliaries

The church at Westmeston, Sussex, close to the Demetriadi family seat, wherein both Flying Officer Richard Demetriadi and his brother-in-law Flight Lieutenant Willie Rhodes-Moorhouse DFC are commemorated.

received orders to join with Blenheims of 25 Squadron in a raid planned for the following day on Borkum, a German seaplane base in the Frisian Islands. Members of 601 Squadron's ground-staff soon arrived, spending the whole night fitting out the Blenheims for this audacious operation – which involved a 500-mile return flight across the North Sea. By 1030 hrs on 28 November, the aircraft were ready, taking off an hour later for Bircham Newton, on the east coast, there to refuel before heading to the enemy coast. At 1525 hrs, 'Front gun attacks were made… by all aircraft, which returned immediately.' Complete surprise had been achieved in what was both 601 Squadron's first operation and Fighter Command's first incursion over German territory. Willie Rhodes-Moorhouse, like his father before him, had now been to war.

The following month, 601 Squadron moved south, beginning a long association with Tangmere, the famous fighter station on the south coast near Chichester. Life, however, continued much the same, like an extended summer camp, not to be taken too seriously. Willie's closest friend on 601 Squadron was Henry Cavendish, as the latter's son – William – relates: -

'During summer months in the late 1930s and even right up to August 1940, ten young fighter pilots would drive or fly down to north Cornwall in their Bentleys and private two-seater planes.

'Accompanied by wives, girlfriends and chums from White's Club, these airmen were Willie and Amalia Rhodes-Moorhouse, Amalia's brother, Richard Demetriadi, Max and Cynthia Aitkin, "Mouse" and Pauline Cleaver, the American Billy Fiske and Rose Warwick, the South African Roger Bushell, Canadian "Paddy" Green, Brian Thynne, Billy Clyde and Henry Cavendish.

'They were welcomed at the cliff-top house Linda Rhodes-Moorhouse built for her fourteen-year-old son, Willie, in 1924. Linda and her Cockney cook, Rose Exton, were joined in the greetings by Willie's aunt, Anne, the VC's sister, and her three attractive daughters, Diana, Silvia and Iris Ryle, who occupied the neighbouring cottage. The girls had shared their childhood with their cousin, Willie, and their mothers, Annc and Linda, at Parnham, the Jacobean manor in Dorset (that practically all female household in his inherited home may have struck Willie as somewhat unusual when he escaped to an all-male boarding school. The girls, conversely, continued their education with a governess in the "School Room").

'The entertainment offered the officers in Cornwall, during their now less frequent and shorter visits, was practically limitless. Besides the usual pastimes of golf, tennis, swimming, backgammon, and listening to wind-up gramophone, guests were expected to go "spratting" with hooks for sand eels, or "prawning" for "Berkeley Boys". Linda and Amalia showed where lobsters, crab and mullet lurked in rock pools.

'At the outbreak of war, to everyone's delight, Diana Ryle and Henry Cavendish became engaged. No-one was more pleased than Willie, for he and Henry, despite the age gap (Henry was six years older), were the closest possible friends, sharing their passion for flying and fast cars. The pair stood out as regular "play boys". Henry would tease Willie for the slightest vanity about his good looks: "Willie is always off somewhere to have raw eggs rubbed into his scalp!" Diana and Henry were married in January 1940 at St Faith's Chapel, Westminster Abbey; Willie was Best Man. First, though, the pair arrived at St Margaret's, where they awaited events before realising it was the wrong church! At St Faith's, the tiny chapel was freezing, men wearing their service greatcoats, the ladies fashionable furs.'

Naturally, 601 Squadron's officers were amongst the wedding guests, which was widely reported in society publications.

In March 1940 there was good news for 601 Squadron: Hurricanes were to replace the Blenheims. Though less charismatic, shall we say, than the Spitfire, the Hurricane, having flown and entered production before Mitchell's fighter, was a single-engined, short-range monoplane interceptor fighter available in greater numbers. Consequently, more of Fighter Command's squadrons operated Hurricanes than Spitfires. While far superior to the Blenheim, and able to turn tighter than the Me 109, the eight-gun Hurricane was inferior to the enemy fighter in respect of speed and height. Nonetheless, Tangmere was in the very front of the line, on the coast with Southampton to the west and London inland, and conversion to the Hurricane meant that 601 Squadron would be a frontline fighter squadron in every sense of the word. Immediately, the 'Millionaires' Mob' began converting to their new mount, and just in time: on 10 May 1940, the 'Phoney War' ended suddenly and violently when Germany unleashed *Blitzkrieg* against the west.

On that day, Squadron Leader Loel Guinness, now 601 Squadron's CO, led twelve Hurricanes to Hawkinge, Fighter Command's closest airfield to France, just inland of Folkestone. Within the formation were Flying Officer Rhodes-Moorhouse and Pilot Officer Demetriadi, both members of Flight Lieutenant Aitkin's Flight. The pilots remained at Hawkinge for the day, which for them passed without event, returning to Tangmere that evening. The following day the process was repeated, Guinness again leading his

The parish war memorial within St Martin's at Westmeston.

pilots to Hawkinge, from where they patrolled over Belgium without encountering any enemy aircraft. Again, Willie and Richard were involved, as was Flying Officer Michael Rowley, with whom we began our story at Madresfield, the 'Real Brideshead'. Next day, 601 proceeded to Manston, but there was no call to arms. A signal was received from HQ 11 Group that three 601 Squadron pilots and their aircraft were to cross the Channel on attachment to 607 'County of Durham' Squadron, another auxiliary unit, based at Vitry-en-Artois. Flying Officer Gerald Cuthbert along with Pilot Officers Richard Demetriadi and C.R. Young were chosen to go, and off they went. Less than twenty-four hours later, Cuthbert was dead, one of three 607 Squadron pilots shot down by Me 109s of 4/JG2 while attacking Hs 123s over Corroy-le-Château. It is highly likely that Richard Demetriadi was also involved in this action, but unfortunately 607 Squadron's records did not survive the Battle of France. We do know that at 1100 hrs on 20 May 1940, while attacking enemy troops between Cambrai and Arras, Richard's Hurricane, N2671, was sufficiently damaged by ground fire to necessitate a forced landing at Merville. We also know that, according to his father Sir Stephen, on this occasion Richard only 'narrowly escaped death… when an enemy machine put a bullet through his oxygen mask which came out through the visor without touching him'. Two days later, 607 Squadron was pulled out of France, returning to England. Pilot Officers Demetriadi and Young had survived their first taste of action, reporting back to 601 at Tangmere. There they found a depleted unit, the bulk of personnel and pilots having proceeded on to operate from bases in France, 'A' Flight from Merville, 'B' at St Valery. Willie was at Merville – the very airfield at which his father had been based. Flying Officer Rhodes-Moorhouse's combat reports tell their own story.

18 May 1940: -

'On offensive patrol over Brussels when about twelve He 111s were sighted flying in pairs just above or in and out of 8/10ths cloud. On attacking one enemy aircraft, the starboard engine issued a lot of black and white smoke, also the aircraft slipped into a steep right-hand turn and dived towards the ground. My machine was hit in several places, one bullet going through the oil tank.'

19 May 1940: -

'About fifty enemy aircraft in three waves, flying west of south were sighted when our fighters were flying in opposite direction at 2,000 feet above. Stern attack was adopted. Then, just within range, I opened fire on the starboard side of the formation when I saw four or five Me 110s approaching from the right and ahead, so I turned towards them and passed through their formation, firing all the time, when my reserve petrol tank was shot, and the whole cockpit filled with petrol. I then dived vertically down to fifty feet and levelled out beside Cambrai, which was being very heavily bombed. I finally landed at Abbeville, re-fuelled and returned to Manston.'

22 May 1940: -

'On sighting enemy aircraft our formation broke up and a dog-fight ensued. After circling about for about five minutes, only seeing Hurricanes, I found myself alone and saw several aeroplanes flying round about 2,000 feet above me – so climbed up, thinking them to be friendly, only to find myself going round in very tight left-hand turns with three Me 109s. After about two turns I found myself on the tail of the one in front of me. My first short burst missed and after the third burst the aircraft dived downwards in a steep left-hand turn with smoke pouring out. I continued going round in right-hand circles until I eventually lost the remaining two Me 109s. I returned to base by myself.'

The battle, however, was already lost, as related previously in this book. Soon Fighter Command was patrolling and engaging the enemy over the French coast, patrolling between Calais and Dunkirk in support of Operation Dynamo. By the end of May, 601 Squadron had claimed the destruction of twenty enemy aircraft and had been well-blooded in combat – and both Richard and Willie had survived. By 3 June, the Dunkirk evacuation was over (again as related elsewhere in this book), and both sides settled down to recuperate before what everyone now knew lay ahead: the Battle of Britain.

On 1 June, 601 Squadron moved west from Tangmere to Middle Wallop in 10 Group, just inland of Southampton. On 5 June, Max Aitkin was promoted to squadron leader and succeeded Loel Guinness in command. Two days later, a composite formation of 43 and 601 Squadron Hurricanes patrolled over Rouen, engaging Me 109s but making no claims; Flying Officer Robinson and Pilot Officer Hubbard were missing from this combat. On 17 June the squadron returned to Tangmere, the month's main activity being training flights and uneventful operational patrols – until 28 June, when Squadron Leader Aitkin destroyed an He 111 at night, a rare feat indeed. The following day, Air Chief Marshal Dowding himself visited Tangmere to award Aitkin an immediate DFC. While Flying Officer Rhodes-Moorhouse flew many sorties that month, there is no record of Pilot Officer Demetriadi having flown at all, or explanation as to his deployment.

The identity of this exclusive club was starting to change. After the Fall of France and Dunkirk air fighting, Fighter Command's squadrons required replacements for casualties sustained. It was now that Trenchard's vision paid off, because most of these new pilots were reservists. So it was that on 21 May 1940, for example, Sergeant Redvers Hawkings of the RAFVR reported to 601 Squadron, followed shortly afterwards by Sergeant Leonard Guy – there would be many more. On 9 June, Flight Sergeant Arthur Pond arrived, a pre-war airman who had become a fighter pilot thanks to Trenchard's initiative permitting a small number of NCOs to fly for four years before reverting to their original trades, thereby expanding further still the trained reserve available in time of crisis. Such personnel, of course, not being of independent or well-connected means, would never have been admitted to the 'Millionaire's Mob' before hostilities, so this is an early example of how the Second World War accelerated social change – and these new pilots would not be found wanting.

We know from surviving records that when next Richard flew, he was Flying Officer Demetriadi, having been promoted, this being a refresher sortie of thirty minutes on 6 July 1940. By this time,

The plaque recording Sir Stephen Demetriadi's gift to the National Trust of land on Ditchling Beacon in memory of his son, Flying Officer Richard Demetriadi.

although four days before the Battle of Britain's official start-date, the brief lull following the Dunkirk evacuation had ended on 2 July, as fighting erupted over Channel-bound convoys (see the story of Sergeant Patrick Hayes and that of merchant seaman Subedar). On 7 July, Willie was in action again, sharing in the destruction of a Do 17, followed by another on 11 July. Meanwhile, Richard continued re-familiarising himself with the Hurricane, making local flights and practising flying in cloud and aerobatics. On 13 July, Flying Officer Demetriadi made his first operational sortie of the Battle of Britain, in Hurricane P3886, unusually a solo and unspecified 'Operational Take-off' between 1935 and 2005 hrs. The date was also significant for another reason: Roger Bushell's American playboy friend 'Billy' Fiske joined 601 as a pilot officer straight from flying training school. Unusually for this period, previously Fiske received no operational training, so his Hurricane flight on 14 July was a first. A few flights and eleven flying hours later, Fiske would make his first operational patrol on 20 July. Although America remained neutral, Fiske was not the only American to cross the Atlantic and volunteer for Fighter Command. Indeed, on 601 Fiske joined fellow 'Yank in the RAF' Flight Lieutenant Carl Davis, an auxiliary and Legionnaire since 1936. Before too long, the squadron would also include pilots from the occupied lands amongst its establishment, indicating that an increasingly socially-diverse and multi-national force fought the Battle of Britain.

Richard was a member of 'A' Flight, commanded by fellow Old Etonian Flight Lieutenant Sir Archibald Hope, the 17th Baronet of Craighall. Over the next few days Richard flew various uneventful interception and convoy patrols led by Hope, although Willie's 'A' Flight had better luck, engaging and damaging the enemy on 16 and 17 July. On the latter date, Squadron Leader Aitkin was posted to the Air Ministry, soon to command a night-fighter unit, being succeeded in command of 601 Squadron by Squadron Leader William Hobson. Although a pre-war Cranwell flight cadet and an experienced biplane pilot, Hobson had only just converted to monoplane fighters and had no combat experience – not an untypical scenario during this early war period.

For Richard, July wore on with a ceaseless round of patrols and convoy escorts, punctuated by night-flying practice. There was cause for celebration on 23 July however: Flight Lieutenant Willie Rhodes-Moorhouse was awarded the DFC, for 'great courage and devotion to duty'. By this time, Willie was credited with the destruction of five enemy aircraft and therefore officially an 'ace'. Naturally, given his father's VC, the Ministry of Information made hay with this award from a propaganda perspective, which was widely reported. The *Sunday Times* also mentioned that Willie had 'a narrow escape in 1937, when with Squadron Leader John Gillan, who made the Edinburgh-London record flight of forty-eight minutes, he was trapped in the wreckage after the plane had crashed. Gillan, who was badly cut, hobbled to a farmhouse, borrowed an axe, and hacked his colleague from the wreckage'. Of her son-in-law, a proud Lady Demetriadi told the *Sunday Graphic* that 'He just lives for flying.' It was certainly a well-deserved decoration.

July passed into August, the routine of sporadic combats, patrols, and training continuing; young Richard Demetriadi flew many times, not meeting the enemy but increasing his flying experience. A pilot, however, Pilot Officer Patrick Challoner Lindsay, an SSC officer who had joined 601 Squadron on 20 April, had been shot down and killed off St Catherine's Point by Me 109s of III/JG27, the 20-year-old's body later washed up on the French coast, the unfortunate pilot buried at Wimereux. This fighting over the Channel was a grave concern for Fighter Command's chiefs, Air Sea Rescue being in its infancy. Even if they safely baled out, unless rescued from the water quickly, especially if wounded, the chances of pilots surviving were slim. Many would be lost over the sea who with a more efficient ASR set-up may well have survived. This was, therefore, a hazardous period of fighting, for more reasons than one.

Timed for when Fighter Command's dawn patrols were running short of fuel, on the morning of Sunday 11 August, Kesselring sent three fighter sweeps over the south-eastern Kent and Sussex coastlines. A high proportion of 11 Group's squadrons were drawn into battle, although the Germans' second initiative, saturating Kent's defences using many individual fighter squadrons, failed to provoke a mass scramble. At 0945 hrs, the radar station at Ventnor reported a huge enemy force assembling over Cherbourg. Air Vice-Marshals Park and Brand, the latter commanding 10 Group, correctly guessed this to be the day's main assault. Immediately, the Spitfires of 609 Squadron were scrambled from Warmwell to patrol base, along with the Tangmere Hurricanes of 1 Squadron. Fifty-three other RAF fighters at those stations in addition to Exeter and Middle Wallop were brought to immediate readiness. This raid would transpire to be the largest yet unleashed against Britain: fifty-four Ju 88s of I and II/KG54, and twenty He 111s of KG27, escorted by sixty-one Me 110s of I and II/ZG2, along with thirty Me 109s of III/JG2. This 'Valhalla's' target was the naval base at Portland, towards which it droned, reaching mid-Channel at 1000 hrs. In response, a total of sixteen Spitfires

Tessa Haughton, Richard Demetriadi's niece, proudly displays her uncle's portrait.

and fifty-eight Hurricanes were scrambled. Not uncommonly, however, information in primary sources differ regarding 601 Squadron's contribution.

According to the 601 Squadron ORB (Form 541), at 0945 hrs, Flight Lieutenant Rhodes-Moorhouse led off Flying Officer Gillan, Pilot Officers Fiske, Dickie and Sergeant Hawkings. At 1000 hrs, 'A' Flight, comprising Flying Officers Demetriadi, Davis, Cleaver, Pilot Officers Smithers and McGrath, and Sergeant Guy, followed on. However, according to a report dated 13 August by Squadron Leader The Hon. Edward F. Ward, who had succeeded Hobson in command the previous day, 'At 1000 hrs… twelve aircraft of 601 Squadron took off…'. If the two flights did take off at different times, they formed up in the air, under the leadership of Flight Lieutenant Rhodes-Moorhouse, the senior officer involved.

By 1009 hrs, German fighter formations were milling about in circles five miles south-east of Portland, 609 Squadron's Spitfires engaging and destroying five Me 110s. As other RAF fighters arrived, a massive dogfight developed between the opposing fighters, which by 1040 hrs covered the whole of Weymouth Bay. Only a handful of Hurricanes and Spitfires managed to intercept the bombers, failing to prevent damage to naval installations and two oil storage tanks being set ablaze.

Flight Lieutenant Rhodes-Moorhouse: -

'I was Blue 1, with Blue Section leading the Squadron. Red Section and Green Section were on my left and right respectively with Yellow Section in the box. We were ordered to patrol St Catherine's Point at 20,000 feet, then told to go to Portland. When just south of Swanage at 19,000 feet, I saw a very large number of E/A milling around some miles to the south, so I turned towards them. At this moment my engine stopped, so I ordered the Squadron to continue without me. By this time, I had found out that I had been running on reserve. I had lost height and the rest of the Squadron. While climbing up to the E/A already mentioned, three Me 109s attacked from my left, so I turned towards them and approached head-on, with E/A and myself both firing. After passing underneath E/A, made very violent right-hand turn and spun down to 14,000 feet. I then climbed again 25,000 feet and circled round, above the main body of aircraft, trying to identify them – and found them to be all Me 109s circling round in sections of three to five, in line astern at various heights. I then dived across this mass of E/A, firing as and when a target presented itself and climbed up the other side (in this attack one E/A was hit but cannot confirm it crashing). I then turned and made a similar dive in the opposite direction. This time I approached a section of three Me 109s from the stern right-hand quarter, firing in front of the leader but not allowing enough deflection. Nevertheless, I hit the two machines directly behind, one going down in flames, the other went down in a steep dive, both of which I saw crash into the sea. Until this point E/A had been so intent on watching each other that I had been unnoticed. But I was then attacked by four Me 109s and thinking I was out of ammunition took cover in cloud and returned to base, just below cloud, to find I had fired 300 rounds in seven guns and 100 in the eighth, which had a broken Pawl spring. I landed at 1110 hrs. I saw a lot of bright green sea-markers in the sea where E/A must have crashed.'

Willie claimed two Me 109s destroyed but unconfirmed in this combat, occurring twenty miles south of Swanage.

Although not involved personally, Squadron Leader Ward's report provides a point of reference for the rest of 601 Squadron: -

'When airborne, orders were received to proceed to Portland. When approximately twenty miles south of St Catherine's Point, enemy aircraft were sighted about twenty miles south of Swanage, in numbers estimated by various pilots as being from fifty to 200, in layers from 15,000 – 25,000 feet. 601 Squadron were ordered to attack the upper layers of fighters, which were identified as Me 109s and Me 110s at 22,000 feet.'

Back at Tangmere, 601 Squadron's pilots claimed the destruction of twelve enemy aircraft with four more damaged. It had been a colossal scrap, a real aerial spectacle, the greatest so far during this crucial summer of 1940.

But four of 601 Squadron's pilots were missing.

Pilot Officer Julian Smithers, an Old Etonian, former stockbroker and pre-war Legionnaire, had been shot down and killed, his body later washing up on the French coast.

Flying Officer James Gillan, an SSC officer, and Pilot Officer William Dickie of the RAFVR were never seen again.

Flying Officer Richard Demetriadi's medals.

The fourth pilot missing was Flying Officer Richard Demetriadi, in Hurricane R4092, UF-U, the youngest pre-war Legionnaire. Richard, as Squadron Leader War's report explained, 'was engaged in the general dogfight which followed the attack. It was observed by another pilot that petrol was leaking badly from Flying Officer Demetriadi's aircraft, but the aircraft was still under control at the time. Nothing further has since been seen or heard of the pilot or aircraft.'

Desolation. Willie, who doubtless felt some responsibility for his younger brother-in-law, the baby of the Demetriadi family, set off by road for Streat Hill Farm, at Streat in Sussex, there to break the worst of news to his wife, Amalia, and father-in-law, Sir Stephen. Two days later, Sir Stephen visited 601 Squadron at Tangmere, concluding that 'When the boats returned and Richard had not been picked up, Squadron Leader Ward and three other machines went out at 7 pm to search the sea. They covered an area of thirty miles, flying at only fifty feet above the sea and could find no trace of Richard. He must have gone down without being able to bale out, which suggests that he had been shot. I fear all hope of his being alive must be abandoned. Whether before paying the supreme sacrifice he brought down any enemy machines that day, and if so how many, will never be known…'

In this fateful action, Fighter Command lost sixteen Hurricanes and a Spitfire shot down, fourteen pilots killed and several wounded. Six RAF fighters force-landed with damage, and five more were shot up but returned to base. During the engagement the Luftwaffe lost six Me 110s, five Ju 88s, one He 111 and six Me 109s destroyed, which was substantially less than Fighter Command's pilots claimed in this chaotic fight. Owing to the high number of RAF losses and German combat claims, it is impossible to say who shot down Richard Demetriadi. What is interesting however, is the disproportionately high number of Spitfires claimed destroyed by the enemy fighter pilots, when only one was lost. We know that Me 109s took part from JGs 2, 27 and 53, and interestingly *Oberleutnant* Helmut Wick of 3/JG2 claimed a 'Curtiss' at 1130 hrs (Continental time), a 'Spitfire' at 1134 hrs, and a 'Hurricane' '40 km Portland' (no direction given), at 1145. It is impossible to say, however, whether this was Flying Officer Demetriadi, but the possibility cannot be discounted. Either way, Richard was missing.

On 15 September, Richard Demetriadi's body was washed ashore near Cayeux-sur-Mer, in which cemetery the 21-year-old was buried, the news eventually filtering back to England via the town's Mayor and French International Red Cross.

The fact is, given that auxiliary squadrons were locally raised, with nepotism a forethought, that pilots were often related. The problem with this was that losses therefore hit these units hard. In the action on 11 August, 601 Squadron had lost a third of its operational strength, including two pre-war Legionnaires. It is perhaps unsurprising that Flight Lieutenant Rhodes-Moorhouse did not fly for a week.

Brian Thynne, a legendary Legionnaire and one-time CO, wrote from Usworth to Amalia: -

'I've only just heard of Richard's loss and send you my very deepest sympathy.

'I'm afraid they have had an awful gruelling down there, and hear on the best authority that they are shortly coming up here for a well-earned and overdue rest. I hope it is true, but how terribly sad that it should not be in time to catch poor Richard.

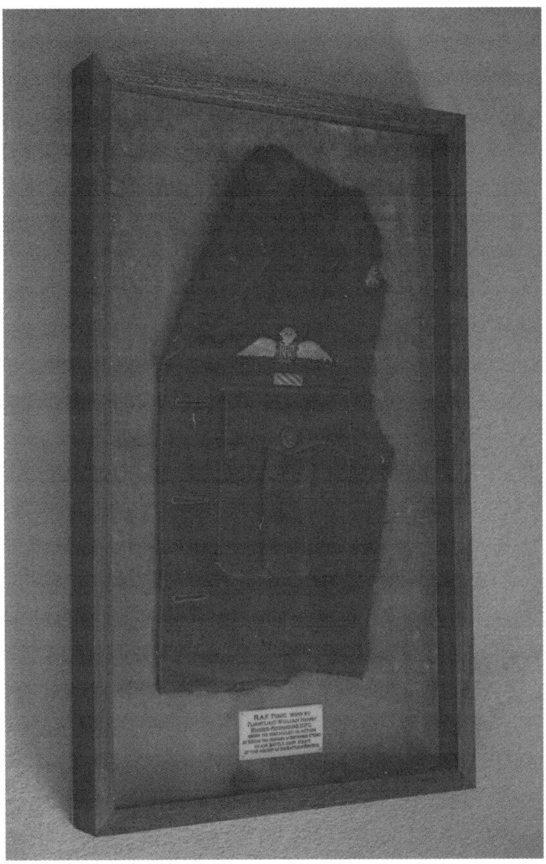

A section of tunic and RAF 'wings' actually worn by Flight Lieutenant Willie Rhodes-Moorhouse when he was killed in action on 6 September 1940, preserved by the family. (W.B. Rhodes-Moorhouse VC Charitable Trust)

'Quite apart from his being such a very charming personality, I shall never forget his grit, determination and fortitude when he first joined the Squadron and was so very airsick. I know how intensely keen he was then and how it was will power, and will power alone, that got him over that handicap.

'I do hope he enjoyed his time in the Squadron as much as we enjoyed having him in it. I don't remember ever having anyone never once for an instant question the wiseness of taking him. In peace, as in war, a first-class officer.'

On 16 August, Tangmere was heavily bombed, the *Luftwaffe*'s focus having shifted from convoys and coastal radar stations to Fighter Command's all-important airfields. In defence of the Legion's base that day, Pilot Officer Billy Fiske was shot down, his Hurricane crashing in flames on Tangmere's runway, the pilot expiring of his grievous injuries the following day; in 1941 a memorial plaque unveiled at St Paul's acknowledged that he was 'An American citizen who died that England might live'. The day after Fiske died, Willie flew operationally for the first time since losing his brother-in-law.

On 18 August, the *Luftwaffe* effort intensified (see the story of Flying Officer Franciszek Gruszka), Willie scrambling twice that hard-fought Sunday in defence of 11 Group's airfields, destroying an Me 109 five miles south of Selsey Bill at 1400 hrs. Two more 601 Squadron pilots were lost however, Sergeant Guy, who disappeared, and Sergeant Hawkings, who was shot down over Pagham and killed. The following day, Squadron Leader Ward was posted to RAF Station Tangmere as an Operations Controller, being succeeded in command of the Legion by the newly promoted Squadron Leader Sir Archie Hope. On that day, 601, having been somewhat battered, was withdrawn to Debden, on the east coast in Essex, for a brief respite, there to receive replacements while maintaining an operational commitment, mainly involving convoy protection patrols once more. On 31 August, 11 Group's airfields were again hit hard, including Debden, which was bombed. In the day's second engagement, 601 claimed another four enemy aircraft destroyed, three more probables (two of which were Me 109s claimed by Willie), and two damaged. However, Pilot Officer Gilbert and Sergeant Taylor were shot down and baled out, as was Sergeant Woolley, who 'suffered slight burns'. Sadly, Flying Officer Michael Doulton, of the Staffordshire ceramics family and a pre-war auxiliary, was reported missing (indeed, no more would be heard of Flying Officer Doulton until his mortal remains were discovered with his wrecked Hurricane by aviation archaeologists at Purfleet in 1984). Two days later, 601 Squadron returned to Tangmere.

On 3 September 1940 – the first anniversary of war being declared Flight Lieutenant Rhodes-Moorhouse, together with his wife Amalia and mother Linda, attended the investiture at Buckingham Palace for Willie to receive his DFC personally from King George VI. It was a proud moment for all, and naturally given great press coverage.

The following day, Flight Lieutenant Rhodes-Moorhouse and 601 Squadron was in action again, over Worthing, claiming a number of enemy aircraft destroyed and damaged, offset against the Polish Flying Officer Jankiewicz being shot down and slightly wounded. Willie had led the squadron, attacking a huge phalanx of enemy aircraft from up-sun, himself claiming a Do 17 destroyed over the sea. The following day was a comparatively quiet one for 601 Squadron. 6 September would not be.

At 0850 hrs that day, Willie led 601 Squadron when scrambled at 0850 hrs to intercept yet another raid bound for 11 Group airfields. Ordered to patrol Mayfield at 15,000 feet, Willie sensibly climbed the squadron 2,000 feet higher, over Redhill-Gatwick sighting fifty Me 109s at 20,000 feet, milling around in *Schwarms* of four or five aircraft, apparently having already fought one combat. No enemy bombers were seen, so rightly assuming this to be an enemy fighter sweep, the Hurricanes climbed to attack – so from the outset were at a disadvantageous tactical position. The 109s pounced, one of a formation attacking the Hurricanes from the rear over-shooting and presenting Pilot Officer Grier a perfect shot – without hesitation, the 109 was given a 'good burst and it immediately exploded and went down, a twisted, smoking, mess'. Grier then chased and destroyed a second 109 over Ramsgate. Flight Lieutenant Michael Robinson blew the cockpit canopy, rudder and fin off another enemy machine. Sergeant Taylor found and damaged a Do 17 over the sea, and Pilot Officer Topolnicki, who baled out slightly wounded, also claimed two 109s destroyed. Flying Officer Humphrey Gilbert also baled out, but was safe. Two pre-war Legionnaires, however, were missing. Soon it was confirmed that the American Flight Lieutenant Carl Davis – Squadron Leader Hope's brother-in-law – had crashed, inverted, in the back garden of Canterbury Cottage, at Brenchley, near Tunbridge Wells, and was dead. The other missing pilot was Willie.

601 Squadron reported that Willie had been 'seen to attack a *Dornier*, which he disabled, and immediately after that his plane was seen to

The commemorative scroll and medal group of Flight Lieutenant Willie Rhodes-Moorhouse DFC. (W.B. Rhodes-Moorhouse VC Charitable Trust)

come down vertically. It straightened out and flew for a few seconds at 3,000 feet, and then went vertically into the ground.

'It would appear from the behaviour of the aircraft that the pilot was either killed or seriously injured in combat, and the aircraft had buried itself at least ten to fifteen feet in the ground of a sewage farm at High Broom, near Tunbridge Wells. Up to the present time, the pilot is still buried in the machine.'

It was to Max Aitkin, close friend and former Legionnaire, that the sad duty fell to deliver the news to Amalia, so soon after her brother's death. The conclusion was non-committal however: Willie was missing, his aircraft yet to be found or his body recovered. Consequently Sir Stephen Demetriadi set off with his daughter and her mother-in-law, Linda Rhodes-Moorhouse, to ascertain his son-in-law's fate. Touring Kentish hospitals proved fruitless, but then it was discovered that a Hurricane had crashed at High Broom on the right date. Further investigation on-site revealed that the machine had completely buried itself, but amongst wreckage on the surface was a plate bearing the numbers '88'. Willie's Hurricane was P8818. He believed his lucky number to be eight. Sir Stephen then arranged for civilian contractors to excavate the site and recover the pilot's remains, which grim task was eventually accomplished.

The ‘mercurial’ Willie Rhodes-Moorhouse was cremated, his ashes buried on top of the hill at Parnham with his father: VC and DFC lying side-by-side. Willie Rhodes-Moorhouse’s life, Linda wrote, ‘had been vivid and, like a meteor, had ended before it dimmed’; he was 26 years old. The loss of this charismatic, hugely popular, highly competent and natural leader hit 601 Squadron hard. The following day the unit was withdrawn to the quieter sector of Exeter – and would lose no more pilots during the Battle of Britain. Willie was the last of the fourteen fatal casualties suffered by 601 Squadron during the Battle of Britain, a figure equalled by four other squadrons and exceeded by just one, another auxiliary unit, 501 ‘County of Gloucester’, which lost nineteen pilots. Group Captain Dundas wrote that ‘Rhodes-Moorhouse had been, perhaps, the most delightful and popular of all the gay spirits of 601. He was the last of the old White’s gang. His loss was a terrible blow.’ How Amalia felt having lost brother and husband in such quick succession can only be imagined; ‘Muggins’ lived out her life at Westmeston, passing away in 2003, having received various offers of marriage but remaining ever-faithful to Willie’s memory.

Today, there are perhaps two things in particular that stand in silent tribute to both Richard Demetriadi – the first pilot of Hellenic origin killed flying with the RAF during the Second World War – and Willie Rhodes-Moorhouse. Firstly, Sir Stephen gave land on Ditchling Beacon, the highest point in Sussex, to the National Trust in memory of his son; walkers there today will hopefully see and be moved by the commemorative plaque as they leave the car park and enjoy the view across the rolling Downs. Secondly, the bronze winged sword installed on Mortham’s tower by Linda in memory of her son – a reminder of a violent time when, regardless of social class or privileged status, the enemy’s bullets were indiscriminate – and we really were ‘all in it together’.

Chapter Six

Pilot Officer Martyn Aurel King

249 'Gold Coast' Squadron
Killed in Action: 16 August 1940

Lanzhou City in Gansu, a province in the People's Republic of China's north-west region, on the Northern Silk Road, is without doubt an unusual starting point for the story of the youngest of the Few – but there we must travel to unravel the short life of Martyn Aurel King.

Historically, the three main religions in China are Buddhism, Confucianism and Taoism, although Christianity and Islam made an appearance during the seventh century. It would not be for another 900 years, however, until Christianity gained traction and popularity, largely owing to the efforts of Protestant missionaries from 1807 onwards. Indeed, after the First Opium War of 1842, Christian missionaries and their schools and hospitals, under the protection of the western powers, played a major role in the westernisation of China throughout the nineteenth and twentieth centuries. The largest Christian mission in China was the China Inland Mission (CIM), founded by Hudson Taylor in 1865, which, between then and 1945, sent 2,680 male and female missionaries to the Orient. Amongst the earliest CIM missionaries were George King and Harriette Black, to whom a son, also George Edwin King, was born on 20 November 1887, in Hankow, China. Young George would later study in England, becoming a medical doctor, returning to China as a CIM medical missionary in January 1911.

Initially, Dr King worked at the CIM hospital at Kaifeng in Henan province. At the beginning of 1915, he founded the Borden Memorial Hospital in Lanzhou, establishing schools there for training Chinese doctors and nurses. On 6 February 1915, in Kaifeng, Dr King married Christina Shaw, an Australian and fellow missionary. A year later, the couple's first daughter, Fern, was born, followed by a son, Raymond, in 1918. Christina died, aged 33, on 27 January 1918. Just short of a year afterwards, on 22 January 1919, Dr King married Ivy Ethel Wallis at the CIM in Shanghai. Two years later, having spent a decade in China, Dr King returned with his family,

Above left: Dr George King and his first wife, Christina, had two children, Fern and Raymond. Christina died prematurely in 1918. Dr King subsequently married Ivy, in Shanghai, the couple pictured here with Raymond (left), Fern and baby Martyn Aurel King. (via Mandy Brown)

Above right: The King children, 'Aurel' seated, middle row. (via Mandy Brown)

which now included baby Gladys, born that year, to England. There, in West Mersea, Essex, on 15 October 1921, George and Ivy's son Martyn Aurel King was born. In 1922 the Kings returned to China, Dr King once more taking charge of the Borden Memorial Hospital. In 1924, George and Ivy suffered a stillborn daughter, and two other daughters died as infants in 1926 and 1927. Two daughters, Hazel Joy (2 July 1925) and Irene Comfort (3 June 1927) survived however, so Martyn Aurel – known to all as Aurel – grew up in a large family.

China was a divided nation at the time: in 1927, civil war finally erupted between Sun Yat-sen's Kuomintang government of the Republic of China and the Communist Party of China. On 24 March, the Nationalist Northern Expedition occupied Nanjing, during which unrest several western missionaries were killed. Western governments consequently advised all expatriates to leave China, and Dr King was put in charge of evacuating all missionaries and their families from Gansu. This group of fifty travelled by raft downstream on the Yellow River towards the coast. On 5 June 1927, Dr King, while helping to rescue grounded rafts, was sucked into a whirlpool and drowned. The highly respected 39-year-old philanthropist's death was deeply mourned by many, a memorial being erected at the hospital he founded and had been an inspiration at for sixteen years.

After George's death, Ivy remained in China, Aurel becoming a boarder at Chefoo School, the CIM school in Shandong Province, northern China. Pupils were largely drawn from the families of CIM missionaries and western businessmen and diplomats. Staff were all CIM missionaries and the curriculum mirrored that of an English public school, with a heavy emphasis on Christian teachings and classics. It was, as one student described it, 'a cloistered, old-fashioned, bible-reading, soul-saving religious community'. Having spent the required four years at Chefoo's preparatory school, Aurel moved up to the Boys' School in the winter of 1931. A successful student, gaining seven credits in his final School Certificate exam, according to the *Chefoo Daily News* (22 August 1940), Aurel 'played forward for the School Football XI and proved a useful bowler at cricket. But it was in rowing that he attained his chief distinction, being selected as Captain of Boats in his last season.'

In 1938, Aurel left Chefoo and returned to England, where he studied business. The 'Old Chefusian' had more exciting plans in mind though: like many other young men, he seized the opportunity to serve and fly by taking an SSC in the RAF. On 14 August 1939, Aurel was commissioned and began *ab initio* flying training at the Civilian Flying School, Hansworth. Then Pilot Officer King completed his mandatory 'square bashing' at 3 ITW, Hastings, between 23 October and 6 November 1939, on the latter date reporting to 6 FTS, Little Rissington, for advanced training. From the outset, Aurel King, the *Chefoo Daily News* also tells us, 'showed himself admirably adapted to flying and was not long before he gained his coveted "Wings"'. Service flying training completed, on 13 May 1940, Pilot Officer King reported for operational training at 5 OTU, Aston Down. At that time, the two operational training units were converting pilots to their operational aircraft types at a rate of eighty each per month. After Germany's attack on the west, the need for replacements became urgent, it being considered that 200 pilots per month were required to make good casualties, and 100 more if raising squadron establishments was considered. Courses were cut and pilots rushed through a syllabus of aerobatics, cross-country, dogfighting and air-firing exercises on the types of aircraft they would soon fly in battle.

Right: Dr King was drowned in 1927. Ivy is pictured here with her four children and two step-children, Aurel at extreme left. (via Mandy Brown)

Below: Pilot Officer Martyn Aurel King – youngest of the Few at 18 years old. (via Mandy Brown)

First, pilots were checked out on the Harvard single-engined monoplane, then allowed to fly the Spitfire, Hurricane or, in the case of those going on to fly 'twins', the Blenheim.

Unsurprisingly there were many accidents. For example, on 9 April 1940, Pilot Officer Lancelot Steele Dixon took off from Aston Down in Harvard P5864 on a cross-country flight. At 10.10 hrs he crashed and was killed performing unauthorised low-level aerobatics over the home of his mother Christine and stepfather, the novelist Rafael Sabatini, on the banks of the River Wye at Winforton in Herefordshire. On 21 May, Pilot Officer Jack Pugh – on the same course as Aurel – was engaged on a similar map-reading exercise in Spitfire P9517; an engine fire caused the pilot to find a suitable field for a forced landing. Finding one, at the last minute, through the smoke belching from his engine, Jack saw a farm labourer, Leonard Deakin, working a horse and plough in the field, right in his path. Instinctively, Jack pulled back on the stick, trying to avoid the unexpected hazard, but the aircraft stalled and crashed, bursting into flames and killing the 20-year-old pilot. Such incidents were grim reminders of the dangerous and uncertain life of a fighter pilot, even when not in the enemy's sights.

Flight Lieutenant James Brindley Nicolson VC with his wife, Muriel, and new-born son, also James.

Successfully and safely converted to single-engined monoplane fighters, on 9 June 1940, Pilot Officers King and J.T. Crossey, and Sergeants F.W.G. Killingback and H.J. Davidson were posted to 249 'Gold Coast' Squadron at Leconfield in 13 Group. One would perish during the Battle of Britain, another before the war's end – again emphasising the uncertain future faced by these young men.

Having been disbanded in 1919 after flying seaplanes during the First World War, on 16 May 1940, 249 re-formed as a single-engined fighter squadron at Church Fenton under the command of Squadron Leader (later Marshal of the RAF Sir) John Grandy. The new unit's authorised establishment comprised sixteen aircraft, and in addition to the CO, two flight lieutenants, fourteen flying or pilot officers, twelve sergeant pilots, six flight sergeants, five sergeants and ninety-five 'other ranks'.

On 17 May, 249 Squadron had been notified that it would not be operating Hurricanes as originally planned, but Spitfires. The squadron was ordered to Leconfield, also in 13 Group. Three days later, 249 Squadron had sixteen fully operational Spitfires on charge. On 10 June, however, the day the four new replacement pilots arrived fresh from Aston Down, the squadron was told to exchange its Spitfires for Hurricanes. Pilot Officer King and Sergeant Killingback joined 'A' Flight, commanded by Flight Lieutenant James Brindley Nicolson, another SSC officer, initially a member of 'B' Flight. On 1 June Nicolson had been promoted to acting flight lieutenant and took over 'A' Flight from Flight Lieutenant Ronald 'Boozy' Kellett, who went on promotion to command the newly formed Polish 303 Squadron at Northolt. Nicolson was an experienced pilot, having flown biplane fighters with 72 Squadron, also based at Church Fenton, from August 1937 until the unit re-equipped with the Spitfire in April 1939 – but, like most, he had no combat experience. This was not, however, for want of

On 16 August 1940, Pilot Officer King's Hurricane crashed in this field, between the Southampton–Salisbury railway and Romsey Road.

trying. Based in the north, 13 Group's squadrons, including 72 and 249, had to content themselves with hoping to intercept lone German reconnaissance bombers by day and night. On 8 July 1940, 249 Squadron's Green Section, comprising Flying Officer Parnall, Pilot Officer Beazley and Sergeant Main, shared the destruction of a Ju 88 off Hornsea with Spitfires of the Catterick-based 41 Squadron. On that day, the squadron also completed a move back to Church Fenton. The advantage of being based in a quieter sector provided an opportunity for continuous practice flying and training in a reasonably safe environment – which, for new pilots like Aurel King, could only be a good thing. During June 1940 in fact, 249 Squadron exceeded all previous records by accumulating 1010.10 hours on training flights, generating a congratulatory signal from Air Chief Marshal Dowding himself.

Between 1710 and 1940 hrs on 15 July 1940, Pilot Officer King made his first operational sortie with 249 Squadron – and his first during the Battle of Britain – when he flew with Sergeant Killingback in a section led by Flying Officer John Young (later the Battle of Britain Fighter Association's long-serving archivist) on an 'interception'. No other details of the sortie are known, but generally speaking it was a bad day for 249 Squadron. Firstly, Pilot Officer Davidson crashed on landing at Acklington, damaging his Hurricane but fortunately not himself; Pilot Officer Meaker ran into an obstruction while scrambling for a night interception, the resulting damage leading to a wheels-up landing. Worse, Sergeant Main crashed and was killed immediately after taking off, also at night. As the squadron diary remarks, it was 'depressing'.

On 5 August, the ORB noted that Squadron Leader Eric Bruce 'Whizzy' King was posted to 249 Squadron, 'for supernumerary duties, to get experience in fighter squadron flying and administration'. Squadron Leader King was born in Dover on 7 June 1911, taking an SSC in 1932, having attended Dulwich College and previously worked for the Asiatic Petroleum Company. He was an experienced pilot, having flown extensively as both an Army Cooperation pilot and flying instructor – but had never flown fighters until posted to 7 OTU on 25 June 1940. Thereafter, King gained extra hours on the Hurricane with 253 Squadron, to which he reported at Kirton-in-Lindsey on 7 July, and then 249 at Church Fenton. There, Squadron Leader King immediately set about flying operational sorties.

On 13 August the Spitfires of 602 Squadron landed at Church Fenton, the pilots lunching and refuelling there before continuing to Westhampnett in the Tangmere Sector, near Chichester. South was where the action was, the Battle of Britain now hotting up – and 249 Squadron's invitation to

After his 'signal act of valour' and eventual escape from his blazing Hurricane, Flight Lieutenant Nicolson's aircraft crashed here, on the playing field of Rownham's School.

join the party arrived by way of a signal at 0730 hrs the following day: the squadron was moving, in a hurry, to Boscombe Down, near Amesbury in Wiltshire. Situated inland of Poole, Southampton and Portsmouth, and between the coast and Bristol, within 10 Group's Middle Wallop Sector, action was guaranteed. Two hours later, transport aircraft arrived to convey a number of airmen and essential equipment to their new station, the remainder of ground personnel leaving by road. At noon, Squadron Leader Grandy led off no less than twenty Hurricanes, Pilot Officer King included, the formation arriving at Boscombe an hour and a quarter later. The CO flew over to nearby Middle Wallop for a conference with the Sector Commander, Wing Commander D.M. Roberts AFC, and while present there was initiated to life in the combat zone when the Sector Station was bombed. The difference in the increased tempo of operations was abundantly clear: 249 Squadron was required to operate from dawn to dusk in addition to providing a section for night interceptions. There was much to organise, the next morning being spent organising aircraft dispersal points, establishing telephone communications, and erecting tented accommodation on the airfield for all ranks.

At 1300 hrs on 15 August, 249 Squadron was ordered to be available for take-off at fifteen minutes notice. Two hours later, 'A' Flight was brought to immediate readiness while 'B' Flight remained at fifteen minutes. At 1715 hrs, the whole squadron was brought to readiness. At 1712 hrs,

Squadron Leader Grandy and Flight Lieutenant Nicolson scrambled with 'A' Flight to patrol the sector's forward airfield of Warmwell at 15,000 feet. At 1719 hrs, the Canadian Flight Lieutenant Robert Barton led 'B' Flight off, Squadron Leader King taking off solo a minute later. Luck would favour 'B' Flight, which got its first glimpse of a massed enemy formation: some sixty Ju 88s of LG1, escorted by forty Me 1110s of ZG2. Over Ringwood, Barton's Hurricanes attacked. Back at Boscombe Down, for no loss, the Hurricane pilots claimed the destruction of five Me 110s. The lone Squadron Leader King encountered and attacked twelve Ju 88s, leaving one trailing smoke from its port engine. This raid was also intercepted by 43, 601 and 609 Squadrons, but in spite of the RAF fighter pilots' determined attacks over Southampton and the Solent, thirty Ju 88s doggedly continued to bomb Middle Wallop, the remainder bombing Worthy Down – the latter being roughly handled by 601 Squadron. It was certainly an encouraging *entrée* for 249 Squadron into their new sector's operational conditions.

On Friday 16 August 1940, the *Luftwaffe* continued the policy of heavily attacking airfields. At lunchtime, four raids were incoming on a broad front, the westernmost of which hit the FAA base at Gosport, damaging installations

Pilot Officer King, whose parachute collapsed, possibly having been deliberately machine-gunned while descending, died in the garden of this house, 30 Clifton Road, Southampton.

and killing six servicemen. At Boscombe Down, 'B' Flight was at a state of readiness, while 'A' Flight was 'available'. At 1305 hrs twelve Hurricanes of both flights, led by Flight Lieutenant 'Butch' Barton, scrambled to patrol the Southampton–Poole line, with Flight Lieutenant Nicolson (Red One, GN-A, P3576), leading 'A' Flight's Red Section, comprising Squadron Leader 'Whizzy' King (Red Three, P3870) and Pilot Officer Aurel King (Red Two, GN-F, P3616).

Flight Lieutenant Nicolson: -

'Our Squadron was heading towards Southampton on patrol from Boscombe Down, flying at 15,000 feet, when I observed three Ju 88 bombers about four miles away, moving across our bows. I reported this to our commander and he replied "Go after them with your Section". Breaking away from the Flight, I led my section of three Hurricanes round towards the bombers and chased hard after them, but when we were about a mile behind I saw the 88s fly straight into a squadron of Spitfires. I used to fly Spitfires myself and guessed it was "curtains" for the *Junkers*. I was right, and they were all shot down in quick time, with no pickings for us! I must confess that this was very disappointing since I had never fired at a Hun in my life and was longing to have a crack at them. So, we swung round again and started to climb to 18,000 feet over Southampton to re-join the squadron. Our Section was still a long way from them when suddenly, very close and in rapid succession, I heard four bangs, the loudest hit I have ever heard. They were made by an Me 110, which hit my machine.'

Climbing, in the tight 'vic' formation, Red Section had been extremely vulnerable to attack from above by an unseen enemy. The twelve Ju 88s raiding Gosport were escorted by eighteen Me 110s, some of which lurked high in the sky over the coast, watching and waiting. Red Section presented an obvious target and the *zestörer* pilots pounced immediately, opening up with their hard-hitting 20 mm cannon. Nicolson continues: -

'The first shell tore through the hood of my cockpit, sending splinters into my left eye, one splinter I discovered later almost severed my eyelid. I couldn't see through the eye for blood. The second cannon shell hit my spare petrol tank, setting it on fire, while the third shell crashed into the cockpit and tore off my right trouser leg. The fourth shell struck the back of my left shoe, shattering the heel and making quite a mess of my foot, but I didn't know anything about that either.

'The instantaneous effect of the shells was to make me dive away to the left in order to avoid further enemy action, then I started to curse myself for my carelessness. I thought "What a fool!"'

What happened next has since passed into legend in the annals of courage: -

'I was thinking of abandoning the aircraft when suddenly an Me 110 whizzed underneath me, in full view of my gunsight. Fortunately, no damage to my windscreen and foresights, so I began to chase the 110, setting everything for a fight. When the Hun was in range I pressed the gun button, he was taking violent evasive action by twisting and turning to get away from my gunfire so I pushed the throttle wide open. Both of us must have been doing 400 as we went down together in a dive. First, he turned left, then right, then left again, finally turning right. I remember shouting at him when I first saw him, "I'll teach you some manners, you Hun!", and I shouted other things as well! I knew I was scoring hits on him all the time I was firing, and by this time it was pretty hot in the cockpit from the effect of the burst petrol tank. I couldn't see much flame but knew it was there alright. I remember once looking at my left hand which was keeping the throttle open, it seemed to be on fire itself and I could see the skin peeling off it yet could feel little pain. Unconsciously I had drawn up my feet under my parachute on the seat, to escape the heat, I suppose. Well, I gave him all I had and the last I saw of him was when he was going down with his left wing lower than the right one, and I gave him a parting burst.

'As he disappeared, I then started thinking about saving myself and decided that it was about time I abandoned the aircraft and baled out, so I immediately jumped out of my seat but hit my head on the framework of the hood, which was all that was left. I again cursed myself for a fool and pulled the hood back – and wasn't I relieved! It slid back beautifully. I jumped up again, but again I bounced back into my seat for I had forgotten to undo the straps holding me in. One of them snapped so I had only three to undo, and I left the machine.

'I suppose that I was about 12 – 15,000 feet when I baled out and immediately started somersaulting downwards, and after a few turns like that I found myself diving headfirst for the ground. After a second or two of this I pulled the parachute ripcord, the result was that I immediately straightened up and began to float down. Then an aircraft, a *Messerschmitt* I was later told, came tearing past me and I decided to pretend that I was dead by hanging limply on the straps. The *Messerschmitt* came back once more and I kept my eyes closed but I didn't get the bullets I was half expecting.

Pilot Officer King's funeral at All Saints, Fawley, near Southampton, attracted a large congregation.

I don't know if he fired at me, the main thing is I wasn't hit. While descending I had a look at myself. The burns on my left hand left the knuckle showing through, and for the first time I discovered that my left foot was wounded, blood was oozing out of the lace-holes, and my right hand was pretty badly burned too. I decided to try my limbs and see if they would work – and thank goodness they did.

'The oxygen mask was still covering my face but my hands were in too bad a state to remove it. I tried but I couldn't manage it. I found too that I had lost a trouser leg and the other was badly torn. My tunic was just like a lot of smouldering, torn, rags, so I wasn't looking very smart! Then after a bit more of this dangling down business I began to ache all over and my arms and legs began to hurt a lot. When I got lower, it was apparent that I was in danger of coming down in the sea and I knew that I wouldn't stand an earthly if I did as I would have been unable to swim a stroke with my hands like that. I managed to float inland and noticed I was heading for a high-tension cable, but fortunately floated over it towards a nice open field. When I was about 100 feet from the ground I saw a cyclist and heard him ring his bell. This surprised me as I realised my descent had been in total silence. I bellowed at the cyclist but don't think he heard me.

'Finally, I touched down in a field – and fell over. Fortunately, the day was very calm and my parachute floated down without taking me along the ground, as they sometimes do. I had a piece of good news almost immediately. One of the people who had come along and witnessed the combat said they had seen the Messerschmitt dive straight into the sea – so it hadn't been such a bad day after all!'

What 'Nick' failed to mention in the above account (which is a transcript of a BBC broadcast) but did include in his official report was that 'when fifty feet up, just before landing, an enthusiastic individual loosed off both barrels of a 12-bore into my buttocks'.

One of the first on the scene was fortunately a doctor and nurse, in the area on their rounds. The cyclist is believed to be a local butcher's boy on his delivery round, who physically assaulted the Home Guard sergeant responsible for shooting the already wounded pilot. Only the arrival of the Hampshire Constabulary's PC Eric Coleman stopped the violence, and, as folklore has it, the ambulance summoned for the pilot actually took away the battered sergeant first – how true this is however, has never been ascertained. Speaking with the constable, Flight Lieutenant Nicolson's first concern

All Saints, Fawley: a quintessential English churchyard.

was dictating a telegram to his expectant wife, Muriel, confirming that he had been shot down but was safe – correcting the officer for misspelling his name with the more common 'h'. By now, a lorry had arrived on the scene, into which 'Nick' was stretchered. The driver then made haste for Royal South Hampshire Hospital in Southampton, PC Coleman riding the footplate ensuring no delays along the way. Upon arrival, the Hurricane pilot was given twenty-four hours to live, such were his injuries, the worst being to his hands, most of the flesh of which had been burned away.

Flight Lieutenant Nicolson's Hurricane crashed on the playing field of Rownham's School, the Me 110 he destroyed reportedly diving into the sea off Calshot.

As the 249 Squadron ORB noted however, 'Red Section unfortunately bought it.'

Squadron Leader King's Hurricane was hit several times, but he was fortunately able to return safely to Boscombe Down, landing at 1410 hrs. Pilot Officer Tom Neil was there and remembered that 'Squadron Leader "Whizzy" King was among us. Excited. Garrulous. Hurrying about. His face creased by sweat and lines of his oxygen mask. Yes, he'd been hit and damaged. No, he wasn't wounded but the others had gone. Both shot down. In flames. The blighters had come down and caught them unawares. Down from behind. Me 110s. "Whizzy" was in a highly emotional state and kept talking about tactics. We'd have to do things differently. Talking quickly and gesticulating.'

Pilot Officer King, however – the youngest of The Few - was dead.

His Hurricane destroyed by cannon fire, King had baled out – but his parachute collapsed and the teenage pilot plunged into the garden of 30 Clifton Road, Southampton – dying in the arms of Fred Poole, a local man. According to 249 Squadron records, this tragedy was caused because 'his parachute had been severely damaged by a cannon shell' – but eyewitnesses reported that the defenceless pilot had been machine-gunned by a German fighter during his descent. On 19 August 1940, however, Squadron Leader Grandy reported that Flight Lieutenant Nicolson's Red Section: -

'… was engaged with an unknown number of Me 109 fighters. Pilot Officer King's aircraft was struck by enemy fire and crashed… There is no evidence that it caught fire in the air. Pilot Officer King baled out and eye-witness accounts state that he was seen to descend normally by parachute but that when at approximately 2,000 feet his parachute appeared to collapse. Pilot Officer King fell to the ground and was killed.

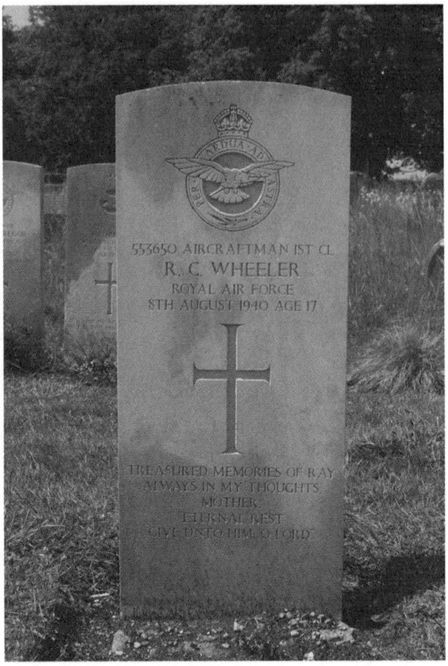

Above left: Pilot Officer King's headstone at Fawley – recently updated to reflect his correct age, the original recording it as 19 years. Research by Geoff Simpson confirmed that Aurel was the youngest RAF fighter pilot in the Battle of Britain.

Above right: Sadly, Pilot Officer King is not the youngest casualty of the 'Finest Hour' buried at All Saints – that mantle belongs to 17-year-old Ray Wheeler, fatally wounded when *Stukas* attacked the RAF high speed launch aboard which he was a signaller.

'The parachute was collected and on examination it was found that a bullet or bullets or metal fragments had passed through the pack before it had been pulled. This apparently damaged the canopy which, however, opened but did not hold for long enough'.

The circumstances of Pilot Officer King's demise actually remained under investigation as late as 17 April 1941, when Squadron Leader (as he was by then) Nicolson, in response to an Air Ministry request for further information, reported under the title 'Shooting of personnel during parachute descents': -

'I am not in a position to state whether Pilot Officer MA King, 249 Squadron, was shot in his parachute after leaving his aircraft or not. The report which was given to me in Hospital was that Pilot Officer King descended normally to 2,000 feet when his parachute caught a balloon cable and collapsed. Squadron Leader J Grandy, who was OC 249 Squadron at the time, told me that one or two bullets had punctured the pack before the rip-cord was pulled and made several holes in the canopy. I did not see Pilot Officer King after we were engaged by the enemy.

'I was informed from several sources that an aircraft believed to be German had made two attacks on me after the opening of my parachute at approximately 10,000 feet (I had delayed pulling the rip-cord for approximately 5,000 feet). It would appear, however, to be beyond the realms of possibility to check whether the aircraft was an enemy one shooting badly or a friendly one investigating my condition, although I heard an aircraft which might easily have been a friendly fighter pass me at close quarters'.

That fateful afternoon of 16 August 1940, the Hurricanes of Flight Lieutenant Nicolson's Red Section had, in fact, been well and truly bounced by Me 109s (not Me 110s), Hauptmann Heinz 'Pietzsch' Bretnütz, Staffelkapitän of 6/JG53 claiming the two Hurricanes shot down, chalking up his eleventh and twelfth aerial victories.

According to the *Chefoo Daily News*, 'At this time the thoughts and prayers of many in the community will be with his mother and two sisters in Chefoo, and his brother, an army doctor, and two sisters in England. Mrs King has only just returned from England and was with Aurel just before leaving… He is the first Chefusian to lay down his life in this war in the cause of freedom, an unpretentious hero, worthy of our honour and gratitude.'

On 21 August 1940, Pilot Officer Martyn Aurel King was buried at All Saints churchyard at Fawley, near Southampton, the funeral attracting great local interest as many people turned out to pay their respects to the pilot only recently confirmed as the youngest of the Few. Aurel, however, was not the youngest serviceman in the churchyard, where he joined Aircraftman 1st Class Raymond Clive Wheeler, the son of Clive and Kathleen Wheeler of 198 Northumberland Road, Southampton, born on 5 January 1923, died on 8 August 1940. According to the *Western Mail* on 13 August 1940, 17-year-old wireless operator Ray, who was 'not a good sailor… volunteered to serve in a launch sent to rescue Nazi airmen shot down in the Channel. The launch was machine-gunned by nine German warplanes and Wheeler was killed. While the launch cruised in rough sea, Wheeler had been so sea-sick that another member of the crew had to support him, but the boy would not give in and continued to send messages until the enemy planes attacked. He carried out his duties very gallantly and stayed at his post to the end, Wheeler's mother was told by the young wireless operator's commanding officer.' Yet another sad story.

While Flight Lieutenant Nicolson recovered in hospital, on 26 October 1940, Wing Commander Victor Beamish, Station Commander at North Weald, where 249 Squadron was then based, recommended 'Nick' for a DFC, describing the incident occurring over Southampton on 16 August, the recommendation concluded that the wounded officer 'has always shown great enthusiasm for air fighting, and this incident shows that he also possesses courage and determination of a high order.' On 29 August, Air Vice-Marshal Gossage, Air Member for Personnel, had written to the Commanders-in-Chief of all three RAF home commands, including Air Chief Marshal Dowding, informing them that the King had expressed surprise that no fighter pilots had been awarded the Victoria Cross. With that in mind, upon receipt of Beamish's recommendation, Dowding approved it – adding his own view that 'I consider this to be an outstanding case of gallantry and endorse the Recommendation for the award of the Victoria Cross.' On 7 November, the Secretary of State confirmed the award. Convalescing at Torquay's Palace Hotel with other wounded airmen, Nicolson was astonished to receive a telegram informing him that he had been awarded his nation's highest award for bravery. The bemused recipient cabled his wife, about to give birth to

Jim Nicolson, the VC's nephew, with the memorial arranged by Richard Hutchinson in the grounds of Sholing Junior School, Southampton, which was unveiled on 15 September 2016. (Richard Hutchinson)

Squadron Leader Alan Jones MBE of Solent Sky Museum, an old campaigner to see the Battle of Britain and the city's aviation past appropriately commemorated in Southampton, and the author with an artefact from Flight Lieutenant Nicolson's Hurricane, picked up by an eyewitness. The occasion was the opening of Nicolson House at Leonardo's, the premises now occupying the site where the VC landed by parachute at Millbrook on 19 October 2018.

their first child, a boy, also James: 'Darling. Just got the VC. Don't know why. Letter follows. All my love. Nick.'

On 25 November 1940, Flight Lieutenant Nicolson, in the company of his wife, mother and two sisters, received the Victoria Cross from King George VI at Buckingham Palace. It would be the only supreme award to a fighter pilot throughout the whole of the Second World War. The problem was, 'Nick' felt that, shot down in his first combat, he did not deserve the medal and now had to earn it. This would profoundly influence the rest of his, perhaps inevitably comparatively short, life. Having recovered from his burns and resumed operational flying, the VC was posted to India, flying Beaufighters against the Japanese, for which he was awarded a DFC. In April 1945, Wing Commander Nicolson was on the staff of HQ RAF Burma, and on 2 May he was a passenger on a 355 Squadron Liberator bombing Rangoon. Over the Indian Ocean, 130 miles south of Calcutta, an engine fire caused the aircraft to crash into the sea. There were two survivors, but

Jim Nicolson with the senior RAF officer present at the unveiling of a further commemorative plaque, this one on 5 April 2019, in Guildhall Square, Southampton. (Richard Hutchinson)

Wing Commander Nicolson was not among them – reported missing, he is remembered on the Singapore Memorial.

The 'garrulous' Squadron Leader 'Whizzy' King, sadly, did not survive the Battle of Britain. On 21 August 1940 he was posted away from 249 to command 151 Squadron at North Weald. Three days later his Hurricane was badly shot up after damaging a Do 17, although King managed to land safely. On 30 August 1940, Squadron Leader King was reported missing from a lunchtime patrol between Eastchurch and Hornchurch. So began an anxious time for his 70-year-old mother, who quickly received the bad news at her Bournemouth home, and brother, a major in the Royal Artillery serving at Pembroke Dock. Soon it was established that 'Whizzy' had been shot down, no doubt ambushed and picked off by an Me 109, his Hurricane crashing at Temple Street, Strood, after a power-dive at full throttle, suggesting that the pilot was already dead at the controls or incapacitated. Squadron Leader King was buried in London's Highgate Cemetery.

As the 249 Squadron diarist said, Red Section had indeed 'bought it'.

For Mrs Ivy King, having to come to terms with her beloved son Aurel's death, there was further suffering: after the Fall of Singapore, together with her two daughters, Ivy was interned by the Japanese – which is, as they say, another story.

Chapter Seven

Flying Officer Franciszek Gruszka (Polish)

65 'East India' Squadron

Missing in Action: 18 August 1940

On the night of 31 August 1939, Nazi Germany invaded Poland in an undeclared act of war. Simultaneously, German troops crossed the frontier along its entire length, attacking guards and forward defensive positions. At dawn, the *Luftwaffe* bombed aerodromes and major strategic assets throughout Poland. In spite of all the diplomatic unrest that summer, the German attack achieved complete surprise.

31 August happened also to be the first day of mobilisation in Poland, reservists reporting to their units and operational squadrons dispersing to various airfields. Few, though, believed that war would actually break out, the reservists expecting little but an inconveniently long stay with the colours ahead of them. The Poles trusted that Britain and France would honour its pledge to support Poland in the event of Nazi aggression, and mistakenly believed that would be sufficient to deter Herr Hitler. Many expected the Soviets to side with the western Allies, unaware of the secret Non-Aggression Pact signed by the foreign ministers of Germany and Russia on 23 August. On that day, Poland's fate was sealed. Although at 1100 hrs on Sunday 3 September 1939 Britain and France declared war on Nazi Germany following Hitler ignoring their ultimatum to withdraw from Poland, the western powers were not geographically positioned to provide military support. In real terms, Poland was on her own.

Sixty-three German divisions attacked Poland, facing fifty-six Polish. The German attack was spearheaded by fifteen mechanised *panzer* divisions, whereas the Poles only fielded two motorised formations. The enemy's superiority of arms was considered 8:1. Moreover, the *Wehrmacht* was a modern force, equipped and armed to current standards, whereas Poland went to war with the equipment of 1925. Importantly, Germany's diplomatic successes of 1938 and 1939 had secured strategic advantages in that Poland's northern frontier and most of the southern was controlled by Germany, and the attack was made simultaneously from north, south, east and west. Offensives on both flanks and steady pressure in the centre provided for envelopment. Nonetheless, by the campaign's ninth day, German losses were such that it was clear that the Poles' determined fighting spirit had been overlooked – a factor emphasised by the propaganda machine preparing German public opinion for news of heavy casualties. This fighting spirit would define the Polish contribution to the Allied cause throughout the hard-fought Second World War.

In 1939, Poland, even more than Britain and France, was ill-prepared for a war in which air power played a crucial role. The immense capital investment required to create and maintain a modern air force was quite simply beyond the means of a newly independent country. The technical inferiority of its air force made Poland vulnerable – but the bravery of her aircrews was beyond doubt. The first German aircraft to be destroyed during the Second World War were two Do 17s shot down over Olkusz by Lieutenant W. Gnys, in total the Polish fighter pilots destroying 126 enemy aircraft during the campaign. The Polish fighter squadrons, including the Fighter Brigade and Army Co-operation units lost fifty pilots and 114 aircraft, while the bomber force suffered 90% casualties in aircrew and aircraft. By 14 September, losses were such that the Polish Air Force was

Franciszek Gruszka serving with the Polish Air Force before the Second World War.

unable to continue operations. Some squadrons lost their last aircraft on that day, others, threatened with being overrun, destroyed their remaining machines. On 17 September, fittingly in a violent thunderstorm, the few remaining Polish aircraft crossed the Rumanian border, ending the air fighting over Poland. On the same day, in another undeclared act of war and a real shock, Russia invaded eastern Poland. Polish Air Force flying schools, experimental and maintenance units evacuated their personnel to Rumania and Hungary.

On 1 October, German troops entered Warsaw. Six says later Polish resistance ceased – although the Polish Home Army would continue fighting a partisan war until the Germans were finally defeated five years later. From a Polish viewpoint the short, tragic, campaign was a consequence of unpreparedness, the outcome, against ruthless and efficient aggression, inevitable. Nonetheless, Poland's defiant spirit, refusing to surrender without a fight, no matter what the odds, set a benchmark of courage that would resonate throughout the Second World War.

It is important to understand the Polish character, fundamental to which is a powerful sense of duty and love of country. For five hundred years, Poland fought two or three defensive wars every generation. Poles know full well, therefore, that material possessions, even the family home, can be lost – instantly. Anything that the enemy can use must be destroyed, so therefore not valued highly. Polish soil, however, cannot be destroyed, and neither can national solidarity, giving rise to an iron will to endure whatever the odds. Consequently, the Polish nation has survived even when forced into exile. This explains why, when Poland had fallen, the Polish Armed Forces trekked west, to continue the fight. It explains why, when the call was made for the Polish Air Force to reassemble in France and later Britain, only the dead, those who were prisoners, or those ordered to remain in Poland, did not respond. For others, not continuing the fight and ultimately liberating Poland was unthinkable.

Organising the evacuation of the Polish Air Force was a huge task. First, crossing into such neighbouring states as Rumania, Hungary, Latvia and Lithuania, the Poles were interned. In Rumania, where the majority of air force personnel were interned, officers and 'other ranks' were immediately segregated. Unsurprisingly, Rumania was unprepared for this influx of personnel, and things were chaotic. When the news was received that General Sikorski had re-formed the Polish government in France and was assembling the Polish armed forces there, this chaos worked to the Poles' advantage: many staged individual escapes, most travelling by boat via Constanza,

Beirut, Malta and Marseilles. On 25 October, British, Polish and French delegates met at the French Air Ministry to decide the best way forward. The Poles argued that their air force should be re-formed in Britain, given their familiarity with British aero-engines but ignorance of French equipment. The French countered that the Poles should be equally divided between Britain and France, believing that Polish squadrons could be quickly formed and would be welcome reinforcements on both sides of the Channel. Finally it was decided that 300 Polish aircrew and 2,000 ground staff would be stationed in Britain, the rest in France. This now meant that a large-scale evacuation had to be organised from the internment camps.

Amongst the Polish airmen interned in Rumania was Franciszek Gruszka, born on 21 January 1910, the second son of a reasonably well off farming family living near Lwow.

Piotr Gruszka: -

'Being only a year younger than my dear brother "Franek", we were very close. The first four years of Franek's primary education were spent at the local school before we together attended a preparatory school in the city. After passing the required entrance exams, we then went to grammar school, science being Franek's leading subject. As we progressed through the school, our lessons changed, which at one point had a neo-classical and Latin emphasis. This was in the hope that at least one, if not both, of us would become a Roman Catholic priest. Franek matriculated on 5 May 1931, there automatically following one year's army service. As I was a year behind him, we feared there would be a parting of our ways forever. After his time at the Military College for Infantry Cadets at Rawa Ruska, between 15 November 1931 and 15 August 1932, he gained air experience on observation balloons at Torun. There he decided that he wanted to pursue a career in the Air Force and become a pilot. He then succeeded in passing entrance exams to the Officer Cadets' Flying School in Deblin. By 11 August 1934, he had successfully completed the course and was a fully qualified pilot with the rank of 2nd lieutenant. His flying, however, was so precise that instead of joining a fighter squadron, as he wanted, my brother was posted to be an instructor at the Flying Training School near Lwow. By then, I was studying at the Humanities Faculty of the University of King Jan Kazimierz, in Lwow, so we shared lodgings.

'One day, when we lived together in Lwow, Franek suggested that I should take a pleasure flight with him. It was a September morning in 1934, and I arrived at the aerodrome early, as we had arranged. Having checked the weather, Franek said that we were to fly at 100 – 200 metres, below the clouds. I was both excited and curious regarding what would be my first flight. By 0700 hrs the plane, a Polish monoplane, was ready. First in climbed Franek, then me, both of us wearing flying suits and helmets. After no time at all we were up to 100 metres. I could see that the airport was getting further and further away, the buildings and trees getting smaller and smaller. Soon we were under the first cloud layer; one second the plane was flying in a horizontal attitude, then, without warning, diving. I felt my stomach coming up into my throat and was just about to shout out in fear when my brother calmly explained that we had hit a vacuum, an air pocket, and had dropped like a stone. Unfortunately, on that flight there were many vacuums and each time I thought that we would crash! We then approached a church steeple at about the same height, swerving to avoid it at the last moment. Then off to Zimna Wodka for Franek to wave to his fiancée, Eugenia. I wondered why we needed to climb so high; suddenly the engine stopped and the plane plunged almost vertically towards some houses. Out of one of them ran some people, one of whom I recognised as "Gena". My brother's skilled hand then changed our direction and we adopted a normal attitude, just above some trees. After waggling his wings in greeting to those on the ground, we returned to the airport. My first flight was one I would never forget!

'My brother had many friends and was very popular. Even before his military days he was known for his great courage and generosity. He liked music and was a splendid mandolinist, me accompanying him on the guitar. He had no match in wrestling and aviation was his passion. I know that he trained his cadets in a most professional manner, for which he was commended.

Flying Officer Gruszka, in England and in RAF uniform, 1940.

'When war broke out, I was called up to defend Warsaw. On 17 September 1939, Franek received orders to escape across the Rumanian border. Having done so, he obtained a Polish passport via the Polish Consulate in Bucharest, and then, via the former Yugoslavia and Italy, arrived in France on 7 October.'

Interned with Franek in Rumania was another young Polish officer and fighter pilot: Boleslaw Henryk Drobinski, more commonly known as 'Gandy' as he was thin: -

'I had toothache so obtained a pass to leave the camp and visit the local dentist. On producing my pass for inspection, the Rumanian guard asked where the others were, "Boleslaw, Henryk and Drobinski"! Immediately I grabbed two others, and off we went to France!'

Piotr Gruszka: -

'On 8 October 1939, Franek registered at the Alien Assembly Point in Paris, but he and three other pilots, namely Wladyslaw Szulkowski, Boleslaw

Flying Officer David Glaser DFC (left), who flew with and spoke highly of his Polish comrades in 65 Squadron, pictured in December 1940 with Sergeant Colin Hewlett – who would be killed in 1942 when his Spitfire inexplicably exploded before landing.

Drobinski and Joseph Szlagowski, decided that the British were more likely to resist the Germans than the French. Consequently they were amongst the first Polish pilots to arrive in Britain, which was in February 1940.'

In England, Franek Gruszka went to Blackpool, where Polish personnel were being collected at the RAF Depot there, which became a clearing and screening centre. In March 1940 he was commissioned as a flying officer in the RAFVR, but had to wait until early July 1940 for a posting to 15 EFTS at Redhill for a flying test. At least the time spent at Blackpool provided an opportunity to start learning English – without an understanding of which, regardless of experience, foreign pilots were of no use to Fighter Command, being unable to understand orders in the air. Having passed his flying test, Flying Officer Gruszka was soon on his way to 7 OTU at Hawarden near Chester, there converting to the Supermarine Spitfire.

On 7 August 1940, probably with around ten hours on Spitfires recorded in his log book, Flying Officer Gruszka reported for duty with 65 Squadron at Hornchurch, there joining a fellow Pole, Pilot Officer Wladyslaw Szulkowski, who had arrived fresh from 5 OTU at Aston Down two days earlier.

Hornchurch was 65's home station, the unit having re-formed there on 10 July 1934. Having previously flown various biplane fighters, by the outbreak of war the squadron was Spitfire-equipped and sharing the sector station with two other Spitfire squadrons, 54 and 74. 65 Squadron had participated in the Dunkirk fighting, and had already been heavily engaged in the early stage of the Battle of Britain, often flying to and patrolling from the coastal aerodrome at Manston.

David Glaser was a pilot officer on 65 Squadron at the time: -

'We were very fond of our two Poles. I was really only a youth and both Gruszka and Szulkowski were experienced and respected pilots in their own air force before the war, I looked up to them. They were having a hard time coming to terms with the language and so on, and I used to try and teach them English during the time we spent at readiness.'

On 9 August, Pilot Officer Szulkowski and Flying Officer Gruszka made their first flight with 65 Squadron, flying with Supermarine test pilot Jeffrey Quill – courageously flying combat sorties to gain first-hand experience of the Spitfire in such operational conditions – to Sutton Bridge for air firing practice. More flying practice followed the next day. On 14 August, Flying Officer Gruszka flew to Manston in a formation led by Flight

The Kent Battle of Britain Museum's excavation of the Grove Marsh Spitfire crash site in 1971. (Kent Battle of Britain Museum)

Lieutenant Gerald 'Sammy' Saunders. Flying alongside the Pole was the Irish Pilot Officer Brendan 'Paddy' Finucane – soon to become a leading ace. Two days before, Pilot Officer 'Gandy' Drobinski also reported to 65 Squadron from 7 OTU: -

'I got to know "Paddy" well, once we practised dogfighting together but Paddy, who was senior to me, stopped the exercise as we had descended to much less than the prescribed height for such an exercise, so keen were we. He was a very quiet kind of man, totally dedicated to being a fighter pilot, spending little time in the bar.'

At 1150 hrs on 14 August 1940, Flying Officer Gruszka scrambled with 65 Squadron from Manston in response to a threat building up over Calais. 32, 610 and 615 Squadrons took off at the same time, collectively these squadrons meeting the whole of JG26 escorting eighty *Stukas*. A massive aerial combat ensued over Dover, involving over 200 aircraft. For no loss, 65 Squadron claimed the destruction of two enemy aircraft and two 'probables'. According to the squadron's ORB, 'One of our aircraft was hit by six cannon-shells in the wing and fuselage but the pilot (Pilot Officer L.L. Pyman, Spitfire R6601) effected a successful forced landing and the machine was only temporarily unserviceable.' This first glimpse of the enemy since fighting over his homeland the previous year must have been quite a moment for Franek Gruszka.

The following day, 65 Squadron patrolled constantly from 0545 hrs onwards. Flying Officer Gruszka joined a patrol between 1545 and 1615 hrs, but the day passed without event for 65. The following day, however, the squadron was 'heavily engaged on War Operations resulting in our claiming four destroyed, two probables, two damaged'. This action was fought late afternoon, when the Spitfires of 64, 65 and 266 Squadrons were scrambled with the Hurricanes of 32 and 111 Squadrons to intercept 150 enemy aircraft which crossed the Kent coast near Dover, splitting into several formations

The leather purse and contents, including a named propelling pencil, recovered from Grove Marsh and which conclusively identified Flying Officer Gruszka as the missing pilot. In 1998 the author arranged for the pilot's medals to be issued to the family (seen here with the Battle of Britain Bar not uncommonly incorrectly displayed on the Aircrew Europe and not 1939-45 Star as intended).

heading north and north-west. 65 Squadron engaged off Deal, taking on the Me 109 fighter escorts. This time Flying Officer Gruszka fired his guns in anger, as he later wrote in his pencil-written diary: -

'Battle of August. I am starting to fight. Many Germans above and just twelve of us (only two Poles, me and Władzio Szulkowski). We attack bombers, German fighters attack us from behind. One of them is closer and closer. I make a sudden turn, get his tail, and fire a series of bursts. He is going down to the clouds, vertical. I cannot go after him, because in the same moment two other Jerries attack me. Have no chance, I hide in clouds.'

The Me 109 was credited as a 'probable'. Pilot Officer Pyman, who had a lucky escape just two days before, failed to return from this engagement.

On 17 August, for reasons soon evident, the *Luftwaffe* flew few sorties – a respite welcomed by Fighter Command, which had lost seventy-eight pilots killed and twenty-seven more severely wounded in the last eight days' fighting. Of these, over half were experienced 'chaps' – pilots who could be replaced in body but not in experience

Flying Officer Gruszka's last journey: Northwood Cemetery, 1975.

by OTU fresh replacements. On this day, Flying Officer Gruszka again patrolled in company with Pilot Officer Finucane.

The next day would be a significant and fateful one for all too many: 18 August 1940, when the *Luftwaffe* pounded 11 Group's sector stations.

At 1054 hrs, Spitfires made the day's first kill, over Manston, when 54 Squadron's Pilot Officer Colin Gray destroyed an enemy reconnaissance machine. By 1230 hrs, the radar showed so much enemy air activity over the French coastal areas that every single available fighter pilot and aircraft were brought to readiness throughout 11 Group. Eight minutes later, 54 Squadron was scrambled from Hornchurch to meet an incoming raid comprising over 300 bandits, followed by nine more RAF fighter squadrons, 65 Squadron scrambling from Rochford at 1250 hrs. Again the enemy's targets were essential sector stations, this time those at Biggin Hill and Kenley. KG1 sent sixty He 111s to attack the former, KG76 forty-eight Do 17s and Ju 88s to bomb the latter. The tactics for Kenley included an audacious low-level strike by 9/KG76, and with the Me 109s of JGs 3, 26, 51, 52 and 54, together with the Me 110s of ZG 26, providing both escort and diversionary fighter sweeps, the scene was set for another fierce combat.

By 1324 hrs, a running battle had developed all the way from Kenley to the coast, tying down many defending fighter squadrons, giving KG1 a clear run in to attack Biggin Hill. Over Cranbrook, five 65 Squadron Spitfires found and shot up a straggling KG1 He 111. The Spitfires were led by Flying Officer Jeffrey Quill: -

'In 65 Squadron we did not fly the useless formation comprising vics of three, but instead our four sections flew in line astern. This could be rapidly opened out sideways and, like the German line abreast *schwarm*, required much less concentration. 18 August, however, was a hectic day and we suffered a fatal casualty: Flying Officer Franek Gruszka. The trouble was that our two Poles, Szulkowski and Gruszka, were inclined to go off chasing the enemy on their own, so determined were they. None of us saw what happened to Gruszka, and back at Hornchurch Szulkowski was very upset that his friend was missing.'

All that was known was that Flying Officer Gruszka was last seen at 1415 hrs, chasing a German aircraft somewhere between Canterbury and Manston.

Michael Wigmore, an 11-year-old schoolboy, had excitedly watched the air battle overhead: -

'A Spitfire's engine was screaming as the plane came down, very close to me. It crashed with a loud thud at a 45° angle and immediately burst into flame. It was completely out of control and the pilot made no attempt to pull out of the dive.'

The RAF fighter, Spitfire R6713, had crashed into the remote Grove Marshes at Wickhambreux near Canterbury. There the aircraft and its pilot would remain undisturbed until 1971, when amateur aviation archaeologists excavated the site. Cutting a very long story short (see *Missing in Action: Resting in Peace?*) the pilot was not actually recovered for burial until the RAF did so on 15 April 1974. As of that day, at long last, Flying Officer Gruszka was no longer missing.

On 17 July 1975, Franek Gruszka was buried with full military honours at Northwood Cemetery, joining there many other Polish comrades who had made the ultimate sacrifice. Poland, of course, was still behind the

Flying Officer Gruszka's funeral was a well-attended occasion organised by RAF Uxbridge and attended by the Queen's Colour Squadron, Central Band of the RAF, and former comrades of the deceased Polish fighter pilot.

Flying Officer Gruszka's grave at Northwood today, pictured in 2019.

'Iron Curtain' back then, the Cold War at its height, so the first Franek Gruszka's family knew of the recovery and funeral was when a shocked Piotr Gruszka heard the news on the BBC World Service. Present at the funeral were three former 65 Squadron pilots who had fought shoulder-to-shoulder with Flying Officer Gruszka: Commander Jeffrey Quill OBE, and Squadron Leaders 'Gandy' Drobinski DFC and David Glaser DFC. Sadly 65 Squadron's other Pole, Szulkowski, could not be present: on 27 March 1941, he had been killed in a mid-air collision. Nonetheless, as Jeffrey said, 'There were at least two coachloads of Poles present from the London community. I had no idea there were so many Poles still over here! They were so proud, and shared the moment with David, "Gandy" and I, when our missing man was at last laid to rest.'

Coincidentally, Franek Gruszka's niece, Barbara Sekowska (now Sykes), later moved to the UK. Via Anglo-Polish friends, Barbara contacted the

Polish Air Force Association in Great Britain and was honoured to receive her uncle's personal effects, recovered with his remains. It was a moving moment indeed in 1995 when Barbara stood at the grave of the uncle she had never known but heard so much about, with her mother, Franek's Gruszka's sister, Katarzyna.

Flying Officer Franek Gruszka was one of 145 Polish pilots who fought with the RAF during the Battle of Britain, seventy-nine of them, like him, in British squadrons, while sixty-four flew with the Polish 302 and 303 Squadrons. With them these men brought experience, an offensive spirit, and a burning desire to one day liberate their homeland. Twenty-nine Polish pilots lost their lives during the Battle of Britain. Many more would die before the Second World War ended. Victory in Europe, however, would see Poland free from one oppressor but under the yoke of another: Stalin's Soviet Union. Thankfully, the 'Iron Curtain' fell in 1989, when Poland was at last able to enjoy freedom for the first time in so many years – a freedom to which the likes of Franek Gruszka contributed greatly, and which was won with no small amount of Polish courage and sacrifice. How easily we forget…

Chapter Eight

Sergeant George Richard Collett

54 Squadron

Killed in Action: 22 August 1940

George Richard Collett was born on 11 March 1916 at 1 Bassett Road, Kensington, London, the son of George Clemson Collett, an insurance agent, and his wife, Elizabeth Mary (née Arkcoll). 'Dick', as he was known, was the couple's second child, joining older sister Rita Eileen, born on 27 November 1914. Little is known of Dick's early life, as his nephew Bill Gulland explains: 'My late mother, Rita, was very close to her brother while they were young and growing up, finding it difficult to talk about Dick. What we do know is that he was an Old Etonian and after leaving school qualified as a chartered accountant, in which capacity he worked for the General Electric Company Ltd in London.' Fortunately, against the odds, Dick's Pilot's Flying Log Book (Form 414) survives, perfectly preserved along with other papers, by Bill, and it is using this document in particular that we can reconstruct some of Dick Collett's life and experiences.

In common with certain other pilots whose stories are included in this book, Dick grasped the unprecedented opportunity to fly presented by RAFVR (see in particular the story of Sergeant Patrick Hayes). While working at General Electric, Dick volunteered in March 1939, learning to fly at 13 Elementary Flying Training School (EFTS) White Waltham. Flying at weekends and studying ground subjects during weekday evenings, Dick found that the *ab initio* syllabus included 'air experience, effect of controls, taxying, straight and level flying, stalling, climbing and gliding, approaches and landings', and 'spinning', all of which, and more, required mastering before going solo. Dick made his first flight, 'air experience' in a Tiger Moth on 16 April 1939, with Flight Lieutenant Fulford instructing. Over the next few days and weeks, flying with a variety of RAF instructors, Dick's experience steadily increased, working through the syllabus. By 31 August 1939 he had soloed satisfactorily and was then mobilised, war imminent, leaving his desk at General Electric and reporting for full-time duty at 1 Initial Training Wing at Cambridge University on 18 September.

George Richard 'Dick' Collett. (Bill Gulland)

'Square bashing' complete, a month later Sergeant Collett, as he now was, reported for more elementary flying training with Brooklands Aviation, 6 EFTS, at Sywell in Northamptonshire. In addition to flying, Dick completed seven hours under the Link Trainer's hood, learning how to fly 'blind', just using instruments, while safely on the ground. On 5 March 1940, Sergeant Collett, having completed a grand total of fifty-five hours in the air, was tested by the Chief Flying Instructor (CFI) and graded 'average'. Two days later, Dick was in Scotland, reporting for advanced flying training with 8 FTS, Montrose.

At Montrose, having previously flown the DH82 Tiger Moth biplane, Dick and colleagues flew more modern monoplanes for the first time. On 13 March, Sergeant Collett was aloft with Flying Officer Porteous for his first air experience in a Miles Master, a type which he subsequently flew extensively. At first the *ab initio* syllabus was repeated, then expanded to include formation flying, cross-country navigation, 'low-level bombing' and reconnaissance exercises. With 91.40 hours as first pilot recorded in his log book, Dick's course at Montrose concluded on 30 June 1940. By then, of course, the war had become a grim reality for many.

On 30 June 1940 Sergeant Collett reported to 7 OTU at Hawarden near Chester, there to learn how to fly the Supermarine Spitfire – every young man's dream. Previously, Dick's monoplane experience exclusively concerned the humble Master, the top speed of which was 242 mph, with a service ceiling of 25,100 feet. At Hawarden his first flight was solo in a Fairey Battle light-bomber, a comparatively heavy machine powered by the same powerplant as propelled the Spitfire – the Rolls-Royce Merlin. For ten minutes Dick stooged around in the Battle, which had a top speed of 257 mph and service ceiling 100 feet lower than the Master. The Battle, however, was expendable, already being obsolete – Spitfires were not. Having demonstrated an acceptable standard of airmanship, and having studied the Pilot's Notes, Sergeant Collett then made that first, heart-stopping, flight in the superlative Spitfire, 'Experience on Type' lasting thirty-five minutes in Spitfire Mk IA R6610. Compared to the ponderous Master and Battle, Dick was flying the airborne equivalent of a finely tuned racing car, with a top speed of 367 mph, capable of climbing 2,150 feet per minute up to 34,400 feet. The difference in performance he experienced can only be imagined.

Toddler Dick with his sister Rita. (Bill Gulland)

While at Hawarden, Dick made twenty-seven Spitfire flights between 1 and 12 July inclusive. Of these, interestingly, five concerned practising set-piece Fighter Command Attacks, a 'Battle Climb', two cross-countries, three aerobatic sorties and just one of air firing. Seventeen flights were practising formation flying – a flawed emphasis indeed. It must be understood that modern monoplane fighters remained comparatively new. The Spitfire had not yet been in operational service for two years. Before the war, it had been anticipated that enemy air attacks would approach Britain across the North Sea, from Germany, involving formations of bombers only, Britain being beyond the range of the German Me 109 single-engined fighter. Consequently Fighter Command's tacticians decided that squadrons should fly in sections of three in a V-shaped formation known as a 'vic', in line astern. When engaging the enemy, the lead section could, by flying in close formation, bring twenty-four guns to bear simultaneously before breaking away, their place in the line taken by the next section and so on. This, of course, assumed that German bombers would fly on without taking evasive action.

Hitler's lightning advance to the Channel coast provided bases for German fighters in north-west France, putting even London within their range. This meant that RAF fighters would not be seeing off unescorted German bombers, but meeting formations escorted by fighters, or engaging purely fighter formations. This changed everything.

By this time, comparatively few RAF fighter pilots had any actual combat experience. Wisely, Dowding had only committed his more numerous and technically inferior Hurricanes to the hopeless battle in France, the smaller, superior, Spitfire force only being sent into battle during the desperate hour of Dunkirk. The Germans, on the other hand, had fought in Spain during the mid-1930s, the Spanish Civil War providing a unique opportunity to experiment with modern weapons and tactics. There the German fighter pilots learned quickly that close formation flying was suicidal, because instead of searching the sky for enemies, pilots concentrated too much on avoiding collisions with their neighbours and were therefore extremely vulnerable. Over Spain, the *Schwarm* was developed, in which German fighters flew in sections of four in a loose line abreast, each aircraft some 200 metres apart. In action, this sub-divided into the *Rotte*, or fighting pair, comprising the leader (*Rottenführer*), whose job was to shoot, and wingman (*Rottenhund*), whose role was to protect his leader's tail, so that the former could concentrate on attacking the target. In this way, German fighter formations were flexible, providing mutual protection without concentrating on formation flying. Unfortunately, although having met the *Jagdwaffe* over France, the inflexible adherence to Fighter Command Attacks and emphasis on close formation flying persisted.

Having made his last flight at Hawarden on 12 July 1940, two days after the Battle of Britain is officially considered to have begun, on 14 July, Sergeant Collett reported to 54 Squadron – a Spitfire squadron based at Hornchurch in Essex. 54 was another regular RAF unit disbanded after the First World War and later re-formed, at Hornchurch in 1930. Over the next few years, the squadron would operate a succession of biplane fighters until receiving the Spitfire in March 1939. Like the other Spitfire squadrons, 54 had been heavily involved in the Dunkirk air fighting, during which it claimed thirty-one enemy aircraft destroyed offset against losing seven Spitfires and four pilots. Moreover, 54 Squadron had already been involved in the early skirmishing over Channel-bound convoys during the Battle of Britain, so was no stranger to air fighting. At Hornchurch, Dick found his new CO to be Squadron Leader James Leathart – known universally as 'Prof' on account of his technical mind and training as an electrical engineer. Over the French coast, Leathart had destroyed a number of enemy aircraft, in addition to executing the dare-devil rescue of 74 Squadron's then CO who had been shot down over France. Escorted by 54 Squadron Spitfires, 'Prof' flew a Master to safely collect Squadron Leader White from Calais-Marck airfield, snatching him from under the Germans' noses. On 11 June, he was appointed to the DSO, a well-deserved award. Another decorated 54 Squadron pilot was the New Zealander Flying Officer Al Deere DFC, who would become a fighter legend and had already inflicted substantial damage upon the *Luftwaffe*, and had survived being shot down and various other adventures. Emphasising the Commonwealth contribution and presence, also on 54 Squadron at this time was another New Zealander, Flying Officer Colin Falkland Gray, also to become a decorated fighter ace, so it was in good company that Sergeant Collett and Pilot Officer Douglas Turley-George, also freshly arrived from Hawarden, found themselves at Hornchurch.

While combat experience was in short supply, pilots, at this time, were not. The various training units maintained a stream of replacements to the squadrons, most of which at this time enjoyed a full complement of pilots. This meant that new pilots could be broken in gently (as was not the case later in the summer of 1940 for certain hard-pressed 11 Group squadrons). On 17 July therefore, Sergeant Collett was able to fly two 'Reccos', familiarising himself with the local area, the first in Spitfire N3192, KL-V, then in P9389, KL-A. The following day, another hour's formation practice was completed, then, on 20 July, Sergeant Collett's name was chalked on the board as operational and a member of 'B' Flight. On that day, Dick flew with other 54 Squadron pilots from Hornchurch to operate from the forward satellite of Rochford, and to Manston the next day, there, close to the coast,

Margate Cemetery. (Anne Wilton)

awaiting the call to scramble. There was also the opportunity for more practice flying, 'Attacks' and 'Dusk Landings' on 21 July.

Across the Channel, on that day Göring met with his *Luftflotten* chiefs, ordering them to devise plans for decisive operations against England, the intention being the destruction of Fighter Command before a seaborne invasion. Although fighting over convoys had begun on 2 July, by mid-July an increasing number of German fighter units were deployed to the Pas-de-Calais, reinforcing JG51, from where they could engage in what was essentially a contest between the opposing fighter forces. On 15 July, for example, the *Geschwader Stab* and I *Gruppe* of JG26 *Schlageter*, moved from Germany, where the fighter group had rested after the Battle of France, to Audembert, near Calais, there re-joining *Generaloberst* Kesselring's *Jafü* 2 of *Luftflotten* 2. On 21 July, the other two *gruppen* of JG26 arrived on the *Kanalfront*, II/JG26 basing itself at Marquise, III/JG26 at Caffiers. A *Jagdgeschwader* (Fighter Group) comprised three *gruppen* (wings), each of three *staffeln* (squadrons), so each *gruppe* represented around forty fighters. The Germans recognised the impracticality of an entire *geschwader*, numbering some 120 machines, operating in concert, and so the *gruppe* was the main tactical entity. This was at odds with Fighter Command's tactics of meeting enemy formations with 'penny packet' formations of either flights of six fighters, or single squadrons of twelve. The Germans also enjoyed the advantage of deciding when and where battle would take place, being able to climb to height over France and the Channel – and in fighter combat, height is everything. Fighter Command's squadrons, on the other hand, insufficient to mount constant high-altitude standing patrols, were scrambled in response to incoming threats, albeit with precious extra minutes' warning from radar, and all too often found themselves sighted and attacked while still clawing for height by the high-flying enemy. As already explained, the *Jagdwaffe*'s tactics were superior to Fighter Command's, and the Me 109 was superior to the RAF's most numerous fighter, the Hawker Hurricane – and equal, and in certain respects also superior, to the romanticised Supermarine Spitfire.

On 22 July, Sergeant Collett practised dogfighting using the cine camera mounted in the Spitfire's wing root, synchronised to shoot when the machine guns were fired. The next day, Dick was off from Rochford to Manston, then back for an overnight stay at Rochford. 24 July would be a busy day…

At 0515 hrs that morning, Sergeant Collett flew the dawn patrol with Pilot Officers Allen and Finnie. After ten minutes the trio landed for some unrecorded reason, taking off again five minutes later for fifteen uneventful minutes. Dick also flew on the day's third patrol, taking off at 0840 hrs.

The grave of *Leutnant* Josef Schauff of 8/JG26 at Margate, possibly shot down by Sergeant Dick Collett on 24 July 1940. (Anne Wilton)

A convoy passing through the Dover Strait had drawn an attack from two *staffeln* of Do 17s, in two waves of six. The first wave reached the ships but missed their targets. 54 Squadron's Green Action, led by Pilot Officer George Gribble, harried the second wave, which jettisoned its bombs and ran back to France. Sergeant Collett took no direct part in the action, and 54 Squadron claimed none of the bombers destroyed, but sighting the enemy for the first time must have been an adrenalin-inducing moment.

Then came, according to the 54 Squadron scribe, 'The Battle of the Thames Estuary'.

This time, a much heavier attack was mounted on a convoy steaming out of the Medway at 1100 hrs, some eighteen *Dorniers* approaching the ships. On what was JG26's first mission against England, ten Me 109s II/JG26 swept ahead of the bombers while forty fighters of Major Adolf Galland's III/JG26 closely escorted the *Dorniers*. Approaching Dover, *Hauptmann* Noack of II *Gruppe* reported a large number of Spitfires (actually only nine of 610 Squadron) over Dover, so aborted the mission and returned to France – where he was killed while landing back at Marquise. At 1120 hrs, 54 Squadron, led by Flight Lieutenant Al Deere, was scrambled. Within minutes, Deere's Spitfires were embroiled with Galland's Me 109s. Sergeant Collett flew in a section of three with Pilot Officers Johnny Allen and Archibald Finnie, as he subsequently reported: -

'I was flying in vic formation at 12,000 feet, acting as rear guard, when I saw about nine E/A on our tails about 2,000 feet above and immediately told my leader, who turned to port. I next noticed white smoke coming from the starboard side of a Spitfire, I think that of Yellow One. I turned left and right and got in a deflection shot on the 109 which was on the tail of this Spitfire; he came off Pilot Officer Allen's tail at once, and as the 109 came up I got in another burst, after which the E/A wobbled badly and his engine stopped.'

This was a classic case of the vulnerable 'Tail End Charlie' section, weaving to and from slightly above and behind their squadron, being 'bounced' first by the ever-watchful high-flying Me 109s. Dick continued: -

'As he dived down, I gave a final burst, after which he was obviously finished. I did not see him strike the sea as my attention was drawn to another 109 which I chased and finally got in my sights and pressed the button, but unfortunately all my ammunition was spent. I had to throttle back to about plus 4 boost to keep on his tail. This last E/A took no evasive action, since he probably didn't know I was there.'

Galland himself later wrote: -

'Over the Thames Estuary we got involved in a heavy scrap with Spitfires… Together with the *Stabschwarm* (Staff Flight) I selected one formation as our prey, and we made a surprise attack from a favourably higher altitude. I glued myself to the tail of the plane flying outside on the left flank and when, during a right-handed turn, I managed to get in a long burst, the Spitfire went down almost vertically. I followed it until the cockpit cover came flying towards me and the pilot baled out, then followed him down until he crashed into the water. His parachute had failed to open.'

There is no record of an RAF fighter pilot baling out into the sea that day. The parachute of *Leutnant* Josef Schauff of 8/JG26 failed to open after he was shot down by a Spitfire over Margate, his aircraft crashing in Byron Avenue, the pilot's body falling in nearby playing fields. It is impossible to say, however, who shot Schauff down. Both Sergeant Collett and Pilot Officer Gray were credited with Me 109s destroyed, and unconfirmed kills were attributed to Flight Lieutenant Deere, Flying Officer McMullen, Pilot Officers Coleman and Turley-George. Eight 109s were claimed as probably destroyed by Flying Officer McMullen, Flight Lieutenant Way (two), Pilot Officer Gray, Pilot Officer Gribble (two), Pilot Officer Turley-George and Flight Sergeant Tew, in addition to two damaged by Pilot Officer Coleman and Matthews. In reality, Schauff's was the only Me 109 lost by III/JG26 in this action, confirming, yet again, the confusion of air fighting as the speed of combat so often deceived the human eye. Little wonder, though, that the 54 Squadron diarist described 24 July 1940 as 'The biggest and most successful day since Dunkirk'.

While Dick shot a 109 off the tail of Pilot Officer Allen, it would seem that his Spitfire was already grievously damaged, as the 54 Squadron ORB reports: -

'The action was marred by the unfortunate loss of Pilot Officer Allen DFC. He was attacked by an Me 109 near Margate; he was seen coming down with engine stopped and appeared to be making a forced-landing under perfect control. The engine came to life again, and he made for Manston, the engine cut a second time and Pilot Officer Allen apparently turned towards Foreness when he stalled and spun straight into the ground. The loss of Pilot Officer Allen, who had destroyed seven enemy aircraft, will be greatly felt by the whole Squadron.'

Sergeant Collett's report continues: -

'I tried by R/T to get a homing vector but could get no reply, so I set course about NW and made landfall close to where I landed. I had only five gallons left so could not try for an alternative landing.'

Dick had 'crashed' (his word) force-landing Spitfire N3192, KL-V, at Sizewell, near Orfordness.

On 25 July, the Record Office at RAF Ruislip wrote to Dick's father: -

'I regret to inform you that according to a communication received from 54 Squadron… your son No 745500 Sergeant George Richard Collett of the

Pilot Officer Finnie's grave at Margate. (Anne Wilton)

above unit was admitted to Ipswich Hospital and placed on the 'Seriously Ill' list on 24 July 1940.

'He was seriously injured when the aircraft of which he was the pilot and sole occupant crashed at Saxmundham, near Martlesham Heath, Suffolk, after an engagement with enemy aircraft.

'Should you propose to visit your son it is desirable that you communicate with the hospital authorities concerned to ensure that he has not, in the meantime, been transferred elsewhere.

'Any change in his condition will be notified to me, and you will be informed immediately.'

This prognosis, however, was a mistake. Certainly, Dick was a patient at East Suffolk & Ipswich Hospital's Churchman Annex Ward, from where, the same day, he wrote to his father and sister (his mother having already died) clarifying the situation and alleviating their anxiety: -

'Shall start by saying I am only slightly hurt, the chief thing being two stitches in the chin, the rest are really aches and pains, which will heal … very rapidly. I should not bother about coming over to see me as it is not worth it, especially as I should be out in about three days. Am very comfortable with nice ward and other HM forces to keep me company.

'Perhaps you may have heard the news on the wireless that an air battle took place over the Channel with the result that we got five certs and nine probables with the loss of two Spitfires. Well, one of the two was me, and the other my Section Leader. We were busy from 5 o'clock in the morning but the big do was at 1 pm.

'I was not shot down but ran out of juice and had to make a forced-landing not far from Lowestoft, which was not a success owing to the engine coughing when just over the hedge, with the result that I hit the dirt rather hard. It was not a complete debit as I did get an Me 109, but having wandered so far after another, when I caught it up I found my ammo had been used up. I had difficulty finding merry England and when I did only had five gallons left, so had to get a move on in the way of a landing. Not very good business trip but I hope it will improve later.

'As luck would have it I was to have 24 hours leave from 1 o'clock yesterday to 1 o'clock today, but that, of course, is knocked on the head and will have to wait a bit. Pity, especially as it is such a nice day today with sun streaming in through the windows.

'Well old things there is no more news I can think of at the moment but will write again giving you an update of my movements before very long. Be good, people, don't get into trouble and don't worry about me as I have literally NOTHING wrong with me and am only here really under observation.

'Heaps of love from old son and brother, Dick.'

While Dick remained in hospital, the 11 Group HQ signalled 54 Squadron following the apparently successful action of 24 July: -

'Air Officer Commanding has read with great interest the combat report of 54 Squadron and congratulates the leaders and pilots on their magnificent fight against superior numbers. He wishes 54 Squadron to know that 65 and 610 Squadrons were also despatched to intercept the same raid and were also engaged with enemy fighters and bombers.'

While the end result, considering actual German losses, was not the body-blow 54 Squadron believed it had delivered to III/JG26, Major Galland, a leading German fighter ace and tactician, a veteran of Spain and the campaigns to date, concluded after the day's events that 'We were no longer in doubt that the RAF would prove a most formidable opponent.'

The day after Dick crash-landed, 54 Squadron was heavily engaged again over the Channel, losing the popular 'A' Flight commander Flight Lieutenant 'Wonky' Way and Pilot Officer Finnie, both shot down by 109s in separate engagements. On 26 July, a much depleted 54 Squadron, including only six surviving pilots from the Dunkirk fighting, left to rest and refit at Catterick. There, on 31 July, 54 was declared 'non-operational' and settled down to receiving and training replacements. The 'rest' would be both brief and busy. By 8 August, when 54 Squadron returned to Hornchurch with a full complement of twenty-two pilots, 153 daylight training hours had been flown at Catterick, and six at night. Touching down at Hornchurch, 54 Squadron felt 'ready for anything'.

Sergeant Collett was pronounced fit and re-joined 54 Squadron on 18 August 1940 – the Battle of Britain's 'Hardest Day' (see Flying Officer Gruszka's story) – flying a short, non-operational 'Air Test' to refamiliarize himself with the Spitfire and local area. That day, 54 Squadron, however, was heavily engaged, as it had been on previous days since returning to Hornchurch. According to the ORB, this was 'A great day! In four sorties the squadron bore the brunt of the Station's thrust against the enemy.' In two hectic air battles, for no loss 54 Squadron claimed eight enemy aircraft destroyed, six probables and eleven damaged, 'A fine performance', generating the following congratulatory signal from no less a personality than the CAS: 'Well done 54 Squadron. In all your hard fighting, this is the right spirit for dealing with the enemy.'

After the exertions of 18 August, the 19th saw 'complete inactivity' for 54 Squadron, an unexpected yet welcome respite, no doubt. That day, Dick took the opportunity to write home: -

My dear old Dad and Rita,

Have not done any flying just yet, but think they will make me permanently operational once my helmet arrives, which should be tomorrow.

The boys have certainly been busy while I have been away, and their bags have increased so will have something to do to put myself in the running. Sunday was exceptionally good for our crowd.

Have bought a nicely mounted picture of the squadron together, with one or two post card copies which I will let you have.

Will be very grateful if you could manage to forward any handkerchiefs that I may have in the laundry, together with a white towel of mine. Hope this will not put you to too much trouble.

Should you be seeing Lew at any time, will be very glad if you could ask him if he has had any luck regarding enquiry for a sports car for me from a pal of his called Dickie. Should like to get fixed up soon with something good and cheap.

Wonder if you have heard from Phyl since her big shift. Wonder where she will get sent onto.

Has Mr Dear telephoned or got in touch with you in any way since I left (illegible)? Expect he must have been kept at Cambridge.

Will come to a close now as it is getting on the late side. Do look after yourselves and be good people.

Heaps of love to you both from your son and brother.

Dick

On 20 August, suitably helmeted, Dick first flew from Hornchurch to Manston with 'B' Flight, now led by Flight Lieutenant George Gribble DFC, from where the Spitfires patrolled uneventfully. At 1415, 54 Squadron was scrambled to intercept an incoming raid over Eastchurch, but cloud prevented a successful interception, although retreating bombers were seen in the distance and Flight Lieutenant Gribble 'chased' nine German fighters back to France (incorrectly identified as 'He 113s' which were nothing but a propaganda ruse and never saw operational service). Finally, the squadron swept around the North Foreland, seeking any straggling enemy machines, but none were found and 54, including Sergeant Collett, returned to Hornchurch. On 21 August, Dick flew down to Manston with 'B' Flight; there were no heavy raids but lone enemy reconnaissance aircraft saw 54 Squadron making six separate sorties throughout the day in an attempt to catch them, two of which Dick participated in before returning to Hornchurch that evening.

On 22 July, the German labour organisation, *Todt*, had begun work on installations around Calais for heavy artillery pieces. By the end of that month, the first battery, *Siegfried*, was installed south of Cap Gris Nez. Other batteries of fifteen, twelve, eleven, and eight-inch guns were soon situated north of Boulogne, at Calais, and Cap Blanc Nez. Between 0800 and 0900 hrs on Thursday 22 August, Convoy TOTEM was negotiating the

Pilot Officer Allen DFC's grave at Margate – both he and Finnie made up the 'Tail-End Charlie' section with Sergeant Collett on 24 July 1940 but did not survive the 'Battle of the Thames Estuary'. (Anne Wilton)

dangerous Dover Strait and fired upon by the German batteries. According to *The Times* report the following day, 'The warships escorting the convoy at once laid smoke screens to conceal the convoy from the enemy. Although some shells fell fairly close to the ships, no ship of the convoy or escort was hit or received damage.' Some hundred shells, in fact, were fired at TOTEM, a Berlin spokesman insisting that 'the long-range guns mounted on the Channel and Atlantic coasts were firing merely for practice'. The batteries' failure to damage TOTEM inevitably led to aerial activity.

At 0535 hrs that morning, Sergeant Collett flew in the six-Spitfire-strong 'B' Flight formation led by Squadron Leader Leathart to Manston, there to await events. Radar plots later confirmed enemy air activity over Calais, so between 1125 and 1205 hrs, 'B' Flight patrolled Manston as a precautionary defensive measure, but no raid developed. Given the heavy attacks on 11 Group's Sector Stations, by this time the fighting was far from just about convoy protection. RAF ground controllers were unable to predict what target a raid was bound for, increasing the pressure on Fighter Command. At lunchtime TOTEM was attacked by the Me 110s of precision bombing unit *Erprobungsgruppe* 210, escorted by Me 109s. At 1235 hrs, 54 Squadron's 'B' Flight was scrambled and battle was joined off Deal. In the ensuing combat, although no German losses correlate to these claims, 'Sergeant Norwell, at "home" again with his 109s, destroyed one, Pilot Officer Hopkin attacked an Me 110 head-on and destroyed it, and Flight Lieutenant Gribble left a 109 in a somewhat unenviable position – trying to do a flick stall at 500 feet.' 'B' Flight were the only

RAF fighters involved in this action, which successfully prevented any damage to TOTEM. 'A' Flight hurried to the scene, scrambling just eleven minutes after 'B' Flight, but arrived to find an empty sky, the fast and furious action over. Afterwards, the Spitfires returned to Hornchurch in ones and twos – except Sergeant Collett and Spitfire R6708, KL-S, who was reported 'Missing'.

According to a casualty report dated 24 August 1940, 'No 54 Squadron were off from Manston to intercept enemy aircraft off Deal. The Squadron became engaged in a dogfight and during the course of this action Sergeant Collett's aircraft was seen diving towards the sea. Since the rendering of signal on 22nd August, no news has been received of the missing pilot and the aircraft was presumed lost in the sea.' The 54 Squadron diary added that it was 'believed that he went down with his aircraft, which sank off Deal'.

Sergeant Collett's Spitfire had undoubtedly been shot down by an Me 109 from I/*Lehrgeschwader* 2, which provided *Erprobungsgruppe* 210's escort. The two claims with the best fit time-wise (Continental time being an hour ahead) are those by *Unteroffizier* Werner Götting (1/LG2) for a Spitfire in the Dover area at 1335 hrs, his first combat victory, and Oberfeldwebel Hermann Staege (2/LG2), for his fourth 'kill' in the same area at 1405 hrs. In addition to Dick, Sergeant Corfe of 610 Squadron was shot down in combat with Me 109s over Folkestone, crash-landing at Hawkinge, 1415 hrs. It is likely, therefore, that these German pilots were responsible for shooting down the two sergeant-pilots, although exactly which is impossible to say.

Immediately, Dick's father was telegrammed with the bad news, the devastating content confirmed by an official letter: -

'In confirmation of my telegram of today's date, I regret to inform you that your son No 745500 Sergeant George Richard Collett of No 54 Squadron, Royal Air Force, is missing, the aircraft of which he was the pilot and sole occupant having failed to return to its base on the 22nd August 1940, after an operational flight.

'This does not necessarily mean that he is killed or wounded. I will communicate with you again immediately I have any further news and would be obliged if you, on your part, would write to me should you hear anything of your son.

'In conveying this information to you, may I assure you of the sympathy of the Royal Air Force with you in your anxiety.'

As time went on, without further news of his missing son George Collett's 'anxiety' can only be imagined. Sadly, any hope that Dick remained alive was crushed on 6 January 1941, with the arrival of another official letter: -

'With reference to my letter dated 22 August 1940, it is my painful duty to inform you that according to a telegram from the International Red Cross, Geneva, quoting official information from Berlin, your son No 745500 Sergeant George Richard Collett of No 54 Squadron, Royal Air Force, previously reported as "missing" is now reported "missing, believed killed in action".

'In conveying this information to you, may I assure you of the sympathy of the Royal Air Force with you in your anxiety.'

On 18 February 1942, another letter arrived, confirming that Dick's body had been buried at Haamstede, Zeeland, Holland. This, however, prompted a

Sergeant Dick Collett's grave at Bergen-op-Zoom, Netherlands. (Paul Neelissen)

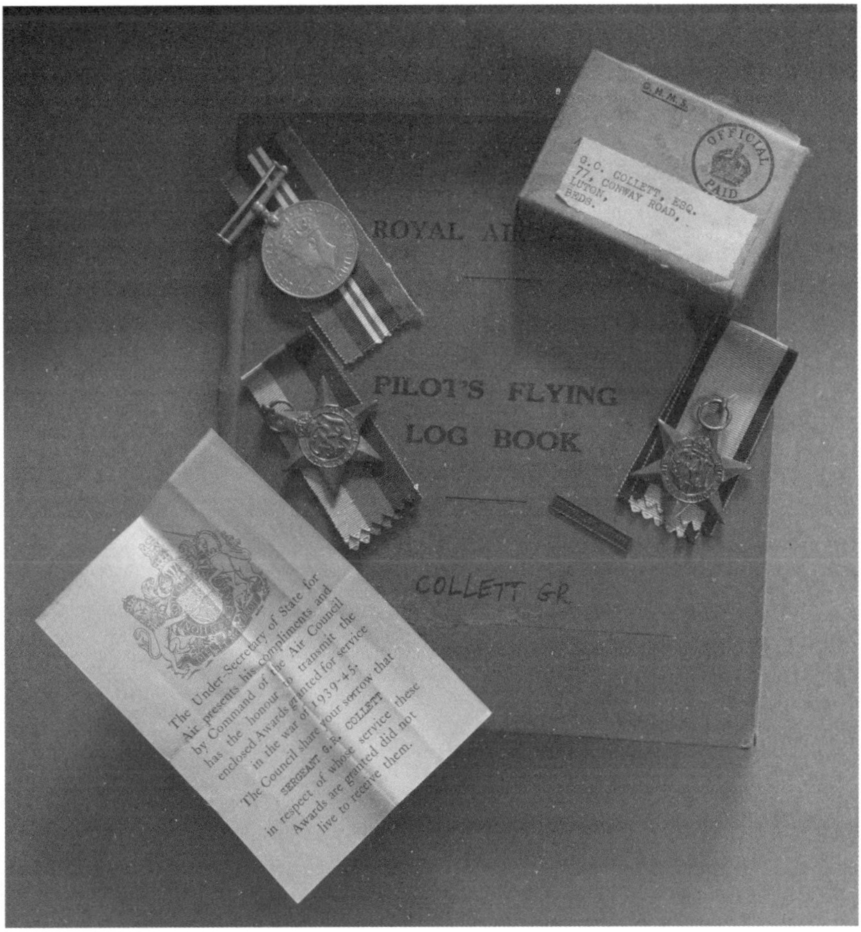

Sergeant Collett's log book and medals, the latter still in box of issue, perfectly preserved.

further enquiry from George, dated 21 February, inquiring as to whether his son had 'crashed in Holland' or had 'his body washed up from the sea on the Holland coast'. The latter had in fact been the case. Eventually, the current had carried Dick across the North Sea, washing the young pilot's remains ashore at Haamstede, on Schouwen Island in the province of Zeeland, where he was buried. The following year, on 14 August 1942, further information arrived, this time from the 'Wounded, Missing and Relatives Department' of the British Red Cross, informing Mr Collett that certain personal effects had been recovered with Dick's body, namely a cheque book, a cigarette case, 'RAF identity paper', two lead pencils, £1.10s., a pocketbook, 'different papers',

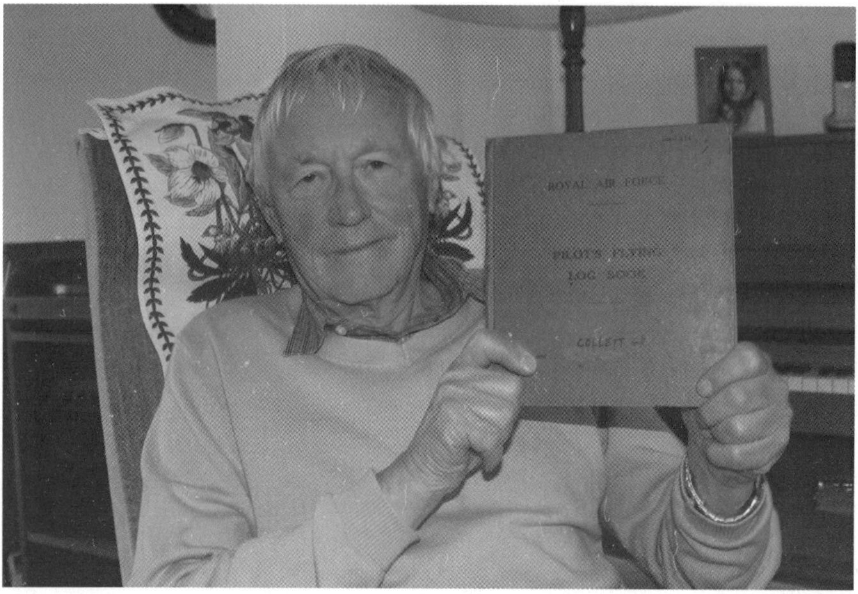

Sergeant Dick Collett's nephew, Bill Gulland, proudly displays his uncle's log book in 2019.

a calendar and two postage stamps. The letter concluded that 'The Dutch Red Cross have expressly asked us to convey their sympathy to the relatives of our airmen who have lost their lives in Holland, and we should like to tell you of the many intimations reaching us of loyal tributes paid by the Dutch people themselves who have covered the graves with flowers and tend them carefully.'

In March 1948, a further communication arrived from the Air Ministry, explaining to Mr Collett that the Graves Registration & Enquiry Service had exhumed Dick from Haamstede, reinterring his remains in the British War Cemetery at Bergen-op-Zoom, 'where facilities are available' for the 'proper care and maintenance' of graves 'in perpetuity, by the Imperial War Graves Commission'.

Today, the grave of 24-year-old Sergeant George Richard 'Dick' Collett can be found at Bergen-op-Zoom, some twenty miles north-west of Antwerp, in the British War Cemetery there, immaculately maintained by the Commonwealth War Graves Commission. The cemetery contains the graves of 1,189 identified casualties, 116 known only 'unto God'.

Dick's headstone bears a poignant epitaph: -

Beloved son of GL Collett & Elizabeth M Collett
Till We Meet Again

Chapter Nine

Aircraftwoman 1st Class Edna Lenna Button

Women's Auxiliary Air Force

&

Aircraftman 1st Class John Joseph Jackson

610 'County of Chester' Squadron

Killed in Action: 30 August 1940

At first the Battle of Britain was a violent and dangerous reality mainly for the aircrew directly at the sharp end, fighting over the Channel. On Fighter Command's inland Sector Stations, daily life and work went on pretty much as before, albeit with a greater sense of purpose and urgency, with everyone bracing themselves for the inevitable onslaught ahead. On such a summer's day, the Station Commander rebuked a Section Officer of the Women's Auxiliary Air Force for the airwomen using gasmask cases as extra 'handbag' storage, and, God forbid, using the airmen's shelter trenches, and not their own airwomen's variety, during practices. Suddenly, bombs began exploding across the airfield, a mass German formation ahead. 'Take cover!' yelled the 'Groupie', heading for the nearest trench and not caring about which sex occupied it. The raid had achieved complete surprise, bombs bursting around and destroying urgently scrambling Spitfires, damaging the runway and airfield installations. As the raiders departed, the Station was wreathed in smoke and flame. Some survivors, including the Station Warrant Officer, reacted swiftly, organising things, barking orders to shocked personnel. The WAAF Section Officer left the trench shared with the Station Commander, looking for her airwomen. The young officer was met with a shocking sight: a row of dead bodies, thankfully their tortured and mutilated features concealed by RAF issue blankets. All were 'WAAFs'. This, however, was not 1940 but the 1969 film *Battle of Britain*, actors Kenneth Moore portraying the Group Captain and Susannah York Section Officer Harvey.

Left: Susannah York added a touch of glamour and played 'Section Officer Harvey' in the 1969 film *Battle of Britain* – which exaggerated WAAF losses on the ground while rightly acknowledging the brave part played by women.

Below: At Biggin Hill, three WAAFs were awarded the Military Medal for their courage and devotion to duty when their Station was heavily bombed. This artist's impression from the *Illustrated London News* shows Corporal Elspeth Henderson maintaining communications while the Operations Room disintegrates around her.

In the background played the dark 'Death and Destruction' piece by composer Ron Goodwin. It was a great, dramatic scene, inspired by events at Biggin Hill on 30 August 1940, emphasising the part played and casualties suffered by those providing essential back-up on the ground.

The 'Section Officer Harvey' character had been based on a real WAAF officer, the 27-year-old Section Officer Felicity Hanbury, commanding RAF

Biggin Hill's detachment of 250 WAAFs. The WAAF had been created on 28 June 1939; until 1941, all WAAFs were volunteers. Unlike today, in those days females did not serve as aircrew or in combat roles. WAAFs therefore engaged with such things as packing parachutes, catering, operations room and communications duties, meteorology, driving, intelligence work and operating barrage balloons. Even so, the advent of air power had put even the civilians in the front line, so all non-combatants were exposed to the same dangers – and WAAFs serving on RAF bases were very much in harm's way during the summer of 1940. On 18 August 1940, one of their number, Sergeant Joan Mortimer, had already shown the fairer sex's mettle under fire, refusing to leave her switchboard post, continuing to pass essential messages, throughout a heavy raid on Biggin Hill – despite being located close the Armoury. Furthermore, before the 'All-Clear' wailed, Sergeant Mortimer, of her own initiative, marked all unexploded bombs on the runway with red flags, ensuring safe landings for the Hurricanes of 601 Squadron. While engaged in this dangerous and

The *Illustrated London News* also reported on Sergeant Joan Mortimer's 'amazing pluck', marking UXBs on the Biggin Hill runway under fire.

uncertain endeavour, a UXB went off close by, winding the WAAF NCO, who, nevertheless continued until the last crater was flagged. Sergeant Mortimer was later awarded the Military Medal for her bravery on that hardest of days, the citation acknowledging her 'exceptional courage and coolness while under attack', which 'had a great moral effect on all those she came into contact with. Her steadfast courage to both remain at her post while under bombardment and undertake action to prevent further aircraft losses was outstanding.' Mortimer had certainly set an inspirational example and no mistake.

According to Section Officer Hanbury (later Air Commodore Dame Felicity Peake) the 'storm broke' on 30 August 1940. As the civilian air raid warning sirens sounded, Section Officer Hamburg was discussing the day's routine with Flight Sergeant Gartside by the WAAF Guard Room. Nothing developed, so Hanbury made towards her office several hundred yards away. When nearby, the Station's alarm sounded and, complying with instructions, Section Officer Hanbury headed at the double to the nearest trench. There she found a WAAF Cypher Officer, Pam Beecroft, the Padre, and Squadron Leader Mike Crossley, the CO of 32 Squadron who had just landed in his Hurricane and been caught helpless on the ground. In the trench the tin-hatted occupants were packed together 'like sardines'. The resulting bombs crashing down felt like an 'earth-quake'. Then, in a lull, the Padre was urgently summoned by a runner to one of the airmen's trenches on the aerodrome's perimeter – which had taken a direct hit. Climbing out of her trench, Section Officer Hanbury went to check on the status of her WAAFs. Rubble and debris impeded her progress, and the whole area near the WAAF Guard Room reeked of gas owing to the ruptured mains. At the side of the road lay a female body – the first dead person Hanbury had ever seen, so steeling herself for that unbeknown experience, the Section Officer approached, thinking that she must 'have a good look at her as I may have to get used to this kind of thing'. Finding her reactions 'controllable', Hanbury found the unfortunate casualty to be a civilian, a young girl who sold tea and wads from the NAAFI wagon. There was worse to come. Reaching the WAAF Guard Room, Hanbury discovered that the airwomen's trench adjacent had been hit. Airmen were already frantically digging to locate and free any survivors, eventually clearing the way for survivors to be rescued. Flight Sergeant Gartside emerged on a stretcher with a broken back, her cheerfulness nonetheless having prevented panic taking hold and keeping up the women's morale – for which she would be Mentioned in Despatches. One WAAF, however, was dead: Aircraftwoman 1st Class Edna Lenna Button.

Above: The same artist also drew Sergeant Helen Turner, still working her switchboard under fire, adjacent to the armoury.

Right: The first WAAF to die in the Battle of Britain was 19-year-old Marguerite Hudson, fatally injured at RAF Driffield on 13 August 1940 and expiring two days later; her grave is in Sheffield but no living family could be found. (Mark Gregory)

Aircraftwoman Button was the 39-year-old daughter of Edmund and Bertha Button of Scotsdale, Tasmania, Australia. A medical orderly, Lenna had insisted upon evacuating all patients from Station Sick Quarters before heading for shelter herself – the last in, when the entrance was hit and the concrete walls collapsed, the gallant nurse was killed. Four days later, news of the casualty was published by Tasmania's *North-Eastern Advertiser*: -

'The war was brought nearer home to this distant portion of the empire with startling and painful suddenness yesterday morning when a cable message was received by Mr Edmund Button, expressing regret that his daughter Edna had been killed in an air raid over England on Friday last. As the sad news was circulated, deep and sincere regret was on all lips, for the bereaved family are widely-known and esteemed, and their daughter, whose career has been watched with interest by friends and admirers, was held in the highest regard.

'The late Miss Button, who was twenty-nine years of age, was born at Scottsdale, and after leaving the State School, put in two years in the Ladies College in Launceston. She then joined the Education Department and for a time was teaching at Scottsdale. Miss Button also temporarily held the position of assistant council clerk at Scottsdale. She had a passion for Missionary Work, and was pleased to accept an appointment at the North Melbourne Methodist Mission, where she stayed for three years, entering whole-heartedly into the task she loved so much. The desire for advancement took her to New Zealand, where she entered the College at Christchurch, and took the degree of Deaconess. Known then as "Sister Lenna" she accepted an appointment at Dunedin and from there went to the Auckland Methodist Mission. This latter position she resigned, for the purpose of proceeding to a college at Birmingham (England). In the meantime, war broke out and the college was not opened. Instead, she engaged in hospital work, and then joined up as a medical orderly in the 8th Brigade of the WAAF, a position occupied at the time of her death.

'A devout Christian and a sincere and earnest worker in the interests of her fellow creatures, she has rendered devoted service to Him whom she served, and the cutting off of a life in its prime is deeply regretted.

'The sincere sympathy of a wide circle of friends will be extended to the bereaved relatives.'

After doing all she was able at the airwomen's trench, Section Officer Hanbury hurried off to Station HQ to see how other sections had fared. Passing by the

Right: The last WAAF, of three, to die in the Battle of Britain was pregnant Carol Lowry, selflessly shielding her mother-in-law during a raid on Eastbourne. (Martin Driver)

Below: The victims of bombing at RAF Biggin Hill were interred at St Mary Cray Cemetery, Orpington, Kent. (Ken Back)

dead NAAFI girl, Felicity noticed that 'someone had put a blanket over her, covering her completely. Somehow this had a greater effect on me than when I had seen her the first time. It seemed so final, almost casual.'

In truth, during the Battle of Britain proper, contrary to the impression generated by *Battle of Britain*, in addition to 'Sister Lena', just two other

The grave of 'Sister Lena', Aircraftwoman Edna Lenna Button, at St Mary Cray. Although the family was located in Tasmania, no photographs of this exceptional lady could be found. (Ken Back)

WAAFs lost their lives during the sixteen-week long conflict. The first was Aircraftwoman 2nd Class Marguerite Hester Hudson, from Wadsley, Sheffield, killed at RAF Driffield when Luftflotte 5, based in Norway, launched its major assault against north-east England on 15 August 1940. Then, there is the sad tale of AW1 Carol Winfried Lawry: whilst shopping with her mother-in-law in Eastbourne on 9 October 1940, a raid occurred, during which pregnant Carol threw herself over her elderly mother-in-law, to protect her; the selfless off-duty WAAF was killed by shrapnel from a nearby exploding bomb. For the family there would soon be another tragedy when Carol's husband, Ken, was killed when the Catalina he was flying in crashed into the North Sea; all nine aircrew aboard were lost.

Returning to the events of 30 August 1940, the RAF Biggin Hill ORB reported that the raid at 1800 hrs, referred to above, was the second of the day: -

'A low-level bombing attack was carried out by the enemy on the Station and very serious damage was done to buildings and equipment. The raiders dropped 16 big HE bombs, estimated 1,000 lbs weight each, of which six fell among the buildings rendering completely useless and unsafe, Workshops, Transport Yard, Stores, Barrack Stores, Armoury, Guardroom, Meteorological Office, and the Station Institute, and shattering by blast part of the Airmen's Married Quarters which was being used as accommodation for WAAF personnel. "F" Type Hangar in N. Camp was also badly damaged.

'One shelter trench received a direct hit and two others near hits. The total casualties were 39 killed and 26 wounded and shocked.

'All power, gas and water mains were severed and all telephone lines running north of the camp were severed in three places.'

Amongst Biggin Hill's fighter squadrons was the Spitfire-equipped 610 'County of Chester' Squadron, the ORB of which matter-of-factly documented: '1255083 AC Burton, 810029 AC Jackson, JJ, & 7589578 Pte. Tarrant, J, killed as the result of enemy action.' These men were amongst those killed in the airmen's trench. So difficult were conditions that work to rescue the living and locate the dead went on throughout the night, RAF teams backed-up by ARP men from nearby Orpington, and even local residents. In total, twenty-three of Biggin Hill's airmen were killed and six badly wounded, of which only one survived. Little or nothing is known of all but one of these casualties – AC Jackson.

Left: Aircraftman Jackson joined the groundcrew at 610 'County of Chester' Squadron. In 1938 he married Hilda, the couple setting up home in Telford, Salop, their first-born, Hazel, arriving in May 1939. (Julian Spragg)

Below: Spitfires of 222 Squadron overfly another of 610 Squadron – Aircraftman Jackson served on the latter as a skilled engine fitter.

Hilda, a War Widow, pictured with Hazel and youngest daughter Jacqueline – born a week after John Jackson's death. (Julian Spragg)

John Joseph Jackson was born at Hulme, Manchester, on 24 January 1917. A working-class lad, upon leaving school he became a 'Papermaker's Labourer'. John joined the RAF aged 19, enlisting as an 'Aircrafthand' on 18 June 1936. The new recruit was posted to the recently formed and local 610 'County of Chester' Squadron of the AAF, equipped with Hawker Hart light bombers and based at Hooton Park in Cheshire. On 5 February 1938, John married Hilda Walker at West Cheshire Register Office, the couple setting up home at 35 King Street, Wellington, Shropshire. Three months later, 610 Squadron re-equipped with Hawker Hind bombers; on New Year's Day 1939, the squadron changed roles, becoming a fighter squadron, receiving the Hawker Hurricane monoplane fighter. Later that month, however, 610 became a Spitfire squadron. These new, modern, fighters, with retractable undercarriages, enclosed canopies and eight machine guns, were very different to the biplanes previously operated. The groundcrews therefore had much work to do learning how best to maintain these new aircraft. By May 1939, John was an AC1 and a fully trained Fitter IIA (Engines), working on 610 Squadron's Spitfires' Rolls-Royce Merlin engines (for a first-hand account by 66 Squadron Fitter IIA Bob Morris, see Pilot Officer Reilley's story). On 27 May 1939, John and Hilda's daughter, Hazel Patricia, was born. Working on Spitfires, happily married with a new-born daughter, life for John was pretty good. On 31 December 1939, AC1 Jackson's character was assessed as 'very good'. By then, having served several years and now in a skilled role, John was established on 610 Squadron and a valuable member of the team.

In October 1939, 610 Squadron moved to Wittering in 12 Group, before heading north again on 4 April 1940, to Prestwick in Scotland. On 10 May,

Hilda, Hazel and Jacqueline pictured with Hilda's mother, Clara Walker, on a visit to John Jackson's grave after the war. (Julian Spragg)

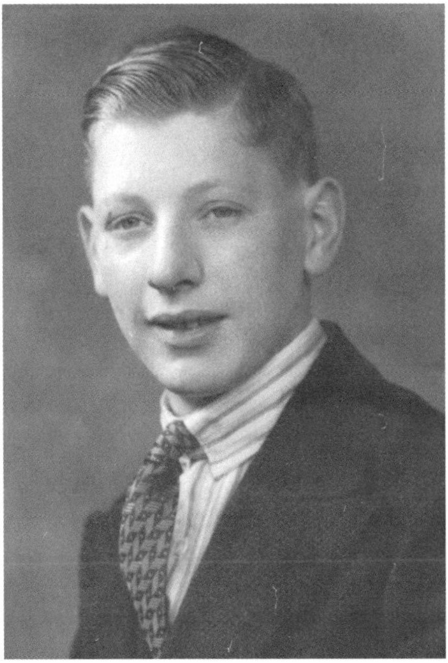

Above left: Aircraftman Jackson's grave at St Mary Cray today. (Ken Back)

Above right: John Joseph Jackson, a working-class Mancunian who joined the RAF as an 'Aircrafthand' in 1936. (Julian Spragg)

when Hitler attacked the west, 610 Squadron flew south, to Biggin Hill in 11 Group. On 26 May, the decision was made for the BEF to retire upon and evacuate from Dunkirk, so Spitfire squadrons were now committed to battle in support of that operation, codenamed Dynamo. To extend its range, 610 moved to Biggin Hill's forward airfield at Gravesend, from where the squadron was heavily engaged in the air fighting over the French coast. Afterwards, 610 remained at Gravesend and fought in the early battles over Channel convoys (see Subedar's story and that of Sergeant Hayes), before returning to Biggin Hill on 8 July. Two days later the Battle of Britain officially began, and 610 Squadron was in the thick of it. From mid-August onwards, the *Luftwaffe* pounded Fighter Command's all-important sector stations, amongst them Biggin Hill. AC1 Jackson, therefore, was at Biggin Hill for the worst attacks suffered by that Station during the summer of 1940. The day after John was killed when the Airmen's Shelter received a direct hit, 610 Squadron was rested and sent north again, to Acklington in Northumberland, there to receive and train replacement pilots and make good losses in ground personnel and aircraft. There the 'County of Chester' Squadron would remain, until returning south, to Westhampnett (Goodwood), at the end of 1940, from where, the following year, the squadron flew as part of Wing Commander Douglas Bader's Tangmere Wing – by which time the Battle of Britain was over and Fighter Command was on the offensive. The sad thing is, therefore, that had John Joseph Jackson not perished on 30 August 1940, he may well have survived the war.

Aircraftwoman Button and Aircraftman Jackson were buried, along with RAF Biggin Hill's other victims of the 30 August raid, at St Mary Cray Cemetery, Orpington, Kent. Lena was a long way from her Tasmanian home; John Joseph's family could at least occasionally make the long journey from Shropshire, but that was no recompense for losing a loving husband and father. A week after John Jackson's death, his widow, Hilda, gave birth to the couple's second child, another daughter, Jacqueline. Grandson Julian Spragg commented, 'I get the impression that afterwards Hilda just got her head down and got on with providing for her two children. It certainly could not have been easy, being a War Widow. Although my mother, Hazel, does not remember her father, I feel sure that at least she saw and touched him – which was denied to Jacqueline. Very sad.'

It is estimated that during the Battle of Britain, 312 RAF personnel were killed on the ground, and 467 injured. Again, this is largely 'hidden history', because rarely do accounts appear concerning these men and women, who served in less glamourous roles. Although the scene referred to earlier from the film *Battle of Britain* exaggerated the facts, it certainly got the point across – and it is one we must not forget.

Chapter Ten

Flight Lieutenant Percy Stevenson Weaver DFC

56 Squadron

Missing in Action: 31 August 1940

Percy Stevenson Weaver was born on 18 September 1916, the son of Ernest Norman Weaver and his wife Katharine, of Lansdown House, Weston Village, Bath, Wiltshire. Ernest ran a long-established family business, Weaver & Son, in the town's Broad Street. Not being fond of the name Percy, the young Weaver was known to all as 'Steve', his nickname being 'Squeak' on account of his initials being 'PSW', as in the *Daily Mirror* cartoon strip, 'Pip, Squeak and Wilfred'. Steve had two elder brothers, George, who served with the Bristol Fire Service, and Norman, who soldiered in the West Somerset Yeomanry; the boys had two sisters, Joan, who died very young, and Phil.

Steve first attended Fair Lea Preparatory School in Weston-super-Mare, then went up to Dean Close School, Cheltenham, in 1929. Academically

Percy Stevenson 'Steve' Weaver, sitting on the grass at left, while at Dean Close, Cheltenham. (Paul Weaver)

he did well, and represented both school and house in most sports, including shooting, competing at Bisley. He was also a bugler in the Dean Close OTC, thought of by his peers, according to his nephew, Paul Weaver, as 'apparently quite introverted and thoughtful, quiet but completely unflappable'. While at Dean Close, Steve owned an old motorcycle, but it failed to make the long journey to the School Corps Camp at Preston, Steve requiring collection from the local railway station by the master-in-charge of the Camp, Mr B. Maxwell Phair. The pair struck up a friendship, the teacher lending Steve his 1930 Frazer Nash HX 846, having satisfied himself that young Weaver was an excellent driver. The car had in fact been used for racing, lapping Brooklands at 90 mph. Mr Phair became a great influence on Steve, encouraging him to pursue a career in engineering.

Like many other youngsters at the time, Steve had become inspired by Sir Alan Cobham's Flying Circus, which toured the country promoting 'air-mindedness' and providing thousands of ordinary people with their first experience of flight – including Steve. Having been bitten by the aviation bug, Steve went straight from Dean Close to an apprenticeship at the De Havilland Aircraft Company in Hatfield. One of his first jobs there was de-coking an engine of the famous Comet racer, which had just won the 1934 England to Australia Air Race. The new apprentice made a model of the streamlined Comet, into which was put a piece of carbon from the de-coking process. The following year Steve invested in a Model 90

Steve Weaver was a bugler in the OTC at Dean Close, seen here during an inspection. (Paul Weaver)

Sunbeam motorcycle, followed by a 2-litre Lagonda and a Frazer Nash, the latter having been raced at Brooklands by Tony Law. By now Steve was a confirmed motoring enthusiast and a regular visitor to the Shelsley Walsh Hill Climb, Donnington Park circuit and Crystal Palace.

In October 1936, Steve left De Havilland and joined the Reserve of Air Force Officers, learning to fly and being commissioned as a pilot officer on 21 December. After successfully completing elementary and advanced flying training, on 13 September 1937 Pilot Officer Weaver was posted to 56 Squadron at North Weald, flying Gloster Gauntlet biplane fighters. A week later, he came off the RAFO and instead took an SSC.

56 was a regular RAF squadron and amongst the most outstanding of the First World War. Even in 1937, when Pilot Officer Weaver joined the unit, the proud memory of the squadron's past was maintained, as Wing Commander Frederick 'Taffy' Higginson told me: 'I joined 56 as a regular NCO pilot on 20 October 1937. In a room at North Weald was displayed the uniform and the VC of McCudden, one of the First World War's greatest aces and a member of 56 Squadron. Every new pilot was made to study the exhibition and salute upon leaving the room.'

In May 1938, 56 Squadron re-equipped with the new Hawker Hurricane monoplane fighter, designed by Sydney Camm. The first squadron to receive the new eight-gun fighter had been 111, which had suffered fatalities owing to engine problems, negatively affecting morale. Rolls-Royce engineers and 56 Squadron engine fitters consequently did much to evaluate the Merlin engine under operational conditions, resolving any issues arising. During this period, each pilot was allocated a personal Hurricane, engine fitter, rigger and mate; all damage had to be signed for, as did aircraft serviceability on the 'Form 700', and the aircraft all spotlessly maintained. Flying regulations were very strict, in fact only Fighter Command HQ at Bentley Priory could authorise the use of spare aircraft.

Having flown with 56 for nearly a year, on 26 August 1938 Pilot Officer Weaver joined the Station HQ Staff at North Weald, serving in an administrative role until 11 February 1939, when, as an acting squadron leader, he was detached to RAF Depot Uxbridge pending a further posting. Three days later, Acting Squadron Leader Weaver returned to North Weald, becoming a Controller in the Sector Operations Room. On 2 September 1939, Steve was enjoying leave with his family, holidaying in the Lake District, when, in the middle of the night, he was recalled to North Weald. At 1100 hrs on Sunday 3 September, Britain and France declared war on Nazi Germany. Three days later, Hurricanes of 56 Squadron were mistaken for

Me 109s over Ipswich by Spitfires of 74 Squadron. In the ensuing incident of so-called 'friendly fire', two Hurricanes were shot down, one pilot being killed. The tragedy became known as the 'Battle of Barking Creek', the circumstances of which remain controversial eighty years later.

After the German invasion of France and the low countries on 10 May 1940, 56 Squadron fought in the Battle of France, for four hectic days 'B' Flight operating from Vitry-en-Artois. During this ill-fated campaign, 56 claimed thirty-five enemy aircraft destroyed, then regrouped at Digby on 31 May, returning to North Weald a day later. Although making a valuable contribution and gaining great experience in 'Ops', Steve Weaver wanted to be flying again – and got his wish on 20 June 1940 when he was returned to 56 Squadron, albeit with a reduction in rank to flying officer. 56 required replacement pilots after action in France and during the Dunkirk evacuation – and already being operational on the Hurricane, 'Squeak' Weaver was an experienced pilot. In fact, he had already reacquainted himself with both 56 Squadron and the Hurricane on 12 June, when he flew P3547, joining a flight from North Weald to Tangmere, from where an operational patrol was made between 1600 and 1835 hrs, a long flight, before returning to North Weald that evening. Back with the squadron proper, Flying Officer Weaver joined 'B' Flight, in which served Pilot Officer Geoffrey Page, a name later to become synonymous with the Battle of Britain, commanded by Flight Lieutenant Edward 'Jumbo' Gracie. After the Battle of France, the squadron's long-serving CO, Squadron Leader E.V. Knowles, was posted away to the Air Ministry, his replacement, Squadron Leader G.A.L. 'Minnie' Manton not arriving until 28 June. Having initially joined the RAF on an SSC in 1931, Manton had been permanently commissioned in 1936, his flying experience having been flying biplane fighters and as a pre-war flying instructor.

Steve – or 'Squeak' as he was known on 56 Squadron – at North Weald before the war. (Paul Weaver)

Since 1937 however, he had flown a desk, being refreshed and converting to monoplane fighters at 5 OTU, Aston Down, the same month he took over 56 Squadron. While Manton lacked experience on modern fighters, and was without combat experience, he was an experienced officer and leader who sensibly deferred to his able flight commanders until sufficiently acclimatised to take 56 Squadron's operational reins.

After the fighting over France, 56, like other squadrons engaged, was now receiving replacement pilots, providing further training. Flying Officer Weaver made his first flight after returning to the squadron on 25 June 1940, an anti-aircraft cooperation sortie. On the same day he also practised 'Fighter Attacks', and the following night flew a night-flying test. On 28 June, 56 and 151 Squadrons flew from North Weald to Manston, from where the Hurricanes provided escort to six Blenheims photographing Dunkirk, Calais and Boulogne, Flying Officer Weaver leading a section of 56 Squadron Hurricanes. 151 was attacked by Me 109s, losing a pilot, but 56 Squadron was unable to catch the enemy fighters. Two days later, 'Squeak' led his section on a similar sortie, again with 151 Squadron, escorting six Blenheims bombing Vignacourt. Two of 56 Squadron's pilots lost the main formation near Le Treport, Sergeants Smythe and Hillwood, encountered five Me 109s, destroying two and damaging a third. On the return journey, six more Me 109s attacked the bombers but were driven off by 151 Squadron which claimed

Pilot Officer Weaver and Gladiator. (Paul Weaver)

A rare photograph of an early 56 Squadron Hawker Hurricane Mk I. (Paul Weaver)

three of them destroyed. Although Flying Officer Weaver had yet to engage, this was all valuable experience.

July began with a variety of training flights, cloud flying, air firing at Sutton Bridge, practice attacks, rearming and refuelling practice, and practice 'attacks' on the aerodrome, so Flying Officer Weaver was kept busy preparing for the battle ahead. These training flights were also punctuated by convoy protection and other patrols, 56 Squadron frequently operating from Martlesham Heath, Manston and Rochford. Flying Officer Weaver's first taste of action came on the dawn patrol of 20 July, when the Controller perfectly guided Blue Section, comprising Flight Lieutenant Gracie, Pilot Officer Page and Flying Officer Weaver, to intercept a Ju 88 off Burnham. The enemy pilot dived for but failed to reach cloud before Gracie emptied all of his ammunition into the lone reconnaissance aircraft, at which Page also fired. The Ju 88 then entered and passed through cloud when it was picked up and attacked by Flying Officer Weaver, who chased his target north-east. The German then began weaving from side to side, stupidly, allowing the Hurricane pilot to catch it. From 250 yards, Blue Three then emptied his ammunition into the bomber. Both Weaver's and Page's Hurricanes were damaged by return fire, forcing both to break away, losing their quarry. Nonetheless, this reconnaissance machine of 4(F)/122, crash-landed in flames at Cocket Wick Farm, at 0550 hrs, its four-man crew being captured.

At dawn on 29 July, 56 Squadron flew to Rochford, encountering a heavy raid on Dover harbour; Flying Officer Weaver reported that at 0745 hrs: -

'The Squadron was sent from Rochford to patrol Whitstable at 5,000 feet. I was flying as leader of Blue Section. R/T communication was bad between the formation leader and base (North Weald). I was receiving well from base but they were not receiving me well. Base informed us of fifty E/A approaching at 2,000 feet a place whose name I could not catch. When at 10,000 feet over Deal we were told to orbit. Blue Three gave warning of aircraft near Dover and Red Four broke away to investigate. I then saw what appeared to be a dogfight over the sea east of Dover. I told the formation leader and went to the scene.

'I saw an Me 109 on the tail of a Hurricane, the latter being on the tail of a 109. I got on the tail of the Me 109 and when he was 600 yards behind he opened fire on the Hurricane in front of him, which emitted white smoke. This may have been Red Three (Flight Sergeant Cooney).

'I fired a short burst at 400 yards which caused E/A to turn away from the Hurricane. I closed and fired at point blank range with intermittent bursts as he turned from side to side. Glycol streamed out from E/A after about eight seconds firing, and after another four seconds firing E/A burst into flames. I did not see him crash as another E/A was on my tail. I tried to turn behind him but lost him and returned alone.

'Sergeant Hillwood (Blue Two) and Sergeant Smythe (Blue Three) both saw this E/A burst into flames. I was hit once in the tailplane.'

Flight Sergeant Cecil Cooney, a pre-war airman who had made the quantum leap from metal rigger to fighter pilot, failed to return and was reported 'Missing'.

August began much the same as July, with practice flights, including aerobatics and air tests, in addition to regular patrolling from Rochford. On 7 August Steve Weaver was promoted to Acting Flight Lieutenant and took over 'A' Flight, Flight Lieutenant Coghlan having been posted

A 56 Squadron Hurricane running up, 1938. (Paul Weaver)

away to Ringway, there to assist with the newly formed airborne forces. On 11 August, Flight Lieutenant Weaver led 'A' Flight on a convoy patrol from which the experienced Sergeant Ronald Baker, another pre-war airman who had become a fighter pilot, failed to return. The squadron diary subsequently reported that Baker was seen to have been 'attacked by a lone Spitfire. He was picked up by a destroyer, but was already dead'. Such incidents of so-called 'Friendly Fire' were, alas, not uncommon, and 64 and 74 Squadron both made many claims for single-engined fighters around the right time and place. On that sortie, 56 Squadron was accompanied by North Weald's incomparable and irrepressible station commander, the Irish Wing Commander Victor Beamish, a Cranwellian, who flew operationally whenever he could, destroying a number of enemy aircraft during the Battle of Britain.

On 12 August the enemy began pulverising coastal Chain Home radar stations, Dunkirk, Dover, Rye and Pevensey all being damaged, Ventnor, on the Isle of Wight especially so. The coastal airfields at Manston, Lympne and Hawkinge were also bombed. This was, although unknown to the defenders, preparatory to the *Adlerangriff* planned for the following day – *Adler Tag*. After a busy day, at teatime three raids comprising some twenty Do 17s were launched against Kentish coastal towns. The speed of the defenders'

An accident which Flight Sergeant Cecil Cooney survived – only to be killed in action on 29 July 1940. (Paul Weaver)

reaction, however, must have made the Germans realise that already the radar stations were functioning again. 56 Squadron was scrambled from Rochford, Flight Lieutenant Weaver reporting that at 1830 hrs, ten miles north of Margate: -

'When airborne, "B" Flight joined us and led us to attack E/A reported approaching Manston. We saw them ten miles east of us, flying north. "B" Flight leader ordered sections into echelon right and led us to attack. I selected the left-hand E/A of the extreme right-hand rear section of the E/A, who were flying in close formation in three lines of sections of three, in vic line astern. I attacked from dead astern, giving a four-second burst at 400 yards, experiencing intense return fire at that range. This burst had no apparent effect. I then closed and gave him a continuous burst at 250/200 yards, using all my ammunition. E/A began to give out black smoke and I broke away. While at 250 yards' range, after about eight seconds firing my windscreen and leading edges began to get coated with oil. On landing, Pilot Officer Joubert and Flying Officer Westmacott confirmed that they had seen the E/A which I had attacked blow up in the air. E/A kept close formation throughout the attacks and adopted no evasive action.'

This 'Do 215' was confirmed as destroyed. The bombers were escorted by a large number of enemy fighters, Sergeant Smythe destroying an Me 109 while Flight Sergeant Higginson damaged another. Interestingly, George Smythe, yet another former aircraft apprentice, and a successful fighter pilot, had fitted

Another early Hurricane mishap at North Weald. (Paul Weaver)

enlarged ammunition boxes to his aircraft, containing an extra 400 rounds. Clearly the 56 Squadron diarist was a master of the understatement, recording that 19-year-old Pilot Officer Geoffrey Page 'baled out but was rescued slightly burned'. Later, Pilot Officer F.B. Sutton remembered that:-

'There was a tremendous explosion on my right, only a few feet away, probably ten yards away, which was Geoffrey. Such a sheet of flame came out of his aeroplane that I couldn't conceive he could have survived, I thought he must be dead already.' Page, though, was still alive in his blazing Hurricane: 'It was like a blast furnace coming straight up at my face and hands. One hand was still on the throttle and I remember looking at it rather fascinated, just watching the burning taking place. Layers of skin were burnt off and rolled up like parchment. I vividly remember screaming in terror when the aircraft was hit, a ball of fire, but as I was losing consciousness a tremendous calm came over me, nature's way of protecting one, and all the fear went. I accepted the fact that I was about to die. I half-rolled the aeroplane and fell out of it. Then there was a thump as the parachute opened. My first instinct was to look up, to check if the parachute was on fire, fortunately it wasn't. I then took stock of my personal situation. First thing I noticed was this awful smell of my own burning flesh. Then I looked down and saw that my trousers had been blown completely off, plus one shoe. Then I splashed

'Taken between May and September 1938, "B" Flight 56 Squadron "shewing off" flight drill practice for an Empire Air Day demonstration for the public. Left to right: Ian Soden, Peter Down, Flight Sergeant Evetts, Leonid Ereminsky, John Hulton-Harrop, Flight Sergeant Cooney or Higginson'. (Paul Weaver)

Two of Steve Weaver's pals at North Weald in 1938. (Paul Weaver)

into the sea, feet first, so thought I'd just float around a bit until picked up. Then I discovered that this life-saving jacket, which for obvious outstanding reasons was known as a "Mae West", had been burnt through, so I had to swim for it. As I was swimming along I remembered that my dear mother had given me a brandy flask, which I had filled up at great expense as a young pilot officer and was in my breast pocket. I got the brandy flask out but couldn't get the cap off, so held it between my wrists and tried to use my teeth. At that point a wave came and washed the flask away before I had taken a sip. I have to say I was pretty angry then.'

Page's 'slight' burns required two years' hospitalisation as one of plastic surgeon Sir Archibald McIndoe's famous 'Guinea Pigs' at East Grinstead. Incredibly, Page recovered, returned to operational flying, became a decorated ace, survived the war, and later founded the Battle of Britain Memorial Trust, the driving force behind the creation of the National Battle of Britain Memorial on the cliffs above Folkestone.

The following day, enemy air attacks on 'Eagle Day' were delayed owing to poor weather. That afternoon, however, 56 Squadron was scrambled from

Rochford and ordered to patrol over Manston at 10,000 feet. At 5,000 feet the squadron was informed of a raid approaching Rochford, and after climbing through thick cloud found a formation of He 111s, escorted by Me 110s, 8,000 feet above. Flight Lieutenant Weaver reported that the attack commenced at 1615 hrs, while he was: -

'leading "A" Flight, which was in the rear of "B" Flight…. Owing to our lack of height it was not possible to catch the bombers, so I climbed as fast as possible towards the Me 110s. These started breaking formation, some of them forming a defensive circle. My Number Three broke away towards a 110 which was above him and to the left. I then realised that a 110 was getting onto his tail, so I pulled up very steeply and tried to fire at this second 110, vertically, from underneath. Commencing fire, I saw Number Three (Pilot Officer Joubert) dive away with a glycol leak, and observed damage to the 110. I then stalled.

'I attacked another 110 from dead astern at about 200 yards, and fired at him for about five seconds. He turned sharply away and dived with glycol pouring out of one of his engines (I believe the port one). I did not continue the attack as there was a 110 on my tail. I broke sharply away and got on the tail of another 110. At about 150 – 200 yards I fired off the remainder of my ammunition (about six seconds), dead astern, and after a few seconds violent twisting and turning, he turned over on his back and went vertically downwards into the clouds with both engines on fire. I broke away and joined up with Yellow Three (Pilot Officer Wicks), who confirmed that this E/A was destroyed.'

Indeed it was, a machine of 3/ZG26 engaged on an escort mission to Southend, this Me 110 exploded over Warden Bay, Sheppey, killing both crew members.

The ORB expands upon the action: -

'In the action, F/O Weaver, P/O Sutton and P/O Mounsden each destroyed an Me 110 and F/O Weaver, F/Lt Gracie, P/O Westmacott, P/O Joubert, F/O Davies and Sgt Hillwood each damaged a 110, F/Lt Gracie also damaging a second. P/O Joubert, F/O Davies and Sgt Hillwood were all shot down and baled out, the former being slightly injured and F/O Davies fairly severely burnt. Sgt Hillwood was practically uninjured having delayed his jump from 12,000 feet to 6,000 feet and swimming 2½ miles to land. F/O Brooker's machine was wrecked when he forced-landed at Hawkinge.'

Pilot Officer Maurice Mounsden of 56 Squadron airborne in 1938. (Paul Weaver)

On Sunday 18 August 1940, the fighting became the most intense yet, as heavy attacks were made against 11 Group's vital sector stations. That lunchtime, Biggin Hill and West Malling airfields were bombed, and Kenley was subjected to an audacious low-level attack by Do 17s of 9/KG76. 56 Squadron was scrambled from North Weald to patrol the Canterbury area. 1, 17, 54 and 266 Squadrons were also airborne, but a thick haze prevented the 11 Group Controller from committing the combined force to fall upon the withdrawing raiders. Instead, the squadrons individually sought out the enemy across Kent. At 1345 hrs, at 21,000 feet over Ashford, Flight Lieutenant Weaver later described the action: -

'I was leading No 2 Section and was put into line astern by the squadron leader (Squadron Leader Manton). I observed approximately five Me 110s below us in a defensive circle and singled one out and attacked. I fired for about six seconds, and broke away when smoke and bits poured from the starboard engine. I then observed an Me 110 below me, I chased it down to about 3,000 feet, full throttle and 12lbs boost. I eventually closed to 200 yards and as E/A was doing evasive tactics fired short bursts, with and without deflection. My guns finished firing, E/A went into a steep right-hand turn and then dived vertically into the ground, bursting into flames, about eight miles south of Ashford on the northern bank of a canal. This was confirmed by both Flight Lieutenant Gracie and Flight Sergeant Higginson.'

Steve Weaver, second right, Maurice Mounsden (extreme left) and friends at North Weald. (Paul Weaver)

This Me 110, of 3/ZG26, crashed and exploded at Bonnington; neither crew-member has ever been found. All five 110s, in fact, were destroyed by 56 Squadron, the Hurricane pilots all landing safely at Rochford.

Late afternoon, fifty-eight KG2 Do 17s were despatched to Hornchurch, while fifty-one He 111s of KG53 droned towards North Weald. The two bomber formations were escorted by 140 Me 109s and 110s, drawn from JGs 3, 26, 51 and 54, and ZG26. Of this impressive fighter force, twenty-five Me 109s of JG51 were closely bound to the Hornchurch raiders, while twenty Me 110s shepherded KG53 to North Weald. The remaining enemy fighters were tasked with a *freie hunt* to soften and divert RAF defences ahead of the bombers. In response, the 11 Group Controller brought thirteen squadrons either to a state of immediate readiness or scrambled them to patrol specific lines. 56 Squadron scrambled at 1700 hrs with orders to patrol Manston, and was the first of Park's squadrons to engage, rapidly reinforced by 54 Squadron's Spitfires. Flight Lieutenant

Weaver reported that at 1720 hrs, 56 Squadron intercepted '200 plus' at 10,000 feet over Bradwell: -

'I was flying Yellow One, leading No 2 Section. After various vectors I saw a large, escorted, formation of bombers approaching Burnham from the east, north of us. I took the lead and flew under the rear section, selecting the extreme left-hand bomber of the rear section. I fired about ten seconds burst into him and saw him begin to burn and break away from the formation. I broke away violently owing to the escorting fighters behind. I then joined in with escorting Me 110s, firing two or three second bursts at several from various angles. No observed effects. My ammunition then ran out. Pilot Officer Mounsden saw the first E/A attacked going down in flames.'

The He 111, a machine of 8/KG53, was flown by *Leutnant* Walter Leber, whose gunners shouted warning of 56 Squadron's appearance before opening fire. Leber could see tracer rounds streaming from the guns of the other *Heinkels* around him – then the temperature of his right-hand motor began rising dangerously. Clearly the cooling system had been hit, so Leber feathered the airscrew and shut the engine down.

Steve was a motoring enthusiast, enjoying fast cars – pictured here in Bath High Street before the war with his Lagonda, a type possessed by various 56 Squadron pilots at this time until changing over to Frazer Nash models. (Paul Weaver)

Unable to maintain formation, the damaged bomber straggled behind and was attacked by a Spitfire pilot, Pilot Officer John Hopkin of 54 Squadron, who wrecked the raider's other engine. With three of his crew too badly wounded to bale out, Leber's only option was to jettison his bombs and make a forced landing. All the time, Pilot Officer Hopkin circled the bomber, but chivalrously did not attack, a gesture much appreciated by Leber who safely crash-landed at Small Gains Farm, Foulness, at 1735 hrs. Those aboard were captured, but the sole crew-member who did take to his parachute later died of his injuries.

It was another highly successful action for 56 Squadron, enemy aircraft also being destroyed by Squadron Leader Manton, Flight Lieutenant Gracie and Flight Sergeant Higginson, while Flying Officer Westmacott, Pilot Officer Mounsden and Sergeant Robinson damaged others – all for no loss. On this hard-fought day, sixty-nine German aircraft were destroyed or damaged beyond economic or practical repair. Ninety-four enemy airmen were killed, forty captured and a further twenty-five wounded. Fighter Command's reaction was a clear indicator that Dowding's force was much stronger than *Luftwaffe* intelligence mistakenly believed.

Certain pilots of 56 Squadron at North Weald in 1939, amongst them Pilot Officers Maurice Mounsden (third left), and Peter Down (fourth left), Flying Officer 'Gus' Holden, and Pilot Officer Montague Hulton-Harrop – the latter tragically killed in a 'friendly fire' incident involving 74 Squadron Spitfires, on 6 September 1939. (Paul Weaver)

Squadron Leader G.A.L. 'Minnie' Manton: -

'From those hectic times I remember well one particular incident… probably because it occurred shortly after I had taken over the squadron following two-and-a-half years at the Air Ministry. Every moment with 56 Squadron, therefore, was new and exciting for me. After only my first or second combat, I was returning to North Weald, trying to gather my wits, when another 56 Squadron Hurricane came alongside and formatted on me. The pilot opened his hood, gave me a great grin, a thumbs up, and then one finger to indicate that he had made a kill: it was "Squeak".'

The introverted boy from Bath certainly appears to have found his calling as a very successful fighter pilot.

After further patrols over the next few days, while carrying out an R/T test with Martlesham Heath at 1815 hrs on 21 August, Flight Lieutenant Weaver and Flying Officer Brooker were warned by the Controller of an enemy aircraft over Ipswich. 'Squeak' sighted it flying north of the town, just before anti-aircraft guns started firing at the intruder. The Do 17 then disappeared into cloud but Flying Officer Brooker regained contact and shot the bomber down, which crashed at Gippeswyk Park, Ipswich. Brooker's machine was also damaged in the combat, the pilot making a crash-landing and escaping with minor injuries.

Clear skies on 24 August heralded a resumption of heavy fighting and attacks on sector stations. During the afternoon, North Weald was hit. 56 Squadron was late getting off from Rochford owing to no scramble order having been received – but Squadron Leader Manton's pilots needed no encouragement when Southend's air raid sirens began wailing and enemy aircraft began passing overhead. At 1605 hrs, at Angels Twelve ten miles east of Bradwell, Flight Lieutenant Weaver, leading Yellow Section, was in action again: -

'I saw many E/A flying east very high over the Thames, I tried to lead the leader of the squadron to them. However, with my Yellow Two, Pilot Officer Mounsden, I became separated from the squadron and being unable to climb up to these E/A climbed over Rochford to about 15,000 feet. I then saw two separate formations flying east, one approximately approaching Bradwell, and one further north. Both were approximately twelve aircraft each. Utilising the sun, I flew parallel to and above this formation, keeping to the south. When nearly level, I turned in and selected the extreme

Steve Weaver's mother, Katherine, pictured in the Lake District on her son's last leave – during the early hours of 3 September 1939, Steve was recalled to North Weald. Later that morning, Britain and France declared war on Germany. (Paul Weaver)

left-hand aircraft. There was no apparent fighter escort. I opened fire at 250 yards and closed to about thirty yards, firing the whole time. I saw bits fall off this E/A. I then broke away and saw him falling out of control, two people jumping out by parachute. Pilot Officer Mounsden saw E/A hit the sea. I then climbed up and delivered another attack, on the E/A Pilot Officer Mounsden had damaged (white smoke pouring out). Owing to intense cross-fire, I used up all my rounds at about 400 yards, with no apparent effect. There was a type of rear gun fire I have not encountered before, and it appeared as a cluster of tracer, only fired once by each E/A I attacked. It was not cannon and I was not hit by it. I received two hits on my aircraft, one of which pierced the oil tank, front centre-section spar, right through self-sealing petrol tank, out the other side and through rear spar.'

This Heinkel belonged to 9/KG53 and ditched in the sea off Brightlingsea. Three of the crew remain missing, but two others baled out and were captured by an RN launch. Squeak's wingman, Pilot Officer Mounsden, damaged an Me 109, and Pilot Officer Marston destroyed another. Returning to North Weald late that evening, the Hurricane pilots found their home station had been badly knocked about, bombing having caused 'considerable material damage', although not to any vital installations. Sadly, ten soldiers had been killed when their air raid shelter took a direct hit.

'Squeak' would not be in action again until 28 August. That morning, while 56 Squadron was still at North Weald, Rochford was bombed.

At 1228 hrs, 56 Squadron was scrambled to protect Rochford from another incoming threat. Squadron Leader Manton attacked, with twelve other Hurricanes over the Thames Estuary, thirty Do 17s of KG2 with a similar number of Me 109 escorting fighters. The CO went after the fighters with Red and Green Sections, while Yellow, led by Flight Lieutenant Weaver, and Blue, took on the bombers. Yellow One opened 56 Squadron's assault on the bombers, firing from close range – but his Hurricane, V7382, was damaged by return fire. Breaking away, Flight Lieutenant Weaver force-landed at Scocles Farm, Eastchurch, walking away unhurt.

That afternoon, by which time 'Squeak' was back at North Weald, large-scale enemy fighter sweeps came in over the Thames Estuary and Kent. 56 Squadron scrambled to patrol Canterbury at 10,000 feet, although considering that the 109s always came in very high, it is difficult to understand why the Controller ordered such an altitude. Clearly the squadron ignored this instruction however, because when at 18,000 feet over Ashford, enemy fighters, Flight Lieutenant Weaver later reported, were sighted just two thousand feet higher, 'milling round in a circle, but came down on us as we climbed'. Over Dover 'a dogfight ensued, E/A breaking away in twos. I chose the rear of a pair of E/A and carried out a beam attack, firing from below and to one side a burst of twenty rounds from each gun at about 200 yards. E/A's nose dropped a little and the pilot jumped out. I saw him hurtling through the air but did not see his parachute open. This was about five miles inland from Dover. Seeing no other E/A and receiving the order to land, I returned to North Weald.'

Steve Weaver at North Weald while serving as an Operations Room Controller in September 1939. (Paul Weaver)

This latest combat victory was an Me 109E-1 of I/JG54, the pilot of which, *Feldwebel* Schöttle, remains missing.

The following day was a quiet one, thankfully, for 56 Squadron, which made but one uneventful sortie that evening. More action followed on 30 August however, when, together with

151 Squadron, a raid approaching North Weald was intercepted. Passing overhead and continuing to Radlett, Flight Lieutenant Gracie's 'B' Flight made contact east of North Weald, several of his pilots later filing combat claims.

31 August 1940 would be another bitterly contested day, as the *Luftwaffe* continued pounding 11 Group's sector stations. By that time, 56 Squadron had lost eighteen Hurricanes destroyed with six more damaged, losing one pilot killed and seven wounded. There would be no respite this day.

Shortly before 0800 hrs on 31 August, the Fighter Command Operations Room at Bentley Priory, Stanmore, was made aware from incoming information from Chain Home radar stations that four enemy formations were incoming, one, comprising solely fighters, approaching Dover, the other three via the Thames Estuary. Thirty Do 17s of III/KG2 headed for Debden, with more of II/KG2 bound for Duxford, intending to execute a simultaneous attack. The Debden raid was escorted by *Hauptmann* Horst Liensberger's Me 110s of V(Z)LG1, the Duxford raid's escort provided by *Hauptmann* Hans Schalk's III/ZG26. This mighty *Valhalla* passed over the North Weald Sector en route to Debden and Duxford. Air Vice-Marshal Park responded by scrambling thirteen squadrons, amongst them 56, Flight Lieutenant Weaver leading off eight Hurricanes from Rochford at 0820 hrs.

By this time over eighty per cent of the Me 109s available in north-west Europe were concentrated in the Pas-de-Calais, amongst them Major Adolf Galland's JG26, tasked that morning with providing a fighter sweep in support of the Debden and Duxford raids. As usual, the lethal 109s were way up there, looking down, this time on Flight Lieutenant Weaver's

Pilot Officer Peter Down scrambles from North Weald in August 1940.

penny-packet force clawing for height over the Thames Estuary. Enjoying the advantage of height and sun, the 109s bounced 56 Squadron near Colchester, executing a perfect ambush. Within seconds, three Hurricanes were spiralling earthwards, doubtless hit without even having seen their assailants. Pilot Officer Mounsden was injured and Sergeant Whitehead baled out; Flight Lieutenant Weaver was reported missing. Flying Officer Westmacott was also injured, attacking a Do 17. In response, Flight Sergeant Higginson shot down *Leutnant* Heinz Ebeling, *Staffelkapitän* of 9/JG26, who baled out well beyond Dover and was rescued by the *Seenotdienst*.

So, what happened to Flight Lieutenant Weaver?

A clue is provided by the Essex County Council War Diary entry for 1009 hrs that day: -

'Crashed aircraft report. British Spitfire found West Point, Osea Island. Pilot believed drowned at 0845'.

A further report was made at 1123 hrs by the Eastern Report Centre: 'Plane now identified as V7373, confirmed pilot drowned.' How though, was this confirmed?

The Situation Report Form, timed 1655 hrs, documents that 'One British plane marked V7373 crashed at Osea Island, River Blackwater, pilot drowned'.

The Comet model made by Steve Weaver, in which a piece of carbon from an engine was inserted, made by Steve Weaver while an apprentice at De Havilland before the war – now preserved by his nephew Paul.

'V7373' was not involved (the aircraft later being lost en route to Malta with 261 Squadron) – and nor was this a 'Spitfire'. Flight Lieutenant Weaver, however, was flying Hurricane V7378.

Squadron Leader 'Minnie' Manton: -

'"Squeak" was posted missing the very day I left the Squadron on posting to command RAF Manston, or at least what was left of it! They rang me from North Weald the next day to tell me the news, such was Flight Lieutenant Weaver's standing in the Squadron.'

On 25 August, Flight Lieutenant H.M. Pinfold had arrived at North Weald, straight from 5 OTU, another officer without combat experience who was promoted to Acting Squadron Leader on 30 August and succeeded Squadron Leader Manton in command. On 2 September, Squadron Leader Pinfold reported regarding the 'accident' involving Flight Lieutenant Weaver and Hurricane V7378: -

'Flight Lieutenant Weaver was patrolling over West Mersea at approximately 0830 hrs on 31st August 1940, when his aircraft was seen to dive vertically into the mud banks on the foreshore.

'There was no trace of the pilot and as he was not seen to abandon his aircraft it is concluded that he is still in the aircraft which is embedded in the mud and completely submerged.

'Contact is being maintained with the authorities at West Mersea but no further information is as yet forthcoming.

'It is believed that Flight Lieutenant Weaver shot down an enemy aircraft before he was himself attacked.'

Just hours after Flight Lieutenant Weaver was reported missing, his DFC was announced (gazetted on 1 October 1940). The citation reads: -

'This officer has displayed great courage and leadership. He has destroyed six enemy aircraft. His excellent example has contributed materially to the fine standard that exists in the squadron.'

Within his Casualty File is a most dignified letter dated 8 September 1940, from 'Squeak's' mother, Katharine, already a widow, in response to the Air Council's letter of 4 September, informing her that her son was missing: 'Will you please convey my thanks to the Air Council for their sympathy,

Right: Paul Weaver with his uncle's DFC.

Below: Flight Lieutenant Weaver's medals, still in boxes of issue, pictured in 2019.

expressed by you, which we very much appreciate in this time of our great anxiety. We shall anxiously await any further information which it will be in your power to send us.'

By 31 October 1940 – the Battle of Britain's final day – the Air Ministry wrote to Mrs Weaver again, confirming that no further news had been received and that 'The aircraft became completely submerged and no trace of the pilot has been found… in the absence of definite news of your son it will be necessary, after the lapse of approximately six months from the date on which he was reported missing, to presume his death for official purposes. When such action is contemplated a further letter will be addressed to you.'

No further news would be received and Flight Lieutenant Weaver's death was in due course presumed and he is remembered on Panel 5 of the Runnymede Memorial to the Missing. Presumably this brave warrior's mortal remains are still entombed in the mud of West Mersea.

The day after 'Squeak' was reported missing, 56 Squadron was withdrawn to Boscombe Down in 10 Group. Although there were further battles ahead before the Battle of Britain ended, the tempo of combat was nothing like the squadron had experienced while operating in the North Weald Sector. That an officer and fighter pilot of such demonstrable ability was lost just a few hours before that move makes the loss even more tragic.

The last word in this thought-provoking chapter goes to Group Captain G.A.L. Manton DSO DFC: -

'While most eulogies tend to go overboard, my recollections of "Squeak" Weaver are all clear and sincere. Of all the boisterous, reckless, young men in the Squadron, he stood out. He was universally liked and because of his irrepressible good humour, enthusiasm for life and everything he did, and his fearless attitude to the battle, he became an absolute lynch-pin in the Squadron. His loss was, I know, felt most deeply at a time when we all tried to shrug off such things for obvious reasons…'

Chapter Eleven

Wing Commander John Scatliff Dewar DSO DFC

RAF Station Exeter

Killed in Action: 11 September 1940

On 18 August 1907, John Scatliff Dewar was born at Mussoori, Lahore Province, India, the third son of a distinguished lawyer, who became a judge, Douglas Dewar, and his wife Edith. Having spent his formative years in India during the British Raj, 'Johnny' moved to England with his family, aged 14, in 1921. The Dewars then lived at 'Almora', Park Avenue, Camberley, where Johnny studied with a private tutor to pass the entrance exam for King's School, Canterbury. An ultimately successful applicant, Johnny became a pupil there in 1922, excelling at sports, winning colours for cricket and rugby, and half-colours for athletics, swimming, water polo and hockey. Becoming Head Boy, he also achieved the rank of sergeant in the King's School OTC, which possibly influenced his decision to become an RAF career officer, entering Cranwell as a Flight Cadet on 14 January 1926, aged 19.

The RAF required officers for specific branches: General Duties (flying), Administrative and special duties, Equipment, Accountant, Medical, Dental, Legal and Chaplains. It was with the first of those categories that Johnny was concerned. Trenchard's vision was that all his officers would be pilots, a skill literally over and above the traditional officer function of leading men into battle on land or sea. Aircrew are a breed apart, as Wells explained: 'From the earliest days of aviation, airmen have been regarded as members of an elite group, largely as a result of the dangers associated with flying. In the early part of the twentieth century, flimsy machines, unreliable engines, and inadequate preparation caused scores of accidents. Aircraft and flying were considered novelties and pilots were often seen as daredevils. In the view of many, it took a special type of man to brave the obvious perils.' It proved an impractical imposition for all officers to become pilots, but not for Johnny Dewar.

Cranwell was modelled upon the two senior services' seats of officer training. These were really an extension of the public-school system, without a background at which entry was impossible, and fees were also payable. A former interwar flight cadet described Cranwell and its traditions: 'The life of the College is resumed with alacrity and care at the beginning of term. One day the place will be wearing a wan and neglected air, while the next day everything will be bustle and confusion. The night seems to bring forth cadets in the same way a conjurer produces rabbits from a hat. But as they come, so they depart, yielding place for others in a never-ending stream: each one, however, leaves his impression for good or bad on the College. Some may be forgotten; others will be talked of by terms of the distant future. Yet one and all will retain indelible memories of their sojourn at Cranwell, and will regard the College with an esteem and affection which is of more value than the cosmopolitan camaraderie of greater seats of learning. For the associations of Cranwell are enjoyed only by a privileged few, who are closely bound together by their careers.' The final sentence is

Above left: Wing Commander John Scatliff Dewar DSO DFC: the highest-ranking RAF officer killed during the Battle of Britain.

Above right: The wedding of John Dewar and Kathleen 'Kay' Bowyer at Highfields Church, Portswood, Southampton, on 10 July 1937. (Paul Heys)

revealing. Johnny Dewar was now entering an elite, the cadre of professional officers in the comparatively small peacetime RAF. As Wing Commander 'Laddie' Lucas wrote, passing out of Cranwell 'opened most doors in the service and set them climbing the stairway to the stars'.

The course upon which Johnny now embarked at Cranwell was of two years duration. Appendix III of Air Publication No 121 described the syllabus: -

Year One

English language and literature, General ethnology, The British Empire, Applied Mathematics, including mechanics and draughtsmanship, Elementary physics, History of the RAF, Theory of flight and rigging, Air pilotage and map reading, Drill and physical training, Air Force Law and administration, Hygiene and sanitation, Workshops and engines, Wireless telegraphy, Radio telephony and signal procedure, and Practical flying.

Year Two

Theoretical and practical instruction in internal combustion engines, Aerodynamics, Practical instruction in rigging, Advanced work in the wood and metal workshops, Outline of wireless telegraphy and telephony, Armament, Practical flying, Air pilotage and airmanship, Meteorology, Outline of the organisation of the Navy and Army, War, strategy and tactics.

Cranwell's first year students flew the Avro 504N biplane, which had a top speed of around 100 mph, progressing the year after to the Armstrong Whitworth Atlas, which was 42 mph faster than the Avro. The Atlas was currently in service with operational RAF squadrons policing the Empire. There were also a few Fairey Foxes and, for those showing the aptitude to become fighter pilots, Armstrong Whitworth Siskin IIIs. All were single-engined biplanes.

An excellent student, nonetheless it was felt by Johnny's instructors that he 'could take his work more seriously'. Flying was his focus, not classrooms. Johnny soloed after ten hours, and later received a rare 'exceptional' rating for his flying ability. On 17 December 1927 he passed out of Cranwell and was permanently commissioned, starting his career as a pilot officer in the General Duties Branch.

On 17 December 1927, Pilot Officer Dewar was first posted to 13 Squadron, an Army Cooperation Squadron based at Andover and commanded by Squadron Leader H.M. Fraser. Army Cooperation was considered highly important, mainly revolving around reconnaissance, communications and spotting for the artillery. At the end of April 1928, Johnny passed the 'short' course at the School of Army Cooperation, scoring 77% in the final exam. He was assessed as 'a good athlete and keen pilot', but, having only recently left Cranwell, 'was inclined to be overconfident'. Nonetheless, the powers that be considered he 'should make a good officer with more experience'.

A flying accident occurred on 31 May 1928, in which Pilot Officer Dewar suffered concussion and minor injuries, as a result of which he was unable to fly for four months, and then restricted to below 10,000 feet with no aerobatics. Interestingly, on 4 March 1929, Pilot Officer Dewar arrived at RAF Leuchars for training on 'Fleet Spotting/Reconnaissance', which included practising deck-landings on aircraft carriers there and at RAF Gosport before the real thing on HMS *Furious*. Having returned to his Squadron, on 17 June 1929, Johnny was promoted to flying officer and considered by his CO to be 'a very good type, keen to succeed, plenty of ability'. The following month, Flying Officer Dewar was posted to the School of Naval Cooperation at Lee-on-Solent. There, Wing Commander D.J. Donald's annual performance review marked him as 'an excellent officer, keen, capable, and very reliable with a good, open, frank personality'. February 1932 saw Johnny on an instructor's course at the Central Flying School, upon conclusion of which he was assessed as 'above average' and posted to instruct at 2 FTS. In September 1932, Johnny sprained an ankle and sustained more minor injuries in another 'prang'. At the end of that year, Group Captain Quinnell's annual assessment was that Flying Officer Dewar was 'Enterprising. With more application should develop into a good flight commander. Plenty of personality and distinctly promising.' Air Commodore R.F.M. Fellowes agreed that he was 'a good type'.

Unusually for an RAF pilot, Flying Officer Dewar next went to sea. In May 1933 he joined 822 (Fleet Spotter/Reconnaissance) Squadron which had recently formed at Netheravon. In July, 822 joined the carrier *Furious*, which then embarked on a training voyage around the British coast. At the end of that year, 822 having returned to Netheravon, another excellent report followed, this time by Group Captain R.C. Mound: 'He has carried out his duties with great enthusiasm, and has done good work… has a pleasing and strong personality and a cheerful disposition… has given great satisfaction.'

John Dewar snapped by Sergeant Laurence Thorogood at Exeter while commanding 87 Squadron in July 1940.

In early January 1934, 822 Squadron re-joined HMS *Furious* at Devonport, sailing on 5 January 1934 for Gibraltar, and thence to Port of Spain, Trinidad. While aboard, on 1 February, Johnny was promoted to flight lieutenant. In April, 822 Squadron returned to Netheravon, Flight Lieutenant Dewar attending a navigation course before 822 again set sail with HMS *Furious*, this time on exercises in the Mediterranean. Transferred to 801 (Fleet Fighter) Squadron, flying Flycatchers, Nimrods and Ospreys, many more voyages followed.

Sometime in 1936, Johnny met Kathleen Bowyer, known as 'Kay', a proficient but diminutive skater at an ice rink in Southampton. Kay, nine years younger than Johnny, was the daughter of an influential local Alderman, Percy Vincent Bowyer (unlike his brothers, who all went to sea and became liner masters and Trinity House pilots, due to ill-health 'PV' instead became an estate agent and valuer based in the city centre, and would twice become Mayor of Southampton). At the end of June 1936, Johnny left 822 Squadron and joined the Aeroplane & Armament Experimental Establishment (A&AEE) at Martlesham Heath near Ipswich, which although not near Southampton, at least was not at sea. On 10 July 1937, Johnny and Kay married at Highfields Church, in Portswood, Southampton, just a short distance from the Bowyer family home at 100 Highfield Lane. The newly-weds then set up their first home in quarters at RAF Martlesham Heath.

There was important work afoot at the A&AEE, which tested new aircraft types, measuring performance against price and thereby informing the Air Ministry's response to aircraft designers' tenders. This was a most exciting time to be involved in such work, given that the Hurricane and

Spitfire, new, fast, modern monoplanes with retractable undercarriage and enclosed cockpits, had only recently first flown and were still being evaluated. Flight Lieutenant Dewar commanded the A&AEE's Armament Flight, responsible for testing the eight Browning machine guns of the Spitfire prototype, K5054. There was, however, a problem: the guns fired perfectly in the butts, on the ground, and at low altitudes, but at high altitude they would not. This was because low ambient air temperature caused the oil in the breech mechanisms to freeze, jamming the guns. Supermarine Test Pilot Jeffrey Quill remembered that: -

'Flight Lieutenant Johnny Dewar… on his first attempt to fire the guns at high altitude, had five guns which wouldn't fire at all, two which fired only four and eight rounds respectively and one which managed to get off 171 rounds before it stopped. The effects of low air temperature were aggravated by the fact that, being mounted remotely in the wings, the guns had to be cocked before take-off. Thus, their breeches were open in flight. As Dewar returned to the aerodrome the oil in the guns progressively un-froze itself and when he touched down on landing the slight jolt immediately resulted in three of his guns firing one round each across the aerodrome and into the peace of the Suffolk countryside!'

Pilot Officer Richard Bowyer, Wing Commander Dewar's brother-in-law, who lost his life in a flying accident on 18 September 1939 and was buried at St John the Baptist, North Baddesley, near Southampton.

On 1 February 1938, Johnny was promoted to squadron leader and on 28 March was posted to RAF Thorney Island, Chichester, on administrative duties. There, close to her family in Southampton, Kay Dewar became a Code & Cipher Clerk, Johnny soon becoming a senior figure in the station operations room. By that time he was an experienced pilot, being one of the few to have flown the Spitfire, which did not enter operational service until Jeffrey Quill delivered K9789 to 19 Squadron at Duxford on 4 August 1938. Quill was based at Eastleigh, still developing the new Spitfire, crossing paths again with Squadron Leader Dewar, the two accomplished airman becoming friends. Indeed, Ray Cobern, then a young boy, recalled the excitement caused when Quill, Dewar and Kay's brother, Richard Bowyer, arrived for Sunday services at St John the Baptist, North Baddesley, in Jeffrey's British racing green Lagonda. The intrepid pair doubtless inspired young Richard, who would himself be commissioned as a pilot officer on 29 March 1939 and begin flying training.

Soon after the outbreak of war, on 10 November 1939, Squadron Leader Dewar was posted to 11 Group Pool for reassignment to a fighter squadron; three weeks later, he took command of 87 Squadron, which was flying Hurricanes in France. When the German attack on the west began on 10 May 1940, 87 Squadron was heavily engaged. Two weeks later, its airfields overrun, the unit was evacuated back to England. On 31 May, the *London Gazette* announced that Squadron Leader Dewar was amongst the first officers to be awarded the 'double' of the DFC and DSO for his services in France. The citations respectively read: -

'This officer has shot down five enemy aircraft and led many patrols with courage and skill', and 'Before intensive operations started, this officer injured his right shoulder in a severe flying accident. Despite this, he flew regularly and led his squadron with skill and dash, more than sixty enemy aircraft being destroyed by them. He remained in command of the squadron throughout the operations, in spite of the injured shoulder, trained his new pilots well and continued throughout to be a very efficient commander, inculcating an excellent spirit in his squadron.'

Upon returning home, of his shoulder injury Johnny simply told his wife, 'Oh, don't worry about that.'

On 5 July 1940, Squadron Leader Dewar led 87 Squadron from Church Fenton in Yorkshire to the new 10 Group station at Exeter. As the squadron's ORB commented, 'By this time the capitulation of France had completely altered the whole strategic situation of this war, and the South West of England suddenly found itself vulnerable to attack, instead of being a safe assignment. There was therefore considerable speculation as to when the *Blitzkrieg* would be launched against England.' Exeter was a civilian airport which had been procured by the RAF and was in the process of changing over to a war and service footing. 213 Squadron had arrived a fortnight

Wing Commander Dewar's service funeral at St John the Baptist.

previously 'and naturally had occupied the best parts of the station. The officers were billeted at the Rougemont Hotel in Exeter, and the men at Farringdon House, not far from the aerodrome.' It was a busy time for 87 Squadron's CO, 'the first bit of excitement from the operational point of view' occurring on 11 July.

Just after 1100 hours on that day, 601 Squadron was scrambled from Tangmere, and half an hour later sighted around fifteen *Stukas* escorted by forty Me 110s approaching Lyme Bay from Cherbourg. More RAF fighters were hurriedly sent off, including nine Hurricanes of 213 Squadron, and three of 87 – amongst them Squadron Leader Dewar. Although these reinforcements arrived too late to prevent the bombing of Portland at 1153 hours, 601 Squadron disrupted the *Stukas*' attack, only one merchant ship consequently being hit. Johnny Dewar reported that he was: -

'Leading a flight of three Hurricanes at 5,000 feet west of Weymouth; sighted nine enemy aircraft approaching Portland from south at 15,000 feet. Commenced climbing south, to get in between E/A and sun. Saw nine more E/A and one group of twelve Me 110s as we were going up. Got level and up-sun of enemy at 12,000 feet. As we approached, some aircraft dived to attack shipping. Enemy did not appear aware of our presence. Saw two other

Hurricanes attacking and swung into Me 110s, which seemed to be flying to form a circle. Saw a Hurricane diving and turning slowly with 110 on his tail, so put four bursts into 110. On last burst the port engine appeared to blow up. Aircraft flicked onto its back and dived almost vertically. Owing to presence of numerous E/A, I did not watch this aircraft hit the sea, but feel certain it must have gone in, four miles east of Shambles. Method of approach was line astern, then "free for all".'

The Me 110 concerned is believed to be the aircraft of 9/ZG 76, which crashed onto the Verne's chalk cliffs with such violence that no trace of the crew has ever been found. The pilot was actually Göring's nephew, *Oberleutnant* H.J. Göring – whose *zerstörer* was the first enemy aircraft to crash in England during the Battle of Britain; it was also the new RAF station at Exeter's first 'kill'. The action, however, was not yet over for 87 Squadron's CO: -

'I went into a full turn to review progress of battle and remove two other E/A trying to get on my tail. Saw a bomb exploding by shipping in the harbour and two E/A diving for ground. One E/A still pursued me. My Hurricane turned easily onto his tail – he was vertically banked. He then dived for ground, going east – I followed but withheld fire as I was getting short of rounds. E/A pulled out about 1,000 feet and continued in "S" turns. I gave him a burst from about 100 yards and vapour came out of both engines. I had to slam throttle back to avoid over-shooting. Vapour then

Kay Leather, as she later became, pictured in 1980 with a 'sweetheart brooch' given to her by her beloved 'Johnny'. (Paul Heys)

ceased to come from one engine and he gathered way again. I was very close and there was no rear gun fire, so I held my position and took careful non-deflection shot, using all ammunition. E/A at once turned inland, going very slowly. Seeing me draw away, he turned seawards again. I went to head him off and he, apparently thinking I had more rounds, turned for land again, sinking slowly. At about 200 feet, another Hurricane came up and fired a short burst at him. He immediately turned and landed on Grange Heath (or near). Both crew got out, wearing yellow jackets. Army was close by. Number of other Hurricane was UW-F (I think).'

This was another machine of 9/ZG 76, which had previously been attacked by 238 Squadron's Green Section; the Hurricane that Dewar reported as having also attacked was Flying Officer Hugh Riddle of 601 Squadron (and whose Hurricane was more likely UF-W). The enemy unit's *Staffelkapitän*, *Oberleutnant* Kadow, and his gunner *Gefreiter* Scholz, were both captured unhurt having force-landed at Grange Heath, near Lulworth. In total, the enemy had lost four Me 110s – an early indication that the type was generally no match for Hurricanes and Spitfires, in spite of its much-vaunted heavy armament – and two *Stukas*. Fighter Command suffered no loss, although, as the 87 Squadron ORB reported, the Australian Pilot Officer Richard Glyde 'had a near escape from a bullet which pierced his central panel of his hood and struck his armour plating – close to his head'.

The following day, 12 July 1940, Johnny Dewar was posted – and became RAF Exeter's station commander. This did not, however, prevent him continuing to fly operationally on occasions with 87 Squadron, now commanded by the New Zealander Squadron Leader Terence Lovell-Gregg. This may have been because although 87 Squadron's new CO had joined the unit in June 1940, he lacked operational experience, sensibly relying upon his flight commanders to lead the squadron in the air while gaining the necessary experience himself. On the other hand, it was also because Johnny Dewar was undoubtedly a 'press on type'. On 13 August, for example, the Exeter Station Commander made up a section of 87 Squadron Hurricanes, with Pilot Officers Glyde DFC and Jay, for an early patrol over the Channel. Twenty miles south of Selsey Bill, a lone enemy bomber was sighted, attacked and shot down into the sea. This was shared by the Section as a Ju 88, but was actually an He 111 of III/KG 27, the crew of which remain missing. Unfortunately during the engagement Glyde's Hurricane was hit by return fire, his aircraft streaming white vapour while returning to Exeter. The next time Squadron Leader Dewar looked, the damaged Hurricane had disappeared, and a search of the Channel proved fruitless.

It was a sad loss: only the previous week, the 26-year-old had joined his CO and other 87 Squadron pilots at Buckingham Palace where all received gallantry awards at an investiture held by King George VI.

On 15 August 1940, the enemy attacked Portland in strength, and a great air battle developed over the south coast – in which Squadron Leader Lovell-Gregg was killed. Three days later, on 'The Hardest Day', Squadron Leader Randolph Mills DFC arrived at Exeter and took command of 87 Squadron. On 25 August, Johnny Dewar – now promoted to Wing Commander – once more led 87 Squadron (a formation not including Squadron Leader Miller) when both Exeter Hurricane squadrons were scrambled at 1730 hours to intercept a raid of over 100 Ju 88s, Me 110s and Me 109s, bent upon destroying Warmwell airfield: -

'Led squadron to patrol Warmwell at 10,000 feet, as ordered. Sighted AA bursts over Portland, but no aircraft. Then sighted a large enemy force coming westwards, along coast. Selected squadron of Ju 88s least escorted, and led in on a quarter attack. Fired about 800 rounds. As I pulled away, I saw the E/A smoking. Flight Sergeant Badger, who was following, saw it burst into flames. It must have fallen near Lulworth. Later confirmed by Observer Corps that one fell there.

'I continued my turn on pulling away, and met about ten 110s head-on, taking a fleeting burst at the last one. By the time I had turned around again, I could see no aircraft near me. Beyond Lulworth there was a huge circle of wheeling aircraft. Every now and then, one dropped out, smoking. The bombers seemed to be making out to sea. Very high over Portland a white

A silver and inscribed cigarette case once belonging to Wing Commander Dewar. (Paul Heys)

Wing Commander Dewar's medals, including the DSO and DFC, and 'wings'. (Paul Heys)

"Verey" light was fired. I flew, climbing towards the coast, turning now and again, to sweep the sky above. During one of these turns I almost collided with an Me 109 turning in the opposite direction. I started to pursue as he went past me, and saw that he was the leader of four. They did not appear to have seen me, so I joined them in the rear. Unfortunately, their high speed prevented me from getting closer than about 600 yards, and although I had +9 on the boost, I could not catch up. As they turned, however, I slowly gained. When about 300 yards away, I opened fire on the rearmost in short bursts. He immediately turned more steeply than the rest, and increased speed, but not before vapour came pouring from him. His manoeuvre carried him to the front of the others and I had to break off action with him. Last seen, he was diving at about 45°, slightly banked, and may also have come down near Lulworth, on land or in the sea. Fumes were pouring from him. I suspect he carried armour, as I fired at least 800 rounds, with almost dead astern shots. The others quickly climbed out of reach. I was greatly handicapped by lack of speed. Seeing no further activity and being short of ammunition, I returned to base without seeing any of my squadron since the first encounter.

'I consider that greater effect would be achieved from an attack, and less losses suffered, if we patrolled in larger numbers, if possible two squadrons going together. Twin-engined bombers can take terrific punishment from the rear and their own shooting has greatly improved. I consider it a mistake to attack from the rear if any other method is possible. With fighter escorts, only fleeting attacks can be made, making it difficult to obtain conclusive results.'

During this engagement, two Ju 88s of II/KG 51 crashed into the sea, along with two Me 109s of III/JG 2; whether any of these were those attacked by Wing Commander Dewar is impossible to say. At Warmwell, two hangars were damaged, the station sick quarters burnt out, and communications disrupted until the following day.

On 12 September 1940, the 87 Squadron ORB recorded: 'Wing Commander Dewar set out from Exeter for a visit to Tangmere and was not heard of again. He had been informed of enemy activity on the route over which he was to pass, and no doubt must have run into more trouble than he could cope with by himself. A very sad loss to 87 Squadron.' Wing Commander Ian 'Widge' Gleed later wrote, 'One afternoon we lost our Station Commander, Johnny. He had borrowed one of our machines to fly to Tangmere for a conference. He was in excellent spirits when he took off. Just after he had left, "Ops" told us there was a *blitz* in that sector. They warned Johnny on the R/T. He gave the usual answer: "Message received and understood." Then nothing more.'

On 12 September, the following telegram was sent to Kay Dewar: -

'Regret to inform you that your husband, Acting Wing Commander John Scatliff Dewar DSO DFC, is reported missing as the result of air operations on September 12th 1940. Letter follows. Any further information received will be immediately communicated to you. Should news of him reach you from any other source, please inform this department. His father has been informed.'

Mr Dewar was puzzled, and wrote to the Air Ministry on 21 September: -

'With reference to your telephone P702 of Sept. 13th stating that my son, Acting Wing Commander John Dewar DSO DFC is reported missing as the result of air operations on 12 September 1940, I beg to state that according to official reports none of our fighter aircraft was brought down by enemy action that day. This being so, I shall take it as a favour if you will kindly let us know the circumstances in which he and his aircraft came to be missing.

'I have not written earlier because in your wire to my daughter-in-law… you stated you would be writing to her, but when I last heard from her she had received no letter from you.'

Mr Dewar was quite correct: on 12 September 1940, enemy air activity was much reduced, and not one RAF fighter was lost in combat.

So, what had happened to Wing Commander Dewar, and when?

On 27 September 1940, the Air Ministry responded to Mr Dewar, confirming that in fact: -

'He took off from Exeter Aerodrome at 3 pm on the 11th September 1940, and proceeded to Tangmere, since when nothing has been heard of him.'

A more detailed explanation is preserved at The National Archives in Wing Commander Dewar's Casualty File, in this report by Squadron Leader R.S. Mills at RAF Exeter, dated 23 October 1940: -

'A/W/C JS Dewar on 11 September 1940, gave orders that he would be flying to Tangmere and the normal procedure for advising Operations at this station was carried out.

'This officer took off at 1500 hrs in Hurricane V7306 and before doing so was advised of enemy activity over Selsey Bill. The route, however, to be flown was from Exeter, via Winchester, then to Tangmere, thus avoiding the balloon barrage over Southampton.

'The flight expected to take some forty minutes in duration and ETA being about 1600 hrs.

'At 1600 hrs, intense enemy air activity developed over the Southampton area and it is presumed that A/W/C Dewar decided to engage the enemy, although there is no definite evidence to support this supposition. A pilot of a rear protective section later reported that he noticed a lone Hurricane had followed his Squadron just before enemy aircraft were engaged.

'S/Ldr RS Mills, acting Station Commander of RAF Exeter, examined the Raid Tracings of Sector Station Tangmere, and formed the opinion that in view of anti-aircraft gunfire over Southampton and intense aircraft activity North of Southampton, that A/W/C Dewar followed one of the operating squadrons and definitely sought engagements as he would have been in the operational area at about that time.'

Ignoring battle was not in Johnny Dewar's nature, so Squadron Leader Mills' assessment was doubtless correct, albeit based on circumstantial evidence. The confusion over the date of his death may have arisen because Johnny's was really an unofficial flight, to visit his wife at Thorney Island. RAF Exeter therefore waited as long as possible in the hope that he would

St John the Baptist, North Baddesley, at which the graves of both Wing Commander John Dewar DSO DFC and Pilot Officer Richard Bowyer can be found.

turn up safe from some remote place, before coming clean on 12 September that their boss was missing.

On the morning of 11 September 1940, the German precision bombing unit *Erprobungsgruppe* 210 had arrived at Cherbourg-Ost airfield, tasked with destroying Southampton's Spitfire production capacity. The main location concerned was, naturally, Supermarine's Woolston-based factory, on the banks of the river Itchen, with final assembly and test flying completed at Eastleigh airport, seven miles to the north. At 1530 hrs, the unit's Me 110 and Me 109 *Jabos* took off from Cherbourg-Ost, bound for Eastleigh, escorted by Me 110s of ZG 76, and Me 109s of JG 2. At 1540 hrs, 213 Squadron scrambled from Exeter and vectored to Selsey Bill, followed over the next ten minutes by 602 and 607 Squadrons from Tangmere. While the latter patrolled base, the Spitfires of 602 Squadron headed out to sea, the Hurricanes of 213 following slightly below and behind. Just before 1610 hours, about forty Me 110s were sighted incoming at 15,000 feet, with an unspecified number of Me 109s some twelve miles behind the main German force. Both RAF squadrons attacked the Me 110s before the Me 109s arrived, but nonetheless bombs began falling on Eastleigh at 1613 hrs – not, as intended, on the Spitfire Final Assembly and Flight Hangars, but on the Cunliffe-Owen Aircraft factory 400 yards away where Lockheed Hudsons from America were assembled and parts made for the new Stirling bomber. Spitfire production was therefore unaffected by this raid, but forty-nine civilians were killed, thirty-eight badly injured, and fifty-four more slightly so.

During the engagement off Selsey Bill, at 1605 hrs, 213 Squadron reportedly claimed the destruction of five Me 110s and two damaged; 602 Squadron claimed, at 1610 hrs, three Me 110s destroyed and one damaged, one Me 109 destroyed and another probably destroyed. It was a fine bag – but somewhat over-exuberant: the available evidence confirms that only one Me 110, of II/ZG 76, was shot down (this aircraft ditching in the Channel); no Me 109s were in fact lost. It appears, however, that the RAF fighters engaged the escorting Me 110s and Me 109s, while the fighter-bombers of *Erprobungsgruppe* 210 reached Eastleigh, at low level, and withdrew safely without being intercepted. 602 Squadron suffered a pilot missing, one slightly wounded, and another landed back at Tangmere with a damaged Spitfire. 213 Squadron lost two Hurricanes: a Polish pilot reported missing, and a flight commander who baled out but was rescued by a passing ship. It was undoubtedly 213 Squadron which Wing Commander Dewar had followed into battle.

Frustratingly, the details of German combat reports available are incomplete, in many cases simply relating the unit, pilot, type of enemy aircraft claimed, time and location. Frequently certain of these essential details are missing from the record, owing to the vast number of documents destroyed during the death-throes of Nazi Germany in 1945. What we do know regarding the action with which we are now concerned is that the following claims exist (continental time): -

Leutnant Kurt Votel	3/JG 2	Hurricane	1646 hours
Oberfeldwebel Hans Tilly	3/JG 2	Spitfire	1650 hours
Oberleutnant Hans Hahn	4/JG 2	Hurricane	1615 hours
Unteroffizier Kurt Bühligen	6/JG 2	Hurricane	1635 hours
Leutnant Heinz Bolze	4/JG 2	Spitfire	1700 hours
Oberfeldwebel Siegfried Schnell	4/JG 2	Spitfire	1705 hours
Oberfeldwebel Siegfried Schnell	4/JG 2	Spitfire	1712 hours
Oberfeldwebel Franz Willinger	8/JG 2	Hurricane	1727 hours
Oberleutnant Wilhelm Herget	6/ZG 76	Hurricane	1700 hours

The only known location is for Herget's claim, which is recorded as five to ten kilometres east of the Isle of Wight, at 5,000 metres. Clearly both sides, as ever, over-claimed, a not uncommon scenario given the speed and confusion of fighter combat. Without doubt Wing Commander Dewar was

The author with the Rev Sally Kerson at the memorial service organised by Wing Commander Dewar and Pilot Officer Bowyer in the Battle of Britain's 75th anniversary year.

en route from Exeter to Tangmere, when he joined in this air battle near Selsey Bill. The likelihood is that one of the *Jagdfliegern* listed shot down V7306 which crashed into the sea.

Nothing further was heard of Wing Commander Dewar until 30 September 1940, when, according to Squadron Leader Mills, 'a body clothed in a shirt was washed up on the beach at Kingston Gorse, Sussex, and subsequently identified as A/W/Cdr J.S. Dewar by means of laundry marks. A tunic was also found near the body, marked JSD and had the ribbons of DSO and DFC… It was established that this officer was killed by machine-gun fire, there being bullet wounds in the back and head.'

This was final, irrefutable, confirmation that Johnny Dewar had lost his life in action on 11 September 1940. As Gleed also wrote, 'We lost a grand Station Commander, and our friend.'

On 2 October, Kay Dewar received a further telegram from the Air Ministry confirming that her husband was no longer missing but confirmed to have lost his life on '12 September 1940'.

According to the artist Sir William Rothenstein, who knew Dewar personally, his friend's body was 'riddled with shot'. Whether Johnny Dewar baled out, badly wounded, discarded his parachute but was not rescued, or, either badly wounded or already dead, had been thrown clear of his Hurricane upon impact, will never be known. At the time, a rumour circulated that

As a result of evidence supplied by the author, in 2019 the Commonwealth War Graves Commission corrected the date of death appearing on Wing Commander Dewar's headstone at St John the Baptist (Sally Kerson).

Johnny had been machine-gunned while descending by parachute, but there was, and is, no evidence to support such an allegation; it is also contrary to a file note of 8 October 1940, stating that the pilot had 'failed to bale out'.

Pilot Officer (later Group Captain) Denis David was a pilot on 87 Squadron, and wrote of Dewar, 'A man of his calibre, leadership and character cannot be replaced – and all who knew him felt this.'

Another distinguished 87 Squadron pilot, Wing Commander Roland Beamont remembered that Johnny was 'a super chap, a marvellous commander and leader who inspired us all with his calm, totally unflappable, manner – he seemed to take the view that it was all rather a joke and certainly not good form for any of us to be in any way concerned about it!'

Wing Commander John Scatliff Dewar DSO DFC was 33 years old and the highest-ranking officer to lose his life in the Battle of Britain. Today his grave can be found in the quiet churchyard of St John the Baptist, where sadly Johnny had joined his brother-in-law, Pilot Officer Richard Bowyer, who had lost his life in a training accident at Hullavington on 18 September 1939. Kay had lost both her brother and husband in less than a year.

In 1980, Joan Reeder of *Woman* magazine interviewed Kay Leather – formerly Dewar – who for a month after her first husband had been reported missing, had barely eaten or wanted to live: -

'I don't remember anything but the delirium. Johnny in blue bathing trunks, coming up out of the sea, with his usual super grin, and holding his arms out. But every time I tried to run to him. I'd wake. I trained as a sheet-metal worker, going off at dawn each day. Bashed away, wanting to feel whacked, find oblivion each night. The other pilots were marvellous, never gave up asking me out, I tried going, but I'd got this phobia, couldn't shed it for years, couldn't bear seeing other married couples together. In the middle of a party, air raid, anywhere, I'd have to lock myself in the loo and cry.

'A letter came to one of Johnny's aunts from the *Manchester Guardian*'s war correspondent. He wrote, "He was a marvellous man. His tranquillity and courage have been comforting to me in bad times since." I thought how much more of a comfort Johnny's courage should be to me, I had the incomparable luck of being married to him. In time that worked. After D-Day, I went on to drive ambulances for the Second Front.

'Nine years after Johnny's death, I married again. There was no comparison with Johnny, he was in a world apart, still is, but Nelson Leather was persistent and kind until his manic depression became obvious… in the end he crashed his car and was killed… left me with a lot of debris but also a daughter, who is the joy of my life, and a granddaughter. But those three years married to Johnny have seen me through the forty I have lived without him. It was war, and he was doing his job, superbly. Now my sixties have brought him nearer, I'm convinced we'll be together again.'

More recently, on 9 July 2015, the eve of the Battle of Britain's 75th anniversary start-date, friends and I organised a graveside memorial service for Wing Commander Dewar and Pilot Officer Bowyer at St John the Baptist. The RAF was officially represented, as was the Royal British Legion and RAF Association, and children from William Gilpin School laid flowers on the pilots' graves. Overhead flew a formation of vintage Chipmunk trainers in a 'missing man' formation, and as the last notes of the *Last Post* faded across the Hampshire countryside, I was reminded of John Pudney's moving lines: -

Do not despair
For Johnny-head-in-air;
He sleeps as sound
As Johnny underground.
Fetch out no shroud
For Johnny-in-the-cloud;
And keep your tears
For him in after years.
Better by far
For Johnny-the-bright-star,
To keep your head,
And see his children fed.

Chapter Twelve

Douglas Cruikshank
Margaret Moon

'Supermariners'

Killed by Enemy Bombing: 24 September 1940

In *The Lion and the Unicorn*, published during the 'Blitz' in 1941, George Orwell wrote, 'As I write, highly civilised human beings are flying overhead, trying to kill me.' It was as early as 1914 that the first German bomb was dropped on England, the small device exploding harmlessly in a Dover garden. From that point onwards Britain was unable to rely on the security provided by being an island nation. Air attacks rapidly intensified and became increasingly efficient, culminating in a one-ton bomb hitting London on 16 February 1918. By the Armistice, German airmen had raided Britain over 100 times in what was an unanticipated development in warfare. No provision had been made to protect the civilian population and 1,413 people died in these attacks. Although the overall death toll equated to that suffered in just one night of the infamous Blitz on Britain, it was sufficient to generate a widespread fear of air power. Indeed, the fear of aerial bombardment in Britain at this time was unprecedented, but unsurprising: close to the continent, from where it was assumed any attack

The only photograph ever taken, by his son Gordon, of Spitfire designer Reginald Joseph Mitchell with the prototype, K5054, at Eastleigh.

would be launched, no part of the British Isles was outside the bomber's range. Furthermore, air power doctrine was developed on the 'knock-out blow' theory, revolving around an air force over-flying conventional armies and navies to deliver an almighty crushing blow to centres of production, transportation and communication, thereby destroying the enemy's ability to wage war. Indeed it was believed that the destruction of production and lowering of public morale through bombing was the pathway to victory. None of this boded well for civilian populations.

In August 1936, Germany's *Condor Legion* provided military support to the fascist General Franco in the Spanish Civil War. Spain became an essential testing ground for German weapons and tactics under combat conditions. While the worth of fighters and tactical air support were proven, the bomber emerged from the conflict supreme, the most feared weapon thus far created. Why? Because of one word: Guernica. A Basque village of 5,000 inhabitants where road and rail networks converged, standing between Franco's forces and the capture of Bilbao, Guernica suddenly became vital to war in northern Spain. The location was extremely vulnerable to air attack, having no anti-aircraft defences and intervention by friendly fighters was impossible owing to heavy losses. The Germans and Italians, the latter having also entered the fray in support of the fascists, mounted a joint air

The Supermarine factory at Woolston on the banks of the Itchen – Southampton's famous 'floating bridge' can be seen bottom right.

attack on Guernica's all-important Renteria Bridge. Twenty-two tons of bombs were dropped, and owing to the general inaccuracy of bombing at this time, the adjacent village was virtually destroyed. This was a somewhat unfortunate consequence, not least for some 400 dead (although casualties were reported at the time to be 1,654), and the raid was propagandised as a deliberate terror attack on a defenceless civilian population. Indeed the global media became virtually hysterical, the terrifying prophecies regarding air power and bombing in particular now apparently a stark reality. Then Italy's *Regia Aeronautica* unleashed heavy bombing attacks on Barcelona. Lasting several days, these represented an opportunity at last to test the theories of Italy's General Giulio Douhet, an enthusiastic advocate of strategic bombing. These attacks caused 1,300 casualties. Initially shocked and demoralised, the survivors recovered surprisingly quickly, their main emotions anger and defiance – which flew right in the face of those believing in the 'knock-out blow'. This unpredicted and stoic reaction by civilians to bombing made the Germans realise that such attacks actually bolstered the enemy population's will to resist, quite the opposite to the expected result. Consequently, German air power doctrine did not revolve around strategic bombing but concentrated on supporting land-based operations. This would prove significant.

When Hitler came to power in 1933, the countdown to war began. After the Munich Crisis in 1938 it was clear that no amount of appeasement would prevent another war with Germany. As tension mounted, the question being 'when' not 'if' war would erupt, between June and the beginning of September 1939 some 3,750,000 people were evacuated from centres of population to the country as a protective measure against air attack. In September, such movements affected around a third of Britain's population. When war was eventually declared on Germany by Britain and France on Sunday 3 September 1939, it was fully expected that Germany would deliver an immediate 'knock-out blow'. At 1127 hrs that fateful morning, Londoners believed Armageddon had indeed arrived when air raid warning sirens balefully wailed across the capital. But it was a false alarm, the first of many. As it happened, there would be no attempt by either side to deliver a decisive air attack. The truth was, neither was actually in a position to do so and both were reluctant to be responsible for unleashing unrestrained aerial warfare. Poland, invaded by Hitler on 1 September, however, suffered. After just one day the Germans achieved total air superiority. On 25 September, the *Luftwaffe* began a two-day pounding of Warsaw, causing immense loss of life. The following year, Norway and Denmark were defeated without

Spitfire Mk Is under construction at Woolston. That Southampton was 'Home of the Spitfire' was one of several reasons making the port a priority target for the *Luftwaffe*.

the need for such an aerial attack, but after Hitler attacked the West, on 14 May 1940 Rotterdam was pulverised – reportedly causing 30,000 deaths (3,000 according to more recent research). Hard on the heels of Guernica and Warsaw, Rotterdam's fate was terrifying news indeed. That the bomber would always get through definitely now appeared to be the case. Soon France had fallen, along with Holland, Belgium and Luxembourg. Britain braced itself for the now inevitable *Luftwaffe* onslaught.

It was not, though, completely one-sided. RAF Bomber Command was retaliating by bombing Germany at night. A raid on Berlin led to Hitler announcing to the Reichstag on 4 September that 'Just now… Mr Churchill is demonstrating his new brainchild, the night air raid… When they declare that they will increase attacks on our cities, then we will raze their cities to the ground. We will stop the handiwork of these night pirates, so help us God!' Having largely confined itself to attacking militarily justified targets, on 7 September 1940 the *Luftwaffe* began the round-the-clock bombing of London to force Fighter Command to battle for destruction *en masse*. That day, 448 Londoners were killed and 1,337 seriously injured. And the bombing continued, relentlessly. The population's spirit, however, was very much that 'London can take it' – winning the admiration of the free world.

Above left: Cyril Russell, of Whites Road, Bitterne, an 18-year-old 'Supermariner' working in the Woolston factory's 'K' Shop – who has left behind a powerful first-hand account of the raids during September 1940.

Above right: A chilling photograph of *Luftwaffe* aircrews planning a raid on Southampton.

London was not the bombers' only destination. Southampton, for example, was extremely vulnerable to air attack and, for reasons we will explore, became an obvious and frequently visited *Luftwaffe* target. On the south coast in Hampshire, seventy miles south-west of London and fifteen north-west of Portsmouth, Southampton is a major port, located at the northern end of Southampton Water, a deep-water estuary formed by the confluence of the rivers Test and Itchen, joined by the Hamble to the south. In the twentieth century, the city's major industry was shipbuilding and repair, the largest employer being Thornycroft's. During the First World War, Southampton became a major embarkation port for the military, in addition to being central to receiving both the wounded and prisoners of war from France. That Southampton was such a well-appointed port was sufficient for it to be targeted by the *Luftwaffe* – based during the Battle of Britain just sixty miles due south, around Cherbourg – but there was another reason: the famous Supermarine factory was located on the Itchen's west bank, at Woolston. It is hard to imagine a more attractive target to *Luftwaffe* planners…

The Supermarine Aviation Works had been born before the First World War, when one Noel Pemberton-Billing decided to combine his passions for flying and boating by producing a flying boat. In 1913 he purchased and set up shop at an old coal wharf at Woolston, where the 'Super Marine Craft' was to be built. Owing to the outbreak of war, however, this visionary flying boat was never built, Supermarine, as the company became known, instead producing warplanes. In 1916, Hubert Scott-Paine became Managing Director and oversaw a reorganisation of the company. New faces appeared at the Woolston works, including a promising designer called Reginald Joseph Mitchell. At this time, the RN commissioned Supermarine to manufacture its flying boats, as a result of which the business maintained an association with this craft well into the 1940s. Between the wars Mitchell oversaw the design and production of the company's entries for the coveted Schneider Trophy, nations competing in this spectacular and hugely popular annual air race at low-level over water. In accordance with competition

Woolston: 15 September 1940.

rules, the country winning the competition three consecutive times kept the prize – which Britain did in 1936 with Mitchell's S.6, which reached a speed of 357.7 mph, setting a world record. The competition had become a matter of enormous national pride and interest, the three victories making Mitchell and Supermarine famous.

Most importantly, the experience gained competing for the Schneider Trophy led directly to 'RJ' responding to the Air Ministry's invitation for aircraft designers to submit tenders for a modern, fast, monoplane fighter, by designing the Spitfire. On 5 March 1936, Mitchell and his team gathered at Eastleigh airport, several miles north of Southampton, and watched Captain 'Mutt' Summers make the Spitfire's maiden flight. Coming off the back of the victorious Schneider Trophy racers, the Spitfire, with its beautiful elliptical wing, was a winner from the outset. True, the Hawker Hurricane had already flown, but Camm's fighter lacked both the charisma and performance of Mitchell's fighter. Whereas the Hurricane resembled a Hart biplane without the top wing, relying upon tried and tested construction materials and techniques, the Spitfire was a revolutionary all-metal design uniting strength and lightness with a Rolls-Royce engine. It was a winning

The shelters on the east side of the railway embankment, on Peartree Green, behind Supermarine's Itchen works, just a few hundred yards north of the main Woolston factory, after the direct hit on 24 September 1940. (Dave Key)

combination. On 3 June 1936 the Air Ministry ordered 310 Spitfires, ordering a further 200 in 1937. On 11 June that year Mitchell died of cancer, never to know the contribution his little fighter would make. The following year, on 4 August 1938, Supermarine test pilot Jeffrey Quill delivered the first Spitfire to an RAF fighter Squadron, 19 at Duxford; it would be just in time. Spitfire production was stepped up, Supermarine's Woolston and nearby Itchen works becoming hives of activity. In May 1940, a local teenager, Terry White, joined the company as a 'handy lad', finding himself 'utterly bewildered by the noise and, it appeared to me, confusion of what was a very, very busy factory' – which would soon fill the cross-hairs of German bombsights.

The first of many bombs fell on Southampton's Millbrook area on the night of 20 June 1940, causing casualties. The city centre was hit on 13 and 14 August, six Sotonians losing their lives, and two days later, Flight Lieutenant James Brindley Nicolson of 249 Squadron performed his 'signal act of valour' over the port, for which he received Fighter Command's sole VC of the Second World War (see the story of Pilot Officer Martyn Aurel King). From then on, the tempo of enemy air activity directed at Southampton increased. On 11 September, the German precision-bombing

Looking west from Peartree Green towards the shelters and damaged Itchen works across the railway embankment. (Dave Key)

The devastated Woolston works and surrounding area following the raid on 26 September 1940.

unit *Erprobungsgruppe* 210 arrived at Cherbourg-Ost airfield, tasked with destroying Supermarine.

At that time, the Vickers Supermarine Aviation Works, as the company was now known, at Woolston was the main base for Spitfire production. The busy factory was located on the Itchen's east bank, immediately north of the floating bridge, which ferried passengers across the estuary, which divided Southampton in two. A few hundred yards to the north was the company's so-called 'Itchen Works'. Both factories fronted the Itchen, a fifteen-foot-high railway embankment rising up across the road behind the Itchen Works. Beyond the railway, to the east, was the open land of Peartree Green, and built-up area of Woolston. Completed Spitfire major sub-assemblies were transported by road to the company's hangars at Eastleigh airport for final assembly and test flying, so to a degree production was necessarily dispersed. In terms of protection, three surface shelters were constructed along the Itchen Work's boundary, but the main shelters were constructed in rows on the railway's far side, access gained via a tunnel just ten feet wide, burrowed through the embankment. While these principal shelters were adjacent and close-by the Itchen Works, the main workforce was located at the Woolston Works, so had a fair distance to cover in a hurry in the event of a raid. What made Woolston personnel especially vulnerable was that warnings were sounded at the last possible minute, so that raids only disrupted production for the minimum length of time. Two practices indicated that it took too long for Woolston workers to reach the shelters, and indeed that the narrow tunnel created a dangerous bottleneck. For this reason, some staff resolved never to use the company shelters – which, as we will see, proved a wise decision.

On the afternoon of 11 September 1940, *Erprobungsgruppe* 210's target was not the Woolston or Itchen Works, but Eastleigh airport, where Spitfires were finally assembled and first flown. There, twin-engined Lockheed Hudson aircraft were also produced, by Cunliffe-Owen. Throughout the Battle of Britain, the *Luftwaffe* demonstrably suffered from inconsistent and often poor intelligence, it being quite likely that the Germans were unaware that Eastleigh was used for anything other than Spitfire production. As it turned out, the raiders successfully reached and bombed Eastleigh – but the Supermarine facility was unscathed. Instead, the Cunliffe-Owen factory was bombed, bringing Hudson production to a standstill and over fifty people killed. Nonetheless, Supermarine was now very much a primary target, and it was just a question of time before both works were attacked.

Neither the Woolston nor the Itchen works exist today. Here we look across the Itchen towards the floating bridge's replacement, the massive Itchen toll bridge. The floating bridge's one-time slipway can clearly be seen.

The enormous air battles on Sunday 15 September, as Göring launched wave after wave of assaults on Britain, represented the Battle of Britain's climax. At about 1739 hrs the sirens sounded across Southampton, sending the populace scurrying for shelter. Eighteen Me 110s of *Erprobungsgruppe* 210, led by *Hauptmann* Martin Lutz, used cloud cover to stealthily approach Southampton before diving at a shallow angle, from 7,000 feet, approaching Woolston from the east. Bofors and other anti-aircraft guns banged away, but the Me 110s dropped twenty-three bombs on Woolston. Again, the Supermarine Works escaped any serious damage, just one skylight being smashed by flying debris. The adjacent residential area suffered though: terraced housing near the Spitfire factory and east of the railway line were devastated; six people were killed, nineteen seriously injured, and twenty-three more were treated for minor injuries at Royal South Hampshire Hospital. In total, thirty-four houses were destroyed; eighty-one so badly damaged that they were consequently demolished; 351 were badly damaged but repairable, 755 sustained minor damage. The charmed life Supermarine was leading was bound to end – and the enemy was determined to succeed in his destructive endeavour.

At 1335 hrs on Tuesday 24 September, Supermarine was again attacked at Woolston, local defence organisations recording how thirty-seven bombers,

All that remains of the Itchen works, the slipway and hard, a few hundred yards north from the Woolston factory site.

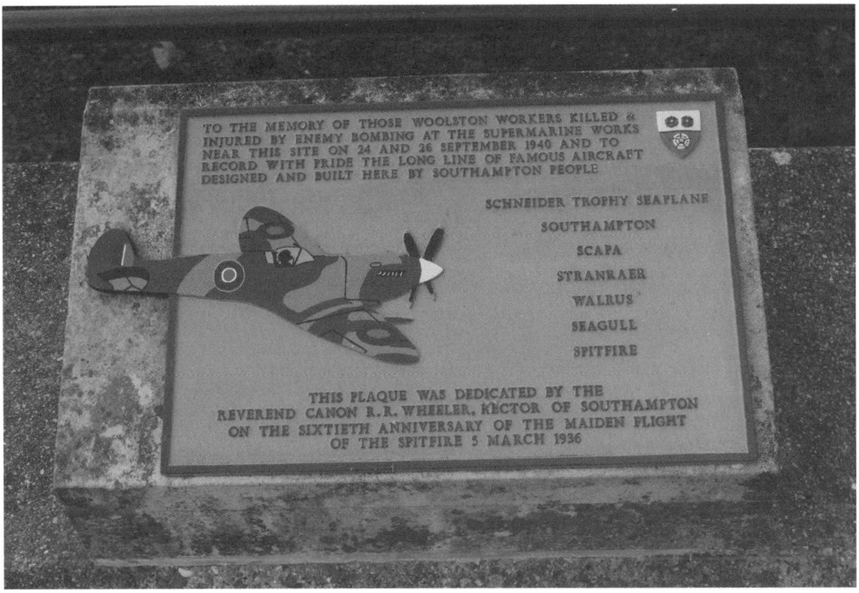

The memorial on the Woolston factory site to those 'Supermariners' who lost their lives during the raids on 24 and 26 September 1940. The works have been replaced by flats and a doctor's surgery.

escorted by fighters, dived from 20,000 feet, attacking Supermarine, the gas works across the Itchen, and the electricity power station next to Southampton's main railway station. Inexplicably, no 'Red Warning' was given, the sirens apparently sounding five minutes after the first bombs exploded. At Supermarine the drill was for the factory siren, signalling immediate evacuation to the shelters, to sound several minutes after the town's warning. On this occasion, before this happened, heavy anti-aircraft fire opened up. Cyril Russell, an 18-year-old 'Supermariner' working in 'K' Shop, next to the floating bridge, remembered that by the time he had exited the building and reached the nearby road, the noise of gunfire was 'terrific'. Looking up, to his left, young Cyril saw the raiders 'with bombs already leaving their racks'. With no time to reach the shelters, which in any case he had previously vowed never to do on account of the distance involved, Cyril flattened himself into the ground. Exploding bombs made the ground 'tremble and kick'. Then the gunfire stopped. The factory was again virtually untouched. At the northern end of the road, close to the Itchen Works, Cyril could see 'a lot of activity', towards which he made haste, joining 'people… with bags marked with red crosses, and metal stretchers… soon people, running, walking and stumbling, came towards

The location of the tunnel through the railway embankment behind the Itchen works, leading to the Peartree Green shelters, where many 'Supermariners' were killed on 24 September 1940.

us from the opposite way. Some looked dirty, others limped, and almost all had that strained, shocked look in their eyes.' Soon the 'cause of their distress' was all too 'apparent': 'The whole bomb load had dropped short, and straddled the railway embankment,' which was untouched, 'but had hit the shelters, the road, and the people making for them.' Cyril's account provides a graphic description: -

'It was obvious there were a lot of casualties; some poor souls had been blown up onto the railway embankment and lay like bundles of old clothing. Others had been blown into the embankment lower down, and were buried, or partly buried, by the earth thrown up from the craters. Here and there a limb protruded, or perhaps just the colour of an overall or jersey could be seen, and it was to these that the survivors who had collected their wits, and we luckier ones from the Woolston factory, turned our attention, tearing away the earth with our hands, lifting them out, trying artificial respiration, calling for stretchers, and, of course inevitably having to leave some lying there when we realised they were beyond our help.'

The use of High Explosive (HE) bombs dictated more damage to life and property in this raid. Forty-two people were killed, sixty-five suffered serious

Where the line of shelters was hit on Peartree Green, pictured in 2019.

injuries, 109 less serious. Again the Supermarine factory itself escaped, with only minor damage to the main building's east corner. In nearby Woolston, the railway bridge was destroyed, and collateral damage on both sides of the Itchen was substantial: eighteen homes were completely destroyed, fifty-three required demolition to finish the job, and 238 more sustained minor damage. Unexploded bombs (UXB) were numerous, causing chaos and dictating evacuation of the factory. Another threat, moreover, was incoming at 1624 hrs, sixteen enemy bombers approaching on the same course as the previous raiders. This time twenty-five tons of HE bombs exploded on the area around Supermarine, including Peartree Green and Radstock Road.

Amongst those killed when the shelter was hit were two teenage 'Supermariners'.

One of four children, with dark curly hair and bespectacled, Douglas Cruikshank was a 14-year-old 'workshop assistant', better known as a 'handy lad', of 6 Osterley Road, at the far end of Peartree Green in Woolston. Douglas's father Ronald was a Supermarine engineer at the Woolston Works, but, unlike his son, was at home when the raid occurred. As smoke billowed across the common immediately after the raid, Ronald dashed out onto Peartree Green, where some of his children had been playing – relieved to find his daughter Jean safe and well, after sending her home Mr Cruikshank hastened towards the main scene of destruction, hoping to find Douglas. That he did – but not alive. Jean did not see her father again until the following morning – overnight his hair had turned white.

That morning, there was also a shock in store for Cyril Russell, when his foreman, Bill Heaver, told him that a particular young girl, Margaret Moon, had been killed: 'He knew that a few weeks previously I had quite a crush on her, and we had gone to the Grand Theatre together. She was a secretary, and known to the lads as "the girl in green" because of the green outfit she wore, with a little fur hat. Her name was "Peggy" Moon, from Canada Road, and a lovelier girl one could not wish to know. Now she was dead, and how grateful I am that I was not the one who found her.'

The 'girl in green' was 19 years old.

This was a phase during the battle when the Germans were targeting the British aircraft industry. The day after Supermarine's shelter was hit, the He 111s of KG55 successfully attacked the Bristol Aeroplane Company at Filton. The next day, 26 September, KG55 achieved what other units had failed to do: destroy the Woolston Spitfire factory. Eight Fighter Command squadrons intercepted the raiders – but only after the target was hammered. On this occasion, the Supermarine Works was gutted, bringing production to a standstill. Although this caused a noticeable reduction in the delivery of new Spitfires over the next few weeks, it was too late to have any real

The grave of 14-year-old Supermarine 'Handy Lad' Douglas Cruikshank, killed on 24 September 1940, in a sad state at St Mary's Extra Cemetery, Southampton. Although descendants of Douglas were traced, no photograph of him could be found.

overall impact. Since July the huge Castle Bromwich Aircraft Factory near Birmingham had also been producing Spitfires, applying the automotive industry's mass production methods. In August, 149 Spitfires had been built at Woolston – and to the Southampton work force's great credit in October no less than 139 came off the line. During the destructive 26 September raid, however, a further forty-five people had been killed and further damage caused to surrounding property.

As the daylight Battle of Britain gave way to the night Blitz on British cities, Southampton continued to find itself a frequently visited target. By the Second World War's end, 630 Sotonians had lost their lives as a result of bombing, with 2,000 injured. Damage to property was substantial, the reconstruction process lengthy.

In total it is estimated that 43,000 civilians lost their lives due to bombing, half of them in London. Nonetheless, it is important to acknowledge that other locations were targeted by the enemy – not least Southampton owing to its status as a valuable deep-water port and association with the legendary Spitfire.

Today, no photographs can be found of either Douglas Cruikshank or Peggy Moon, their graves neglected at Southampton's St Mary's Extra Cemetery. As Cyril Russell rightly said, 'What a waste!'

Nineteen-year-old typist Margaret 'Peggy' Moon was another 'Supermariner' killed when the shelters were hit on 24 September 1940, and also buried at St Mary's Extra. No known photograph of Peggy, Cyril Russell's 'Girl in Green', exists today.

Chapter Thirteen

Pilot Officer Rogers Freeman Garland Miller

609 'West Riding' Squadron
Killed in Action: 27 September 1940

Rogers Freeman Garland Miller was born at Redlands, Radipole, Weymouth, on 15 July 1920, the second son of Thomas Charles, a farmer, and Frieda Esther Miller, both of that address and who had married in Weymouth during 1915. 'Roger', as he was widely known, was the couple's second son, John Garland having also been born at the same Dorset farmhouse on 31 August 1916. A sister, Lola, known to all as 'Sally', was born on 19 November 1925, and the Millers relocated to farm at Alveston Pastures, near Stratford-upon-Avon in Warwickshire. It was there that the family would be beset by tragedies.

John Miller attended King Edward VI School in Stratford between 20 January 1931 and 28 July 1934, after which he went into farming. Younger brother Roger attended the same school between 5 May 1932 and 4 April 1939. The School's Archivist, Richard Pearson, is able to tell us that Roger: -

'always had a particular affinity for rowing, and was a member of the most successful crew that the school ever put in the water. His friend, Richard Spender, wrote that "Roger was always remarkable for his perfectly natural and cheerful readiness to help, whether in small or big matters. This was all the more to his credit because his nature was in some ways rather sensitive, and he appreciated the various difficulties which arose in a rowing club. His unfailing good temper and good sportsmanship helped us to meet all the vagaries of fortune". Roger won the trophy for the Brickwood Sculls three years in succession, and returned it for further competition, although tradition entitled him to keep it. It continues to remain on display in "Big School". Roger had the fine physique and long reach which made a good oarsman, plus a natural instinct for leadership – he was Captain of Boats – inspiring those under him. "Towards other younger and less experienced boys",

Spender also wrote, "he was always considerate and sympathetic. Always a good companion, he entered into the humorous side of life in a club with great enjoyment".

'Roger was a great sportsman, excelling at rugby and playing a prominent part in many other sporting activities, winning sixteen cups and eight medals. In spite of his success, however, he remained remarkably unassuming, caring more about doing his best for the team than any personal recognition. He was wing three-quarter in the 1st XV (winning his colours), a member of the Shooting VIII, and Sergeant-at-Arms for the Debating Society, while throwing himself enthusiastically into a number of small parts in numerous productions by the Dramatic Society. It was written later of him that he had been one of the most popular boys at school (often he could be heard playing a ukulele in the Prefects' Study), a friend to every colleague, and the delight of his schoolmasters. He was the first boy to arrive with speed and noise at school on a motor cycle, and later the first to arrive by car – an Austin 7.'

Thomas Miller at his farm, Alveston Pastures, near Stratford-upon-Avon in Warwickshire. (Carey Parkinson)

While Roger was at King Edward's, his parents celebrated the birth of a daughter, Rebecca Rosalind Garland, at Alveston Pastures on 9 July 1937. Less than eight months later, poor Rebecca succumbed to pneumonia, dying where she had entered the world on 9 March 1938. The Millers were great friends at this time with the Thornley farming and brewing family of Radford Hall, some twelve miles from Alveston Pastures, at Radford Semele, near Leamington Spa; the families worshipped at St Nicholas's there, in which churchyard little Rebecca was laid permanently to rest. It would be the first tragedy to befall the hitherto happy family.

Life for the living, though, goes on.

At King Edward's, Roger was also Band Sergeant in the OTC, and decided upon a career in the RAF. Unfortunately, his application to become a Flight Cadet at Cranwell as a Direct Entrant was unsuccessful, so instead, together with brother John, he took an SSC, beginning elementary flying training on 12 June 1939. More advanced flying training was completed at Little Rissington in the Cotswolds, before Pilot Officer 42419 R.F.G. Miller reported for instruction at 5 OTU, at Aston Down, near Stroud in Gloucestershire, on 5 April 1940. At this time, Aston Down was one of two Spitfire conversion units, preparing new pilots to fly the type operationally (see Prologue). However, Fighter Command was also equipped with the twin-engined Bristol Blenheim, and it was to this type that Pilot Officer Miller converted. The Blenheim had initially been designed as a civil airliner, first flying in 1935, its performance sufficiently inspiring the Air Ministry to order a modified version as a light bomber for the RAF. With a speed of over 250 mph, the Blenheim was faster than the biplane fighters still equipping the world's air forces at that time; consequently, the aircraft was also pressed into service as a fighter, with the addition of a pack of four forward-firing Browning machine guns. As the 1930s progressed, the German Me 109's appearance, with a speed far exceeding that of the Blenheim, made the type obsolete as a day-fighter, a role subsequently fulfilled by the faster Spitfire and Hurricane. Nonetheless, certain squadrons remained equipped with the Blenheim fighter version, and required replacement pilots to make good losses. Having successfully completed the course, therefore, on 8 May 1940, Pilot Officer Miller, together with Sergeant Alan Feary, a VR pilot, reported from Aston Down to fly Blenheims at Northolt with 604 'County of Middlesex' Squadron of the AAF. Three days later, on 11 May 1940 – the day after Hitler attacked the west – Pilot Officer Miller was posted again, this time to Manston and 600 'City of London' Squadron, another AAF Blenheim unit, where he joined Pilot Officer John Curchin,

Alveston Pastures before the Second World War. (Marion Clayton-Wright)

with whom he had trained at Aston Down. Roger made his first flight with his new squadron on 12 May, an R/T test. On 15 May, together with a Flying Officer Smith, Pilot Officer Curchin and Sergeant Feary, Roger flew from Northolt to St Athan, from there to Manston, and back to Northolt. Such flights were important practice, and other similar sorties, including night-flying, followed.

On the continent, Hitler's unprecedented rampage through the Netherlands, Luxembourg and Belgium, into France, reaching the Channel ports in short-order, soon threatened Lord Gort's BEF with envelopment. On 26 May 1940, the reluctant and almost unthinkable decision was made for Gort to retire on and evacuate the BEF from the port and beaches of Dunkirk. Air Vice-Marshal Park and 11 Group then had to deal with another unprecedented circumstance: the provision of air cover for the seaborne evacuation, Operation Dynamo. Previously, Air Chief Marshal Dowding had only committed Hurricanes to the Battle of France, preserving his Spitfires for home defence. Now, there was no choice but to commit the smaller, precious, Spitfire force to battle, and over the French coast RJ Mitchell's iconic fighter would meet the Me 109 for the first time.

Owing to the losses suffered both by Hurricane squadrons in France and Spitfire units during Dynamo, replacement pilots were rapidly required for these units. The OTUs were unable to provide sufficient new pilots (again, see Prologue), so, acknowledging that the Battle of Britain ahead would primarily be fought by single-engined fighter types, replacements were posted to such squadrons from all over the RAF and even the FAA. So it was that on 11 June 1940, Pilot Officers Miller and Curchin, and Sergeant Feary, reported to fly Spitfires with 609 'West Riding' Squadron at Northolt. 609 was another elitist pre-war AAF territorial unit, locally raised, but now, after the Dunkirk fighting and as replacements arrived, largely comprising SSC and VR pilots, and including foreign nationals, the identity of these units was substantially changing, becoming increasingly diverse and consistent with the composition of other fighter squadrons.

609 had been formed at Yeadon on 10 February 1936, the ninth of the AAF's twenty-one squadrons. Initially equipped with the Hawker Hind biplane light-bomber, these were replaced by the Hart fighter version. In August 1939, when still a part-time squadron, 609 received the Spitfire. When war and mobilisation came, 609 flew first from Catterick, defending northern England, moving first to Acklington, then to Drem, near Edinburgh, providing cover to RN bases, convoy protection patrols, practice flights

Alveston Pastures today. (Marion Clayton-Wright)

and searching for unidentified aircraft on the radar screen. The squadron's first action was fought on 29 January 1940, when an He 111 attacking a merchant ship off the mouth of the Tay was damaged. On 27 February, Red Section shot an He 111 down which crashed into the sea.

Interestingly, having completed his service flying training on 27 April, on 5 May, Pilot Officer David Crook, a pre-war auxiliary of 609 Squadron, re-joined the squadron at Drem. Called up for full-time service in August 1939, just as 609 received Spitfires, Crook had not flown one of the new fighters when his training began in October. It is surprising, therefore, that he was not posted to an OTU for conversion to type, but returned straight to 609 Squadron. Before the formation of OTUs, that was how things were done, conversion to the type of aircraft a pilot would fly operationally being undertaken on the squadron. Crook's first Spitfire flight was on 6 May, but he did not go with the squadron to Northolt on 19 May owing to a knee injury. Subsequently, 609 Squadron, excluding Pilot Officer Crook, participated in Operation Dynamo, its pilots, like most in Fighter Command, with little or no combat experience, and none involving the Me 109 – which was a very different proposition to a lone German bomber. During just three days of fighting over Dunkirk, 609 lost five pilots killed; it was a rude awakening.

Around his neck, Pilot Officer Roger Miller proudly wore the silk 1st IV colour rowing scarf awarded to him at King Edward's (not an affectation or a pose, but a very necessary precaution to avoid painfully chafing the neck while searching the sky for threats). On 66 Squadron, the older and perhaps more worldly-wise Pilot Officer 'Dizzy' Allen's neck-scarf was the perfumed silk of a seventh veil dancer stolen from a London nightclub! Nineteen-year-old Roger now found himself pitched headlong into a man's world – only the previous year having still been a schoolboy. Tony Pickering, a Hurricane pilot with 501 Squadron, remembered: 'I was eighteen during the Battle of Britain. I came from a small village where everyone knew everyone else, we went to school, did our homework in the evenings and went to church on Sundays. We were innocents, really, the RAF was a bit of a shock, all these chaps who were going around nightclubs, and girls – it was something to touch a girl's arm at a dance then, not like it is now!'

On 29 June 1940, Pilot Officer Crook re-joined his depleted Squadron at Northolt: -

'A great change had come over the Squadron since I had left them only seven weeks before. We had a new CO and there were several new pilots to replace the Dunkirk losses. The old easy-going outlook on life had vanished, and everybody now seemed to realise that war was not the fairly pleasant affair that it had always seemed hitherto. Altogether the general mood now appeared to be one of rather grim determination.'

Being locally raised, with personnel not only often being friends but also related, these early casualties not only changed these squadrons' identities but hit them hard.

When Pilot Officers Miller and Curchin, and Sergeant Feary, reported as replacement pilots to 609 Squadron at Northolt, they had yet to fly a Spitfire, prompting the remark in the unit's ORB that 'None are trained'. Based in 11 Group, in south-east England, it was obvious that squadrons there required combat-ready pilots, because they could soon expect to be engaged with the enemy once more, requiring all hands to the pump and with no time to train replacements. Like Pilot Officer Crook, however, there was no option but to provide conversion experience on the squadron. Upon arrival the new pilots found their fellow pilots absent – to 609 was given the honour of escorting the Prime Minister to Orleans on his mission to try to persuade the French to continue fighting. There the Spitfires remained overnight, returning to Northolt the following day, flying several further such sorties over the next few days as these forlorn negotiations continued. France surrendered on 22 June 1940. 'Surrender', fortunately, was not a word in the British Prime Minister's vocabulary.

When Pilot Officer Miller made his first Spitfire flight cannot be ascertained, but his first operational flight was made in Flight Lieutenant Frank Howell's 'A' Flight, Spitfire L1065, between 0735 and 0810 hrs on 2 July 1940: 'Patrol and Reconn over Abbeville. Returned due to low cloud at 1,000 feet'. That evening, 'A' Flight, Pilot Officer Miller again flying L1065, reconnoitred Rouen-Dieppe-Abbeville, contacting no enemy aircraft but experiencing 'Heavy AA fire'.

On 4 July 1940, 609 Squadron was ordered from Northolt to relocate to Middle Wallop, inland of Southampton, in 10 Group, the intention being for the 'West Riding' Spitfires to provide some protection to that port – also home of the Supermarine factory building Spitfires – the naval installations of Portland and Portsmouth, and the aircraft factories inland at Yeovil and Filton. It was intended that the squadron's aircraft should land at the forward airfield at Warmwell, near Weymouth, proceeding to the Sector Station at Middle Wallop the following day. Owing to confusing and conflicting orders however, the move was chaotic, the aircraft not arriving at

Pilot Officer R.F.G. 'Mick' Miller. (Richard Pearson)

the Sector Station until 6 July. It was then decided that the operational flights would remain 'indefinitely at Warmwell', with the HQ and Servicing Sections being located at Middle Wallop. While this deployed the Spitfires closer still to the coast, there was a feeling that dividing the squadron in this way would reduce efficiency. Consequently it was agreed on 7 July that only one flight would remain at 'readiness' at Warmwell, south of the Wareham to Dorchester railway line, throughout the day, while the squadron would be based in its entirety at Middle Wallop, where the pilots would also be accommodated.

Of interest is that next day, Flying Officer John Newbury, and Pilot Officers Michael Staples and the half-French half-Armenian Pilot Officer Noel le Chevalier Agazarian, reported to 609 Squadron as further replacements, these pilots having already converted to Spitfires at 5 OTU. They were, in fact, the squadron's first replacements supplied by an OTU, the ORB documenting that 'Having all done a few hours on Spitfires, these pilots should be operational very shortly.' That replacements were needed was emphasised in harsh terms on 9 July when Flying Officer Peter Drummond-Hay, a married man, failed to return from an engagement off Portland when Green Section intercepted some Ju 87s but were bounced by Me 110s. Pilot Officer Crook shared a room at Middle Wallop with the missing pilot: -

'Peter's towel was still in the window, where he had thrown it during our hurried dressing eighteen hours before. Now he was lying in the cockpit of his wrecked Spitfire at the bottom of the English Channel… I took my things and went to sleep in Gordon's room next door.'

Flight Lieutenant 'Pip' Barran broke the news to Mrs Drummond-Hay, while after spending the night in Pilot Officer Gordon Mitchell's room, a depressed Crook spent the following day, 10 July, the Battle of Britain's official start-date, with his wife in London. He returned a day later to the shattering news that both Barran and Mitchell – the latter an old school friend – were missing from another clash with *Stukas* attacking a convoy off Portland. 609's new CO, 27-year-old Squadron Leader 'George' Darley, clearly had no mean task ahead overcoming the battering his new squadron's morale was taking.

609 was the sole Spitfire squadron operating from Warmwell until 12 July 1940, when joined there by those of 152 'Hyderabad' Squadron. Facilities at this forward aerodrome were basic, first opening as RAF Woodsford in May 1937 as a pre-war camp for units practising firing at the nearby Lulworth Cove bombing and gunnery ranges. The Watch Office lay halfway along the northern boundary, overlooking the grass airfield towards a row of dispersal pads on the western half of the base; two Bellman hangars were erected in the south-east corner, with seven blister hangars added later. Amongst 152's armourers was 19-year-old Aircraftman Ray Johnson: -

'The Station Commander, a Group Captain, paraded all Warmwell personnel about a week after our arrival. Until then we had operated from

609 Squadron at Warmwell after their big fight over Weymouth Bay on *Adler Tag*, 13 August 1940. Standing, from left: PO 'Red' Tobin (American); FO P. Ostaszewski-Ostoja (Polish); FO Henry Goodwin; FO E. Hancock; PO M.J. Appleby; FL F.J. Howell; SL H.S. Darley; FL H.J. McArthur; Sgt A.N. Feary; FO T. Nowieski (Polish); FO C.H. Overton; kneeling, from left: PO M.E. Staples; PO D.M. Crook; PO R.F.G. Miller.

the concrete apron in front of the hangars, but his speech altered all that; it went something like this: "One of these days in the not too distant future, the Hun is going to appear over those Purbeck Hills and knock three kinds of shit out of us. Therefore 152 Squadron is going to disperse to the far side of the airfield and thus try to ensure that as little damage as possible is occasioned. The hangar will only be used for major inspections and repairs". He was right about us being hit. We were, several times.'

Throughout this time, Pilot Officer Miller flew on 'A' Flight commitments, patrolling base, convoys and Portland. The 13th of July dawned overcast, a Channel convoy steaming westwards attracting sporadic attacks and the attention of German reconnaissance aircraft. By early afternoon, the ships were entering Lyme Bay, and just before 1500 hrs the three Spitfires of 609 and the Middle Wallop-based Hurricanes of 238 Squadron were scrambled to provide protection. Owing to having sensibly adopted a zig-zag course, the convoy, however, was behind schedule, so the Hurricanes found no ships – only about fifty enemy aircraft, equally surprised by the convoy's non-appearance. 238 Squadron destroyed a *Dornier* and damaged another, while the main enemy formation, Me 110s of V/LG1 adopted a defensive posture; Pilot Officer Miller, Yellow Three, reported: -

'I was on patrol with Yellow Section (led by Flying Officer John Dundas, Yellow Two was Pilot Officer Overton) at 4,000 feet looking for Convoy CRUMB which was not in position stated. Suddenly I noticed a large number of A/C circling at a great height on our starboard beam. I informed Yellow Leader and he told me to lead. I climbed right to one side of E/A, into the sun until I was 1,000 feet above. I waited for an E/A to break from the very wide circle in which they were milling. It was straight below and towards me. I fired a short burst ahead of him and he flew straight into it and disappeared underneath me. I regained height and waited again. Then a Do 17 came out of the circle across me. I gave three one second bursts from quarter beam ahead and then followed him round and opened again from 200 yards, following him closely and firing continuously up to fifty yards, throttling right back. This attack started from quarter ahead and developed through a quarter attack to more or less astern. I was overshooting and broke away as my ammunition was expended and there were so many Me 110s about. This A/C was later seen diving with the starboard motor on fire, going south.'

Although in what was his first action against the enemy, Pilot Officer Miller's attack on the Me 110 was inconclusive, pilots of 238 Squadron confirmed seeing the Do 17 heading out to sea 'with his port engine on fire and losing height rapidly'; it was credited as a 'probable'. Flying Officer Dundas destroyed an Me 110 with 800 rounds, but Pilot Officer 'Teeny' Overton was unable to gain sufficient height quickly enough and was unable to engage. Nonetheless, considering 609's run of bad luck to date, this result was certainly a 'good show'.

The rest of July continued much in the same vein, training flights for new pilots, interception patrols, clashes over convoys (none involving Pilot Officer Miller) and still further casualties: on 27 July, Pilot Officer Buchanan failed to return from a scrap with *Stukas* and Me 109s over Weymouth Bay.

During August 1940, 609 Squadron's personnel composition changed further still with the arrival of two Polish pilots, Flying Officers Nowieski and Ostaszewski – soon dubbed 'Novi' and 'Osti'. Furthermore, three volunteers from neutral America appeared, namely Pilot Officers Mamedoff, Tobin and Keough. Three of the remaining auxiliary pilots were posted away, leaving Flying Officers Dundas and Goodwin, and Pilot Officers Appleby and Crook, 'sole champions of the Auxiliary attitude in the Squadron'.

On 8 August, so much did the fighting intensify that 609 Squadron considered it to be the date on which the 'Nazi *Blitz* began'. What actually developed was heavy *Luftwaffe* attacks on Convoy CW9 – codenamed Peewit. Having sailed from the Medway on the previous evening's tide, the ships hoped to negotiate the Dover Strait hidden by the cloak of darkness. Their presence was detected by the new German *Freya* radar at Calais, leading to an attack by E-Boats – which sank three ships and damaged several more. As daylight dawned, *Luftflotte* 3 ordered a major attack, spearheaded by the Stukas of *Fliegerkorps* VIII, the objective being Peewit's total destruction. Isolated attacks during the early morning were dealt with by RAF fighters, the ships reaching Brighton around 1000 hrs. *Stukageschwader* 2, 3 and 77 were now being briefed to smash the convoy as it steamed south of the Isle of Wight after high noon. Escort was to be provided by a *gruppe* of Me 110s, and two *gruppen* of Me 109s. Soon a massive combat ensued, involving over 150 aircraft of both sides, lasting just twenty minutes. Earlier, 609 had reached Peewit too late to intercept a raid, but 'B' Flight, led by Squadron Leader Darley, pitched into the fighting that afternoon, the four pilots who managed to engage destroying five enemy aircraft. 'A' Flight, including Pilot Officer Miller, drew the short straw, having to patrol over base and missing the action. Nonetheless, it was a good day for

609 Squadron's chalk board at Warmwell on 13 August 1940, showing the 'score' after the 'Stuka Party' over Weymouth Bay – Pilot Officer Miller flew in 'A' Flight's Yellow Section with 'Teeny' Overton and Mike Staples.

609 Squadron, scoring victories without loss. It was, as Flying Officer John Dundas, a journalist, recorded in the ORB, 'a bad day for the navy'. Of the twenty merchantmen which set forth from the Medway, seven now lay on the seabed, while six more had put into various ports severely damaged; four escort and rescue vessels had also been damaged.

On 12 August, 609 Squadron 'had its second experience of massed German fighter formations – this time off Portsmouth and the Isle of Wight.' Pilot Officer Miller, flying Spitfire L1096, reported that at 1230 hrs, Angels 27, three miles South of Portsmouth, 609 Squadron encountered 'sixty-plus' Me 109s, 110s and Ju 88s: -

'I was Green Three. I became separated from the remainder of my Section when bandits were sighted as my machine was slower than my Section Leader's. So, I climbed for height on my own, positioning myself in the sun. I was unable to climb above the top layer of 110s, so I singled out three large bombers which were circling 4,000 feet below me at 20,000 feet. I dived down on them and did a beam attack on one which developed into a stern attack. I kept on flying until I overshot him… I climbed up again into the sun and dived on some 110s which were circling below me, but before I had time to open fire two 109s appeared above me on my tail, so I half-rolled away and pancaked. E/A by now was 15-20 miles out to sea. Machine was damaged – "heavily plastered". 110s and 109s had a higher ceiling than my Spitfire and I was unable to climb above them.'

The Me 110 attacked by Pilot Officer Miller was claimed as damaged. Significantly on that day Roger – or 'Mick' as he was known by his squadron mates (probably after the famous racing greyhound 'Mick the Miller') – was flying Spitfire R6915 – which can be seen today preserved at the Imperial War Museum in London.

It was on this day that the second tragedy struck the Millers: Pilot Officer John Garland Miller, of 149 Squadron, was killed. On the night of 11 August 1940, ten Wellingtons had taken off, P9244 captained by John and flown by Pilot Officer J. Body, detailed to attack enemy industrial targets at Gelsenkirchen. Upon return to Mildenhall at 0355 hrs on 12 August, according to the subsequent casualty report, 'The aircraft had asked for and been given permission to land on the flare path. It made a very low approach which was not on a direct line to the flare path and struck one of the masts of the wireless transmitting station near the top. The aircraft struck the ground very heavily and immediately caught fire… The wireless masts are seventy feet high and there was a single flashing red light on at the time of the crash. The flare path was almost directly into wind but aircraft have to pass fairly close to the wireless masts. The direction in which the flare path is sited gives aircraft the longest landing run with an approach which is unobstructed by trees. It is considered that the accident was due to an error of judgement on behalf of the pilot in approaching the flare path too low and too wide and trying to swing into the flare path from a line of approach which took him over the wireless masts.'

In addition to Pilot Officers Miller and Body, all of their crewmates, namely Pilot Officer Houseman, and Sergeants Scott, Cocks and Swift, were killed.

It is unknown when Roger discovered that his brother had been killed. From John's casualty file, preserved at the National Archive, we know that a letter from the Air Ministry to Mr Thomas Miller dated 14 August 1940 confirmed the content of an earlier telegram notifying him of his eldest son's death. It is reasonable to assume, therefore, that Mr Miller would have been made aware on 12 August, and that word would have reached Roger at Warmwell the same day. With the Battle of Britain hotting up, Roger had no option but to literally soldier on.

13 August 1940 would be a significant day – *Adler Tag* ('Eagle Day'). The *Adlerangriff* ('Attack of the Eagles') was, however, postponed until afternoon because of unfavourable weather. According to the 609 Squadron ORB, 'Thirteen Spitfires left Warmwell for a memorable tea-time party over Lyme Bay, and an unlucky day for the species Ju 87, of which no less than fourteen suffered destruction or damage in a record Squadron "Bag", which also included five of the escorting Me's. The enemy formations, consisting of about forty dive-bombers in four vic formations, with about as many 110s and 109s stepped up above them, heading northwards from the Channel, was surprised by 609 Squadron's down-sun attack. All thirteen of our pilots fired their guns.' Twelve of the Spitfire pilots made combat claims, amongst them Pilot Officer Miller, who made out the following report of a combat occurring five miles west of Dorchester: -

'I was flying Yellow Two, "A" Flight was scrambled to 17,000 feet when Red Four saw E/A flying below us. Red Leader led us into the sun in line astern, and we dived down astern on the nearest formation which comprised about twenty Ju 87s in vics of thirteen and seven. I selected a vic of three on the starboard side, opening fire at 300 yards, firing for five seconds.

Pilot Officer David Crook's Spitfire being turned around after the Weymouth fight on 13 August 1940.

The E/A did a steep climbing turn to the right then dived down with black smoke coming from its engine. Last seen diving in a wide spiral towards the clouds. I broke off to the right, diving, and did another stern attack on another formation below. I singled out three which were flying in extremely tight vics, opening fire at their leader at about 300 yards. As all three rear gunners were firing at me I yawed slightly from side-to-side, spraying all three. Before I broke away, the port E/A commenced a slight climbing turn to the right but was not smoking. As all my ammunition was expended, I pancaked.

'Before I made my attack I saw Yellow One shoot down one Ju 87 in flames.

'I was sixth to go into the attack and before I opened fire I observed at least five E/A going down smoking heavily. Red Section completely demolished a section of three.'

One Ju 87 was considered 'confirmed', the other accredited as a 'probable'. By the end of the day, forty-seven German aircraft had been destroyed against thirteen RAF fighters, three defending pilots being killed. The end result, therefore, was not the knock-out blow envisaged for *Adler Tag* by Göring, whose *Luftwaffe*'s ability to achieve aerial superiority was looking increasingly questionable.

The next day, the ORB described how 'Middle Wallop Station was raided by three twin-engined enemy bombers, who scored direct hits on our hangar and made a shambles of the offices. While attempting to close the hangar doors, Corporal Smith RW, LAC Thornley, H, and LAC Wilson, K, were killed, and Corporal Appleby, FH, admitted to hospital, injured.' In response, Sergeant Feary destroyed the Ju 88 concerned, and both Flying Officer Dundas and Pilot Officer Crook made further claims. Middle Wallop was attacked again the next day by a force of over fifty Ju 88s escorted by Me 110s. Less damage was achieved than by the previous day's lone raider, and in retaliation 609 Squadron claimed five of their assailants destroyed and two 'probables'. The day was not without loss though, as Flying Officer Henry MacDonald Goodwin, an Auxiliary pilot from Worcestershire, was shot down and killed over the Solent.

Pilot Officer Miller did not fly between 14 and 17 August 1940, it being likely that he was granted a '48' to attend his brother's funeral: on 15 August, Pilot Officer John Garland Miller was laid to rest alongside his baby sister Rebecca at St Nicholas's. The loss was the second tragedy to befall the Millers – but would sadly not be the last.

Readiness, September 1940. Pilot Officers 'Shorty' Keough (American), Geoff Gaunt and David Crook await the call to scramble from Warmwell; none would survive the war.

Although there is no record of it in either the 609 Squadron ORB or on the Aircraft Movement Card (Form 78), according to the diary of Flight Sergeant 'Tich' Cloves of 609's groundcrew, on 30 August 1940, 'A' Flight practised a 'quick scramble… Pilot Officer Miller, Spitfire L1096, was so eager to do his best, didn't wait for the starter trolley to be pulled clear, turned and damaged his rudder on it. New rudder required.' This aircraft was an early Mk I, test-flown at Eastleigh by Supermarine's George Pickering on 5 September 1939, and had been on the strength of 609 Squadron since 7 September 1939. Like other Mk Is, L1096 was upgraded in the field during the Battle of Britain to Mk IA configuration with the Constant Speed airscrew improvement, a great advantage over the previous two-pitch example. These early aircraft, however, lacked the automatic start of subsequent marques, requiring a cumbersome battery accumulator to be plugged into the aircraft, thus firing the engine. It was this that Pilot Officer Miller hit when swinging round into wind.

On 1 September, Pilot Officer Miller was in the 'A' Flight formation led by Flying Officer Dundas which was scrambled at 1100 hrs – this was a call from 11 Group for 10 Group reinforcements. At 1105 hrs, 'B' Flight also scrambled, the squadron making its way to and patrolling Guildford. Patrols of Brooklands and Windsor became a daily occurrence for the next week, although no interceptions occurred. On 7 September – 'Black Saturday' – the

Germans famously changed tack, switching attention away from 11 Group's airfields to bombing London. On that fateful day, at lunchtime Pilot Officer Miller patrolled Brooklands uneventfully with 'A' Flight, while 'B' Flight was successfully in action that evening. On the great day, 15 September, Pilot Officer Miller did not fly, but 609 Squadron was again in action over London, claiming two enemy aircraft destroyed in addition to a probable and a damaged. Pilot Officer Geoffrey Gaunt, a cousin of the Hollywood star James Mason, was shot down in flames. That afternoon, a 609 fought a second successful combat over Rye, after which a congratulatory signal was received from the CAS: 'Well done, once more'. Over the next week or so, patrols over both their own area of responsibility and that of 11 Group were continuous but largely uneventful.

On 24 September, again the Germans changed tack, this day heralding another change of target emphasis. Now it was British aircraft factories, including those in the West Country, which were in the enemy bombsights. Amongst the targets that day was the Supermarine factory on the Itchen at Woolston which was first attacked by the precision bombing unit *Erprobugsgruppe* 210 led by the brilliant *Hauptmann* Martin Lutz. Eight minutes later, twenty-four civilians and Supermarine workers were dead with another seventy-five injured. The effect on Spitfire production, however, was negligible. A further attack came in that afternoon, causing more damage and loss of life, 609 Squadron intercepting a formation of Me 110s and Do 17s over the Isle of Wight; the 609 Squadron 'Intelligence Combat Report', more commonly known as Form "F", provides the wider detail of this action fought between 14,000 and 17,000 feet: -

'Approaching coast on way to patrol Swanage at 15,000 feet, Sorbo Leader, Red One (Squadron Leader Darley), was told bandits had turned NE towards Southampton at 20,000 feet. He noticed AA fire over town and saw two loose enemy formations of Do 17s at 14,000 feet, and a rear formation of 12-15 Me 110s at 17,000 feet about three miles behind. He climbed 609 Squadron to attack first *Dornier* formation by sections, from quarter diving from 18,000 feet down-sun. This tactic completely broke up the formation.

'Red One attacked a Do 17 and an Me 110, receiving return cannon fire from the latter, which missed. Engagements inconclusive.

'Red Two (Sergeant Feary) and Red Three (Pilot Officer Staples) both sent *Dorniers* into the sea off the South coast of the Isle of Wight.

'Yellow Leader (Flying Officer Dundas), having damaged if not destroyed a *Dornier*, had an exhilarating dogfight with an Me 110 in which he found that he could easily hold his climb and turn inside him. He gave him a long burst at short-range after he had straightened out and sent him

An Me 110, with one of which type Pilot Officer Miller collided head-on in combat over Dorset on 27 September 1940. The German pilot miraculously baled out while his gunner and the Spitfire pilot were killed.

spinning into the sea. Having attacked the same *Dornier* as Red Two, he selected and damaged another.

'Yellow Four (Pilot Officer Ogilvie) damaged a Do 17 which went down towards the sea but levelled just above the water and may have escaped. Blue Section, acting as above guard, did not see E/A until they were too far out to catch.

'Green One (Pilot Officer Curchin) twice attacked a single-engined fighter, at which Green Two (pilot not known) also gave a burst. It went into the sea fifteen miles south of the Isle. This E/A and others with it were marked like Me 109s but were of different shape, resembling the French Morane.

'Sorbo Leader and Yellow Leader both comment on the accuracy of our AA fire and state it was very helpful in locating E/A.'

Pilot Officer Miller: -

'I was flying Yellow Three. My Section attacked from the starboard quarter. As Yellow One and I were attacking the same aircraft, I pulled up and attacked another aircraft from quarter beam above. I gave a two second burst which appeared to enter his cockpit. Red Two then attacked this aircraft, he followed it until it crashed five miles south of the Isle of Wight. I singled out another Do 17 and positioned myself to do a beam attack. As I turned towards him, he turned towards me and climbed very steeply. I attacked quarter in front and from below. I fired about three seconds. He was smoking heavily from starboard engine. Return fire from nose heavy. As I positioned myself for another attack, an Me 109 dived on my tail, shooting from long-range. He climbed away, but I was not able to find any more bandits, so I pancaked. Do 17 was last seen with white smoke coming from starboard engine, slowly losing height.'

The German bomber was claimed as a 'probable'.

On 25 September it was clear to the defenders that something was very much afoot. Firstly, aerial reconnaissance photographs revealed that nearly half of the improvised vessels assembled at Boulogne, Calais and Dunkirk, ready to transport Germany's invasion force across *Der Kanal*, had disappeared – providing clear evidence that the once-imminent threat of invasion had passed. Secondly, radar picked up some 200 enemy aircraft moving from the Pas-de-Calais west along the French coast. What the defenders did not know was that this redeployment was in readiness for a resumption of heavy day and night attacks on the West Country – beginning that day.

Reconnaissance had indicated to the German planners that there were no fighters based at Filton, home of the Bristol factory producing Blenheims and a variety of essential aero-engine types. Filton was also home to the new Beaufighter prototype, although whether German intelligence was aware of this is unknown. At 1100 hrs, diversionary raids were made on Plymouth, Falmouth, Swanage and Southampton, on both flanks of the main effort: at 1115 hrs, fifty-eight He 111s of KG55 *Greifen*, escorted by Me 110s, droned north over the Dorset coast, while simultaneously Portland was dive-bombed by Ju 88s. 10 Group incorrectly anticipated the target to be Westland Aircraft at Yeovil, scrambling three squadrons to the area. The *Heinkels*, however, passed ten miles east of Yeovil, travelling further north and reaching their undefended Filton target at 1145 hrs – just after Me 110s of *Erprobungsgruppe* 210 had marked the target. It was a perfectly executed attack. Some 100 tons of bombs were dropped, bringing all production to a standstill, causing 250 casualties in the factory and 107 more further afield. The railway line to South Wales was blocked, telephone lines cut; eight brand new Beauforts and Blenheims were destroyed with many more damaged.

Above left: The grave of *Gefreiter* Georg Jackstedt's gunner, *Gefreiter* Emil Liedtke, at Brookwood. (Kev Barnes)

Above right: The Miller family graves at St Nicholas, Radford Semele, near Leamington Spa, Warwickshire.

After turning south, homeward bound, the enemy formation was at last attacked by RAF fighters – amongst them Middle Wallop's 238 Squadron Hurricanes and Warmwell's two Spitfire squadrons.

609 Squadron reported: -

'A big battle just before noon, in which over 200 *Dorniers* and *Heinkel* bombers (author's note: there were no *Dorniers*, as was the case on previous days of combat when the type's presence was claimed), escorted by at least 30 *Messerschmitt* fighters, were chased and caught just south of Bristol. The city's AA fire, though well meant, was more than disturbing our pilots, none of which, however, were hurt. The Squadron obtained a very good bag, at the expense of only one machine (P/O Ogilvie's) damaged by enemy fire.'

Pilot Officer Miller had scrambled with the squadron at 1110 hrs in Spitfire X4107: -

'I was flying Red Five. Bandits were sighted over Yeovil and turned west, towards Bristol. My Section carried out a beam attack in echelon to break up E/A formation. I fired two second burst at 400 – 50 yards. Me 110s above started to dive on us, but promptly climbed rapidly again before in range. I saw no return fire from E/A. I climbed up again, positioning myself in the sun. I carried out a beam attack on main formation (five seconds, 300 – 150 yards). Me 110s diving down opened fire at long-range but broke away before coming close. I broke away and climbed. I then saw three E/A in straggly formation 3 – 4,000 feet below the main formation. I carried out a beam attack on the middle one, firing round to astern (rest of ammunition, 300 – 100 yards). Blue Two (Pilot Officer Agazarian) also fired at this machine, which crashed west of Bournemouth. Three of the crew baled out. It looked like a He 111. One He 111 flew low over the port, machine-gunning, but I had run out of ammunition, so pancaked.'

The *Heinkel* destroyed by Pilot Officer Miller and Agazarian was also attacked by the Hurricane of Pilot Officer Jackie Urwin-Mann of 238 Squadron. This raider was an He 111-P (2803), G1+LR, of 7/KG55, flown by the unit's *Staffelkapitän*, *Oberleutnant* Hans Bröcker, who remained at the controls and was killed when his bomber crashed on a clifftop house, 'Chatsworth', in Westminster Road, Branksome Park, Poole. *Oberleutnant* Heinz Scholz baled out but was found dead; *Unteroffizier* Josef Hanft also baled out, but expired before being recovered from Poole harbour; *Unteroffizier* Günter Weidner was killed due to parachute failure, but *Unteroffizier* Kurt Schrapps landed safely in the sea off Branksome Chine and was captured unhurt.

Roger Miller's sporting trophies preserved at King Edward VI School, Stratford. (Richard Pearson)

In total, 609 Squadron claimed the destruction of seven enemy aircraft destroyed, two probables and three damaged. In reality, the total of enemy aircraft collectively destroyed by RAF fighters in this action was five, with three more crash-landing in France; another was destroyed by AA fire over Bristol.

26 September started well for 609 Squadron with a congratulatory signal for the previous day's effort from the Secretary of State for Air. That afternoon, KG55's He 111s, escorted by ZG26's Me 110s, were back again – this time executing a precision carpet-bombing attack on the Supermarine factory at Woolston. In a single pass over their target, seventy tons of accurately dropped bombs brought production to a standstill, destroyed several new Spitfires and damaged twenty more. Thirty-seven factory workers died in addition to fifty-two in the wider area. 609 Squadron engaged the enemy over Christchurch after the bombing, a force of 'sixty bombers and twelve fighters'. 'A' Flight remained top cover, warding off enemy fighters, while 'B' Flight harried the bombers. Pilot Officer Miller was in the 'A' Flight formation, but was not amongst the 609 Squadron pilots who later filed combat claims.

Surprisingly, *Luftwaffe* intelligence analysis of reconnaissance photographs following the raid on Filton wrongly interpreted the damage as slight. Consequently, on 27 September, nineteen Me 110 fighter-bombers of *Erprobungsgruppe* 210 preceded the main force of thirty KG55 He 111s, escorted by twenty-seven Me 110s of II/ZG26, in another attack on Bristol's Filton factory. This time 10 Group was ready for them, especially given that the previous day 504 Squadron's Hurricanes had wisely moved from Hendon to Filton. Action was soon joined as the raiders were intercepted and forced to turn about before reaching their intended target.

At 1115 hrs, 609 Squadron was scrambled from Warmwell, Pilot Officer Roger 'Mick' Miller flying his usual X4170. The squadron ORB, however, lamented that 'For the second time in three days, 10 Group Control positioned the Squadron so badly that they had little or no chance of catching any of the bombers over the coast. Both flight commanders' R/T having failed, Pilot Officer RG Miller led the Squadron into an attack on the escort of fighters that were seen circling over Warmwell.'

Pilot Officer David Crook: -

'I was flying behind Mick and he turned slightly left to attack a 110 which was coming towards him. But the German was as determined as Mick and refused to give way or alter course to avoid this head on attack.

Their aggregate closing speed was at least 600 mph and an instant later they collided. There was a terrific explosion and a sheet of flame and black smoke seemed to hang in the air like a great ball of fire. Many little shattered fragments fluttered down and that was all. Mick was killed instantly.'

Also following Pilot Officer Miller was Pilot Officer 'Skeets' Ogilvie: -

'The 110 turned out to get his cannon working on Mick, and they hit head on. There was a terrific explosion, a sheet of flame and a column of black smoke. I glimpsed a Spitfire wing fluttering out and the white of a parachute with something on the end. It was ghastly. Somehow, I shot straight up, half-rolled, and coming down saw a 110 float under me. I pressed the button and kept it pressed and he went straight down in a sheet of flame. The whole vicious action lasted only a few moments.'

609 Squadron had engaged a defensive circle of III/ZG26 Me 110s south of Blandford Forum, soon after the enemy formation had crossed the Dorset coastline, heading north. Pilot Officer Miller, leading 609 Squadron's charge, had singled out a 9/ZG26 machine flown by *Gefreiter* Georg Jackstadt, raking the enemy fighter with machine-gun bullets in his first pass. Jackstadt broke formation, pursuing Miller at whom he fired several short bursts of heavier cannon-fire. The nimble Spitfire however turned and attacked the German head-on. Jackstadt met the challenge, both pilots giving no ground and firing continuously. At the last second, both pilots decided upon exactly the same course of action, pulling away upwards, with the disastrous result that their machines collided. Jackstadt's gunner, *Gefreiter* Emil Liedtke, screamed loudly immediately before the point of impact, upon which the 110's right wing collapsed, the aircraft catching fire and spinning away. Unable to jettison his damaged canopy, Jackstadt smashed out the Perspex panels of his burning cockpit, but was unable to force his way through the small aperture. Miraculously, the German pilot suddenly found himself thrown free, due to centrifugal force – losing no time deploying his parachute and watching with horror as his aircraft, with Liedtke still aboard, smashed into the ground on the boundary of two farms at Piddletrenthide. Jackstadt was rapidly taken into custody upon alighting by parachute, and entertained to a glass of lemonade at Doles Ash Farm before being taken away by the local bobby. After a night in the cells, Jackstadt was treated at Dorchester Hospital, and then escorted by two armed soldiers to London by train, doubtless bound for Colonel Alexander

Roger Miller's camera, also preserved at King Edward's, but I wonder what became of his photographs? (Richard Pearson)

Scotland's 'London Cage', the infamous interrogation centre housed in Kensington Palace.

According to Squadron Leader Darley's report on the incident, written three days afterwards, 'The two aircraft collided head-on, the Me 110 exploding in mid-air and the Spitfire going into a vertical dive with flames coming from the front part of the aircraft. A parachute was seen to leave the Spitfire, but it could not be definitely established at the time whether or not a person was in the harness. The wreckage of the Spitfire was subsequently discovered spread over a wide area and was brought to RAF Station Warmwell.'

Pilot Officer Miller – who was undoubtedly killed instantly – was found to have fallen to earth near Dorchester. At 0820 hrs the following morning, a telegram was sent to Mr Thomas Miller informing him of his second son's death in action: 'Regret to inform you that your son, Pilot Officer Rogers Freeman Garland Miller, is reported missing and believed to have lost his life as the result of air operations on September 27th 1940. Letter follows. Any further information received will be immediately communicated to you. Should news of him reach you from any source, please inform this department.' Having lost their eldest son, John, just six weeks previously, how the Millers felt is simply unimaginable.

Pilot Officer David Crook: -

'I remember walking into the Mess for lunch and sitting down and suddenly recollecting that at breakfast, only a few hours before, I had sat next to Mick at this very table and we had chatted together. And now, here we were at the next meal, everything was quite normal, and he was dead.

'That was one thing I could never get accustomed to; seeing one's friends gay and full of life as they always were, and then, a few hours later, seeing the batman start packing their kit, their shaving brush still damp from being used that morning, while the owner was lying dead in a shattered aeroplane "somewhere in England".'

Squadron Leader Darley wrote to Roger's parents: -

'During the time that I have been in command of the squadron I have had ample opportunity of judging your son's excellent qualities as an officer and as a pilot. He was unfailingly cheerful in all circumstances and we all feel his loss very much indeed and extend our sympathies to you and your family.'

The 609 Squadron ORB grimly noted that the popular young Pilot Officer Miller's loss was 'deplored by his associates'.

The *Stratford-upon-Avon Herald* report of Roger's death in action read: -

'One of the few, as the Prime Minister has said, to whom so much is owed by so many – yet the people of Stratford remember him as a schoolboy

Supermarine Spitfire Mk IA R6915, in which Pilot Officer Miller damaged an Me 110 on 12 August 1940, which can be seen today at the IWM London. (Peter Trimming/Imperial War Museum/CC BY-SA 2.0)

only last year. He was a charming personality, and he will be mourned by a host of friends.' One of whom wrote: 'Great as is our sense of loss, we who knew him cannot fail to be very grateful for having been privileged to be his friend and very proud of his fine record of unselfish service.'

The 20-year-old Spitfire pilot's funeral service and cremation was held at Perry Bar, Birmingham, and presided over by the Rev'd J.E. Hughes of St Nicholas's, Radford Semele, assisted by Rev'd Cecil Knight, the headmaster of King Edward VI School. On 3 October 1940, Roger's mortal remains were laid to rest at St Nicholas's, alongside those of his brother and baby sister.

In July 1941, the Millers were informed that Pilot Officer R.F.G. Miller had been posthumously awarded a Mention in Despatches for 'gallant and distinguished service'.

Roger's niece, Carey Parkinson: -

'With both sons killed, there was no point keeping the farm, so my grandparents sold Alveston Pastures in 1944, retiring to a house called "Pud Hill", at Woodchester, near Stroud. There they remained until my grandfather's death, aged seventy-four, in 1958. Afterwards, my grandmother, Frieda, moved to London, buying a mansion flat in Maida Vale; she was younger than Tom and thoroughly took to London life. My grandmother died in 1971, also aged seventy-four, and joined Tom, Rebecca and the boys at St Nicholas's. They were, of course, distraught at the death of both sons in such quick succession, but in those days, you grieved in private and just got on with it. My mother, the boys' surviving sister, Sally, joined the WRNS, meeting my father, coincidentally a FAA pilot.'

Richard Pearson, the King Edward VI School Archivist, adds: -

'For very many years, at the Battle of Britain Thanksgiving Service, held in the Guild Chapel in Stratford-upon-Avon, and conducted by the Chaplain of the Stratford Branch of the Aircrew Association, Roger was remembered by name. He is commemorated on the Alveston War Memorial, and also on the KES Boat Club Memorial in the Garden of Remembrance, and in the Memorial Library at King Edward VI School.

'In 2006, during a visit to the school Archive, John and Roger Miller's sister, Sally Brown, presented all the cups and medals that Roger had won at KES, and also the camera that he had apparently often carried in his Spitfire.

'The Brickwood Sculls Trophy was presented in 1928 by Sir John and Lady Brickwood as a prize for rowing; in 2011, the Brickwood Cup for Open Sculls was reintroduced in memory of Rogers Miller during the annual rowing on Benefactors' Day, and was presented by his niece, and Sally's daughter, Carey Parkinson.'

Strangely, both Pilot Officers Rogers and John Miller are also commemorated on the Australian War Memorial – although their birth certificates prove beyond doubt that neither had an antipodean connection. A possible explanation for this is that the abbreviation RAAF for Royal Auxiliary Air Force has been misinterpreted as 'Royal Australian Air Force', but even so, while Rogers belonged to an Auxiliary squadron, John did not, and in any case the Auxiliary Air Force did not become 'Royal' until 1947. This error has been pointed out and accepted by the Australian authorities, whose records have recently been corrected.

Of Pilot Officer Miller's friends on 609 Squadron, many did not survive the war. His Flight Commander, Flight Lieutenant John Dundas DFC, was shot down over the Solent on 28 November 1940, seconds after he shot down the German ace Major Helmut Wick; neither pilot was ever seen again. Pilot Officer Noel le Chevalier Agazarian was shot down and killed over the western desert and is buried far from home in Libya. Flight Lieutenant David Crook, a married man with children, was reported missing in 1944 when his Spitfire crashed into the sea off the Scottish coast, probably due to oxygen system failure.

The last line in this tale however goes, appropriately, to Roger's friend Richard Spender, who wrote and dedicated this verse: -

How brilliantly you flew for such short years,
Roger, across the small horizon of my life,
Like laughter, borne on shining wings!
Now you have sped into the Sun
And stand ennobled in proud robes of flame.
We can no longer see you.
For the light that clothes you is too fine a fire
For our dull, ordinary eyes.
But every day we shall remember you
In the brave glory of the golden sun...

To RGM (Fighter Pilot, killed in action, 1940)

Chapter Fourteen

Pilot Officer Philip Melville Cardell

603 'City of Edinburgh' Squadron
Killed in action: 27 September 1940

Philip Melville Cardell – commonly known as 'Pip' – was born on 26 September 1917, the eldest son of Harold Stanley and Elsie Louise Cardell, farmers of Manor Farm, Great Paxton Street, St Neots, Cambridgeshire. His brother Edmund, known to all as 'Ted', followed a year later, their sister Margaret being born in 1924. According to the *Biggleswade Chronicle* on 11 October 1940, Pip 'was a general favourite. He was always cheerful, bright, energetic and kind. He was educated at Paxton Park. After leaving school he joined his father and became a very efficient and capable farmer, with an excellent knowledge of both the practical and scientific sides of the industry. He thoroughly enjoyed various kinds of sport: hockey, badminton, golf and lawn tennis in particular. Sometime before the war started, he and his brother entered the RAF Volunteer Reserve for preliminary training. Mr Cardell was a Society Steward at St Neots Methodist Church.'

Pilot Officer Phillip Melville 'Pip' Cardell.

Pip's uncle, Jack Gawthrop, had been in the RFC during the First World War; stationed in America, he was an engineer working on the interrupter gear synchronising the firing of a nose-mounted machine gun through the turning propeller arc. Whether Uncle Jack's tales inspired his nephews to answer the call and join the VR, volunteering for pilot training, is unknown, but it is certainly possible. Either way, Pip and Ted became Reservists in May 1939, being mobilised on 1 September 1939. Their father struggled to cope on the farm alone, so requested that one of his sons be released from the RAF to help out, farming being a Reserved Occupation, meaning, since 1938, that both agricultural students and farmers were exempt from conscription. This had not stopped the Cardell boys volunteering, but their father's request, given the importance of food production, led to Ted, who suffered from airsickness, being released back to the farm. Pip remained in the service, soon swapping his tractor for a Spitfire.

After 'square bashing' and *ab initio* flying, Sergeant P.M. Cardell, as he then was, was posted to 15 FTS at Lossiemouth on 29 December 1939. With him was 19-year-old Sergeant Jack Stokoe, a miner's son from County Durham: -

'Only a year before the Battle of Britain began, my contemporaries and I were pursuing our civilian careers while learning to fly with the RAFVR in our spare time. The majority of us were eighteen – nineteen-years old. Being aircrew, when called up in September 1939, we were automatically given the rank of sergeant, which at first caused some dismay amongst the ranks of professional sergeants, many of whom had taken twenty years to reach that exalted rank!

'Most of us had only 50-60 hours flying on elementary types like Tiger Moths and Magisters when we were called up. After a brief spell at ITW to instil some discipline into us, we had about 100 hours on Harvards at FTS, which included a few trips actually firing guns.'

No 6 Course concluded at Lossiemouth on 10 June 1940, when Pip was commissioned, and, with Sergeants Jack Stokoe, Bill Read and others, was posted to 5 OTU at Aston Down near Stroud for conversion to Spitfires. Pilot Officer David Scott-Malden also reported for duty at 5 OTU, his route to a Spitfire's cockpit having been slightly different. A Cambridge graduate with a First in Classics and a former member of the Cambridge UAS, after flying training David had been posted to No 1 School of Army Cooperation at Old Sarum in Wiltshire. Flying Lysanders however was not exactly what he had in mind, and so he eagerly answered Fighter Command's call for volunteers. David's diary entries at Aston Down perfectly capture the atmosphere of those dramatic days: -

Wednesday 12 June 1940 Had a test on a Harvard and passed successfully into Spitfire flight. First solo an indescribable thrill. Felt a pretty king man.

Friday 14 June 1940 Paris falls. Astonishing to think of it in the hands of the Germans. Reynaud declares "Will fight on even if driven out of France". Marvellous days doing aerobatics in Spitfires.

Monday 17 June 1940 The French give up hostilities. Cannot yet conceive the enormity of it all. I suppose it will not be long before we are defending England in earnest.

Thursday 20 June 1940 Reports of another raid in South Wales. Fired eight Brownings into the River Severn for the first time. This getting up at 0430 am is beginning to tell.

Pilot Officers Richard Hillary and Noel le Chevalier Agazarian, both Oxford graduates (and of whom more later), were on the next course at Aston Down. In his classic memoir *The Last Enemy*, Hillary described his first Spitfire flight: -

'The Spitfires stood in two lines outside "A" Flight's pilots' room. The dull-grey-brown of their camouflage could not conceal their clear-cut beauty, the wicked simplicity of their lines. I hooked up my parachute and climbed awkwardly into the low cockpit. I noticed how small was my field of vision. Kilmartin swung himself onto a wing and started to run through the instruments. I was conscious of his voice but heard nothing of what he said. I was to fly a Spitfire. It was what I had most wanted through all the long, dreary months of training. If I could fly a Spitfire, it would all be worth it. Well I was about to achieve my ambition and felt nothing. I was numb, neither exhilarated nor scared…

'I taxied slowly across the field, remembering suddenly what I had been told: that the Spitfire's prop was long and that it was therefore inadvisable to push the stick too far forward when taking off; that the Spitfire was not a Lysander and that any hard application of the brake when landing would result in a somersault and immediate transfer to a Battle squadron. Because of the Battle's lack of power and small armament, this was regarded by everyone as the ultimate disgrace.

'I ran quickly through my cockpit drill, swung the nose into wind, and took off. I had been flying automatically for several minutes before it dawned

Brothers 'Pip' and Ted Cardell when both were sergeants in the RAFVR. (via Ruth Cornes)

on me that I was actually in the air, undercarriage retracted and half way round the circuit without incident. I turned into wind and hauled up on my seat, at the same time pushing back the hood. I came in low, cut the engine, and floated down on all three points. I took off again. Three more times I came round for a perfect landing. It was too easy. I waited across wind for a minute and watched with satisfaction several machines bounce badly as they came in. Then I taxied rapidly back into the hangars and climbed out nonchalantly. Noel, who had not yet soloed, met me. "How was it?" he said. I made a circle of approval with my thumb and forefinger. "Money for old rope", I said. I didn't make a good landing for a week.'

Soon afterwards, Hillary and Agazarian became aerial rivals, culminating in both flying a Spitfire between the arches of the Severn railway bridge. This, however, was nothing new for student pilots at 5 OUT. Pilot Officer (later Air Vice-Marshal) David Scott-Malden: -

'I remember very clearly that we treated flying under the Severn Bridge rather as a parting gesture when already posted to a squadron and reasonably safe from any complaints to the authorities. There are several large arches in the railway bridge, and two smaller ones on the Welsh side. I had long arguments with my great friend George Barclay about whether a Spitfire could get through one of the smaller arches. He decided that it could get through on the diagonal, i.e. with the wings at 45° to the horizontal, and we watched while he did so, with some relief at seeing him emerge safely the other side! Personally, I played it safe and used one of the larger arches… it would certainly not be recorded in anyone's log book, not if they were wise.'

Sergeant Jack Stokoe: -

'Upon conclusion of our course at Aston Down, with just ten to fifteen hours on Spitfires recorded in our log books, Pilot Officers Cardell and Read, the latter having also been commissioned, and I were posted to 263 "Fellowship of the Bellows" Squadron at Drem on 23 June 1940.'

When the Second World War broke out, 263 Squadron had been equipped with obsolete Gloster Gladiator biplanes, which it subsequently operated against the *Luftwaffe* during the following year's ill-fated Norwegian campaign. Tragically, on 8 June 1940, while being evacuated, all of the squadron's officers and a sergeant-pilot were killed when HMS *Glorious* was sunk by a Hipper-class battleship. Just two days later, 263 re-formed at Drem, equipped with Hawker Hurricanes. It has been reported elsewhere that when Pilot Officer Cardell arrived at Drem, 263 was flying a twin-engined Westland Whirlwind, but this is not strictly true: the 'Crikey', as it was known, did not arrive at Drem until 6 July 1940. In advance of that, pilots were given the option of remaining with 263 and flying twins, or being posted away to remain on singles. Pilot Officers Cardell and Read, and Sergeant Stokoe, all chose the latter, consequently being posted to fly Spitfires with 603 'City of Edinburgh' Squadron on 3 July.

603 Squadron was another Auxiliary unit, locally raised on territorial lines and formed at Turnhouse, near Edinburgh, on 14 October 1925. Having flown the DH9A, Wapiti, Hart, Hind and Gladiator biplanes, 603 received Spitfires in September 1939, the same month it was called to full-time service. Soon deployed as a defensive facility to the north of Scotland, 'A' Flight operated from Dyce to provide protection to the RN, while 'B' Flight went to Montrose as a defensive resource for the FTS based there. The squadron was therefore responsible for the great stretch of Scottish coastline between the Firth of Tay and Aberdeen. Flying consisted of patrolling and searching for lone German reconnaissance bombers, and innumerable day and night training flights. Action was comparatively rare, although on

28 October 1939, Spitfires of both 602 and 603 Squadrons engaged and shot down the first German aircraft to crash on British soil during the Second World War, a *Stab*/KG26 He 111 forced to crash-land near Edinburgh.

Pilot Officer Richard Hillary joined 603 Squadron's 'B' Flight on 6 July 1940. Pilot Officer Cardell, 'still bewildered, excited and a little lost', was a member of 'A' Flight. There being no shortage of pilots, new pilots had the luxury of accumulating more flying experience on Spitfires before being declared operational. Pilot Officer Read did not fly operationally until 18 July 1940, when his Yellow Section inconclusively attacked a Do 215 near Aberdeen; Sergeant Stokoe did not fly operationally until 29 July, when his Red Leader, Sergeant Caistor, sighted and attacked an He 111 twelve miles west of Aberdeen, which quickly jettisoned its bombs and scuttled off into cloud; Red Two, Pilot Officer Read, and Red Three, Sergeant Stokoe, did not get close enough to fire their guns. Pilot Officers Hillary and Cardell would not join an operational sortie until the following month.

On 20 August 1940, both flights of 603 Squadron were ordered back to Turnhouse. The pilots rightly sensed that a move was in the offing, and so it proved: Squadron Leader 'Uncle' George Denholm was to take his Spitfires south, to relieve a battered squadron at Hornchurch in 11 Group. There was

'Ted, Pip, Margaret, Jack, Edna, Harold, and Shirley, Xmas 1939'. (via Ruth Cornes)

great excitement, the squadron's youngest pilot, Pilot Officer 'Brody' Benson, according to Hillary, 'hopping up and down like a madman…' shouting "Now we'll show the bastards! Jesus, will we show 'em!".' The move took place on 27 August.

Sergeant Jack Stokoe: -

'By 27 August 1940, I had about seventy hours on Spits and was therefore most fortunate. I could have gone straight to a front-line fighter squadron from OTU, as indeed so many pilots did, and if so I would not have rated my chances of survival very highly. I had even already seen, but not actually engaged, two German reconnaissance bombers over northern Scotland. This was all invaluable experience which stood us in good stead.'

Four of 603's Spitfires were unavailable for the move south until that evening, so Pilot Officers Cardell, Benson, Pinckney and Hillary remained behind after the squadron had taken off, to fly the aircraft to Hornchurch later. At 1600 hrs, Benson led the small formation off, Cardell and Hillary to each side, Pinckney in the centre, navigating.

Twenty-four 603 Squadron pilots flew to Hornchurch that day; only eight would survive.

Benson's formation landed at Hornchurch at 1900 hrs and were shocked to find not just one section at readiness but four whole squadrons. Their own was already in action and soon Spitfires began returning with gun-smoke-stained wings. It was a rude awakening to the increased tempo and trauma of combat over south-east England: from this first sortie, Pilot Officer Don MacDonald failed to return. The following day, both Flight Lieutenant John Cunningham and Pilot Officer Benson – the latter having been so confident of what punishment 603 Squadron would dish out to the Germans – were both killed. On 29 August, Pilot Officers Read and Hillary and Sergeant Stokoe flew operationally. On the first sortie, between 1515 and 1700 hrs, Pilot Officer Hillary scored his first victory, an Me 109 destroyed, while Read claimed a 'probable'. Both flew on a second patrol between 1810 and 1930 hrs, during which Sergeant Stokoe claimed a 109 'probable', and Hillary another destroyed.

Sergeant Stokoe: -

'On 29 August I flew on our patrols, intercepting Me 109s on two of them. I claimed one damaged but the trimming wires of my own aircraft were shot away.'

Pilot Officer Hillary did not escape unscathed either. Separated from the squadron and without radio contact, the Spitfire pilot tacked onto Squadron Leader Peter Townsend's 85 Squadron Hurricanes, which was flying in open, or search, line astern formation, covered by a section of three 'tail-end Charlies', weaving from side-to-side at the squadron's rear. Hillary approached from behind and also began weaving. Townsend, a professional airman and experienced fighter pilot, was unimpressed, as he later told me: 'The sudden appearance of Hillary's Spitfire, the frontal view of which was not dissimilar to a 109, caused us momentary confusion in identifying an enemy attack when it came over Winchelsea. We lost Flight Lieutenant Hamilton, a Canadian and super flight commander, purely because the 109s were identified a fraction of a second too late. Hillary should have known better.' The 603 Squadron pilot was also shot-down, force-landing his Spitfire, unhurt, near Lympne.

Sergeant Stokoe: -

'The following day we made four more interceptions, during the course of which I was credited with having destroyed an Me 109 and damaged another. Again, however, my own aircraft was damaged, by a cannon-shell in the windscreen, and my hand was slightly cut by splinters.'

Pilot Officer Pip Cardell with his 603 Squadron Spitfire. (via Ruth Cornes)

The fighting was intense, with several pilots, including Squadron Leader Denholm, being forced to take to their parachutes. On 31 August 1940, 603 Squadron's Pilot Officer Waterstone was amongst the thirty-nine RAF pilots killed that day. At this time, the situation was critical, the enemy effort firmly focussed upon knocking out Fighter Command's all-important sector stations – amongst them Hornchurch. On that day, 603 Squadron received three replacement pilots direct from 6 OTU, namely Flying Officer B.R. MacNamara and Pilot Officers F.J. MacPhail and W.P.H. Rafter. The scene greeting them must have been horrendous: on that day, the Sector Stations at Hornchurch and Biggin Hill had been hit twice. The Hornchurch Station ORB records a vivid picture: -

'Mass raids continued to be made against our aerodromes, again starting early in the morning. The two attacks were delivered at 0830 and 1030 respectively and were directed at Biggin Hill, Eastchurch and Debden. The third attack was delivered at Hornchurch, and although our squadrons engaged, were unable to break the enemy bomber formation, and about thirty *Dorniers* dropped some 100 bombs across the airfield. Damage, however, was slight, although a bomb fell on the new Airmen's Mess which was almost completed. The only vital damage, however, was to a power cable, which was cut. The emergency power equipment was brought into operation until repair was effected. Three were killed and eleven wounded. 54 Squadron attempted to take off during the attack and ran through bombs. Three aircraft were destroyed, one being blown from the middle of the landing field to outside the boundary, but miraculously all three pilots escaped with only minor injuries.

'The fourth attack of the day was also directed at Hornchurch, and once again, despite strong fighter opposition and AA fire, the bombers penetrated our defences. This time, however, their aim was inaccurate, and the line of bombs fell from them towards the edge of the aerodrome. Two Spitfires parked near the edge of the aerodrome were written off, and one airman was killed. Otherwise, apart from the damage to dispersal pens, the perimeter track and the aerodrome surface, the raid was abortive and the aerodrome remained serviceable. Our squadrons, which had a very heavy day, accounted for no less than nineteen of the enemy and a further seven probably destroyed, 603 Squadron alone responsible for the destruction of fourteen enemy aircraft. Although we lost a total of nine aircraft, either on the ground or in combat, only one pilot was lost.'

Sergeant Stokoe: -

'On 1 September came three more interceptions of twenty-plus bandits, one of which, an Me 109, I shot down in flames over Canterbury.'

According to the 603 Squadron Intelligence Report, Jack had been attacked by a single Me 109 at 3,000 feet over Canterbury, while the squadron was patrolling the Manston area. This was also Pilot Officer Cardell's first recorded operational flight with 603 Squadron, but forced to land at an unrecorded location in Spitfire L1020 owing to 'oil trouble'. He was, nevertheless, back in the air the following day, in Spitfire X4274, participating in the second sortie described below by Jack.

Sergeant Stokoe: -

'On 2 September, I was involved with two more interceptions, during the course of the last of which I damaged two enemy aircraft but was myself shot down in flames, fortunately baling out. On that occasion, as I was attacking an enemy aircraft I remember machine-gun bullets, or maybe cannon shells, hitting my Spitfire, followed by flames in the cockpit as the petrol tanks exploded. I thought "Christ! I've got to get out of here and *quick*!" I undid the straps and opened the hood, but this turned the flames into a blowtorch. I was not wearing gloves, as during our hasty scramble I had forgotten them, but had to put my hands back into the fire to invert the Spitfire so that I could drop out (no ejector seats in those days!). I remember seeing sheets of skin peeling off the backs of my hands before I fell out of the aeroplane. I was then concerned regarding whether the parachute would function or whether it had been damaged by fire, but I pulled the ripcord and fortunately it opened perfectly.

'I landed in a field, but the Home Guard queried whether I was an enemy agent! A few choice words in English soon convinced them I was genuine, and thereafter I was rushed into the emergency hospital at Leeds Castle, suffering from shock and severe burns to my hands, neck and face.

'I was in hospital for six weeks before returning to operational duties on 22 October, with further combat successes. A second tour of duty with 54 Squadron followed, which included a second bale out (over the sea!). I was then seconded to a training unit but returned to "ops", flying fighters, later in the war.

Holy Trinity, Great Paxton, Huntingdonshire.

'The point about the incident when I was shot down over Kent on 2 September is that at the time 603 Squadron was suffering such heavy casualties that administration got pretty chaotic. For four days after baling out, although quite safe in hospital, I was officially posted "Missing in Action"!'

During those early days of action with 11 Group, 603 Squadron had to learn quickly, and rapidly determined not to be 'bounced'. Squadron Leader Denholm would fly on a reciprocal of the course given by the Controller, until at 15,000 feet when he would turn the squadron about, still climbing. This way 603 Squadron often saw the enemy striking inland below them, and, enjoying the advantage of height, were in a perfect position to intercept. Breaking away from the officially accepted vic of three aircraft, Denholm devised a new system whereby a pair of Spitfires would fly together, offering mutual support. Recent exhaustive research by John Alcorn suggests that 603 was actually Fighter Command's top scoring squadron in the Battle of Britain; if this is so, and I believe it is, George Denholm's tactical awareness and application of original thought must take the lion's share of credit for this accolade. Moreover, unlike many squadron commanders, 'Uncle George' led his squadron, virtually without exception, on every sortie during the Battle of Britain, in addition to performing numerous administrative tasks.

The day after Jack Stokoe went down over Leeds Castle, Pilot Officer Cardell was up again with the squadron, participating in the action during which Pilot Officer Hillary fell victim to *Hauptmann* Erich Bode, *Kommandeur* of II/JG 26 – and also dropped from the fight in flames. Miraculously, Hillary was thrown clear of his blazing Spitfire and although terribly burned managed to deploy his parachute. Two hours later he was rescued from the Channel by the Margate lifeboat, close to death. Cared for by the remarkable surgeon Sir Archibald McIndoe, Hillary subsequently became a 'Guinea Pig' at East Grinstead's now famous Burns Unit. Tragically, while training to be a night fighter pilot, Hillary would be killed in 1943.

Given the casualties and intensity of combat, it was no longer possible for 603 Squadron to break new pilots in gently. Pilot Officer Cardell was now on the board for many sorties, and on 5 September the inexperienced Pilot Officer Rafter flew his first patrol – only to be shot down and wounded within a few seconds of meeting the enemy.

Squadron Leader George Denholm: -

'After an engagement, the Squadron would come home either individually or in ones and twos in intervals of about two minutes. About an hour after landing I used to check to see if anyone was missing. Sometimes a phone call would be received from a pilot who had perhaps forced landed elsewhere, or baled out and was safe, which was always news well received. Other times we would be informed by recovery team of the identity of a crashed Spitfire and pilot.'

On 11 September, poor weather in the morning delayed the enemy's main effort until the afternoon. At 1500 hrs, the He 111s of I and II/KG26 left their French bases, rendezvousing with their 200-strong fighter escort, heading for London via the Thames Estuary. At 1516 hrs Squadron Leader Denholm scrambled with 609 Squadron, Pilot Officer Cardell flying

Spitfire X4323. From 1530 hrs onwards, RAF fighters attacked the raiders – albeit after they had bombed their dockland targets. The Me 110 escorts withdrew southwards, forming a defensive circle over Croydon, covering the bombers' shortest exit route, out over the Kentish coast between Dover and Dungeness. Inaccurate routing on the incoming journey, however, led to a substantial number of escorting Me 109s expending too much fuel and having to break off early – leaving the *Heinkels* with little protection. Unsurprisingly the bombers suffered heavy losses: ten were shot down and twelve more damaged. Pilot Officer Cardell was amongst the successful 603 Squadron pilots, intercepting an He 111 half-a-mile north of Margate at 1610 hrs: -

'I saw an He 111 going east, on which I made one stern attack, opening fire at 300 yards, closing to forty yards. Then I did four quarter attacks, when white smoke came from one of the engines. Having fired all my rounds, I broke off the attack.'

Pip claimed a 'probable', but was credited with a 'damaged'.

On 16 September, Flying Officer Peter Grenfell Dexter DFC, a 22-year-old South African who had taken an SSC in December 1938, joined 603 Squadron at Hornchurch. Dexter had initially flown Lysanders with 16 Squadron as an

Above left: Pilot Officer Cardell's unique grave marker at Holy Trinity: the sundial he built at the family farm.

Above right: The medals, including coveted Battle of Britain Bar, of Pilot Officer Cardell (Philip Harvey)

Army Cooperation pilot, serving in France. On 21 May 1940, while flying a tactical reconnaissance of Arras/Cambrai/Amiens, Dexter was attacked by Me 109s. Remarkably, he subsequently destroyed one using his sole forward-firing gun, while his rear gunner shot down another. Although his aircraft was badly damaged, Dexter returned safely to base, later being awarded the DFC for his gallantry and skillful flying. After the Fall of France, 16 Squadron was stationed at Redhill, Peter volunteering to fly fighters and reporting to 7 OTU Hawarden for conversion to Spitfires on 22 August. On 3 September he joined 54 Squadron at Catterick, but after five operational sorties was sent south to Hornchurch. The day after arriving, Pilot Officer Dexter joined 603 Squadron's afternoon scramble, making no combat claim. On 23 September, Pilot Officer Cardell flew for the first time since making his first combat claim on 11 September, as did Pilot Officer Dexter, but were not amongst 603's successful pilots that day. Neither would fly again until 27 September.

The gallant Flying Officer Peter Dexter DFC sadly did not survive the war: on 14 July 1941, the South African collided with another Spitfire over France and was killed.

On that fateful day, at 0815 hrs, a large formation of German fighters swept over southern England, and were engaged by certain of 11 Group's squadrons. The enemy were in no rush to withdraw however – ensuring that when the next raid was incoming, Air Vice-Marshal Park's fighters would be on the ground, being refuelled and rearmed. Just before mid-day, the radar screens were alive with activity, as a big raid assembled and struck out for the Kentish coast. At 1146 hrs, Squadron Leader Denholm, operating from Hornchurch's forward airfield at Rochford, scrambled with nine other 603 Squadron Spitfires, including Pilot Officers Dexter (N3100) and Cardell (N3244), to patrol Hornchurch. At noon, some 300 bandits crossed the coast between Dover and Lympne, heading for Chatham. The bombers, Ju 88s of I and II/KG77, having arrived late at their intended rendezvous, were without fighter protection. Some 120 Spitfires and Hurricanes fell on them, destroying eleven raiders, but the bombers' frantic assistance shouts brought Me 109s and 110s rushing to the scene, a huge air battle developing over 'Hellfire Corner'.

When at 18,000 feet over Maidstone, 'four Me 109s', according to the squadron's Form "F", 'went across the bows' of 603 Squadron. 'The Squadron chased them and they turned east. When in mid-Channel, two of the 109s turned about, flying back towards England.'

Pilot Officer Dexter reported at 1200 hrs he was mid-Channel, flying at between 100 and 500 feet: -

'I was flying Number Two in the Guard Section.... after the Squadron had engaged the enemy, I saw one Me 109 returning to France. I turned and engaged it. Another Me 109 attacked me from the rear but a Spitfire, which I later identified as one flown by Pilot Officer Cardell, came to my assistance. Pilot Officer Cardell and I chased the two aircraft towards France and shot them both down about ten miles off the French coast. One enemy pilot baled out. As we circled the pilot, five more Me 109s came towards us out of the sun.

'After a short engagement I could see Pilot Officer Cardell heading for home. I followed him and tried to contact him over the R/T, but he had removed his helmet, and appeared to be having difficulty with the aircraft.

'A quarter of a mile off Folkestone beach, at a height of 300 feet, Pilot Officer Cardell baled out. His parachute did not open. I saw him hit the water and rise to the surface almost immediately.

'Five minutes elapsed, and no apparent effort at rescue had been made from the shore, so called up my home base to ask them to have something done, but got no reply. I decided to "crash-land" on the beach and organize a rescue boat myself. It took some time to get the boat launched, and we reached Pilot Officer Cardell at least 35 minutes after he hit the water. Artificial respiration was applied in the boat, and for thirty minutes after we got him to the shore, but he showed no signs of life... I phoned a report to Operations as soon as possible.'

Dexter's frustration is more evident in the 603 Squadron's Form 'F', which describes how 'Pilot Officer Dexter DFC and Pilot Officer Cardell were together when Pilot Officer Cardell was fired at by two Me 109s. Pilot Officer Cardell baled out from 500 feet, 400 yards out to sea off Folkestone. His parachute failed to open, but he came up immediately and was floating head-up, well above the water. The machine crashed near him. Pilot Officer Dexter circled for ten minutes, calling up "Rival" and 603 Squadron but got no reply. There were several people on the beach and he tried to attract their notice. As they showed complete apathy and no boats put out, he crashed his machine on the beach and after much waste of time, got a boat from a fisherman – but by then Pilot Officer Cardell was drowned. A naval launch arrived on the scene an hour later.'

Given that Pilot Officer Cardell had removed his helmet and was struggling to control his Spitfire, it is likely that his head injuries were suffered when attacked by the 109s. Notwithstanding that and that he had baled out very low, his parachute failing to open, a doctor present declared the cause of death to be drowning.

Pilot Officer Dexter had performed an incredibly gallant act, trying to save his friend – yet more distinguished conduct from an exceptionally brave young pilot.

Flying Officer Dexter's grave at Samer Communal Cemetery, France. (via Kev Barnes)

On 30 September 1940, Mr Cardell received the usual formal letter from the Air Council confirming details of the earlier telegram dated 28 September, notifying him of his eldest son's death in action – the day after his twenty-third birthday. Pip's body was taken home and buried in Holy Trinity churchyard, Great Paxton. There, where his grave can be found today, Pilot Officer Cardell has a unique memorial – no headstone but a sundial, moved from a pond he constructed in the garden of Manor Farm (although, strangely, on the privately-erected accompanying plaque, his date of death is incorrectly given as 1 September 1940).

For Pilot Officer Dexter, the war went on. On 30 September, promoted to Flying Officer, he destroyed another 109, but was himself shot down on 2 October, having destroyed a further German fighter, baling out wounded. After a period of hospitalisation, he returned to 603 Squadron in April 1941, moving to 611 Squadron at Hornchurch in June. By now, Fighter Command was taking the war across the Channel, the so-called 'Non-Stop Offensive' in full swing, so a very different scenario to the defensive battles of 1940. After more combat success, on 14 July Flying Officer Dexter collided with Sergeant Panter of 54 Squadron over Boulogne. Both took to their parachutes, Panter landing safely and becoming a prisoner, but the gallant Dexter was found dead in his parachute. The South African, also 23, was buried at Samer Communal Cemetery in France, yet another serviceman a long way from home. Further words would be superfluous.

Chapter Fifteen

Oberleutnant Lothar Siegfried Stronk

8 Staffel, Jagdgeschwader 53 'Pik As'
Killed in Action: 2 October 1940

Lothar Siegfried Stronk – known as Siegfried – was born during the First World War, on 12 February 1915, at Turawa, Upper Silesia, the son of Anton Stronk, a teacher, and his wife Martha. Eventually, Germany defeated, the guns fell silent, on 11 November 1918, but it was a troubled peace into which Siegfried's younger brother Wolfram was born on 17 November 1919 and the Stronk brothers would spend their formative years.

On 7 May 1919, the terms of the Versailles Peace Treaty were announced, provoking a strong reaction from the German people – who considered the Allies' conditions too harsh and the Treaty nothing more than a *Diktat*. In particular, the Germans were incensed at the infamous 'War Guilt Clause' in which they were forced to accept sole responsibility for causing the war. Furthermore, Germany was expected to pay enormous reparations, and lost its overseas colonies and some German territory. Traditionally Versailles has been considered unreasonable and a primary cause of the Second World War. More recent interpretations, however, disagree, signposting evidence that Germany planned the First World War two years before it began, arguing that the subsequent global conflagration owed more to the Allies' failure to enforce the Treaty than its actual provisions. Be that as it may, the fact is that German nationalists were infuriated by Versailles and the apparent capitulation of their new democratic Weimar government. These volatile circumstances, coupled with hyperinflation, saw Germany descend into the darkness of revolutionary politics. This is not the place to recount the rise of Hitler and the Nazis, but that such an extreme right-wing political party came to power and waged a racial war, ultimately concluding in Germany's virtual destruction, remains a tragedy for mankind as a whole.

Returning to Versailles, relevant to our story is that the Air Clauses were intended to prevent a resurrection of the German Flying Corps. Consequently, Germany surrendered over 15,000 aircraft and 27,000 aero engines.

Oberleutnant Siegfried Stronk. (Florian Stronk)

The Treaty however did not prevent Germany possessing or manufacturing civil aircraft. The opportunity was immediately seized, therefore, to develop and expand civil and commercial aviation, including airlines, flying clubs and schools to train both air and ground crews. Behind this innocent façade the foundations of a new – illegal – air force were soon being laid. As early as 1920, General von Seeckt, the Chief of the Army Command at the *Reichswehr Ministerium*, was convinced that German military aviation must be revived. Certain officers whose names were later to become famous as commanders in Hitler's *Luftwaffe*, including Sperrle, Kesselring and Stumpff, were given responsibility for various aspects of military aviation and secreted away in von Seeckt's ministry.

By 1926, Germany was widely considered the most air-minded nation in Europe. The German society for aviation enthusiasts, the *Deutscher Luftsportverband*, founded in 1920, exceeded 50,000 members by the end of that decade. Again, von Seeckt was behind this, encouraging an interest in gliding to circumvent Versailles. Thus Germany had no shortage of air-minded youngsters eager to aspire to powered flight – and who already had air experience. Although the Paris Air Agreement of 1926 considerably restricted the number of service personnel permitted to fly, von Seeckt succeeded in creating a secret cadre of trained aircrew. These men were trained in the schools set up for the commercial airline *Deutsche Lufthansa*, and in a top-secret military flying training school at Lipetz in Russia. When Adolf Hitler and the Nazis came to power in Germany in January 1933, no time was lost in creating the new *Luftwaffe* – and many who had become intoxicated by gliding with the Hitler Youth were enthusiastic volunteers. Among them was Siegfried Stronk.

Between 1933 and 1939, Germany's neighbours considered the new *Luftwaffe* to be the greatest threat to their national security. The aeroplane, even more than the tank, was viewed as *the* offensive weapon of the future, the very embodiment of both the totality and the brutality of modern industrial warfare. Indeed, air power was seen as fundamental to the achievement of Hitler's expansionist aims in foreign policy. At first Hitler intended to achieve *Lebensraum* in the east. Britain, he thought, would either ally itself with him or at least not intervene. It soon became clear, however, that Britain was trying to prevent this. From that point on Hitler had to consider a major war against Britain and mobilise German resources rapidly. Initially, therefore, the *Luftwaffe* was conceived as a comparatively short-range force in anticipation of war with Germany's Polish neighbour to the east and French to the west. But it was the people of Britain who feared German air attack more than any other nation. The concern was increased when Nazi Germany withdrew from the League of Nations and the disarmament conference in 1933. The following year, Baldwin, who had famously endorsed the view that 'the bomber would always get through', told the House of Commons that Germany's progress in military aviation meant that the aerial defence of Britain no longer began at the White Cliffs of Dover but at the Rhine. In 1935, Hitler was sufficiently confident to blatantly contravene Versailles and reveal to the world his new *Luftwaffe*.

Hitler's deputy, Göring, a Great War fighter ace, was made head of the new German air force. This was a turning point, as with the Deputy *Führer's* political influence the *Luftwaffe's* status increased in terms of rearmament. At its inception this new independent air service's strength stood at 1,888 aircraft of all types, and 20,000 personnel, supported by thirty to forty airframe and engine manufacturers. The *Luftwaffe* immediately began improving its aircraft and testing them in competitions all over Europe and in large-scale air exercises at home. Influenced by the same factors as British aircraft designers, the emphasis on German aircraft development in the mid-1930s revolved around the monoplane. By 1935 the prototypes of many German aircraft which would become so familiar in the Second World War began appearing. In 1920 Professor Hugo Junkers opened a factory in Dessau; in 1922 Ernest Heinkel built an aircraft factory at Warnemuende; Claude Dornier began production in Friedrichshafen; in 1924 Heinrich Focke and George Wulf founded the Focke-Wulf aircraft company at Bremen. While all of these would produce bombers and fighters providing the mainstay of the *Luftwaffe* throughout 1939-45, most important to this story is the fact that Professor Willy Messerschmitt took over the *Bayerische Flugzeugwerke* (BFW) at Augsburg and began producing sporting aeroplanes. By 1934, Messerschmitt had designed a monoplane, the Me 108 *Taifun*, as an entrant in an international aviation contest, the *Challenge International de Tourisme*, held in Poland. The 108 came fifth, sixth and tenth, but its overall performance was impressive. Already, though,

Messerschmitt was working on a new monoplane fighter incorporating the features found in his *Taifun* – and from 108 to 109 would be a short step.

During 1933, the technical department of the *Reichsluftministerium* (RLM), known as C-*Amt*, reported on the conclusions of their research into the application of modern technology to air combat. C-*Amt* considered that to meet future needs of German air power, four types of military aircraft were needed: a multi-seat medium bomber, a tactical bomber, a single-seat fighter and a two-seater fighter. The single-seater, which would replace the existing He 51 and Ar 68 biplane fighters, was required to have a top speed of at least 250 mph at 19,690 feet, achieving that height in seventeen minutes with a maximum operational ceiling of 30,000 feet. Thus far the German requirement was almost identical to the RAF's specifications F.36/34 and F.37/34. Submissions were made by Arado, Focke-Wulf, Heinkel and BFW. Designs by the first two companies were immediately rejected, leaving Heinkel's He 112 and Messerschmitt's Me 109. Messerschmitt's new fighter first flew in May 1935 – six months before the Hurricane and nearly a year before the Spitfire.

Messerschmitt's new monoplane fighter was based entirely upon the principal of producing the smallest and therefore lightest airframe around the most powerful engine – initially a Rolls-Royce Kestrel. The so-called 'Augsburg Eagle' featured a metal-alloy framework, flush-riveted stressed metal covering, leading-edge wing slots in conjunction with slotted trailing-edge flaps which increased the wing area on demand, retractable main undercarriage, and an enclosed cockpit with a jettisonable canopy – another farsighted consideration. As there was no requirement for wing-mounted armament, the 109's wing was extremely thin, the main spar being situated at the mid-chord point. In fact, it became necessary to strengthen the join of the wings and fuselage. Torque also caused landing problems, exacerbated by the

Major Werner Mölders – the 'father' of modern air fighting.

narrow track undercarriage. The 109 was initially armed with two nose-mounted 7.92 mm machine guns and, like the first Hurricanes and Spitfires, a wooden fixed-pitch propeller. After extensive testing at Tavemünde, the 109 was officially declared the winning design and awarded a production contract. In April 1937, *Jagdgeschwader Richthofen* became the first unit to replace their obsolete He 51s with the new 109. Messerschmitt's fighter therefore entered operational service before both its British contemporaries. At some stage during the mid-1930s, Siegfried Stronk joined the *Luftwaffe* as an aircrew volunteer – and would soon see action.

German intervention in the Spanish Civil War began in August 1936, when twenty Ju 52 transport aircraft and six He 51 fighters were despatched to assist Franco's fascist forces. More fighters followed, with pilots to fly them. It soon became clear, though, that such a small number of German fighters could make no impression on the conflict's outcome, not least because the He 51 was inferior to the Russian- and American-built fighters flown by the Republicans. The decision was therefore reached to send a powerful German force – the *Condor Legion* – to Franco's aid. For the *Luftwaffe* Spain became an essential proving ground for the new monoplanes, which did not arrive in theatre until the early summer of 1937. Air superiority was soon achieved and maintained, thus providing an early indication of the monoplane's superiority. As *Condor Legion* veteran and expert German fighter pilot Adolf Galland wrote, the Me 109s 'were mainly intended to combat the numerous Curtiss and Rata fighters, either as lone wolves or when escorting bombers formations. The Me 109 was definitely superior to them and shot down a great number, the record for "kills" being held by *Leutnant* Harder, until eventually Mölders topped his figure.' Upon arrival in Spain, Werner Mölders succeeded Galland in command of 3/J 88, which was converting to Me 109s. With a full complement of 109s Mölders was instrumental in working out the mechanics of combat tactics with the new monoplane fighter. He was uniquely placed to do so, achieving fourteen personal victories over Spain in the process.

Mölders realised that fighter combat was fast and furious, a cut and thrust affair often lasting but a matter of minutes. Given the high speed and manoeuvrability of the new monoplane fighters it was quickly realised that inflexible formation attacks – such as those being practised and rigidly enforced by Fighter Command – were inappropriate: fluency and fluidity was required. Pilots needed to keep a sharp lookout – because enemy fighters could appear and attack in a very short time – and be able to break and respond to any given tactical situation, whether in defence or attack.

What was required now, Mölders discovered, was a combat formation based on the fighting pair, not a squadron of twelve aircraft flying cohesively in sections of three and in close formation. The pair, or *Rotte*, comprised leader and wingman. Before battle was joined the *Rotte* operated as part of a *Schwarm* of two *Rotten*. This section of four cruised in line abreast, each aircraft some 200 yards apart, slightly stepped up, permitting pilots the freedom to search for the enemy instead of concentrating on avoiding collision with their neighbour. When battle commenced, the *Schwarm* broke into two *Rotten*. The leader's job was to shoot down the enemy while his tail was protected by his wingman, or *Rottenhund*. Air Vice-Marshal Johnnie Johnson, officially the top scoring RAF fighter pilot of the Second World War, commented on the *Schwarm*: 'We used to see the 109s flying this loose, flexible, formation, alert, like the four fingers of an outstretched hand. I always thought that they looked aggressive, ready for anything, like a pack of hunting dogs.' Mölders' new tactics allowed the *Condor Legion* to achieve air superiority in 1937 – which it never lost. The balance sheet indicated 72 German combat losses against 327 Republican aircraft destroyed. Upon return from Spain, Mölders wrote a new manual of fighter tactics for the monoplane which became standard operating procedure throughout the

Experte Adolf Galland describes his latest victory as Werner Mölders looks on, at General Theo Osterkampf's birthday party in Le Touquet.

Luftwaffe – earning for himself the nickname *Vati* – father – of the German *Jagdwaffe*. Although his life would one day become inextricably connected with the Me 109 and Werner Mölders, Siegfried Stronk did not fly fighters in Spain. He served there with the *Condor Legion*, but as the pilot of an He 111 reconnaissance bomber with *Aufklarangsgruppe* 88.

After Spain, the *Luftwaffe*'s expansion gathered momentum. In 1937 its front-line strength was between 2,000 and 2,500 aircraft of all types. By August 1938 it was 2,900. That year Germany produced 5,235 military aircraft – 8,295 in 1939. Britain's figures for the same years were 2,827 and 7,940.

According to Air Ministry Pamphlet 248, 'the German conception of the employment of fighter aircraft was not in a very developed stage on the eve of war. The majority of the fighter force was intended for deployment over the battle area… In support of ground units one of the main functions of the single-engined fighter units was to prevent or hinder activities by enemy reconnaissance aircraft. In addition, single-engined fighter units were intended to protect and escort bomber and dive-bomber formations operating against enemy ground targets.' From this it is clear that the *Luftwaffe* had not considered the kind of protracted strategic offensive air operations that became necessary during the summer of 1940. The intention was to fight a series of short, sharp, wars using fast-moving ground forces supported by flying artillery – *Blitzkrieg*. German air policy concentrated on attack. This is confirmed by the fact that at the outbreak of war 40% of

Pilots of JG53 with an Me 109 bearing their famous 'Ace of Spades' insignia, after the Battle of Britain.

Luftwaffe units were bomber or dive-bomber units, while only 25% were fighters. So, although much has rightly been made of the opportunity provided by Spain, not even the Germans had got air power doctrine right as yet. Even though the *Luftwaffe* had the most up-to-date combat experience, and overall was equipped with excellent aircraft, it was not a flawless foe. Still, from a perspective of day-fighter warfare, in the event of contact with enemy fighters the German pilots had a huge edge: Mölders had rewritten the book of fighter tactics, based on his experience in Spain, and these tactics were now standard operating procedure throughout the *Jagdwaffe*. Moreover, as the British Air Ministry observed, 'There is no doubt that in 1939 the Me 109 was superior to any Allied fighter except the Spitfire which, however, was then only available to the RAF in small numbers.' Exactly when Siegfried Stronk first converted from twin-engined bombers to the single-engined Me 109 fighter is unknown, but we do know that during the Battle of Britain *Oberleutnant* Stronk served with JG53.

JG53 *Pik As* (Ace of Spades) was formed on 1 May 1939 when the *Geschwaderstab* (group staff flight) and both I and II/JG133, each a *gruppe* (wing) of three *staffeln* (squadrons) was redesignated *Stab*, I and II/JG53. When the Second World War broke out, I and II/JG53 was based in western Germany, at Wiesbaden-Erbenheim and Mannheim-Sandhofen, responsible for the defence of the sector from Saarbrücken to Trier. In command of 3/JG53 (the third squadron in the first wing) was *Hauptmann* Werner Mölders. On 9 September 1939, I/JG53 opened the unit's account by destroying a French reconnaissance aircraft, another Bloch being shot down later that day by 3/JG53. On 21 September, Mölders achieved his first aerial victory of the war when he claimed a French Curtiss fighter, after which he was promoted to command the latest wing of JG53, the new IIIrd *gruppe* at Wiesbaden-Erbenheim. On 22 December 1939, it would be pilots of III/JG53 who had the *Geschwader*'s first fight with the RAF, when two 73 Squadron Hurricanes were destroyed over Metz.

When Hitler attacked the west on 10 May 1940, defending the northern flank of the rapidly advancing army dictated that little action was at first experienced, thanks to the swift defeat of the Dutch. By 14 May however, *Panzergruppe* von Kliest had poured from the Ardennes, German forces had captured bridgeheads across the Meuse, and JG53 was redeployed to Sedan in correct anticipation of RAF counter-attacks on the Meuse crossing points. In the subsequent fighting, 170 Allied bombers were claimed destroyed, thirty-five of them by I/JG53. After this threat was neutralised, JG53 remained at Sedan, adding a further fifty aerial victories to the tally before the month's end. The unit's leading ace was Mölders, who on 29 May 1940 became the first member of the *Luftwaffe* to receive the coveted *Ritterkreuz*, the Knight's Cross, after scoring his twentieth victory two days before. By 3 June, the British Expeditionary Force had been evacuated from Dunkirk, the *Luftwaffe* then mounting Operation Paula against French airfields and aircraft factories around Paris. On that day, JG53 destroyed fourteen French machines for the loss to two 109s. Two days later, the final assault on Paris began, *Fall Rot* (Plan Red), JG53 claiming a further eleven victories – but Mölders was shot down by a French fighter and captured, spending a short period as a prisoner before France surrendered. During the Battle of France, the *Jagdwaffe* had achieved total aerial supremacy, making the army's unprecedented advance possible. JG53 claimed the destruction of 185 enemy aircraft destroyed, offset against 32 aircraft lost, seven pilots killed and nine wounded. They were good odds.

When the Battle of Britain began, JG53 was based first at Poulmic in Brittany, then on Guernsey, forced to watch from a distance as the latest round of aerial fighting began. Exactly when *Oberleutnant* Stronk joined III/JG53's 8th *Staffel* is unknown, but as we know that he did not fly fighters during the Fall of France, it is likely that for some reason he transferred from twins to singles and joined 8/JG53 as a replacement for losses suffered during the fighting to date. On the evening of 8 August, JG53 II/JG53 escorted *Stukas* on yet another attack on the already battered Convoy Peewit. Over Swanage, the 109s clashed with 10 Group fighters, *Hauptmann* Gunther von Maltzahn, *Kommodore* of II/JG53, claiming a Spitfire destroyed, while *Hauptmann* Heinz Bretnütz (6/JG53) destroyed another, and *Unteroffizier* Richard Vogel (4/JG53) a Hurricane. Three days later, JG53 joined in the fighting over Portland (see the story of Flying Officer Richard Demetriadi), sweeping in advance of a huge raid comprising over fifty Ju 88s, twenty He 111s, sixty Me 110s and further Me 109s from JG2. More fighting followed next day, when 120 fighters, including those of JG53, escorted 100 Ju 88s of KG51 to attack Portsmouth. Over the Needles, the Spitfires of 152 and 609 Squadrons attacked the bombers, engaging JG53's 109s, which rushed to defend their charges. In the ensuing combat, four RAF fighters were claimed, but III/JG53 lost its *Kommodore*, Hauptmann Harro Harder. So it went on, with JG53 escorting Ju 87s attacking coastal targets. After horrendous losses the *Stuka* was withdrawn from the Battle after 18 August, and the whole thing rethought. General Adolf Galland, at the time *Kommodore* of JG26 *Schlageter*, wrote, 'The accompanying fighter pilots were blamed for the painfully high losses, although the limitations

Limited range was a huge problem for the Me 109 pilots during the Battle of Britain, this 109 running out of fuel at the French coast. *Oberleutnant* Stronk was forced to ditch in the Channel and await rescue by the *Seenot.*

of the Stuka in action were obvious enough in the Battle of Britain… When the fighter force failed to achieve air supremacy, the bomber force was ordered to attack British fighter bases and to bomb aircraft and motor industries. While, in particular, Portsmouth, Portland and numerous targets on the British east coast were bombed, attacks on convoys and fighter sweeps continued.' The General observed that the *Luftwaffe* was 'far from achieving air supremacy. One of the main reasons for this was that the sort range of the Me 109 allowed only little penetration and in consequence also reduced the bombers' range.' Therein was the rub.

Like the Spitfire and Hurricane, the Me 109 was designed and intended as a short-range defensive interceptor – not as a long-range offensive or escort fighter. These fighters simply lacked the fuel and range for such a role. Although the *Luftwaffe* had the twin-engined and heavily armed Me 110 *Zerstörer*, potentially better suited to this role, in practice the 110 had been found to be no match for the fast and nimble British fighters. As General Galland said, the scenario whereby 109s had to protect the supposed 110 'destroyer' was 'farcical'. Experience had convinced German fighter leaders that the most effective way for them to protect the bombers was by flying free-ranging fighter sweeps in advance of the main formation and over the target, clearing the way of RAF fighters. Without visible protection, this did not, however, necessarily find popularity with the bomber crews. 'Extended Protection' was possibly the answer, with some fighters remaining with the bombers and authorised to intercept any approaching RAF machines, with fresh fighter units meeting the bombers on their way back, sometimes over the English coast.

On 19 August, Göring called his principal officers to his country estate, *Karinhall*, increasingly concerned at the ongoing failure to defeat Fighter Command. The problem was this perennial sticking point of range, the 109 only having sufficient fuel for a few minutes of combat over England if sufficient petrol was to be preserved for the return flight. The *Luftwaffe* chief's post-conference memorandum supported 'Extended Protection' and recognised the effectiveness of free-range fighter sweeps: 'In the actual conduct of operations, commanders of fighter units must be given as free a hand as possible. Only part of the fighters are to be employed as direct escorts to our bombers. The aim must be to employ the strongest possible fighter forces on free-lance operations in which they can indirectly protect the bombers… No rigid plan can be laid down for such operations, as their conduct must depend upon the changing nature of enemy tactics and weather conditions.' It was also now decided to move virtually all of *Luftflotte* 3's Me 109s from the Cherbourg area to the Pas-de-Calais, in the *Luftlotte* 2 area, the idea being that with only twenty-two miles of water between Calais and the Kentish coast, the escorting fighters would have longer over England – a full twenty minutes over London. So it was that JG53 flew north-east, III/JG53's new base being Le Touquet.

Having turned away from attacking convoys and coastal radar stations, Göring's focus had been Fighter Command's airfields. Certainly these attacks were damaging, but at no time was Fighter Command rendered ineffective, and nor was Air Chief Marshal Dowding ever forced to consider committing his entire force to battle *en masse*. On the contrary, Fighter Command maintained its defensive responsibilities throughout the country, and the rotation of squadrons in and out of the battle area meant that overall strength was preserved. *Luftwaffe* estimations that Fighter Command was on its knees were therefore woefully inaccurate. On the night of 24/25 August, a German bomber had inadvertently bombed central London at night, owing to a navigational error, contravening Göring's exclusive right to order attacks on the enemy capital. Churchill was determined to 'return the compliment', so the following night saw fifty Hampdens and Wellingtons of Bomber Command bound for Berlin. A cloud-covered target, however, saw most of the bombs fall harmlessly in countryside south of the 'Big City', although two people were injured and a chalet destroyed in a Berlin suburb. Hitler was furious and promised his people that Germany would reply 'with increasing force'. Göring now took personal control of the Battle, meeting his *Luftflotten* commanders, Kesselring and Sperrle, pressing his view that the current focus on Fighter Command's sector stations should be 'abandoned in favour of a large-scale assault on the English capital'. It appeared obvious that Fighter Command would not be destroyed on the ground, and London was considered the only target of sufficient importance to force Dowding to commit his 'last reserves of Spitfires and Hurricanes'. Göring then visited his *kommodoren* on the Channel coast, berating his fighter leaders on this occasion for the bombers' high losses. Göring now demanded inflexible close escort, completely denying his fighter leaders' tactical initiative or the ability to continue their (actually highly effective) fighter sweeps. Frustrated though the fighter leaders were by this turn of events, there was a degree of optimism, as General Galland explained: 'We fighter pilots, although discouraged by a task beyond our strength, were looking forward impatiently and excitedly to the start of the bomber attacks. We believed that only then would the British fighters leave their dens and be forced to give us open battle.'

At 1100 hrs on Saturday 7 September 1940, seventy enemy aircraft crossed the coast at Folkestone and separated, one formation flying along the coast to Hastings, the remainder fanning out over east Kent. Dover and the forward fighter airfield at Hawkinge were dive-bombed. Then the enemy withdrew, leaving the defenders' radar screens devoid of plots for several

A Me 109E-4 fighter-bomber of the type flown by *Oberleutnant* Stronk.

vexing hours. At 1554 hrs, enemy air activity was noted over the Pas-de-Calais, the unprecedented number of plots making clear that this would be the heaviest attack so far. On the cliffs at Cap Gris Nez, Göring and his entourage watched proudly as 348 bombers, escorted by a staggering 617 fighters, roared overhead. This massive 'Valhalla' occupied a twenty-mile front and was stacked a mile-and-a-half high, wave after wave London bound. At 1617 hrs, eleven 11 Group squadrons were scrambled and by 1630 hrs all of Air Vice-Marshal Park's fighters were up. Both 10 and 12 Groups were called upon for assistance, the sheer size of the raiding force suggesting that London – not airfields – was the target. That Saturday afternoon, Londoners witnessed aerial combat on an unprecedented scale. Through sheer weight of numbers, the Germans reached their target, starting large fires in the docklands and the East End. Vast areas were devastated and 1,800 Londoners lost their lives that day. During the fighting, Fighter Command lost twenty-seven aircraft, with fourteen pilots killed. Somewhere in that huge battle was *Oberleutnant* Stronk – who recorded his first aerial victory, a Spitfire (unfortunately the exact details of height and location are unavailable). For any fighter pilot, this was, of course, a significant moment.

That night, the bombers returned, for another relentless attack lasting over eight hours. The next day things were quieter, as both sides regrouped, but again bombs rained down on London after dark. Further daytime attacks followed. On 11 September, III/JG53 fought an interesting action when scrambled to intercept a British raid. That evening, a formation of five 53 and six 59 Squadron Blenheims joined with 826 Naval Air Squadron Fairey Albacore biplanes, escorted by Thorney Island-based Blenheims of 235 Squadron (Coastal Command), to attack German shipping off Calais.

Sutherland Avenue, Biggin Hill, the crash site of *Oberleutnant* Stronk's Me 109. (John Nelson)

Me 109s of I/JG52 and III/JG53 responded, claiming the destruction of five Albacores and four Blenheims. One of the former was claimed by *Oberleutant* Stronk, representing his second 'kill'. As so often is the case however, owing to the confusion and speed of combat, actual losses bear little resemblance to claims, with just one Albacore being lost and three damaged, while two 235 Squadron Blenheims failed to return. The British claimed the destruction of two Me 109s during this engagement, but no record of any such loss can be found.

The daylight battle for London reached a terrifying crescendo on Sunday 15 September. But by that time frustrations were mounting in the *Luftwaffe* camp, because with the invasion fleet scheduled to sail in five days, Fighter Command still showed no sign of being beaten. Indeed, Hitler was losing confidence in his boastful *Reichsmarschall*'s ability to deliver his promises, prompting Göring to launch yet another day of massive attacks on London – one which he hoped would at last end decisively in his favour. By the end of this tumultuous day, the defenders sensed a turning point in their favour. Fifty-six German aircraft had been destroyed, less, in fact, than on both 15 (seventy-five) and 18 August (sixty-nine), but it was obvious that, relentless though the attack was, Britain was robust in defence and such losses could not be absorbed indefinitely. The Battle was far from over, but the tide had turned.

On 29 September 1940, Siegfried Stronk wrote to his best friend Gerhard von Szymonski, a fellow pilot, the pair having served together at Bad Vöslau near Vienna in 1939 and earlier in 1940: -

Dear Szy!

Thank you very much for your letter. I was very happy that you did not forget me. With two old Upper Silesians this would rarely happen anyway.

Now, we have switched roles in relation to our activity. You now see from your own view how miserable one feels at home. But calm down, every useful man is brought to the front again. This is especially true for the hunt. The losses are sometimes enormous. I recommend that you switch to 109! In the present war, this is maybe the last time there will be true fighter combat, true hunting.

The destroyers shoot down what they can, whenever they can get in a shot, but even more so they get shot down themselves.

We are, whenever the weather permits, used daily as escort to London. I can tell you, for the 109 a pretty criminal act, because with we have to watch our fuel to the last minute and drop (or not, as once with me), and secondly, the Channel is causing a great deal of trouble for the return flight. Any simple cooler hit, or otherwise harmless thing in a dogfight over London and you're done – meaning an emergency-landing in England or swim in the Channel. The latter I have recently experienced, not because of a hit, but simply due to running out of fuel.

In the middle of the Channel I had to make a belly landing, which went very well despite high waves. The 109 always sinks immediately, but I was equally fast getting out. Swimming and cursing – quite funny – not! Since I had radioed in my location before the rather watery landing, a 109 came after about half an hour, so I fired red and green flares, but unfortunately this pilot also ended up paddling in the water with me.

After ten minutes, a rescue seaplane arrived, which broke two struts while landing, but still managed to get me out, up in the air again and brought me home. I have to say getting out feels much better than getting into the water. Big piece of luck I reckon. Ricki doesn't know yet and shouldn't know for now.

Otherwise, of course I am doing fine. I only have three aerial victories. I am disadvantaged by having missed the whole experience of the fighting in France. But I'm also pretty satisfied, because most rookies are shot down without having shot down anything – and shooting down enemy planes is far from easy. Well, I am sure you will experience it yourself.

Nothing else to report.

Siegfried's letter is an illuminating historical document, providing a German fighter pilot's view of the Me 110's poor performance, and,

Sutherland Avenue in 2019. (David Evans)

of course, the frustrations of limited range and danger imposed by a two-way sea-crossing. What is also interesting is the reference to *Luftwaffe* Air-Sea Rescue – *Seenot. Luftwaffe* aircrews were better equipped than their RAF opponents to survive in the water: they were equipped with a flare pistol and cartridges. Also, although not mentioned, it is likely that the sea around him was coloured by fluorescent dye, with which German aircrew were provided and could deploy. Rescue aircraft were usually He 59 biplane seaplanes, painted white, emblazoned with a large red cross and given civilian registrations. After such a machine was destroyed by the RAF on 1 July 1940 however, these aircraft were camouflaged and given *Luftwaffe* registrations. The *Luftwaffe* also far-sightedly deployed rescue buoys, *Rettungsbojen Generalluftzeugmeister*, known to the RAF as 'lobster pots'. These housed four bunks and everything downed airman would require to survive in an emergency. In reality, these floating sanctuaries often broke loose, so were of little value practically, but this does demonstrate how much further along the way the Germans were in providing for the rescue of downed airmen. The final thing of interest in Siegfried's letter is his reference to three aerial victories – details of two can be found, this emphasising the frequently incomplete sources available to the historian, especially from the German side owing to the destruction of records in 1945.

By the time Siegfried wrote his letter, the German daylight bombing offensive had all but been defeated, the emphasis changing to night attacks. There was a change too in tactics for the German fighter units. Fighter sweeps, successful though they could be, had failed to draw the RAF to battle, 11 Group's controllers recognising that these incursions were no threat unless squadrons were scrambled to intercept. Far better, then, to let the enemy waste fuel but do no harm. Having previously been frustrated by the close escort role, this was a disappointment to the German fighter pilots. To provoke a reaction from the defenders, Göring ordered that one *staffel* in every *gruppe* would become fighter-bombers – *Jabos*. This affected one third of the available fighter force, and was an unpopular decision with senior fighter leaders, who already lacked sufficient resources, to achieve aerial superiority. For so long, auxiliary fuel tanks had been requested, to extend range, but instead bombs arrived. The tactical thinking, however, was that if German formations included *Jabos*, the RAF would have to consider every sweep a threat and react to it. This would directly concern *Oberleutnant* Stronk – because 8/JG53 was chosen as the IIIrd *Gruppe*'s dedicated *Jabo Staffel*.

The first of these raids occurred on 20 September, when a sweep was ignored by Fighter Command – until suddenly bombs exploded in the City of London. Monitoring British radio frequencies, *Luftwaffe* intelligence reported a confusion of orders and counter-orders after the 'harmless' fighters dropped their bombs. Two Spitfire squadrons from Hornchurch were scrambled and battle joined, the RAF fighters climbing desperately while the Me 109s enjoyed all the advantages of height and sun. By close of play, four RAF pilots were dead with others wounded, while only one Me 109 was destroyed.

General Galland: -

'The fighter-bombers were put into action in so great a hurry that there was hardly any time to give the pilots bombing training, and most of them dropped their first bomb in a raid on London or on other targets in England. We had a total of 250 fighter-bombers. The Me 109 carried a 500lb High Explosive bomb… No great effect could be achieved with that… the fighter pilots were "browned off" with carrying cargo and glad to get rid of their bombs anywhere.

'The fighter-bomber raids were carried out in the following way: each *gruppe* escorted its own bombers. The approach altitude was about 18,000 feet. At the start, we let the fighter-bombers fly in bomber formation, but it was soon apparent that the enemy fighters could concentrate fully on the bombers, so we distributed them in small units throughout the entire formation and thus brought them fairly safe over their target area. This type of raid had no more than nuisance value. The passive behaviour towards enemy fighters, the feeling of inferiority when we attacked, because of loss of speed, manoeuvrability and rate of climb, added to the unconvincing effect of single bombs scattered over wide areas, combined to ruin the morale of the German fighter pilot, already low because of the type of escorting that had previously had to be undertaken.'

On the subject of morale, *Oberleutnant* Ulrich Steinhilper of 3/JG52 commented that 'we began to openly discuss the subject of *Kanalkrankheit* – "Channel Sickness" ... some court-martials had been instituted for pilots who had returned too frequently with mechanical faults which could not be found by the ground-crews.'

Because of the high altitudes that the Me 109s swept in at, these threats could only be met by Spitfire squadrons, given their aircraft's superior performance.

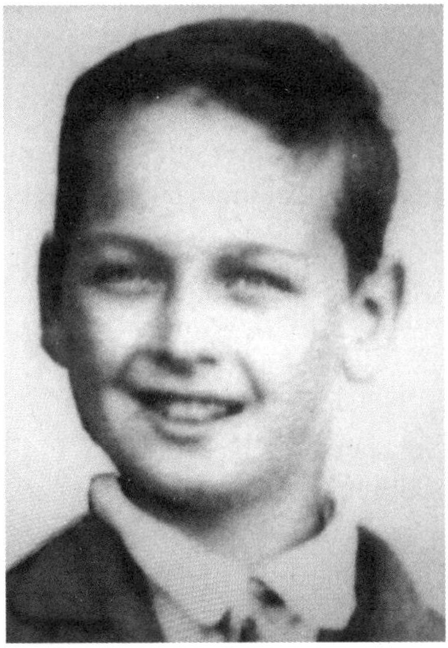

Biggin Hill schoolboy John Nelson. (John Nelson)

The strain was telling for both sides. Pilot Officer Geoffrey Wellum DFC of Biggin Hill's 92 Squadron: 'During September and October the 109s were always active in the Biggin Hill Sector, and caused problems. I recall that they were always above us as we never seemed to be scrambled in time to get enough height. Our climb was always a desperate, full-throttle affair, but we never quite got up to them. I did manage to get a crack at two Me 109s on one patrol, but although I saw strikes I could only claim them as damaged.'

On the morning of 1 October 1940, Portsmouth and Southampton were attacked, followed by wave after wave of fighter sweeps penetrating to South London, which Me 109 *Jabos* bombed from high altitude, causing negligible damage. It was simply impossible for a 109 to bomb accurately from high altitude. Escorting fighters would frequently be at 30,000 feet, the fighter-bombers operating at 25,000 feet, attacking London, according to the official RAF history, 'with seemingly little regard for specific targets'.

On Wednesday 2 October, clear skies saw *Jafü* 2 despatch numerous formations of fighters and fighter-bombers throughout the day to attack London and Biggin Hill, as usual from very high altitude. At 0920 hrs that morning, 603 Squadron was scrambled from Hornchurch to intercept an incoming threat. Squadron Leader Denholm's pilots' combat reports describe the action: -

Flying Officer John Haig, 'A' Flight, 1020 hrs, 'Above 8/10 cloud, Croydon area': -

'When at about 29,000 feet we sighted about ten Me 109s below. We dived on them and I fired a good burst at one Me 109 as it dived away to port. I saw a white glycol stream just starting to issue from it, and I then broke away and did not see it again. On landing I discovered that Pilot Officer Goldsmith, who was my Number 2 in my Section and just behind me in the attack, saw the Me 109 streaming with glycol and also clouds of black smoke started and it went down out of control.' This 109 was claimed as damaged.

Pilot Officer Henry Matthews, 'A' Flight, 1020 hrs, 'West of Croydon': -

'When patrolling at 28,000 feet, the Squadron was ordered into line astern and dived to the right after enemy, but owing to the difficulty of getting into line astern in the rear section, I climbed to lose speed and sighted four Me 109s to the left. The last one I attacked from close astern. The Me 109 was hit and dived down with smoke and glycol issuing from it. No evasive action was taken or was any attempt made to get away. Height 25,000 feet.' This 109 was claimed as a 'probable'.

Sergeant George Bailey, 'A' Flight, 1020 hrs, 'five miles south-west of West Malling': -

'After meeting E/A at 26,000 feet, I lost height and saw E/A in cloud; after coming through cloud I saw AA fire and the sighted enemy again and opened fire on it from astern, he then began to lose height with a stream of glycol coming from the machine. I followed it to about fifty feet, when I lost sight of it.' This Me 109 was claimed destroyed at 4,000 feet, but although leaking glycol and unlikely to get home, the outcome of the combat appears inconclusive.

Flight Lieutenant John Boulter, 'B' Flight, 1005 hrs (this time is incorrect, should be 1020 hrs), 'Above cloud, approximately over Biggin Hill': -

'The Squadron went into line astern and dived on a formation of Me 109s. I attacked the rear aircraft of a pair which had become separated from their formation and were climbing. I fired two bursts of approximately two seconds, closing my range. On the second burst it slowed suddenly, pieces flew off both wings, the port wheel dropped down, and white vapour came from underneath the aircraft. I left it to engage the leading aircraft and saw the one I had fired at turn over and go into an inverted dive.' This 109 was claimed as damaged.

Flying Officer Peter Hartas, 'B' Flight, 1020 hrs, 'Over Biggin Hill': -

'When I was on patrol with 603 Squadron, flying at 30,000 feet, we saw two Me 109s about 2,000 feet below us. The CO dived and attacked one of them to my port. I attacked the other, which immediately turned to starboard and dived steeply. I followed it down and fired three bursts of three seconds, and after the second a thin spiral of white smoke started trailing from the enemy aircraft. This grew thicker and was pouring out when I finished my third burst. Almost immediately after the third burst the enemy aircraft turned slowly on its back and dived vertically into the cloud, which was then only about 1,000 feet below. I then broke off, but was through the cloud before recovering from the dive. I came below the clouds immediately over an aerodrome which I assumed to be Biggin Hill. Having circled this once, I saw a fire burning to the south-west. On examination this turned out to be an aircraft on a road.' Again, this Me 109 was claimed as destroyed.

Pilot Officer Ludwik Martel (Polish), 'B' Flight, 1020 hrs, 'Over Biggin Hill': -

'When on patrol with 603 Squadron I saw an Me 109 coming underneath from the starboard quarter, the Squadron being 1,000 feet below me. I dived and made a stern attack and saw glycol smoke come out of the Me 109, which took evasive action. I then saw two Me 109s in my rear-view mirror, so I half-rolled and dived away.' This Me 109 was claimed as damaged.

In addition to the foregoing, Me 109s were also claimed destroyed by Pilot Officers Brian Carbury ('Near Croydon') and Peter Dexter ('South of Croydon'). Unfortunately, again indicating the incompleteness of sources available to historians, neither combat report is preserved at the National Archives.

Pilot Officer Dexter was himself shot down over Croydon at 1030hrs, baling out with a badly wounded leg and receiving treatment at Croydon Hospital. 603 Squadron had clashed with III/JG53, two pilots of 9/JG53, *Leutnant* Erich Schmidt and *Unteroffizier* Robert Wolfgarten, claiming to have destroyed two Spitfires each. In reality, Pilot Officer Dexter's was the only Spitfire lost in this action, so either one, or even both, could have been responsible for shooting him down.

During this combat, *Oberleutnant* W. Radlick, the *Staffelkapitän* of 9/JG53 was shot down and baled out, but was killed when his parachute failed to open; his aircraft crashed near 'Swallowfields', Limpsfield Common. It was the *Jabos* of 8/JG53, however, with which 603 Squadron scored most success. It appears fairly certain that Sergeant Bailey was responsible for shooting down *Oberleutnant* W. Fiel, whose 109 crash-landed at Addelsted Farm, East Peckham; *Gefreiter* H. Zag was also captured having force-landed at Forge Farm near Goudhurst. The final *Jabo* pilot was *Oberleutnant* Siegfried Stronk – who was killed, his aircraft crashing at Sutherland Avenue, Biggin Hill. From the incomplete evidence available, with the exception of Fiel, it is impossible to say who shot down who. It is possible that Stronk was shot down by either Flight Lieutenant Boulter or Flying Officer Hartas – or probably both, their combat reports suggesting that they attacked the same 109, unaware of the other's presence (as so often happened).

At the time, John Nelson was a pupil at Biggin Hill School: -

'The day began much the same as most others since the summer holidays had ended. No sooner than we arrived at school than the siren on top of the hose-drying tower behind the Fire Station sounded the warning of an impending air raid. We all filed down the steps to the shelters below what is now a supermarket car park. Afterwards, when the danger had passed, we emerged into the bright afternoon light and our headmaster, Mr Frank Hicks, indicated to several of us "usual suspects" to stand over to one side. "Earlier this morning," he said, "after being attacked by a Spitfire, a German *Messerschmitt* blew up in the air overhead and pieces have fallen in gardens mostly along the other side of Sutherland Avenue. I'm telling you now that you're not to touch any of it." A wry smile flickered across his face – some hope!

'Dismissed, we all stampeded towards the back gate of the school and out into Sutherland Avenue. My brother, Peter, and I went home, which was immediately opposite the school gate, to get something to eat. Our mother knew what had happened. As she had been alone, she had been very kindly invited to share our neighbours' Anderson Shelter. When a large piece of fuselage crashed down into our Bramley apple tree, the boy of the family, who had left school, asked if he could have it – and she gave it to him. But it was ours. It fell in our garden but he refused to give it back, and never did. It lay in long grass in his garden for years afterwards.

'Later on, we joined other boys in Sutherland Avenue on the usual hunt for souvenirs. The pilot, who had almost certainly been killed in the mid-air explosion, had plummeted down into the front garden of "Lindenwood", where Miss Chew had previously run a small private school. His body, which had been covered over, was taken away on a truck sent out from Biggin Hill airfield. Mrs Win Aldridge, a nurse at the local First Aid Post returning home from duty, had checked and confirmed that the unfortunate pilot was indeed dead, and noted that on his belt was an empty leather holster – perhaps a Luger was not very far away, but we never found it.

John Nelson's prized souvenir from the Sutherland Avenue Me 109 crash site – other items can be seen in the Kent Battle of Britain Museum at Hawkinge. (John Nelson)

'Further along was a bungalow called "Hainault", the temporary residence of the Pastor of Biggin Hill Baptist Chapel, Mr Felmingham. Fortunately, he was not at home when the main part of the aeroplane crashed through the roof of his front bedroom. By the time we got there a soldier, standing on guard at the gate with a rifle and fixed bayonet, told us to keep away. With trees and shrubs in full leaf in the front garden there was not much to see, so we went off searching for bits elsewhere.

'That evening a truck load of RAF personnel arrived in Sutherland Avenue and manhandled the tailplane, which had landed in one of the back gardens where the land begins to slope steeply towards The Grove, onto the road. They then cut out the swastikas on both sides, loaded everything onto the truck and drove away.

'A day or so later the security situation at "Hainault" was more relaxed. The guard on duty was a member of the Pioneer Corps, enjoying every minute of it. Someone living close by had found him an old kitchen chair and, with rifle propped up against the hedge, he sat with a regular supply of tea and biscuits. He still asked us to keep out, but while a couple of lads diverted his attention with sweets, Woodbines and an exchange of family photos, the rest of us managed to get to the wreckage from Mr Foxlow's garden next door.

'The nose of the aircraft was embedded into the floor of the front bedroom with the remains of a double bed around it. The engine and cockpit rose up at an angle of about 45° towards the rear right-hand corner of the room. Still hanging at a crazy angle on the left-hand side wall was a framed biblical text, closely missed by a thick black streak of engine oil. Overall there was an unusual, sickly-sweet smell, possibly coming from spilt engine coolant.

'There was no time to stand around, the object of the exercise was to get away with as much as possible. There were live machine-gun bullets everywhere and these were quickly harvested, and together with any other loose bits of aeroplane crammed into jacket and trouser pockets. The position of other parts, attached by electrical wiring, were noted and removed on a subsequent visit with wire cutters.

'With access to most of the gardens between Sutherland Avenue and The Grove, we were able to find various other bits and pieces. Notable amongst these were the discovery by Colin Martins of the complete instrument panel and the control column lying close together in a wooded area. John Aldridge found the aircraft's First Aid kit, containing phials of morphine which were promptly confiscated by our GP, Dr Mary Pease. The kit also contained a large triangular bandage on which were printed various instructions as to its various uses. John De'Ath somehow acquired the cockpit canopy, and my own collection, apart from an armoury of bullets, included the radio aerial with porcelain insulator in an aluminium cone, a badly damaged bank of electrical circuit breakers, which I had cut away from the cockpit, and several rectangular black magnets, probably from the generator.

'One weekend, all of the souvenirs were collected together and exhibited in John Aldridge's garage. A modest entrance fee was charged and a grand total of nine shillings was collected and donated to the St John's Ambulance.'

While *Oberleutnant* Stronk's Me 109's wreckage provided a source of great excitement for Biggin Hill's schoolboy population, news of the airman's death was devastating when received in Germany: Siegfried was a married man – and his wife, Maria, was pregnant. Daughter Erika was born on 8 January 1941, never knowing her father. In November 1942, Maria married Siegfried's best friend, Gerhard von Szymonski, who survived the war. So too did Siegfried's younger brother, Wolfram, who had served with distinction as a *panzer* commander in *Fallschirmpanzerkorps* Hermann Göring, seeing action in France, North Africa, Italy and on the *Ostfront*.

Decorated with the *Ritterkreuz*, Wolfram survived the war but not unscathed: he was severely wounded fighting near Warsaw, losing a leg, and owed his life to his brother-in-law Gerhard von Szymonski, who arranged for him to be flown to Berlin for emergency medical treatment.

Initially, 25-year-old *Oberleutnant* Siegfried Stronk was buried at St Mary Cray Cemetery, near Orpington in Kent. After the war his remains were interred at the German Military Cemetery at Cannock Chase, Staffordshire, where his stark headstone of Belgian granite incorrectly records his date of death as 5 October 1940.

Oberleutnant Stronk's grave at Cannock Chase, Staffordshire. (Glenn Gelder)

During the Battle of Britain, according to German historian Hans Ring, the *Luftwaffe* lost 2,585 aircrew either killed or missing in action, with a further 735 wounded and 925 captured. Siegfried Stronk's is one story of many, therefore. Sadly, the vast majority of these individual stories will go unrecorded, untold and ultimately forgotten. Today, many artefacts of the *Luftwaffe* assault on England in 1940 can be seen at the inspirational Kent Battle of Britain Museum, where the remains of over 700 aircraft, of both sides, destroyed between 10 July and 31 October 1940 are displayed – including items from *Oberleutnant* Stronk's 109. John Nelson still preserves one of the switches he removed from the cockpit, his prized souvenir of that fateful day when a German *Jabo* crashed on Sutherland Avenue.

At rest with Siegfried Stronk at Cannock Chase is a *Gefreiter* Walter Schumann, whose story is unknown but who died before repatriation, on 25 October 1945. Coincidentally, and perhaps appropriately, Walter Schumann was born on 23 April 1913 – Siegfried Stronk's great-nephew Florian shares that same birthday, albeit in 1974.

Life goes on.

Chapter Sixteen

Pilot Officer Harold Ingham Goodall
Sergeant Robert Bett Mirk Young
(New Zealand)

264 Squadron

Killed in Action: 8 October 1940

Some readers may be surprised to know that the Battle of Britain was not just fought by the Spitfire and its more numerous Hurricane stablemate, but also certain other aircraft types. There were more Spitfires and Hurricanes than any other fighter type, which naturally therefore did the lion's share of the fighting, but those squadrons equipped first with twin-engined Blenheims, and as the battle wore on the new Beaufighter, put up a brave defence in Britain's night skies. The Boulton-Paul Defiant's story, though, is a particularly brave – yet tragic – one.

The Defiant was a twin-crewed, single-engined fighter – with a difference: it had no fixed forward-firing armament, just an air gunner in a turret with four machine guns behind the pilot. The aircraft was developed before the war, when the RAF only expected to intercept unescorted German bombers approaching the east coast over the North Sea. The idea was that the Defiant pilot, without having to personally worry about firing, could concentrate on positioning his fighter below and slightly in front of any target, providing his gunner an unmissable shot. Operating in concert, a formation of Defiants could bring multiple guns to bear.

In 1935, the Air Ministry's specification F.9/35 invited aircraft designers' tenders for a two-seater day and night turreted fighter with a top speed of at least 290 mph. The powered turret was to provide a 360° field of fire – but only in the upper hemisphere, the gunner unable to shoot forwards because of the propeller arc. When firing forward, the angle was always elevated at least 19°. Cutting a long story short, on 28 April 1937 the Air Ministry ordered eighty-seven Defiants straight off Boulton-Paul's drawing board, the prototype not actually making its maiden flight until 11 August.

Above left: Pilot Officer Harold Ingham Goodall. (Andy Long)

Above right: As a child, Harold Goodall was 'aviation minded'. (Linda Bell)

In June 1938, the Assistant Chief of the Air Staff (ACAS), Air Vice-Marshal Sholto Douglas, informed Air Chief Marshal Dowding that he must form nine squadrons of Defiants for day fighting. Dowding, however, as Air Member for Research & Development before taking over Fighter Command, was technically minded and had been heavily involved with producing the specification resulting in the Spitfire and Hurricane. During the First World War, Douglas had flown the two-seater Bristol fighter, a highly successful type, and consequently supported the Defiant programme. The Bristol Fighter, though, had an advantage the Defiant lacked: a forward-firing armament. Some have argued that the Defiant's electrical-firing system permitted the pilot to personally fire the guns, facing forward, but as previously explained the shot had to be oblique, not direct, which greatly complicated things in what required split-second decisions and timing. In 1938 it was never envisaged that Britain would be within the range of single-seat, fast and highly manoeuvrable enemy fighters, and some, owing to the high speeds involved, even rejected the notion that fighter v fighter combat, as in the First World War, was even now possible. In the event, both assumptions proved flawed.

After some high-level arguments, in June 1939 the requirement was reduced from fifteen to nine squadrons. Still not satisfied, Dowding continued fighting the issue. Ultimately, only two squadrons would be Defiant-equipped: 141 and 264. By the outbreak of war, though, only three production aircraft had reached the RAF, and those for trials only. Consequently, given later events, it has been argued that the Defiant's lengthy development and time taken to enter service contributed to making the type obsolete before ever firing a shot in anger. Why? Because although the Defiant's top speed was 304 mph, the enemy now had modern bombers not much slower (He 111, 273 mph, Ju 88, 292 mph), and the Me 110 twin-engined heavy fighter flew at a maximum speed of 295 mph. Moreover, the more manoeuvrable Hurricane, which entered service in 1937, had a top speed of 335 mph, while the nimble Spitfire, following on a year later, hurtled along at 353 mph.

At this stage, the Me 109, with a top speed of 354 mph, was not really a consideration, because no-one anticipated Hitler's unprecedented advance to the Channel coast of May 1940 – which in the event changed everything. Acquisition of French airfields, putting even London within the Me 109's limited range, meant that German bombers would be escorted by this excellent fighter – a circumstance beyond that considered by the F.9/35 specification. This made the Defiant, described by Group Captain John Wray as 'The Flying Brick Shit House', vulnerable in daylight skies shared with the 109 – although when the turreted-fighter concept first arose and tenders invited from designers, this circumstance was unimaginable. It is important to understand this backdrop which underpins this story.

Harold Ingham Goodall was on 14 July 1915 at Stoke in Coventry, the son of John and Harriet Goodall, both originally from Tupton, Chesterfield. Growing up, Harold was fascinated by aviation. His cousin Muriel, eight years his junior, remembered how, to amuse her on a family visit when he was 12 or 13, Harold ran into the living room holding an Easter egg aloft, enthusing 'Look, Muriel, it's just like a Zeppelin!' Between 1929 and 1934, Harold attended Lawrence Sheriff, a grammar school in Rugby, where he excelled, becoming Head of House and School and achieving numerous sporting and academic accolades. Afterwards, Harold studied law at Birmingham University, graduating with a *Legum Baccalaureus* (LLB) and becoming articled to Seabroke, Marshall & Davies in Rugby.

Aviation, however, still captivated the young lawyer, who, in May 1939, joined the RAFVR, learning to fly at 6 EFTS, Sywell. Mobilised when Germany invaded Poland on 1 September 1939, after the mandatory introduction to the service at 1 ITW, Cambridge, Sergeant Goodall then successfully completed advanced flying training at 10 FTS, Ternhill, being commissioned on 12 May 1940 and being posted to 264 Squadron at Duxford on the 22nd.

Sergeant-Observer Robert Bett Mirk Young. (Andy Long)

264 Squadron had been formed at Sutton Bridge on 30 October 1939, commanded by Squadron Leader S.H. Hardy, who had formerly served at Fighter Command HQ, Stanmore. It was a fortnight later that Fighter Command ordered the new unit to be equipped with the Defiant aircraft, this being confirmed by the AOC 12 Group, Air Vice-Marshal Leigh-Mallory, when he visited the squadron on 16 November. Five days later, 264 moved to Martlesham Heath, and on 25 November Squadron Leader Hardy left to visit the Air Fighting Development Unit (AFDU) at Northolt and actually fly a Defiant. On 2 December, four 264 Squadron engineers attended the Boulton Paul Aircraft Factory in Wolverhampton for a four-day course on maintaining the Defiant. All pilots had soloed on the Battle monoplane by 20 December, and slowly but surely Defiants began arriving, but following engine failures being experienced on landings, all Defiant aircraft were grounded on 28 January 1940 while Rolls-Royce engineers resolved the issue. Work soon resumed to introduce the type into operational service, and on 24 February 1940 a section of 264 Squadron flew to Northolt for affiliation exercises with Wellington bombers – it being perceived that the Defiant could also perform as an escort fighter. Eventually, on 20 March 1940, 264 Squadron signalled HQ 12 Group that two sections of three aircraft were operational, these six Defiants thereafter contributing to convoy protection patrols out of Wittering and Bircham Newton. On 24 March, Squadron Leader Phillip Hunter succeeded Squadron Leader Hardy in command, and it would be Hunter who would soon lead 264 Squadron into battle.

Training and familiarisation with the Defiant continued into spring 1940, with tactical exercises and night-flying practice introduced into the mix, while various VIPs visited to look over the new aircraft, including the Belgian Air Attaché. This early flying was not without mishap: on 23 April, Pilot Officer Greenhouse and his gunner, LAC John Bromley, crashed after their aircraft caught fire over Orfordness. Air-to-air firing was also carried out, at Sutton Bridge, the results of 27 April considered 'very good'. On 10 May, Germany attacked the west, and 264 Squadron was moved to Duxford, from where it was operational from 1800 hrs that fateful day. On 12 May, 'A' Flight, led by Squadron Leader Hunter, flew to Horsham St Faith to refuel and rendezvous with the six Spitfires of 65 Squadron's 'B' Flight. Taking off at 1310 hrs, in vic sections of three, each section of Defiants following one of Spitfires, by 1355 hrs the formation had crossed the North Sea and was patrolling The Hague. The ORB reported: -

'An aircraft, afterwards recognised as a Ju 88, was seen approaching and dropped one bomb near three destroyers at 1410 hrs. Red Section cut him off as he turned to port (inland) and dived almost to ground level. An overtaking attack was commenced, then each machine made a "cross-over" attack in turn. Tracer bullets could be seen entering the *Junkers*, smoke poured from its port engine and it crashed in the middle of a field full of cows and surrounded by dykes. Meanwhile, Yellow Section, with a section of Spitfires, had sighted a He 111 at 3,000 feet, which promptly dived to ground-level. While three Spitfires attacked from behind, Yellow 1 carried out a cross-over attack from the starboard side, when smoke immediately issued from both engines… the machine crashed in a field, ending up against a hedge.'

This was, of course, exactly the kind of combat envisaged for the Defiant – unescorted bombers, and Squadron Leader Hunter's team had not disappointed. The following day, however, came a reality check. This time, it was the turn of 264 Squadron's 'B' Flight and the Spitfires of 66 Squadron's 'A' Flight, the fighters taking off at 0430 hrs and heading over the North Sea to harass enemy transport aircraft ten miles north of The Hague. At 0515 hrs, the Dutch coast was crossed, the RAF formation proceeding inland on a northerly course when Dutch AA fire opened up, forcing the fighters to take evasive action. Then a number of Ju 87s dive-bombing a railway line were spotted by the leading Spitfire pilots, who led the whole formation into attack. Four of the dive-bombers, from 12(St)/LG1,

A Boulton-Paul Defiant of 264 Squadron. (Andy Long)

were destroyed. Then… disaster. High above, keeping a watchful eye on the *Stukas*, lurked the Me 109s of 5/JG26, which lost no time in surprising the British fighters. Within a matter of seconds, five of the six Defiants were shot down – one spectacularly exploding in mid-air. Three 264 Squadron aircrew were killed; five wounded and/or captured; two crash-landed and evaded. Only one aircraft, flown by Pilot Officer H.S. Kay, survived the encounter. In response, 264 Squadron shot down just one of their assailants, *Leutnant* Karl Boris, who baled out west of Dordrecht. The Spitfires fared somewhat better than the Defiants, with just one of their number being damaged.

On the day 'B' Flight was massacred over the Dutch coast, the Defiant's manufacturer telegrammed 264 Squadron, referring to the previous day's success: 'Squadron Leader Hunter and squadron. Congratulations on first blood.' Some might consider the timing somewhat unfortunate. The following signal was received from Air Vice-Marshal Leigh-Mallory on 15 May: 'I want to congratulate 264 Squadron most heartily on the success of their operations over Holland which have proved the success of the Defiant as a fighter. I much regret the loss that "B" Flight suffered in the second operation. The courage and determination displayed were of the highest order and create for 264 Squadron a tradition that any squadron might well be proud of.' And from the CAS himself: 'You have done magnificent work during the last 48 hours in Holland and Belgium and fully justify the confidence placed in you. Keep it up.' While the bravery of the crews in the somewhat quirky aircraft are beyond reproach and can only be admired, considering the balance sheet it is difficult to see anything 'magnificent' about it. Such, then, was the position when Pilot Officer Harold Goodall joined 264 Squadron on 22 May.

By that time, things were looking bleak in France, it becoming patently obvious that the *Blitzkrieg* was unstoppable – in no small part owing to the aerial supremacy achieved over the battlefield by the Me 109. On 23 May, Squadron Leader Hunter and his operational crews flew to Manston, from where they patrolled over the French coast during the days ahead. On 26 May, the situation had deteriorated to such a catastrophic extent that the decision was made for the BEF to retire to and evacuate from Dunkirk. From that point onwards, the purpose of air operations was to provide cover for this desperate undertaking. On 27 May, Squadron Leader Hunter himself came into contact with the Me 109 for the first time; espying eight 109s, Hunter ordered his aircraft into line astern, the 109s on this occasion did attack from the rear – and paid the price. Two German fighters, of I/JG1, were shot down. The following day, 264 Squadron engaged twenty-seven 109s over the Channel, Hunter ordering his men to form a defensive circle. In the ensuing combat, the Defiants claimed six Me 109s destroyed – but

The Defiant's turret, armed with four Browning machine guns.

lost three of their number in the process. On 29 May, in addition to claiming two further 109s destroyed, 264 Squadron was attacked by twenty-one Me 110s – fifteen of which Hunter and his pilots claimed destroyed. That evening, Hunter's Defiants claimed eighteen Ju 87s and an 88 destroyed, generating a further congratulatory signal from Air Vice-Marshal Leigh-Mallory. This success 264 Squadron partially ascribed to the enemy having mistaken their Defiants for Hurricanes, attacking from the rear and paying the price.

On 1 June, back at Duxford, 264 Squadron's operational pilots were given a hard-earned 24 hours' leave, and took no further part in the Dunkirk fighting, which concluded on 3 June. That day, the last in a line of visiting VIPs, 264 entertained none other than the 'Father of the Royal Air Force' himself, Marshal of the RAF Lord Trenchard – an honour indeed. Replacement aircrew were also arriving at Duxford, nine air gunners from New Zealand on the day of Trenchard's visit, four more the following day, including LAC Robert Bett Mirk Young, the 22-year-old son of John Carville Young and Emma Harriet Young of Palmerston North. It was a good day to arrive on 264, because the squadron had cause for celebration: Squadron Leader Hunter was appointed to the DSO, and Flight Lieutenant Cooke awarded the DFC. On 7 June, Pilot Officer Kay, survivor of the 'B' Flight massacre, was also awarded the DFC, and Sergeant Thorn, along with Corporal Lippett and LACs King and Turner, all received DFMs. These awards and the Dunkirk action confirmed 264 Squadron as a fighting unit.

Pilot Officer Goodall, being a new pilot, had first to convert to the Defiant, so had not participated in the Dunkirk fighting. Now he teamed up with LAC Young as his gunner, the pair joining five other 264 Squadron machines practising air firing on 12 June. Five days later, Goodall and Young safely carried out night-flying practice. By 11 July, one day after the Battle of Britain officially began, Pilot Officer Goodall and LAC Young were considered 'operations', and as such flew their first patrol from Duxford between 0830 and 1025 hrs, in Defiant L7024, which became their regular mount. The patrol was uneventful, and, owing to a full complement of aircrews, it would be a week before the pair flew again, this time a convoy patrol. Further equally uneventful patrols followed on 19 and 21 July. Next day, 264 Squadron was withdrawn to Kirton-in-Lindsey, from where convoy patrols were flown on 2 and 7 August. On the latter date, Robert Young was promoted to sergeant-observer, receiving his air gunner's brevet on 15 August. A week later, 264 Squadron was deployed to Hornchurch, in 11 Group, during what was a very busy time in the Battle of Britain, with the *Luftwaffe* pounding Air Vice-Marshal Park's airfields. Given that the other Defiant squadron, 141, had been virtually wiped out the previous month while operating in daylight from West Malling, this decision is difficult to comprehend.

Immediately upon arrival at Hornchurch, 264 Squadron were up patrolling Manston, and prowled over the Thames Estuary next day. On 24 August, 264 was again in action, Flight Lieutenant Campbell-Colquhoun being shot up by 109s but living to tell the tale. At lunchtime, the Defiants were refuelling when a big raid came up, the fighters taking off hurriedly – difficult because of the two-crew boarding procedure. Unable to coordinate a squadron attack against the twenty Ju 88s, the Defiants attacked independently, claiming five enemy aircraft destroyed and another damaged. Three Defiants, however, were missing – including Squadron Leader Hunter and his gunner Pilot Officer King, last seen pursuing a Ju 88 towards France. There was more action to come.

Having not flown operationally since 7 August, Pilot Officer Goodall and Sergeant Young were on the board for 264's next sortie on 24 August – which would be a traumatic one. At 1540 hrs, the squadron was ordered off to patrol base as a raid was approaching from the south-east, Harold flying L7024, their usual machine. Seven Defiants scrambled, two of which collided on the ground, such was the panic – bombs were already exploding on the airfield as the remaining five fighters took off. Some miles north-east of Hornchurch, contact was made with a large formation of Ju 88s and Me 109s; ORB: -

'Squadron Leader Garvin attacked the main formation and succeeded in destroying two Ju 88s by overtaking and converging attacks. Pilot Officer Welsh attacked a straggler some 400 yards behind the main formation and shot it down in a crossover attack, he also damaged an Me 109, which attacked with two others. Pilot Officer Young, separated from the main formation, found a solitary He 111 which he destroyed in an overtaking attack. Flight Lieutenant Banham and Pilot Officer Goodall combined in damaging a Ju 88, which they last saw diving towards the London balloon barrage'. Pilot Officer Goodall, Red 2, reported that having followed Squadron Leader Garvin, 'I saw a formation of Ju 88s. I carried out a No 1 Attack from the port side, firing several bursts. The enemy aircraft started to dive, issuing forth white to black smoke. I followed him through cloud and found him underneath. I attacked him from the front and saw bursts entering the cockpit. The enemy aircraft dived away very steeply. I was unable to follow him down.'

A Flight of 264 Squadron on patrol.

The bomber was awarded as a 'damaged', shared with Flight Lieutenant Banham. The Defiants did not escape unscathed: Pilot Officer Gaskell was shot down by a 109, his gunner, Sergeant Machin, dying of wounds. On 24 and 25 August, seven new Defiants were delivered to 264 Squadron, but these aircraft required forty-eight hours work by the unit's maintenance section before they were serviceable. Certain modifications were required and most of the new machines even had the wrong plugs. Work during the night was seriously hampered by air raids, during which no light was allowed in the hangars. This is another indication of the essential role played by groundcrews in difficult conditions.

26 August would be a busy day for 11 Group. With the enemy air assault still focussed on attacking 11 Group's airfields, Air Vice-Marshal Park had gathered his strength about the sector stations around London. After the usual reconnaissance aircraft making their dawn appearance, the first substantial raid, consisting of over fifty bombers escorted by over eighty Me 109s and 110s, crossed the Kentish coast north of Dover at 1130 hrs, bound for Biggin Hill, Kenley and other targets. In response, Air Vice-Marshal Park scrambled forty Hurricanes and thirty Spitfires, a running battle developing from Canterbury to Maidstone. In anticipation of further incoming raids, 264 Squadron was scrambled from Hornchurch at 1142 hrs with orders to orbit Thames Haven. Flight Lieutenant Banham, Pilot Officer Hughes and Sergeant Thorn took off at 1145 hrs, Flight Lieutenant Campbell-Colquhoun, Flying Officer Stephenson, Pilot Officers Goodall and Barwell hurrying after them five minutes later. At 12,000 feet between Hearne Bay and Deal, the Defiants, alone, intercepted twelve Do

17Zs of 7/KG3, based at St Trond in Belgium, heading for Manston, heavily escorted by fifty Me 109s of JG3.

Flight Lieutenant Banham: 'I was Red Leader 264 Squadron, when approaching Dover at 12,000 feet we sighted twelve Do 17s in vics line astern and I opened fire at the leading bomber of last section. I saw my gunner get in a long burst at 100 yards; I then broke away and turned in towards the leading section and got a long burst in at 100 yards on No 2 of first section. I was then hit myself near the cockpit and my machine was on fire. I lost control, and telling my gunner to jump, as I turned aircraft on its back, I fell out and was picked up in the sea. Sergeant Thorne and gunner confirm seeing second Do 17 I fired on go down in flames.'

Shot down by a 109, Flight Lieutenant Banham, rescued after ninety minutes in the sea, was luckier than his gunner, the 27-year-old 'Brummie' Sergeant Barrie Baker – who remains missing.

Flight Lieutenant Campbell-Colquhoun was Yellow 1: -

'On patrol approaching Dover at 11,000 feet I saw nine Do 17s in three vics. Approaching enemy aircraft from starboard side I carried out several attacks from beam. I saw one Do 17 break formation and commence a shallow dive, smoking from starboard engine. I returned to base owing to gun stoppages.'

Pilot Officer Goodall was Yellow 2: -

'When over Manston at 11,000 feet we climbed up to attack a formation of nine Do 17s. During this climb and before we were in range of the Do's, I was attacked by an Me 109 from behind and above. My gunner got in two short bursts and appeared to hit the Me 109, which dived away and was not seen again. Immediately after this I attacked a Do 17 with an overtaking beam attack at 250 yards, and got in two fairly long bursts at point blank range. Pieces fell from the starboard engine which burst into flames. Just as the machine went into a dive one of the crew baled out. I saw the machine go down in flames.

'I immediately attacked another Do 17, which had broken formation and my gunner got in a short burst which appeared to hit. I saw the Do 17 dive into cloud and lost it as I was being attacked by Me 109s. I landed with three guns jammed and damage to my machine.' L7024 was considered damaged 'Category 1', requiring repair off station, and would not be flown again by the Goodall and Young combination. One Do 17 was accredited as destroyed.

Do 17s preparing for a raid on England. (Peter Taghon)

Although their personal combat reports do not appear to have survived, the 264 Squadron ORB reports that 'Pilot Officer Hughes in his first engagement with the enemy successfully destroyed two Do 17s by converging attacks. Sergeant Thorne and Sergeant Barker put up a magnificent show by destroying two Do 17s in the action, and while attacking a third machine they were attacked by an Me 109 and their machine developed oil and glycol leaks. Taking evasive action, they spun away and were preparing to make a crash-landing near Herne Bay when the Me 109 again attacked them at 500 feet. The aircraft caught fire but before crashing Sergeant Barker fired his remaining rounds into the enemy which crashed a few fields away.'

The Me 109 destroyed by Sergeants Thorne and Barker was a fighter of 4/JG3, which crashed on Chislet Marshes, south of Grays Farm, Reculver, at 1225 hrs; the pilot, *Unteroffizier* W. Finke, was killed.

Thorne and Barker were the most successful Defiant crew of the Second World War, and, having already received DFMs for their contribution to the Dunkirk fighting, both received a Bar to their medals for their bravery that day.

Pilot Officer Stephenson, however, was 'set on fire by a 109 and baled out. He was picked up in the sea and later taken to Canterbury Hospital with minor injuries. His gunner, Sergeant Maxwell, is missing.'

From German records, we know that a German *experten*, *Hauptmann* Günther Lützow of *Stab*/JG3, claimed two Defiants in this combat, recording his eleventh and twelfth victories, while *Oberleutnant* Friedrich-Franz von Cramon, also of *Stab*/JG3, claimed a Defiant as his second kill.

There this combat would probably have rested, just one of numerous during those sixteen weeks of high drama, except for one thing: in 2008, recreational divers discovered the wreck of a Do 17 on the Goodwin Sands, lying in fifty feet of water, on top of a chalk bed. Sonar scans were undertaken by the RAF Museum working in partnership with Wessex Archaeology and the Port of London Authority, and the aircraft was identified as being *Werke Nummer* 1160 – a 7/KG3 aircraft shot down during the action involving 264 Squadron on 26 August 1940. The wrecked *Dornier* was eventually recovered from the seabed by commercial diving company Seatech in June 2013. The bomber was then conveyed to the RAF Museum's site at Cosford in Shropshire, there to begin the lengthy and complex process required to clean and conserve the aircraft, ensuring its long-term preservation and display. At the time of writing this remains ongoing, but one day this 'Flying Pencil' will be exhibited as a unique and poignant reminder of the young men from both sides and many nations who lost their lives during the Battle of Britain.

Darren Priday, Manager of the Michael Beetham Conservation Centre at RAF Cosford, responsible for conserving the bomber, confirms that no plate bearing the all-important *Werke Nummer* has been found, and owing to the wreck's overall state it is considered 'very unlikely to positively identify the aircraft as WN1160'. Far from having been conclusively identified during a sonar survey, then, as the *Telegraph* reported on 10 June 2013, that this aircraft is 1160 appears to be little more than educated guesswork. But, for the record, what do we know of 1160, and who shot it down?

A Do 17 over England. (Peter Taghon)

Aboard the bomber, the fuselage code of which was 5K + AR, were four crew-members: the pilot, *Feldwebel* Willi Effmert, a married 24-year-old from Bad Salzuflen near Hanover; the observer, *Unteroffizier* Hermann Ritzel, 21, from Frankfurt am Main; the wireless operator, *Unteroffizier* Helmut Reinhardt, 27, from Bochum, and the flight engineer *Gefreiter* Heinz Huhn, 21, from Lotterfeld in East Prussia (now Loznik, in Poland). Two of the crew baled out but were drowned, namely *Unteroffizier* Reinhardt and *Gefreiter* Huhn, whose bodies washed ashore on opposite sides of the North Sea. The pilot, *Feldwebel* Effmert, looked to force-land on the Goodwin Sands, six miles east of Deal, which were exposed at low tide. Upon impact, the aircraft somersaulted, but both occupants, the pilot and *Unteroffizier* Ritzel, survived and were captured. We know that 1160 disappeared into the sea; another 7/KG3 Do 17 lost in this engagement (WN 2646) force-landed on rocks at Foreness Point, the crew of which did not bale out but were either captured or picked up dead.

Although the combat report of Pilot Officer Des Hughes and Sergeant Freddie Gash is not amongst those preserved at the National Archives, according to the *Telegraph*'s story of 16 June 2013, Hughes, who survived

Conservation of the Goodwin Sands Do 17 is being overseen by Darren Priday, Manager of the RAF Museum's Michael Beetham Conservation Centre at Cosford.

the war and eventually retired as an air vice-marshal, in his unpublished memoir wrote that two crew-members baled out of a Do 17 he and Gash destroyed. The newspaper therefore accredited the 'kill' exclusively to Hughes and Gash. However, given the volume of claims by 264 Squadron, offset against actual 7/KG3 losses that day, there was a significant over-claiming factor, meaning that crews had probably engaged the same target independently without realising that other fighters were doing likewise. In this case, it is clear that Pilot Officer Goodall and Sergeant Young, who also described two crew-members baling out of the Do 17 they destroyed, attacked the same machine. If the aircraft recovered has been correctly identified as 1160, then they too had a hand in its destruction – which has been previously overlooked.

The question remains: is this really Do 17 WN1160? There are, of course, countless aircraft, of both sides, missing over the sea in this area,

One of the Goodwin Sands Do 17's engines and propeller displayed at the RAF Museum, Cosford – appropriately adjacent to the sole surviving and complete Defiant fighter (a Defiant replica can be seen at the Kent Battle of Britain Museum).

the crews of most unrecovered. Their last resting places, with their aircraft wrecks, are protected sites under the provisions of the Protection of Military Remains Act, 1986, which prohibits any interference, preserving them as officially recognised war graves. Without positive identification, therefore, it is difficult to understand how or why permission was given by the Ministry of Defence to raise the aircraft from the seabed. The Goodwin Sands remains at the centre of a controversial plan to dredge the area to stockpile sand for construction work on Dover's Western Docks. Somewhat surprisingly, in July 2018, the Marine Management Organisation granted a dredging licence to Dover Harbour Board for the removal of a staggering three million tonnes of aggregate. The licence was issued on the grounds that appropriate measures were proposed to protect the marine environment, minimise inconvenience to other waterway users and 'mitigate impacts to any other relevant matters'. This is incomprehensible. This rampant hoovering of the seabed will undoubtedly disturb the last resting places of fallen airmen, of both sides, not to mention souls lost in shipwrecks spanning centuries. Needless to say, many feel strongly about the issue of this licence, the resistance coordinated by the Goodwin Sands SOS (Save Our Sands) Group, which called for the project to be suspended. On 8 March 2019 the pressure group won a significant victory in the High Court when Joanna Thomson's lawyers were granted leave to proceed to a Judicial Review of the MMO's decision. At the time of writing, the result of that review is eagerly awaited, and it can only be hoped that respect and decency will prevail over commercial self-interest.

Returning to the events of 1940, on 27 August 264 Squadron operated from Rochford, although there were no engagements and Pilot Officer Goodall and Sergeant Young did not fly that day. The next, 28 August 1940, saw the squadron's final reduction as an effective daylight fighting unit while operating from Rochford, as the ORB described: -

'At 0830 hrs, twelve machines were sent to patrol Dover at 12,000 feet. Twenty He 111s were engaged near Folkestone, heavily escorted by German fighters. The Squadron attacked but was split up by the Me 109s and the cross-fire from the *Heinkels*. One of the He 111s was destroyed by Pilot Officer Carnaby, his first engagement, and one damaged by Sergeant Lauder. Squadron Leader Garvin had a fuse blow in his turret and while Flight Lieutenant Ash was replacing it, his aircraft was hit by a cannon shell and caught fire. Both baled out, but Flight Lieutenant Ash was dead when found. Squadron Leader Garvin suffered minor injury. Pilot Officer Whitley and Sergeant Turner, one of the most successful crews in the Squadron, were killed when their machine crashed and burst into flames. Pilot Officers Kenner and Johnson crashed and were killed. Pilot Officer Bailey made a forced landing after being shot down by an Me 109. Both he and his gunner, Sergeant Hardy, were unhurt. Eight machines returned to Hornchurch. Only three were serviceable.'

Again, the damage had been executed by high-flying Me 109 escorts. The bravery and tenacity of 264 Squadron is underlined by the ORB's next line: -

'At 1245 hrs a large enemy formation was reported approaching Rochford. Permission was sought for the three serviceable machines to take off. This was refused by Operations. At about 1300 hrs, the Section was ordered to scramble. Enemy aircraft were then almost overhead at 18,000 feet. The Section was just airborne when four sticks of bombs dropped across the aerodrome. One of our aircraft was slightly damaged. It was too late for the Section to engage the enemy.'

So far, Pilot Officer Goodall and Sergeant Young had played no part in the day's events, until taking off in their replacement aircraft, N1630, on a patrol of Hornchurch with Flight Lieutenant Banham and Pilot Officer Barwell. The enemy was not encountered, the section returning to Hornchurch at 1715 hrs. At 1800 hrs, a signal was received withdrawing 264 Squadron from the front line. On 1 September, the handful of surviving aircraft and crews once more flew to Kirton in Lindsey. From there, again, the squadron flew convoy patrols and trained replacement crews, in addition to starting night patrols. On 13 September, eight 264 Squadrons, including Pilot Officer Goodall and Sergeant Young, flew from Kirton to operate from Northolt and contribute to the 'night operational flying defence of London'. At this time, night defences were primitive, airborne interception radar and coordination with ground controllers and searchlights embryonic, and dedicated night-fighting aircraft had yet to reach the squadrons in numbers. Consequently, and for some time yet, single-engined day-fighters, including the Defiant, were pressed into service after sunset. Proved unsuitable for daylight operations when Me 109s were present, it would be at night, as the nocturnal *Blitz* on British cities began, that the Defiant would make an essential contribution. That said, the Defiant was being used as a 'catseye' fighter, meaning that interceptions were reliant upon the crew themselves, looking for clues such as searchlights, AA fire, bomb explosions, or the glowing exhausts of enemy aircraft to guide them to a target. Consequently,

Above: The Do 17's inverted wing and centre section.

Below: Close-up of the Do 17's port undercarriage.

only limited success would be achieved by Defiant crews, while the radar-equipped Blenheim Mk IF really held the fort until arrival of the purpose-built Bristol Beaufighter.

That night, 'B' Flight commenced night-flying operations, Pilot Officer Goodall and Sergeant Young in Defiant N1630, patrolling the Maidenhead to Halton line. The ORB reported that 'Pilot Officer Barwell and Pilot Officer Goodall both had a "Tally Ho" (which is to say both pilots sighted an enemy aircraft), but the enemy evaded the searchlights and were not seen again. The guns were not fired. Some difficulty was experienced with the R/T and with Northolt Control.' Interestingly, that night, Flight Lieutenant Smith and Pilot Officer Robinson, carrying out night-flying practice, were stalked by an He 111, which followed them into the Kirton satellite of Caistor, opening fire with its nose-gun. The Defiant was not hit but twelve bullet holes were later counted in the Chance Light, although fortunately none of the Flare Path Party were hit.

A few days later, while 'A' Flight largely operated from Caistor, 'B' Flight moved to Luton 'due to the unsuitability of Northolt', continuing to patrol the Halton to Maidenhead, and Maidenhead to Guildford lines. It was not easy. Without modern navigation aids and considering the blackout

Above left: Pilot Officer Goodall's grave at Parkstone Cemetery, Poole, Dorset. (Andy Long)

Above right: Sergeant Young's grave at Northwood Cemetery.

below, this was exhausting and dangerous work, especially given ongoing problems with ground communications. Pilot Officer Goodall and Sergeant Young's next flight was on the night of 20 September, when they patrolled uneventfully, although on their subsequent sortie, on 24 September, the transmitter broke down at Luton, making operations 'very difficult'. The pair flew a further patrol four evenings later, but contacting the enemy in the night sky was proving extremely difficult.

At 2150 hrs on 8 October 1940, Pilot Officer Goodall and Sergeant Young took off from Luton in Defiant N1627 to patrol the Maidenhead to Halton line at 'Angels 10' (10,000 feet). At 2120 hrs, Pilot Officer Goodall called up Control, reporting that he was investigating a suspected 'bandit some distance away' (accident report dated 18 October). Nothing further was heard from the Defiant. However, 'at 2140 hrs, Operations at Northolt reported that a Defiant aircraft had crashed near Marlow.' Further investigation revealed that this was N1627, in which both pilot and gunner lay dead. It was ascertained that the 'colour cartridge of the hour had been fired', suggesting that the Defiant crew were uncertain as to whether the aircraft they stalked was friendly or hostile. Sadly, the latter was the case: the Defiant's wreckage was found to be riddled with bullet-holes.

Twenty-five-year-old Pilot Officer Harold Goodall was buried in Parkstone Cemetery at Poole, Dorset, where his mother and next-of-kin resided. Twenty-two-year-old Sergeant Robert Bett Mirk Young was laid to rest at Northwood Cemetery – a long way from home in New Zealand. Suffice it to say that to have survived the virtual destruction of 264 Squadron during the daylight battles, only to be killed in action in these circumstances was a travesty.

Chapter Seventeen

Sergeant Peter Roy Charles McIntosh

605 'County of Warwick' Squadron
Killed in Action: 12 October 1940

Peter Roy Charles McIntosh was born on 9 August 1920, the son of John Gilchrist and Florence McIntosh, at Crofton Park, Brockley. Two years later the family moved to 220 Lower Addiscombe Road, Croydon, where Peter spent his formative years. His sister Mary (later Cooper) recalled those happy days: -

'Like his friends, many of who also sadly perished during the war, Peter had a happy growing up. He attended Woodside Primary and then Whitgift Middle School in Wellesley Road, Croydon. At Whitgift he enjoyed being a cadet, especially on field days – getting lost but if lucky being on the winning side – summer camps and tattoo days. In the long summer holidays, we had a choice of three airfields to visit by bicycle: Croydon, Kenley or Biggin Hill. Biggin Hill was a long way to go but from the road the planes could be seen on the ground. Kenley was closer but although we lay for hours in the long grass, often no plane was espied. Croydon even offered real cream ices on the roof of the airport building but we hadn't much pocket-money so rarely enjoyed the delicacy. I actually had very little interest in aviation so stopped going after a while, but Peter was always able to sufficiently enthuse some friend or other to accompany him.'

After leaving school, Peter became a clerk with the Eagle Star Insurance Company. A cockpit, however, was preferable to a desk for this aviation-minded youngster, who joined the RAF Volunteer Reserve as AC2 745004 on 7 February 1939. As previously explained elsewhere in this book, the RAFVR was an essential initiative arising from the 1936 Expansion Plan, aimed at 'Citizen Volunteers' who would remain in their civilian occupations while learning to fly at local centres during weekends, while studying ground subjects on weekday evenings. In the event of emergency, this trained reserve could be mobilised to expand the ranks of the RAF. On the outbreak of war,

Sergeant Peter Roy Charles McIntosh. (via Colin Brown)

Peter was called up, leaving his desk for good, and completing mandatory 'square bashing' at 1 ITW, Cambridge. Between 1 January and 21 May 1940, Sergeant McIntosh completed both his elementary and advanced service flying training before learning to fly Hurricanes with 6 OTU at St Athan. His conversion course complete, on 7 July, Peter reported for flying duties with 151 Squadron's 'B' Flight at North Weald – just in time for the Battle of Britain (see also the story of Pilot Officer Jack Hamar DFC, which provides the background on 151).

Unusually, Peter made his first flights with 151 on the very day he arrived at North Weald, a formation practice flight followed by a 'Sector Recce'. Two more practice flights followed the next day, and on 15 July, Peter made his first 'Fighting Patrol', when 151 was scrambled to intercept a lone and unescorted German bomber attacking shipping in the Dover area. An attack was made by certain pilots but the results were unclear owing to bad visibility and the target escaped into cloud. From then on, Peter flew regularly, the usual pattern being flying to Manston or Rochford at dawn, from where convoy protection sorties were flown. This pattern continued throughout August, Sergeant McIntosh often flying several sorties in a day, but although the Squadron was sometimes engaged, Peter and his flight were never in the right place at the right time. On 30 August, however, 151's CO, Squadron Leader 'Whizzy' King (see Pilot Officer Martyn Aurel King's story) was shot down and killed, by which time the squadron was operating from Stapleford, and there was more 'trade' the next day: 'P/O Ellacombe damaged an Me 109 and Flight Lieutenant Smith destroyed an Me 109. Yellow Section claimed an Me 109. On the second patrol P/O Ellacombe damaged an Me 109, Flight Lieutenant Blair damaged a Ju 88, Pilot Officer Smith damaged a Do 215. Pilot Officer Czajkowski was missing from this patrol and is now in Shoeburyness Hospital with bullet wounds. He claims an Me 109 destroyed. On the third patrol, Pilot Officer Patullo destroyed a Do 215, Pilot Officer Smith destroyed a Do 215 and damaged another.

Pilot Officer Ellacombe force-landed and is in hospital with burns.' What the ORB does not mention is that Sergeant McIntosh, who flew on every patrol that day, also damaged an Me 109. Peter later reported that the Squadron had intercepted thirty Do 215s and 'some' Me 109s at 1300 hrs, 16,000 feet east of North Weald: -

'The Squadron attacked the formation of 215s in line astern from below and behind. I was Number 4. I broke away downwards and to the left after firing for eight seconds. Our leader I think climbed up behind them and saw two Me 109s behind me. I did a steep climbing turn and dived onto the second 109 and gave it a five second burst at full deflection. After firing I dived away as the first one had turned on me, I think the 109 flew into my burst.'

Peter was credited with a 'damaged'.

On 1 September, 151 Squadron was removed to the quieter sector of Digby, where Peter would make just one local flight on 6 September. A week later he was posted back to the combat zone, joining 605 'County of Warwick' Squadron at Croydon, Peter's hometown and the very airfield which so inspired him as a child. There the pilots were accommodated in two-bedroom houses adjacent to the airfield, and Peter's family rejoiced at

A 605 Squadron Hurricane being rearmed and refuelled at Croydon during the Battle of Britain's height.

the opportunity to have him nearby. The Battle of Britain was now entering its critical stage however, leaving little time for socialising.

605 'County of Warwick' Squadron was an AAF unit formed on 5 October 1926 at Castle Bromwich, as a day-bomber squadron recruiting personnel from the Birmingham area. Having flown biplane bombers, on New Year's Day 1939, 605 was redesignated a fighter squadron and re-equipped with Gloster Gladiators. Shortly before the outbreak of war, the Squadron moved to Tangmere and converted to the Hawker Hurricane. From there, 605 flew north, to Drem in Scotland, in February 1940, from where it flew to France in May 1940, reinforcing the AASF for a week before returning to Scotland. On 7 September 1940, the Luftwaffe changed tack from bombing 11 Group's sector stations and attacked London. On that day, 605 flew south, to Croydon, there to relieve 111 Squadron, which had lost eleven pilots. That evening, 605 Squadron had an indication of what was ahead when 'Heavy bombing of London docks' commenced, 'continuing all night. Large fires at Peckham gas works could be seen from Croydon.' With thunder-crashing violence, the Second World War hit London's East End – hard. The following day, 605 was in the thick of it, Flight Lieutenant Archie McKellar DFC's 'B' Flight intercepting a large formation between Maidstone and Tunbridge Wells, as did Pilot Officer Christopher 'Bunny' Currant's 'A' Flight, which was simultaneously bounced by high-flying 109s. The Hurricane pilots made a number of combat claims but Pilot Officer Jon Fleming, a New Zealander, was shot down in flames, baling out 'badly burned and suffering from shock'. That first evening of battle, 'Flight Lieutenant McKellar, Pilot Officer Humphreys and Pilot Officer Forrester stole or borrowed the Station Bedford truck, which Flight Lieutenant McKellar drove to enable them to enjoy the fleshpots of London' – and who could blame them? However, 'Owing to air raids

Christopher 'Bunny' Currant – ultimately a wing leader and fighter ace.

they never slept a wink and returned in truculent mood having found no consolation for lack of sleep, whereas we at Croydon slept soundly!'

Over the next few days, the Battle of Britain now at its height with the *Luftwaffe* pounding London round-the-clock, 605 Squadron was heavily engaged on a daily basis. On 13 September, Sergeant McIntosh reported to Croydon, on which date Pilot Officer Currant, who had so ably commanded 'A' Flight despite his junior rank, was promoted to flight lieutenant. A regular air force officer, 'Bunny' had flown fighters since 1937, and had fought with the Squadron in France; a highly successful Fighter Pilot, he later wrote poetry as an outlet for his wartime experiences, including this one, entitled simply 'Croydon: September 1940'.

Once again he took to the air, and Croydon was the base
To fight it out in fear and sweat so many times each day
To smell the burn of cordite flash, to see the flames of war
High above the fields of Kent the dive, the zoom, the soar.
Returning from a clash of foes one day he came across
A sight which burnt deep in his soul and never can be lost.
A pilot dangling from his chute towards the earth did drift
He circled round this friend or foe so hopelessly alone
To keep away whoever dared to fire on such a gift.
It was a useless gesture, though, as round and round he flew
He saw as in an awful dream first smoke and then flames spew,
Curl up his back as arms he waved and burn the cords of life
Snapping the body from the chute, snatching him from
wartime strife.
With sickening horror in his heart, he landed back at base.
He cried himself to sleep that night in thanks to God's grace
That he was spared yet once again to live and fight this fight
Against the things he saw as black, for things he believed
were right.

In 1995, Wing Commander Currant DSO DFC, told me that: -

'At the time of this event, the battle over London and south-east England was in full flow. We were busy. Oh boy, we were busy! There had been reports from RAF pilots of being shot at as they floated down in their parachutes by Me 109s. I was racing back to Croydon having expended all my ammunition in a great big mêlée of *Heinkel* and *Dornier* bombers,

Me 109s and 110s, Hurricanes and Spitfires. I had attacked a number of bombers from above, from the side, from below and head-on. It was a frantic whirl of in-fire-break-down or up-and-in again and again. And then there was no ammunition, all gone, head for home like mad. As I flew westwards, south of London, I came across this pilot in his parachute, yellow Mae West prominent. Ours or theirs I could not tell. I knew about the attacks by 109s and so flew round and round to stop any swine rom attacking this pilot. I was determined that no bugger would get this lad. No-one did. They'd got him already as he had almost certainly baled out of his plane on fire. Clothing wet from petrol, embers glowing, fanned by the air as he floated down. Yes, I wept myself to sleep that night. Who wouldn't?'

Revealingly, 'Bunny' added: -

'You always felt it would be the other chap, which is typical of combat life. You have to think like that. You were always very tense and apprehensive until you got into the aircraft and started to take off, then that feeling disappeared. Then there was the exhilaration of what was coming, which was quite a different feeling from when you were sitting around waiting to be told to take off. One was always very frightened, but you just carried on in spite of it.'

On 14 September, Sergeant McIntosh made his first flight with his new squadron, practising formation flying with the highly competent and popular 'B' Flight commander, Flight Lieutenant Archie McKellar. Next came *the* day, the great air battle over London and southern England now commemorated annually as 'Battle of Britain Day'. Although a pilot of some experience by now, Peter was new to 605 and not rostered to fly on 15 September. 605 was, however, heavily engaged. Pilot Officer Bob Foster: -

'That particular day we had the "Invasion Imminent" warning, codename CROMWELL. We sat in our cockpits at immediate readiness, ready to scramble immediately, from an hour before to an hour after dawn. As we were facing east, we actually watched the sun rise. It was a beautiful day. We sat awaiting the call for a couple of hours, expecting the invasion when it did. It never came. We just sat there and in the end were reduced to "fifteen minutes readiness", meaning that we could leave our aircraft while remaining available to take off within a quarter of an hour. So we went back to the nearby house we were billeted in or went to the Mess. There was a lot of tension when just sitting around, then a bit of a let-down when nothing actually happened.'

While the invasion did not materialise that fateful day, as the 605 Squadron ORB reports: -

'Enormous enemy bomber and fighter formations crossed the coast towards London morning and afternoon. In the morning the fight took place around Croydon aerodrome, 605 Squadron doing conspicuously well. Flight Lieutenant Currant destroyed two Do 17s and damaged another; Sergeants Wright and Howes each destroying another and Flight Lieutenant McKellar destroyed two Me 109s. Pilot Officer Jones baled out at West Malling, slightly injured. In the afternoon three waves of enemy bombers and fighters approached from the SE, the first escorted by the Me 109s, the second and third unescorted. Most of 605 Squadron's attacks were upon the first formation, around Maidstone. Again, the Squadron did exceedingly well, Flight Lieutenant McKellar destroying a Do 17 and probably destroying a He 111, Flight Lieutenant Currant destroying an Me 109, damaging two Do 17s and a He 111, Pilot Officer Cooper-Slipper destroying a Do 17, Sergeant Howes probably destroying a Do 17 and Sergeant Watson damaging a Do 17. During this engagement Pilot Officer Cooper-Slipper had a remarkable escape. His control was shot away and his aircraft hit a Do 17 amidships. Pilot Officer Cooper-Slipper's aircraft, minus port wing, spiralled down

'Bunny' at the launch of the author's *Through Peril to the Stars*, Great Malvern, 1993.

and he baled out, landing unhurt other than small bruises, near Marden. He returned to Croydon later in the evening, apparently unshaken, with two German Mae Wests and a complete rubber boat, given to him by Maidstone Police! A very noisy night from AA fire and bombs whistling around. Two bombs landed within 200 yards of our sleeping quarters; neither yet exploded. Flight Lieutenant McKellar did a night patrol in bright moonlight and damaged, if not destroyed, a He 111. Further reports are awaited from the Observer Corps with great interest.'

By close of play, this massive effort by the *Luftwaffe* to bring Fighter Command to battle for destruction had failed. The British press eagerly reported the Air Ministry's figures of 185 enemy aircraft destroyed for the loss of thirty fighters and ten pilots. In reality, the Germans had lost fifty-six aircraft, less, in fact, than on 15 August when their losses totalled seventy-five, and on 18 August (sixty-nine). Nonetheless, 15 September 1940 represented the major turning point for the hard-pressed defenders, it now being abundantly clear in messes across *Der Kanal* that the RAF was not and would not be destroyed, and in Berlin it was recognised that Göring was unable to deliver on his boastful promises of only a few weeks before. If it was sensed in the vapour-trail criss-crossed air that the back of the enemy assault had been broken, the Battle of Britain remained far from over.

16 September dawned 'a dull, drizzling, day', no doubt welcomed by both sides after the previous days herculean exertions. On the dawn patrol over Folkestone, Pilot Officer Watson was hit by a 109, forcing him to land at Detling, and received hospital treatment. Sergeant McIntosh flew on that sortie, but owing to poor weather, the next two days saw little flying. On 19 September, Peter was scrambled four times throughout the day, but no raids were intercepted. The weather remained poor next day, the 'rough seas', the 605 Squadron diarist decided, being responsible for delaying 'Germany's invasion plans'. On the evening of the 22nd, a wet and cold day, Peter again patrolled uneventfully with his Squadron. 23 September was one of high winds and broken cloud, 605 Squadron clashing with Me 109s on the dawn patrol, one of which was damaged by the Polish Pilot Officer Witold Glowacki. The next day, he was dead. On the 24th, another wet and cloudy day, Pilot Officers Muirhead and Glowacki patrolled over Beachy Head, stalking a Do 215 in and out of cloud, sharing the bomber's destruction, which fell into the sea off Cap Gris Nez. Emerging from cloud near the enemy-occupied French coast, the two Hurricanes were bounced by 109s, Muirhead hedge-hopping twenty-one miles inland over France before

shaking off his pursuer; Glowacki was never seen again, undoubtedly shot down over Boulogne by 3/JG51's *Oberleutnant* Michael Sonner.

On 26 September, Peter joined the 605 Squadron formation which flew down to operate out of Hawkinge in anticipation of being required to defend a large convoy intending to pass through the Dover Strait. In the event, the Hurricanes were not required and so returned to Croydon. On the morning of 27 September, 605 Squadron found itself patrolling over north-east Kent and, 8,000 feet higher than the Me 109s, which the Hurricane pilots lost no time in 'jumping', destroying one and damaging several others. That afternoon, Sergeant McIntosh was scrambled with the squadron, which found five Ju 88s south-east of Croydon which were followed to the coast; one was destroyed, three were shared with other units, and the fifth was seen to crash near Winchelsea. 28 September saw Peter fly on three of the day's four scrambles, the squadron being bounced twice by high-flying 109s, leading to critical comments being levelled at Group Controllers. Nonetheless, Flight Lieutenant Currant destroyed a 109, and Pilot Officer Hope survived being shot down and baling out. On the 29th, Peter flew once, uneventfully on a day of fog and poor visibility which saw 605's CO, Squadron Leader Walter Churchill, a pre-war auxiliary member of the squadron, posted to command the new all-American 'Eagle' Squadron, his place at 605's helm taken by the newly promoted Squadron Leader Archie McKellar DFC. The month's last day was again foggy, and although patrols were flown, no enemy aircraft were encountered.

By 1 October, the German daylight bomber offensive had been defeated, the battle moving into its final phase. In the main, the German bombing effort shifted to nocturnal operations, chiefly to continue the progressive

Aviation historian Colin Brown points to the spot where Sergeant McIntosh's Hurricane crashed at Littlestone Golf Course on Romney Marsh, Kent.

destruction of London, and secondly, although of much lower importance, to interfere with production at the Midlands' great arms centres. The OKW also agreed that daylight bombing operations should continue, but on a much reduced scale, by either lone aircraft engaged on nuisance raids when weather conditions were favourable, or by Ju 88s escorted by large numbers of fighters. The aircraft industry was the target of these raids; an invasion was no longer the enemy aerial offensive's aim. In terms of fighter operations, since the previous month Göring had included fighter-bombers – *Jabos* – in fighter sweep formations, which indiscriminately dropped their bombs from high altitude. RAF controllers were unable to tell whether an incoming fighter sweep included *Jabos*, meaning that all had to be met. The volume of these raids, most against London and the south-east, stretched Fighter Command to the limit. Indeed, 11 Group had to mount standing patrols of either one or a pair of squadrons over the Maidstone Line, barring the way to London. Immediately an incoming threat was detected, those airborne units would be ordered to 30,000 feet, there to contain the enemy fighters and provide top cover for friendly squadrons scrambled and climbing to reinforce. Only the Spitfire could meet the 109 on equal terms at high altitude, so this very much became the Spitfire squadrons' responsibility – which, as 92 Squadron's Pilot Officer Geoffrey 'Boy' Wellum remembered was 'exhausting'. The new enemy tactics required a much higher state of preparedness throughout 11 Group in particular, and the standing patrols increased a squadron's operational flying hours from forty-five to sixty hours daily.

Peter McIntosh flew two patrols, uneventfully, on 2 and 3 October, the latter a most miserable, foggy, day which saw 605 Squadron released from 1800 hrs until dawn on 4 October, the first such occurrence since the unit's arrival at Croydon and which was appropriately celebrated by 'an excellent dinner at "The Greyhound", Croydon'. Peter did not fly again until the afternoon of 10 October, when in thundery weather 605 Squadron patrolled at 25,000 feet 'and got iced up for the first time since last winter'. Fog persisted the next day, although Peter patrolled twice, the 'Squadron for the first time adopted new tactics of flying in echeloned or staggered pairs astern when over 25,000 feet, with one pilot weaving in front and another behind. It was considered successful, and possibly confusing to the enemy as being like the German fighter tactics.' Equally surprising was how long, lacking direction from on high, it took squadrons to reject the pre-war Fighter Command formations, which, in the words of 19 Squadron's Flight Sergeant George 'Grumpy' Unwin DFM were 'Bloody useless'. That said, without a standard operating procedure, *ad hoc* local arrangements could also be confusing to other

Fighter Command squadrons – and 'Friendly Fire' was in any case not uncommon. There was no choice but to experiment – on the job.

Fog also greeted 605 Squadron at dawn on 12 October. Mary Cooper: 'Peter telephoned home at about mid-day, telling us that he would be on Ops during the afternoon, but would phone again later.' That day, however, seven attacks were made by the *Luftwaffe*, five penetrating via Kent to London. During the morning, a fighter sweep reached London, including three 2/LG2 *Jabos*, one of which dropped a SC250KG bomb from 20,000 feet, killing five people in Piccadilly. At 1215 hrs, Squadron Leader McKellar scrambled from Croydon, leading off Flying Officer Hope, Pilot Officers Hayter and Ingle, and Sergeants Budzinski and McIntosh, in company with the Hurricanes of Northolt-based 615 'County of Surrey' Squadron. At 1315 hrs, the Hurricanes met the enemy over Dungeness, as Pilot Officer Alec Ingle, Green One, reported: -

'The Squadron was in sections, vic astern. At 25,000 feet, the Squadron paired into six sections, staggered line astern. After patrolling on various vectors, the Squadron was heading SE at 23,000 feet, towards Dungeness, when three small formations of Me 109s passed about 1,500 yards ahead, heading NW. We held formation in a SE direction for about one minute, when four enemy aircraft appeared out of the sun ahead of and dived on us. The leading sections, not already engaged, did a diving turn to the right and engaged the enemy aircraft below them, who were at that time being engaged by 615 Squadron. Various enemy aircraft broke out of the engagement and headed SE. I picked an isolated and unengaged one and chased it towards the coast. I expended all my ammunition on it in five equal bursts, in astern attacks, and after the third one saw oil come out of the starboard side. When about four miles out from the coast of Dungeness at about 1,500 feet, I broke off the engagement and watched the enemy aircraft descend into the sea in a shallow dive some ten to fifteen miles east of Dungeness. While chasing this aircraft I saw another enemy aircraft plunge into the sea about two miles off Dungeness. I returned to base at 1340 hrs.' Sergeant Howes also shot a 109 down into the sea off Dungeness, but back at Croydon 605 had a pilot missing.

Mary Cooper: -

'When Peter neither telephoned or came to see us, our father called the Squadron and received the devastating news that Peter was missing. There was no other official news throughout the next day, but we knew from other

Sergeant McIntosh's grave at Shirley Cemetery, Croydon. (Joel Diggle)

pilots that there had been a combat over the Kentish coast. Our father and elder brother then travelled by car to tour the country area over which the combat had been fought. They stopped and questioned people regarding whether they had seen a British fighter crash on the day in question, and were eventually directed to Littlestone Golf Course, near New Romney, by a farmer who had seen a plane come down there. They subsequently returned home with a piece of fuselage bearing the number P3022, which identified the aircraft concerned as Peter's Hurricane. When approached by my father the Air Ministry said it had no personnel available to search for missing aircraft, and so, needless to say, in our house there was much bad feeling against the authorities. In the event, father still had difficulty persuading them that he had found Peter's crash site. Eventually, my brother's remains were recovered by the RAF and brought home. Ten days after his death in action, our dear Peter was buried in Shirley churchyard.'

There is little doubt that Sergeant Peter McIntosh was yet another RAF fighter pilot hacked down in a surprise attack by none other than Major Werner Mölders, *Kommodore* of JG51 – possibly the greatest ace of all – who claimed a Hurricane over Dungeness. Peter's was the only Hurricane lost at that time and place.

In sum, Peter McIntosh flew at least 108 operational flights with both 151 and 605 Squadrons during the Battle of Britain. On the day he was killed, *Generalfeldmarschall* Wilhelm Keitel announced the OKW's decision to postpone the invasion of England until the spring or early summer of 1941, and that in the meantime efforts would be made to 'improve the military conditions for a later invasion'. Thanks to young pilots like Sergeant McIntosh, that proposed invasion never happened.

A letter to the British press from Mr McIntosh criticising the authorities' efforts to establish the fate of pilots missing in action was never published.

Chapter Eighteen

Pilot Officer Hugh William Reilley (Canadian)

66 Squadron

Killed in Action: 17 October 1940

66 Squadron, known affectionately as 'Clickety-Click', was a regular RAF fighter squadron with a long and proud history. Before the war, 66 shared Duxford in 12 Group with 19 Squadron, the latter having become the RAF's first Spitfire-equipped squadron in August 1938; 'Clickety-Click' followed three months later to become the second. By the outbreak of the Second World War on 3 September 1939, 66 Squadron, therefore, was one of the RAF's most experienced Spitfire squadrons – and the Spitfire was, as Bob Morris, a Fitter (Engines) on 66 Squadron put it, 'a young man's dream!'

Bob Morris had joined the RAF before the war, studying aeronautical engineering at the RAF Technical School, Halton. Because of the urgent need for personnel after war was declared, activities such as time off and sport were cancelled and replaced by more technical training. In May 1940, Bob passed out as an Airman 1st Class and was posted to 66 Squadron at Coltishall: -

'I knew neither the location of Coltishall or what aircraft 66 Squadron had. Coltishall, I discovered, was in Norfolk, and my first glimpse of 66 Squadron was from the bus which travelled alongside the airfield a short distance – what a thrill to see… *Spitfires*!

'In 66 Squadron, I found the set-up was that there were two groups of technical people looking after the aircraft. Trades in the RAF were sub-divided into five, the technical people being in the first, and we did all major work on the aircraft. Group Two were flight mechanics, semi-skilled, who looked after the aircraft's daily requirements, like Daily Inspections, oil, petrol, tyre pressures etc. In our group there was a Fitter Engines and a Fitter Airframe, and in the second a Flight Mechanic Engines and Flight Mechanic Airframe, the latter two always staying with the same aircraft. The Flight

Above left: Pilot Officer Hugh Reilley. (Chris Reilley)

Above right: Bob Morris, a Fitter II (Engines) on 66 Squadron during the Battle of Britain.

Mechanic Engine would start up the Spitfire's Rolls-Royce Merlin engine first thing in the morning, so when the call to scramble came the engine was already nice and warm. We Fitter IIEs never had an aircraft of our own, as there were less of us, so we could be called upon to work on any of the Squadron's Spitfires. We used to do the 30, 60, and 90-hour inspections, and when each aircraft had reached the maximum number of flying hours per its particular type of engine, we would also do the necessary engine change. My first jobs were mainly inspections, as opposed to repair work. I remember a pilot getting into the cockpit and I helped him to get going, pulled the chocks away and set him up to fly. As he taxied out, I thought to myself "I bet he doesn't know that this is my first attempt!" Perhaps he wouldn't have taken off so confidently had he known!

'We shared Coltishall with the Hurricanes of 242 Squadron, but we were not there for long as we moved down to Kenley in 11 Group, right down in the thick of it, the Battle of Britain having started by this time. We arrived there on 3 September 1940, to find a shambles, hardly a single building remained standing. As we drove around the aerodrome to our assembly point, I saw a car park full of vehicles – all riddled by gunfire or shrapnel.

There were shelters destroyed, buildings flattened. We had to learn very quickly about air raids, which were incoming thick and fast. Once I looked up and saw five parachutes descending. We were soon dispersed around the edge of Kenley airfield with plenty of space between each aircraft. We could not put the aircraft either in a hangar or in a group for fear of them being wiped out together. That meant we had to work on them out in the open, often without any cover when a raid occurred. They had built some blast pens at Kenley, but nowhere near enough, so you could be quarter of a mile away from the nearest shelter. It is perhaps surprising, however, that you do get used to it, almost blasé. We used to carry on working after the siren had gone, right up until when the Germans were practically overhead. If you then left your aircraft and lay down on the ground some distance away from it, the chances of being killed by a bomb were remote. Strafing was more hazardous, but the greatest danger was bomb-blast, i.e. what got thrown up into the air. If it exploded near a road, building or runway, huge slabs and chunks of concrete and masonry would come falling down on you. You therefore tended to lie there and keep your fingers crossed that when all the rubbish came down, none of it hit you.

'We were only at Kenley for a week, but that short time was absolutely devastating: we lost eight pilots, so by the end of the week were practically out of action.'

Pilot Officer Hubert 'Dizzy' Allen was a pilot in 66 Squadron's 'B' Flight, to whom the Spitfire was 'the very pink of perfection' and who survived the carnage at Kenley; of casualties, he later wrote that 'Whereas we had had to withstand only a few losses among our pilots when paddling around in Cambridgeshire and Norfolk, now we had to become used to greeting many newly joined pilots. Some came from other squadrons, for various reasons – one arrived when his squadron had been bombed on take-off and his unit was more or less written off, certainly decimated. Others came from nowhere and went to heaven or hell, or to limbo. Some we liked, some we didn't like. Either they were possessed of, or managed to attain, the peculiar style which we preferred, or they weren't.'

Bob Morris: -

'On 10 September 1940, 66 Squadron moved to Gravesend, which was no more than a civilian flying club airfield. We were the only squadron there, at what was Biggin Hill Sector Station's satellite. At Gravesend we looked down the Thames, opposite Tilbury, and I remember bombs hitting large floating oil tanks in the river there. I always admired the sailors of the little boats,

Bob Morris pictured at the launch of the author's *Battle of Britain: The Photographic Kaleidoscope, Volume III*, at Worcester in 2000. Bob was passionate about the Spitfire and immensely proud of 66 Squadron and his part in the Battle of Britain, during which he got to know Pilot Officer Reilley well and thought highly of him.

tugs and the like that used to pull out those tanks which were on fire, to stop the flames spreading. Fortunately, we were not bombed at Gravesend. There was only one hangar there, our dining room, a small hut for flying control and a pilots' crew room, and that was it. Without much to hit on a grass airfield, we would have been hard to put out of action anyway.'

'Dizzy' Allen: -

'Gravesend was immensely to our liking. It was a pre-war airport, not a regular fighter station, and lacked all the pretence which goes with the latter. Our pilots' dispersal room was an old clubhouse, furnished with not uncomfortable armchairs, and integral to its design was a bar. Behind the room were the kitchens and so on, and in the room was a microphone intended to relay the scramble order around the airfield. We immediately got hold of a gramophone and our favourite records, and installed them within easy reach of the microphone. From dawn to dusk our kind of music sighed round the airport, breaking our neighbours' eardrums – assuming they hadn't been already broken by the roar of the Merlins being run up, or on take-off; but we also used the microphone for the scramble order, to allow the mechanics time to get the engines started ahead of our sprint to the Spitfires.'

Acting Flight Lieutenant Bob 'Oxo' Oxspring commanded 'B' Flight at Gravesend: -

'An hour before dawn, we crawled out of bed, forced down some breakfast and got shaken into wakefulness as we were transported to dispersal in a hard-arsed lorry. We arrived to the cacophony of Merlin engines being warmed up and tested all round the airfield by the reliable fitters. Having chalked up the allocations of pilots to aircraft and formation compositions, we donned our Mae West lifejackets, collected our parachutes and helmets and trudged out to our aircraft. Detailed walk-round inspections such as are the mode today would have been an insult to our conscientious groundcrews, many of whom had been up all night rectifying faults and repairing battle damage.'

Oxspring had joined 66 Squadron at Duxford in December 1938, making his first Spitfire flight on 2 February 1939. By the time 'Clickety-Click'

Hugh Reilley (third left) and his friend Robert Monro Buchanan before leaving Canada to join the RAF. Buchanan would become a Hudson pilot – shot down and killed by the German ace Gordon Gollob in July 1940. (Chris Reilley)

moved to Gravesend, 'Oxo' had shared in the destruction of a Do 17 and personally destroyed an He 111 – but now the tempo of combat would increase to an unprecedented intensity. Years later, Group Captain Oxspring also wrote of replacement pilots: -

'After the clobbering we had suffered in the few days since moving south, we had absorbed the hard lessons meted out. The squadron was now flying with mounting confidence, but the brunt of the fighting fell on the more experienced surviving pilots. In the two months since the battle started, Fighter Command had sustained such heavy losses that the supply of trained fighter pilots was exhausted. Our replacements began to arrive from the Operational Training Units before they finished their courses. They could only muster little more than ten hours' flying on a Spitfire which, though unavoidable, was grossly insufficient. With such a background they could scarcely fly the aircraft, let alone fight in it. None had even fired their guns and tragically they became lambs for the slaughter. Within the next ten days, seven of these chaps arrived to fill the gaps, and none lasted more than three weeks.'

Amongst 66 Squadron's replacements was a Pilot Officer Reilley, possessed of more experience that a pilot fresh out of OTU, who arrived from Biggin Hill-based 92 Squadron on 15 September 1940 – now commemorated as 'Battle of Britain Day' and remembered as the daylight battle's crescendo.

Hugh William Reilley was one of over 100 Canadians who fought in the Battle of Britain, having been born at Victoria Hospital, London, Ontario, on 28 May 1918, the only son of Hugh William, an American, born in Smith, Virginia, and Annie Reilley, a Scot. The Reilleys actually lived at 960 Cass Avenue, Detroit, but Annie Reilley had decided on a move to South London, Ontario, for her child's birth, to be closer to her brother, John Miller and his family. After Hugh's birth, the Reilleys returned to Detroit, but separated there a decade later. Thereafter, Annie and young Hugh went to live in South London, close to brother John and his wife Rose. Annie died prematurely on 25 May 1930, after which sad event young Hugh was taken in and brought up by his aunt and uncle. It was in South London, Ontario, therefore, that Hugh Reilley spent his formative years. Having initially attended Tecumseh Public School, between 1933 and 1938, he studied at London South Collegiate High School and excelled at rugby and tennis. After leaving school, Hugh, according to family records, worked at the Highland Golf Club, probably as a caddy, and at the 'Winery', also in London, although his job there is unknown.

Pilot Officer Reilley with a Harvard aircraft during training at Brize Norton. (Chris Reilley)

Far away in western Europe, another war between Britain and Germany was looking increasingly unavoidable. The prospect of achieving an SSC and learning to fly with the RAF gained traction in the Commonwealth countries, with many young men gravitating to England from far-flung corners of the dominions and Empire. Amongst these intrepid adventurers was Hugh Reilley, who, together with his friend Robert Monro Buchanan, left Montreal in May 1939, bound for England and the RAF.

On 20 September 1939, Hugh Reilley took the King's shilling and an SSC. Joining No 1 Initial Training Wing at Jesus College, Cambridge, two days later, there his introduction to the service was undertaken before starting flying training, first at the civilian Bristol Flying School, Filton, and then 10 Elementary Flying Training School at Yatesbury. From there, on 25 March 1940, it was up to Brize Norton and 46 Course at 2 Flying Training School, learning to fly the Harvard monoplane. On 20 April 1940, Pilot Officer Reilley married Marjory Etta Fleming – universally known as 'Molly' – the couple having met at a London ball thrown by Lord Beaverbrook, the Canadian-British publisher and politician. Mrs Reilley remained at her home in Park Road, Uxbridge, while her new husband completed his training in Oxfordshire. Although 46 Course concluded on 11 July, Pilot Officer Reilley was for some reason deferred for further

20 April 1940: after the wedding of Pilot Officer Hugh Reilley and Marjory Etta Fleming, known to all as 'Molly'. (Chris Reilley)

training, spending until 3 August on the subsequent 47 Course. A week later, he reported to 7 OTU at Hawarden, near Chester, one of two Spitfire training schools. Having successfully converted to the type, with a handful of Spitfire hours recorded in his flying log book, the young Canadian was posted to 64 Squadron at Leconfield on 2 September. The following day he flew the first of several uneventful operational patrols from Leconfield, thus qualifying for the Battle of Britain Clasp to the 1939-45 Star and inclusion amongst the fabled Few.

From 7 September 1940 onwards it had been decided to rotate squadrons in and out of the combat area, allowing battered formations to rebuild to strength, receiving replacement pilots who could obtain further experience in a quiet zone. When back on 'top line', these squadrons could be redeployed to southern England, but equally combat-ready pilots from these units were also transferred independently as replacements to frontline squadrons. Consequently, on 12 September, Pilot Officer Reilley was posted from 64 in 12 Group to 92 Squadron at Biggin Hill in 11 Group. 92 was a first-rate and very experienced fighter squadron, heavily committed at that time at what was the Battle of Britain's height. After its disastrous week at Kenley, though,

Squadron Leader Rupert 'Lucky' Leigh (centre) with some of his 66 Squadron pilots at Gravesend, September 1940. From left: PO H.W. Reilley, PO C.A.W. Bodie, FL G.P. Christie; PO A.B. Watkinson, FLT R.W. Oxspring and PO H.R. Allen.

66 Squadron at nearby Gravesend was more in need of replacements, and so our Canadian hero packed up his troubles once more and joined 'Clickety-Click' three days after arriving at 'Biggin-on-the-Bump'.

At Gravesend, Pilot Officer Reilley found that 66 Squadron was commanded by former Cranwellian and flying instructor Squadron Leader Rupert 'Lucky' Leigh, and was assigned to Flight Lieutenant Bob Oxspring's 'B' Flight. Amongst 'Clickety-Click's' pilots, he also found a fellow Canadian: Pilot Officer George Corbett, from Saskatchewan. Corbett's family had moved to live in England before the war, the air-minded George becoming a de Havilland apprentice and learning to fly with the RAFVR. When war broke out, however, he was visiting Canada, so terminated the vacation and hurried back to England. Back home, mobilised, George completed his service flying training at Hullavington, and after converting to Spitfires at 5 OTU, Aston Down, joined 66 Squadron on 26 July 1940. On 9 September, 66 Squadron was engaged over Kent when Pilot Officer Corbett made his first combat claim, an Me 109 'probable' over Rye, but was in turn shot down over East Grinstead and baled out slightly wounded (contrary to the Squadron Operations Record Book which states that Corbett 'forced-landed and received slight injury at Cowden').

After a week's sick leave, Pilot Officer Corbett returned to 66 Squadron, meeting Pilot Officer Reilley, who had made his first operational flight on 17 September. After the climax on 15 September, the weather deteriorated, providing both sides a little respite, although defensive patrols continued. On the 17th, 66 Squadron flew just one patrol, Squadron Leader Leigh taking the squadron off at 1520 hrs, Pilot Officer Reilley flying as Red Two to Flight Lieutenant Oxspring. The sortie was uneventful, the Spitfires returning safely to Gravesend at 1705 hrs.

Further patrols followed over the next few days, throughout which the weather was bad, with cloud-base often descending to 2,000 feet. On 23 September the weather improved and so too did enemy activity, although this maintained the pattern of operations since the great climax on 15 September, with nuisance attacks by single aircraft and free-ranging fighter sweeps at high altitude to the outskirts of London. These fast-moving fighter formations were difficult to intercept. Indeed, on 23 September, Fighter Command surprisingly made as many sorties as it had on 'Battle of Britain Day', and yet only three or four of the twenty or so squadrons scrambled to meet these threats actually engaged. Certainly, radar provided advance warning of intruders, this usually being ten to twenty minutes before the Germans crossed the English coast. Insufficient information however, regarding position, numbers or height, and the inability to distinguish fighter from bomber formations, made interceptions hard work – not assisted by the cloud cover at this time, neutralising the ever-watchful Observer Corps. When interceptions did occur, RAF fighters were often disadvantaged because they were still climbing, whereas the Me 109s were already, as always, high up there, watching and ready to pounce. Moreover – and this is the rub – above 25,000 feet the Me 109 was demonstrably superior to the Hurricane, and with fuel-injection coupled with cannon and machine-gun armament enjoyed advantages over the Spitfire. This was a very dangerous and exhausting period for Fighter Command.

On 23 September, having scrambled from Gravesend with Pilot Officer Cooke at 0911 hrs, Pilot Officer Reilley, again flying as Red Two, reported that at 0955 hrs, twelve miles east of Chatham, 'The Squadron was attacked by Me 109s at 28,000 feet. We all split up immediately and this resulted in my being left alone. I was cruising at 20,000 feet when two Me 109s appeared out of cloud. I managed to get in one burst just beneath the cockpit, from behind. There then appeared more planes on the scene and I was unable to follow the hit Me 109, but he seemed to turn over on his side and plunge earthwards with black smoke trailing behind. The other 109 disappeared,

Another well-known Gravesend photograph; from left, standing: FL R.W. Oxspring, SL R.H.A. Leigh; PO C.A.W. Bodie. Seated, from left: FL K.M. Gillies, PO A.B. Watkinson, PO H.M.T. Heron, PO H.R. Allen, FO Hewitt (Adjutant), and PO H.W. Reilley.

and the new arrivals turned out to be friendly aircraft. In the engagement, as I attacked the first E/A, the second turned a left-hand circle and directed an accurate burst of machine-gun fire, but due to deflection did not hit my aircraft.' Returning to Gravesend at 1025 hrs, Reilley claimed his first combat success: an Me 109 probably destroyed.

The following day, a new phase in the Battle of Britain began, the enemy's focus now being firmly on aircraft factories, the Supermarine works in Southampton attracting attention from the crack *Erprobungsgruppe* 210, heralding a renewed assault of West Country targets. Around 1130 hrs, some 180 enemy aircraft appeared, the ratio of fighters to bombers being 2:1, their targets Kentish coastal towns, although little damage was done. At 1120 hrs, Pilot Officer Cooke led Pilot Officers Reilley, Pickering, Corbett, Watkinson and Sergeant Corbett when scrambled at 1120 hrs. Later, Pilot Officer Reilley reported that: -

'"B" Flight took off at 1120 hrs and joined "A" Flight. After a short chase, the Squadron then proceeded to Biggin Hill and joined 72 and

92 Squadrons. We then proceeded to about 20,000 feet and made an attack on two stray Me 109s. In the ensuing jumble the sky appeared full of Me 109s, a conservative estimate would be forty-eight. They were split up by various squadrons and I saw four 109s about 300 feet below me, at the time I was at about 17,000 feet. I dived on them, attacking one to the side. I made a quarter attack and gave him a burst, and he broke away from the action. The remainder of section tried no offensive action and the one I shot tried only to join his section. I prevented this by a head-on attack, a bit below, and saw all my bullets enter the machine. I could just see him stagger before I was far behind. The visibility was very poor from about 400 – 800 yards and as more aircraft were milling about, my attention was taken and I was unable to look for my Me 109. I was unable to get into any other engagement and returned to my base at 1235 hrs.'

The Me 109 was claimed as 'damaged'.

Later that day, 'B' Flight was aloft again, when, as Pilot Officer Reilley reported, several miles north of Hastings an He 111 was intercepted at 1720 hrs: -

'E/A sighted at about 700 feet below on our starboard side, coming in from the Channel, proceeding approximately NNW. We turned south, keeping E/A between us and coast. The weather was very misty and E/A did not see us until we were about one mile away, he then turned and tried to make out to sea. We carried out a stern deflection burst, Red One going in first, and myself, Red Two, following. Red Three was looking out for fighters. I followed Red One in all attacks and during the engagement saw dirty white smoke coming from the engines. After our ammunition was finished I formed up on Red One. Red Three reported that he saw E/A at about 500 feet losing height and dropped his bombs.'

The *Heinkel* was claimed as a shared 'probable'.

Having damaged an Me 109 and shared an He 111 probably destroyed, it was a lucky day for Pilot Officer Reilley – even more so because his son, Chris, was born that day.

Having not flown on the previous two days, at 1450 hrs on 27 September Pilot Officer Reilley was up again with 'B' Flight. At 1500 hrs, nine formations comprising some 160 bombers and fighters in roughly equal numbers crossed the English coast between Dover and Brighton, London bound. At 1520 hrs, Pilot Officer Reilley reported: -

'The Squadron went into line astern and made attacks on Ju 88s and Do 215s. 109s peeled off on our rear section, they were a good 1,000 feet above. Two of the 109s became separated and I was in a position to attack one. I gave him a three second burst while climbing up, just beneath his tail. He staggered but tried to climb steeply, to get out of range. I then climbed and was able to get a deflection shot from just above his cockpit. My burst shattered the whole glass and killed the pilot. The 109 didn't spin but seemed to float down. I did follow him down and saw the plane hit the ground and burst into flames in the wooded area near Wrotham. Some Hurricanes were as usual on the spot where it crashed but definitely did not fire because they weren't close enough, the 109 crashed without their assistance. The Squadron took off at 1450 hrs and landed at 1540 hrs.'

This Me 109 was credited as destroyed, although which enemy casualty this was remains unclear. Hugh Reilley's friend George Corbett had a lucky escape on this sortie, when his Spitfire was hit by AA fire, causing the pilot to make a forced landing near Orpington – fortunately he was unhurt.

Although a number of patrols were flown on 28 and 29 September, it was not until the 30th that 66 Squadron was again in action. On this day,

Spitfire R6800, the usual mount of Squadron Leader Leigh.

four major attacks were launched against targets in East Kent, while, again, the West Country's aircraft factories were assaulted. At 1258 hrs, 66 Squadron was scrambled to intercept the third incoming raid, comprising 180 enemy aircraft which crossed the coast over Lympne at 1310 hrs, heading for London. Pilot Officer Reilley's combat report describes the action as 'Clickety-Click' engaged: -

'The Squadron went into a defensive circle, with a few bombers below and squadrons of escorting fighters above. We engaged several of the E/A fighters and we were mostly split up. I climbed to 27,000 feet and went down to search for any returning aircraft. Eventually I spotted five enemy bombers a good way below. I dove down to attack. There were many enemy fighters a good three – four miles away. The bombers were flying parallel to the coast, NE. The formation was already damaged. Two Me 110s were forming a rear-guard, but they were all very close together.

'I made a quarter attack on a 110. I saw my bullets enter his fuselage but not much damage was done. I manoeuvred into a position and made a head-on attack on the leading Do 215. I was above and managed to smash all the glass canopy, but by this time the 109s were too close for comfort, so I dove down below cloud and landed at 1358 hrs.'

Both the Me 110 and Do 215 were claimed as 'damaged'. Pilot Officer Reilley's combat reports really give a powerful insight into fighter combat – how units scattered once the action began, and how, for the fighter pilot, war was an individual affair: alone and isolated after the first contact, a climb to height and a look-see, then a solo return to the fray – miles above the earth, in the cold, clean, air. This is not from the *Boy's Own Paper* but real life, an authentic glimpse at the violent, traumatic, past.

Bob Morris: -

'By this time, we were finding the living conditions at Gravesend a bit trying. We had half a day off every ten days. We used to spend that half-day fast asleep. We were exhausted working such long hours, from dawn to dusk. At Gravesend there were no billets, so a restaurant about three-quarters of a mile away, called "Laughing Waters", adjacent to a big lake, was commandeered. We were taken there in our usual mode of motorised transport, a Bedford three-tonner. The building was just a shell, nothing on the floor and all we had to sleep in was two blankets. It was a mighty cold place with two blankets on the floor, on the edge of a lake! The only thing not taken away were the rowing boats, so every morning to get warm we rowed around the lake.

'Fortunately, we were not at "Laughing Waters" for very long before our billet was moved to Cobham Hall, the Earl of Darnley's estate. We slept in the servants' quarters, but at least we had beds. We were quite near Cobham village, and it was strange, wherever we were the officers would find a restaurant or similar for their evening drinks while we "Other Ranks" would find a pub. We never went into theirs, and they never in ours. Our entertainment was to walk to Rochester or Strood, to the cinema, then walk back again. We also went to dances at the Co-op Hall in Gravesend.

'During the day, it was long hours, work, work, work, and then more work. Non-stop. At Gravesend we used to watch the German aircraft coming in, heading for London or elsewhere, their trails in the sky, and how relieved we were when they passed overhead and went straight on! During that September, as we were so close to the river, there would often be a ground mist, lasting all day. You could have a day with thick fog in which no aircraft could take off, or no bombing could take place because the Germans could not see us. We used to get all our work done by early afternoon on such days, and then, inevitably, a football always seemed to appear from somewhere and a game would start on the edge of the aerodrome. We never picked a side, you just joined in with whichever side appeared to be winning, and that was the direction you kicked! On one occasion we were busy playing in thick fog – you could only see about half-way across the airfield – when we heard these German aircraft circling round above us, seeking a target. Suddenly, right through the fog, came a parachute flare, which landed on the football pitch – someone kicked some dirt onto it and we just kept on playing – the German then flew off. No-one ran for shelter, that was how used we had become to it all. You never heard anyone talk about defeat.'

And so the hard routine went on, for groundcrews toiling out in the open to keep the 'kites' on 'top line', and the pilots flying multiple daily sorties to counter the high-altitude fighter sweeps – these (as explained in detail in Pilot Officer Whitbread's chapter) could not be ignored owing to the presence within these formations of fighter-bombers. After 30 September, though, the German *kampfgruppen* were unable to continue sustaining such heavy losses, leading to another change of tack. The slower He 111s and Do 17s were largely withdrawn to night-bombing, and indeed the main destructive focus switched to the hours of darkness, given the primitive British nocturnal defences. During daylight, in addition to the fighter and fighter-bomber sweeps, small formations of fast, well-armed, Ju 88s continued to attack targets mainly connected with the British aircraft industry, while lone bombers, usually Ju 88s, made harassing attacks in favourable weather, hidden by cloud. So, while these raids lacked the numbers and ferocity of September, the skies over southern England remained an aerial battlefield as the autumn wore on.

The beginning of October began with poor flying weather, low cloud and reduced visibility, limiting operations. On 4 October the highly competent and popular commander of 'A' Flight, Flight Lieutenant Ken Gillies, was shot down intercepting a lone He 111 over the east coast. Reported missing, as Bob Oxspring commented, 'His loss was a grievous blow; the feeling was, "If Ken 'bought it', what chance have we got?"' Sadly, Gillies did 'buy it', his body being washed ashore at Covehithe on 21 October 1940.

The following day, although Pilot Officer Reilley did not fly, 'B' Flight was again in action, intercepting Me 109s and Ju 88s. A number of enemy aircraft were claimed destroyed, including by Sergeant Ward, in addition to a 'probable'. Pilot Officer Kendal was shot up and slightly injured, as was Pilot Officer 'Bogle' Bodie, who returned to base uninjured; Bob Morris: -

'I remember "Bogle" coming back with his port mainplane knocked about by a cannon shell. I had to rip part of the aileron off, which he took as a souvenir. I always remember a Spitfire returning with a horrible

Another view of R6800 at Gravesend, clearly showing the squadron leader's pennant. It was while flying this aircraft that Pilot Officer Reilley would be shot down and killed on 12 October 1940.

whistling noise – it had a bullet hole right through the propeller blade! We did not have a new propeller, however, so we smoothed out the hole and drilled corresponding holes in the other two blades – the aircraft then flew another fortnight with that same airscrew! We had to drill the other holes because when a propeller is assembled it is finely balanced to prevent vibration.'

Only two sorties were flown owing to the weather on 6 October, the following day seeing 10/10 cloud at 1,500 feet. Both flights patrolled, Me 109s being sighted on one occasion, Pilot Officer Heron getting shot up, but no claims were submitted by the Spitfire pilots. On 8 October, there was little improvement weather-wise, although 'B' Flight was bounced by Me 109s over Upchurch. Hugh Reilley's fellow Canadian, Pilot Officer George Corbett, was flying as wingman to Flight Lieutenant Oxspring, who, blissfully unaware of the surprise attack, glanced at his Number Two only to see his Spitfire suddenly explode in flames. In Oxspring's words, 'George didn't stand a chance and a few days later this gallant Canadian was buried near where he fell.' Later that day, 'A' Flight was also bounced by high-flying Me 109s, losing the 'promising' Sergeant Rufus Ward. Clearly, although the daylight bombing assault had been defeated, the fighter war remained very much ongoing. And so October continued, with variable weather and occasional violent clashes between the Spitfires and 109s high over Kent.

Although unproven, it is likely that Pilot Officer Reilley was another of Major Werner Mölder's victims.

On 17 October, four fighter sweeps intruded over Kent, comprising some 300 German fighters and fighter-bombers. At 1510 hrs, four raids totalling eighty Me 109s headed for East London, Kenley and Biggin Hill. 66 Squadron was scrambled from Gravesend at 1455 hrs to patrol over Maidstone. Flight Lieutenant Oxspring's subsequent report describes events: -

'Throughout the patrol we were warned by Operations that there were enemy fighters about, but all we saw were friendly. It was after we had been to investigate some aircraft we had seen, and which proved to be Spitfires, that I noticed Pilot Officer Reilley, who was Red Four and doing the duties of look-out above the Squadron was no longer with us. I called him up but there was no reply. I also called up Red One, who replied that he had not seen Pilot Officer Reilley for some minutes. The Squadron had landed at 1605 hrs and Pilot Officer Reilley was still missing. I afterwards learned from the Intelligence Officer that he had crashed one mile south of Westerham at approximately 1545 hrs.'

So, what happened to Pilot Officer Reilley?

It is so important to understand just how high the Me 109s were operating, just beneath the stratosphere, high in the rarefied air. From such a vantage point the German fighter pilots watched, the climbing RAF fighters easily espied when silhouetted over white cloud. It is a misconception to think of fighter combat as heroic dogfights, each combatant attempting to outwit and outmanoeuvre his opponent. Such combats, reminiscent of the slower-moving biplanes of the First World War, were comparatively rare in the Second, given the high speeds of the aircraft involved. Instead, it was about ambushing an opponent, a surprise attack – the 'bounce' – by an unseen assailant, who spotted the opportunity, pounced, fired, and away in a high-speed diving attack, called a 'Dirty Dart' by 19 Squadron Battle of Britain survivor Wing Commander David Cox DFC. From German records, it is clear that Pilot Officer Reilley was shot down and killed by none other than Major Werner Mölders – the great German ace, *Kommodore* of JG 51 and the so-called 'Father of Modern Air Fighting' himself. The 'weaver' or 'arse-end Charlie', flying to and fro, alone, to the rear and slightly above the squadron, acting as a look-out, was extremely vulnerable. Repeatedly when studying these aerial combats, the weaver is the first to be picked off, unseen, as in this case, by his peers, who flew on oblivious. So, it is clear what happened: the opportunity was seen and grasped by Germany's leading fighter pilot and leader, who, leaving his formation as top cover, a lone aircraft more likely to achieve a successful, surprise, attack, dropped like a stone, picked off Pilot Officer Reilley – the weaver – and disappeared into the blue, unseen.

Pilot Officer Reilley crashed at 1525 hrs, in Spitfire LZ-N, R6800, the usual mount of his Squadron Commander, Squadron Leader Rupert Leigh, at Crockham Hill, Sevenoaks. The 22-year-old Canadian, a married man with a new-born son, was killed.

Bob Morris: -

'Having lost so many pilots at Kenley, replacements arrived at Gravesend, although several of these were also killed. Amongst them was one I had got to know quite well, Pilot Officer Hugh Reilley. By this time, however, we were quite accustomed to losses, it sounds terrible to say now but I think you can get used to anything. I remember I was on my half day, fast asleep on my bed at Cobham Hall, as we usually were on our half days off, when the Sergeant stuck his head round the door and said "Everybody on Half Day – outside, best blue, best greatcoat, webbing belt round your waist and get in the lorry!" He did not tell us what for, but we got dressed and piled onto the lorry, which took us to the church near Gravesend. It was then we realised that we were going to be the guard of honour at Pilot Officer Reilley's funeral. We sat in the church for the service. A four-wheeled trailer was hitched up to our truck, and the coffin was placed on this trailer, which we marched behind, through the middle of Gravesend to the cemetery, where the burial took place.'

Group Captain Bob Oxspring: -

'Our favourite pub was the "Leather Bottle" at Cobham, the regulars of which were largely dockers from Chatham. They were very generous and adopted 66 as 'their' squadron. When Hugh Reilley was buried, they and their families turned out in large numbers, lining the route through Gravesend, paying their respects as the cortege passed.'

Bob Morris: -

'On the way back, someone mentioned that Pilot Officer Reilley had got married and his wife had recently given birth to a little boy. In 1983, I attended a 66 Squadron reunion at Kenley, there meeting a family-man in his forties – Reilley's son!'

Naturally proud that his father was one of the Few, Chris Reilley, however, has understandably been frustrated by persistent inaccurate references claiming that Hugh was an American, risking prosecution by the neutral

Above: Pilot Officer Reilley's medals, including the Canadian Memorial Cross issued by the Canadian government. (Chris Reilley)

Right: The memorial on the site of Gravesend airfield commemorating those killed flying from there in the 'Finest Hour' – including Pilot Officer Reilley. (Chris Reilley)

Chris Reilley with his father's grave at Gravesend Cemetery. (Chris Reilley)

US government for volunteering to fight for Britain. Indeed, this mistaken belief was even shared by 66 Squadron survivors, no doubt arising because although Hugh was born in Canada, the family lived at that time in Detroit. The fact is, as proven by Hugh William Reilley's Birth Certificate, Chris' father was, in fact, a Canadian.

Conducting his own research into his father's RAF service, in 1979, Group Captain Oxspring wrote to Chris: -

'They were hectic days, and gallant chaps came and "bought it" so quickly – largely because of grossly inadequate flying experience.

'Because of casualties in September 1940, I became commander of "B" Flight on 14 September, and your father was one of my pilots. He always wore a white pair of flying overalls, which our Squadron did pre-war. Mine were worn out and of course before Dunkirk the RAF had been told to wear uniform for combat in case we were taken POW… in any event white overalls were purchased individually by pilots and were never RAF issue… I only knew him for four weeks, tragic, but a week seemed like a year then.'

PILOT OFFICER HUGH WILLIAM REILLEY (CANADIAN)

Wing Commander 'Dizzy' Allen also wrote, in 1981: -

'He was with 66 Squadron for such a short time, we were losing a lot of pilots – shadowy figures came and vanished, so to speak. Now what I can tell you is that his Dad was Canadian, he joined 64 Squadron early in September 1940, did not stay with them long before he was posted to 66. More than likely 64 was resting up north while we were running out of pilots in the front line, so they sent him to us as reinforcement. He could not have gained much experience of combat when placed in the hot seat, but we had to accept what you might call "rookies" and hope to God they could cope. He always wore white flying overalls which I had made up – so it would be fair to suggest that he wasn't prepared to conform any more than I was. He was mousey blond with crinkled hair, and left his mark – why should I remember? There must have been thirty pilots with us for short periods before they were shot down… He joined us on the big day, 15 September 1940, but I am sure we would not have ordered him into the air on that day. Without much question, he would have been detailed to fly in the Squadron formation a day or so later… he was posted as killed in action on 17 October 1940. How that happened, I simply do not know. We used to call him by his Christian or nick-name, I seem to remember we called him "Pat".'

Pilot Officer Hugh Reilley's story is sadly typical of so many young replacement pilots, provided an unexpected opportunity to fly through the RAF's Expansion Plan, and in this case the SSC route. His early combat success marked him as a potentially excellent fighter pilot – a surprising number of pilots never made a combat claim. This story also emphasises the contribution made by pilots from the Commonwealth and Dominions, who had travelled to England by various means to fight with the RAF in a desperate hour of need.

Today, Pilot Officer Reilley's grave can be found at Gravesend Cemetery, his name recorded on the memorial plaque at Gravesend Sports Ground commemorating those who lost their lives flying from there during the Battle of Britain. For some, including Pilot Officer Hugh William Reilley, Gravesend was a very long way from home.

Epilogue

Over the years, history's emphasis has been on the Battle of Britain's survivors, especially, of course, the Few, those august members of the Battle of Britain Fighter Association. This has made possible a rich legacy of recorded memories. At the time of writing only six of the Few remain alive, all over 100 years old. One day all will be gone, and with them our first-hand link with the past. This dictates that the time has come for historians to shift our focus. What we now need to increasingly explore are the stories of casualties – and not just those suffered by the Few. As indicated by some of the stories in this book, others also served – the emergency services, for example, come readily to mind – and what about Bomber Command's losses during our 'Finest Hour'? Examples of all, ideally, must be researched, recorded and shared. Who were these people? What were their backgrounds and experience before untimely death? Who was left behind? What did they look like? All of these questions and more require answers, and there is no shortage of potential subjects. This is really 'hidden history', history not considered through the usual 'top down' lens of politicians and great leaders, or even war heroes, but from the bottom up, frequently concerning the anonymous masses, or in other words the 'also rans', as 19-year-old Battle of Britain Hurricane pilot Peter Fox famously described himself and friends. That said, the stories of successful fighter pilots can also be found in this book, so it is really about a collective whole.

In my opinion and experience, there is a much greater awareness of the Battle of Britain today than, say, thirty years ago. Indeed, the 'Finest Hour' has become a great source of pride and fundamental to Britain's national identity. This raised awareness, I have no doubt, owes much to the comparatively recent phenomenon of social media. In tangible terms, the superb National Battle of Britain Memorial, on the cliffs near Folkestone, provides a fitting and dignified focal point for remembrance and education. Nearby, at Hawkinge, is the world-famous and unique Kent Battle of Britain Museum, at which, amongst other things, the remains of over 700 aircraft

Above: The debt we owe: Cross of Sacrifice at Hawkinge Cemetery – wherein the graves of a number of the Few can be found.

Right: Sergeant Peter Fox of 56 Squadron, who famously and self-effacingly described himself and peers as 'also-rans'.

Above: The National Battle of Britain Memorial at Capel le Ferne, near Folkestone – with the Wing education and visitor centre behind, opened by HM the Queen in 2015.

Below: The National Memorial, maintained by the Battle of Britain Memorial Trust, overlooks the Channel and 'Hellfire Corner'.

Above: The National Memorial site includes the Sir Christopher Foxley-Norris Wall, recording the names of the Few, and a moving poem by Battle of Britain Spitfire pilot William Walker.

Below: Once Fighter Command's HQ in the Battle of Britain, now luxury apartments, Bentley Priory also hosts an excellent museum dedicated to the Few.

destroyed in the Battle of Britain can be seen. At Bentley Priory, once Fighter Command's HQ, a superb museum now exists, firmly focussed on the human experience. The Imperial War Museum Duxford, of course, provides the opportunity to see Spitfires, Hurricanes and other 'warbirds' fly.

Above: The Kent Battle of Britain Museum is a must-visit location, where the remains of over 700 aircraft destroyed during the Battle can be seen – and much else besides. (Kent Battle of Britain Museum)

Left: William Walker: a Spitfire pilot who survived the 'Finest Hour' – and to whom goes the last word in this book.

Indeed, given the number of companies now restoring or completely rebuilding these vintage aircraft, there is no shortage of opportunities to see these wonderful machines in flight. The Battle of Britain Bunker at Uxbridge, from where Air Vice-Marshal Park controlled 11 Group during the Battle, has recently been refurbished to provide a quality visitor experience. There are many more places, on and off the beaten track, where the Battle of Britain can still almost be touched, whether a polished museum or forgotten field in rural Kent where once an aircraft crashed. A closer, perhaps even spiritual, connection, can be experienced in the many churchyards and cemeteries in which the 'Finest Hour's' casualties can be found – and, of course, at the imposing memorial to the many missing at Runnymede.

The reason why it is so important to remember the Battle of Britain are the stories in this book, the casualties concerned representative of all who perished in the 'Finest Hour' – including *Oberleutnant* Siegfried Stronk, a German Me 109 pilot whose loss was as devastating to his family as any others, regardless of sides. There remains an infinite amount of research still to be done, to discover and collate as much information as possible on the lives and times of our 'Finest Hours' lost souls. For me personally, I very much doubt that quest will ever end.

The concluding word I give to my old friend, the sadly now late Flight Lieutenant William Walker (1913-2012), who flew Spitfires with 616 'South Yorkshire' Squadron during the Battle of Britain: -

'Looking back to the time when so many of us had such high hopes and felt invulnerable, it is terribly sad that some would not survive a year, would never see the enemy who killed them, all their hard work and training pointless. While they are just casualties of war in the records, they are a reminder to me of many happy days of friendship that are well-worth recalling and should be remembered. They were the most exhilarating days – but one lost so many friends who were all so young.'

Bibliography

The following primary sources are available for inspection at the National Archives: -

Operations Record Books

54 Squadron	AIR27/511
65 Squadron	AIR27/592
66 Squadron	AIR27/598
87 Squadron	AIR27/12
149 Squadron	AIR27/1000
151 Squadron	AIR27/1018
249 Squadron	AIR27/1498
264 Squadron	AIR27/1553
601 Squadron	AIR27/2068
603 Squadron	AIR27/2079
605 Squadron	AIR27/2088
609 Squadron	AIR27/2102
610 Squadron	AIR27/2106
615 Squadron	AIR27/2123
5 OTU	AIR27/682
4 FPP	AIR29/458
RAF Biggin Hill	AIR28/64
RAF Exeter	AIR28/261
RAF Kemble	AIR28/418

Combat Reports

54 Squadron	AIR50/21
65 Squadron	AIR50/25

66 Squadron	AIR50/26
87 Squadron	AIR50/37
151 Squadron	AIR50/63
264 Squadron	AIR50/104
601 Squadron	AIR50/165
603 Squadron	AIR50/167
609 Squadron	AIR50/1771
615 Squadron	AIR50/175

Casualty Packs

Pilot Officer A Bird	AIR81/2452
Pilot Officer PC Cardell	AIR81/3461
Sergeant GR Collett	AIR81/2721
Flying Officer RS Demetriadi	AIR81/1320
Wing Commander JS Dewar	AIR81/3230
Pilot Officer WML Fiske	AIR81/1473
Pilot Officer HI Goodall	AIR81/3702
Flying Officer F Gruszka	AIR81/2628
Pilot Officer JR Hamar	AIR81/2446
Sergeant PS Hayes	AIR81/1037
Flying Officer PJC King	AIR81/3091
Pilot Oficer MA King	AIR81/1442
Pilot Officer RFG Miller	AIR81/3460
Pilot Officer HW Reilley	AIR81/3822
Flight Lieutenant WH Rhodes-Moorhouse	AIR81/3117
Sergeant Observer RBM Young	AIR81/3702
Personnel casualties, RAF Driffield, 15 August 1940	AIR81/1428

Many documents can now be downloaded online from the National Archives: -

nationalarchives.gov.uk

Published Sources

'AHE', 'Cranwell and its Traditions', *Journal of the Royal Air Force College* (1930), pp. 12-15

Allen, Squadron Leader H.R., & Forbes, Wing Commander A (Eds), *Ten Fighter Boys*, Collins, London, 1942

Allen, Wing Commander H.R., *Fighter Squadron: A Memoir, 1940-42*, Kimber, London, 1979

Anon, *The Rise & Fall of the German Air Force (1933 to 1945)*, Air Ministry Pamphlet No 248, Issued by the Air Ministry (ACAS [I]), 1948

Anon, *The Second World War, RAF 1939-45, Flying Training, Volume One, Policy & Planning*, MLRS Books, Smalldale, 2009

Bekker, C., *The Luftwaffe War Diaries*, Corgi, London, 1972

Bissell, A., *Southampton's Children of the Blitz*, Centenar Publishing, Bournemouth, 2010

Branson, N., & Heinemann, M., *Britain in the Nineteen Thirties*, Weidenfeld & Nicolson, London, 1971

Calder, A., *The People's War: Britain 1939-45*, Pimlico, London, 1992

Caldwell, D., *The JG26 War Diary, Volume One 1939-42*, Grub Street, London, 1996

Clapson, M., *The Routledge Companion to the Twentieth Century*, Routledge, London, 2009

Cluett, D., Bogle, J., & Learmonth, B., *Croydon Airport and the Battle for Britain 1939-40*, Sutton Libraries & Arts Services, Sutton, 1984

Cornwell, P.D., *The Battle of France: Then & Now: Six Nations Locked in Aerial Combat September 1939 to June 1940*, Battle of Britain International Ltd, Harlow, 2007

Cornwell, P.D., & Vasco, J., *Zerstörer: The Messerschmitt 110 & its Units in 1940*, JAC Publications, Norwich, 1995

Crook, Flight Lieutenant D.M.C., *Spitfire Pilot*, Faber, 1942

Cull, B., *First of the Few: 5 June – 9 July 1940*, Fonthill Media, Stroud, 2013

Cull, B., *Battle for the Channel: The First Month of the Battle of Britain 10 July – 10 August 1940*, Fonthill Media, Stroud, 2017

Dean, Sir M., *The Royal Air Force & Two World Wars*, Cassell, London, 1979

Dempster, D., & Wood, D., *The Narrow Margin: The Battle of Britain*, Arrow, London, 1969

Donnolly, M., *Britain in the Second World War*, Routledge, London, 1999

Elderton, Sir W., 'Merchant seamen during the war', *Institute of Actuaries*, 1946.

Foreman, J., *RAF Fighter Command Victory Claims of World War Two*, Red Kite, Walton-on-Thames, 2003

Franks, N., *Air Battle for Dunkirk: 26 May – 3 June 1940*, Grub Street, 2006

Galland A., *The First and the Last: Germany's Fighter Force in the Second World War*, Cerberus Publishing, Bristol, 2001 (first published 1954)

Gilbert, M., *The Second World War: A Complete History*, Phoenix, London, 2009

Gleed, Wing Commander I.R., *Arise to Conquer*, Grub Street, 2010

Graves, R., and Hodge, A., *The Long Weekend: A Social History of Britain 1918-1939*, Hutchinson & Co, 1985

Gregg, P., *A Social & Economic History of Britain 1760-1980*, Harrap, 1982

Honeysett, J., *Death in the Afternoon: The Bombing of Vickers Supermarine Works, Southampton, 15th, 24th and 26th September 1940*, Hamble Village Press, Southampton, date unknown

James, J., *The Paladins: A Social History of the RAF up to the Outbreak of World War 2*, Futura, 1990

James, T.C.G., *The Battle of Britain* (RAF Official History), Frank Cass, 2000

Jefford, J., 'Aircrew Status in the 1940s', *Royal Air Force Historical Society Journal*, No 42, 2008, pp. 57-93

Kemp, A., *Southampton At War 1939-45*, Ensign Publications, Southampton, 1989

Lisiewicz, Squadron Leader M. (Ed), *Destiny Can Wait: The Polish Air Force in the Second World War*, William Heinemann, London, 1949

Mason, F., *Battle Over Britain*, Aston Publications, Bourne End, 1989

Mason, P.D., *Nicolson VC: The Life and Times of James Brindley Nicolson VC DFC RAF*, Geerings, Ashford, 1991

Morgan, E.B., & Shacklady, E., *Spitfire: The History*, Key Publishing, Stamford, 1987

Moulson, T., *The Millionaires' Squadron: The Remarkable Story of 601 Squadron and the Flying Sword*, Pen & Sword, 2014

Mowatt, C.L., *Britain Between the Wars 1918 – 1940*, Methuen, 1955

Mulvagh, J., *Madresfield: The Real Brideshead*, Doubleday, 2008

Neil, Wing Commander T.F., *Gun Button to 'Fire'*, Kimber, London, 1987

Orange, V., *Park: The Biography of Air Chief Marshal Sir Keith Park*, Grub Street, 2001

Orange, V., *Dowding of Fighter Command: Victor of the Battle of Britai*n, Grub Street, 2008

Overy, R.J., *The Air War 1939-1945*, Europa, London, 1980

Overy, R.J., *The Battle of Britain*, Penguin, London, 2004

Oxspring, Group Captain R.W., *Spitfire Command*, Kimber, London, 1984

Peake, Dame F., *Pure Chance*, Airlife, Shrewsbury, 1993

Pope, R., *War & Society in Britain: 1899-1948*, Longman, London, 1991

Price, Dr A., *Battle of Britain: The Hardest Day, 18 August 1940*, MacDonald & Jane's, London, 1979

Prien, J., *Jagdgeschwader 53: A History of the 'Pik As' Geschwader, Volume 1, March 1937 – May 1942*, Schiffer, Pennsylvania, 2004

Priestley, J.B., *English Journey*, Victor Gollancz, London, 1934

Pugh, M., *We Danced All Night: A Social History of Britain Between the Wars*, Bodley Head, London, 2008

Quill, J.K., *Spitfire: A Test Pilot's Story*, John Murray, 1983

Ramsey, W.G. (Ed), *The Blitz: Then & Now, Vols I and II*, Battle of Britain Prints International, London, 1987/8

Ramsey, W.G. (Ed), *The Battle of Britain: Then & Now, Mk V*, Battle of Britain Prints International, London, 1989

Rhodes-Moorhouse, L., *Kaleidoscope 1886 to 1960: The Story of a Family in Peace and War*, Arthur Barker, London, 1960

Robinson, A., *RAF Fighter Squadrons in the Battle of Britain*, Arms & Armour, London, 1987

Russell, C.R., *Spitfire Odyssey: My Life at Supermarines 1936-1957*, Kingfisher Railway Productions, Southampton, 1985

Sarkar, D., *Through Peril to the Stars*, Ramrod, Malvern, 1993

Sarkar, D., *A Few of the Many: Air War 1939-45, A Kaleidoscope of Memories*, Ramrod, Worcester, 1995

Sarkar, D., *Spitfire! Courage & Sacrifice*, Victory, Worcester, 2006

Sarkar, D., *The Few: The Story of the Battle of Britain in the Words of the Pilots*, Amberley Publishing, Stroud, 2009

Scatliff, C., *Gentleman Warrior: The Life of Wing Commander John Scatliff Dewar DSO DFC*, privately published, Ontario, Canada, 2001

Stevenson, J., *British Society 1914-45*, Penguin, London, 1984

Wakefield, K., *Luftwaffe Encore*, Kimber, London, 1979

Waugh, E., *Brideshead Revisited: The Sacred & Profane Memories of Captain Charles Ryder*, Chapman & Hall, London, 1945

Wells, M.K., *Courage in Air Warfare: The Allied Aircrew Experience in the Second World War*, Frank Cass, London, 1995

Willis, J., *Churchill's Few*, Guild Publishing, London, 1985

Wright, R., *Dowding and the Battle of Britain*, Corgi, London, 1970

Wynn, K.G., *Men of the Battle of Britain: A Biographical Directory of the Few*, Frontline Books, Barnsley, in association with the Battle of Britain Memorial Trust, 2015

Ziegler, F.H., *The Story of 609 Squadron: Under the White Rose*, MacDonald, London, 1971

Documentaries

Willis, J., *Churchill's Few*, Yorkshire Television, 1985

Websites

Battle of Britain Memorial Trust: battleofbritainmemorial.org
Battle of Britain Monument: bbm.org.uk
Kent Battle of Britain Museum: kbobm.org
The Supermariners: supermariners.wordpress.com
Greeks in Foreign Cockpits: greeks-in-foreign-cockpits.com

Acknowledgements

Certain stories in this book were researched some years ago, the following members of the Battle of Britain Fighter Association having kindly contributed to that process; sadly, all are now deceased: -

Air Vice-Marshal F.D.S. Scott-Malden CB DSO DFC
Air Commodore E.M. Donaldson CBE DSO DFC
Group Captain G.L. Denholm DFC
Group Captain G.A.L. Manton DSO DFC
Group Captain R.W. Oxspring DFC
Wing Commander H.R. Allen DFC
Wing Commander C.F. Currant DSO DFC
Wing Commander R.W. Foster DFC
Wing Commander N.P.W. Hancock OBE DFC
Wing Commander F.W. Higginson OBE DFC
Squadron Leader B.H. Drobinski VM KW DFC
Squadron Leader E.D. Glaser DFC
Squadron Leader J. Stokoe DFC
Lieutenant Commander J.K. Quill OBE AFC FRAeS

Also: -

Mr Bob Morris, Fitter IIE, 66 Squadron

The help and support of the following relatives of casualties whose stories appear in this book has been invaluable (in no particular order), many of whom were traced by my genealogist friend Michelle Baverstock: -

Chris Reilley; Paul & Judy Miller; Carey Parkinson; the late Dorothy & Dennis Hessling; Ruth & Geoff Cornes; Andrew & Peter Dewar; the late

ACKNOWLEDGEMENTS

Fred & Enid Hamar; Paul Weaver; Piotr Gruszka & Barbara Sykes; Mandy Brown, Charlotte Walsh & Michael Sturdee; Jim Nicolson; the late Marjorie Whittaker; Kevan Hulcoop & Michelle Jarvis; Bill & John Gulland; Steve Collett; Michael Taylor; the late Mary Cooper; Brian Sedgwick & Linda Bell; Tessa & Michael Haughton; Rupert Ryle-Hodges; William Cavendish; Julian Spragg; Professor Dr Detlef Stronk & Florian Stronk.

I am most grateful to the Venerable Ray Pentland, Chaplain to the Battle of Britain Fighter Association, and Group Captain Patrick Tootal OBE of the Battle of Britain Memorial Trust for supporting the project and providing the book's foreword. I am also grateful to the Trust's Wing Commander Andy Simpson and Major (Ret'd) Jules Gomez, Site Manager, Battle of Britain National Memorial.

I must also thank the following friends who have all contributed in some essential way: -

Andy Long; Dave Brocklehurst MBE, Kent Battle of Britain Museum; Richard Pearson, Archivist, & King Edward VI School, Stratford-upon-Avon; Dave Baverstock; Glenn Gelder; Peter Dove; Geoff Simpson; Sam Styles; Stephanie Hume, Australian War Memorial; David Abbott; Marion Clayton-Wright; Paul Heys; Allan White; Edward McManus of the Battle of Britain Monument; Andy Jones, Solent Sky Museum; Richard Hutchinson; Ken Back; Thomas Games and Donna Davies; Dave Key; John Honeysett; David Evans & Rita Radford; John Nelson; Mark Gregory; Patricia Driver & Martin Driver; Colin Brown; Marcel Boven; Paul Neelissen; Hannah Sarkar; Anne & Howard Wilton; Debbie Coulson & Peter Dalkin, both of the RAAFA (Tasmanian Division); Dave Key of the 'Supermariners'; W.B. Rhodes-Moorhouse VC Charitable Trust; Nick Hector; Dimitrios Vassilopoulos of 'Greeks in Foreign Cockpits'; Darren Priday, RAF Museum; James Sarkar; Will Matley; Joel Diggle; Philip Harvey; Kev Barnes and the Commonwealth War Graves Commission.

As always, Martin Mace and team at Pen & Sword made production of this book a seamless experience.

Other books by Dilip Sarkar

(in order of publication)

Spitfire Squadron: No 19 Squadron at War, 1939-41
The Invisible Thread: A Spitfire's Tale
Through Peril to the Stars: RAF Fighter Pilots Who Failed to Return, 1939-45
Angriff *Westland: Three Battle of Britain Air Raids Through the Looking Glass*
A Few of the Many: Air War 1939-45, A Kaleidoscope of Memories
Bader's Tangmere Spitfires: The Untold Story, 1941
Bader's Duxford Fighters: The Big Wing Controversy
Missing in Action: Resting in Peace?
Guards VC: Blitzkrieg 1940
Battle of Britain: The Photographic Kaleidoscope, Volumes I-IV
Fighter Pilot: The Photographic Kaleidoscope
Group Captain Sir Douglas Bader: An Inspiration in Photographs
Johnnie Johnson: Spitfire Top Gun, Parts I&II
Battle of Britain: Last Look Back
Spitfire! Courage & Sacrifice
Spitfire Voices: Heroes Remember
The Battle of Powick Bridge: Ambush a Fore-thought
Duxford 1940: A Battle of Britain Base at War
The Few: The Battle of Britain in the Words of the Pilots
Spitfire Manual 1940
The Last of the Few: Eighteen Battle of Britain Pilots Tell their Extraordinary Stories
Hearts of Oak: The Human Tragedy of HMS Royal Oak
Spitfire Voices: Life as a Spitfire Pilot in the Words of the Veterans
How the Spitfire Won the Battle of Britain
Spitfire Ace of Aces: The True Wartime Story of Johnnie Johnson
Douglas Bader
Spitfire: The Photographic Biography

OTHER BOOKS BY DILIP SARKAR

Hurricane Manual 1940
River Pike
The Final Few: The Last Surviving Pilots of the Battle of Britain tell their Stories
Arnhem 1944: The Human Tragedy of the Bridge Too Far
Spitfire! The Full Story of a Unique Battle of Britain Fighter Squadron
Battle of Britain 1940: The Finest Hour's Human Cost
Letters from The Few: Unique Memories of the Battle of Britain
Johnnie Johnson's 1942 Diary: The War Diary of the Spitfire Ace of Aces
Johnnie Johnson's Great Adventure: The Spitfire Ace of Ace's Last Look Back
Sailor Malan - Freedom Fighter: The Inspirational Story of a Spitfire Ace
Spitfire Ace of Aces – The Album: The Photographs of Johnnie Johnson
The Real Spitfire Pilot
The Real Hurricane Pilot
Bader's Big Wing Controversy: Duxford 1940.
Bader's Spitfire Wing: Tangmere 1941
Spitfire Down
Forgotten Heroes of The Battle of Britain
Faces of The Few
Spitfire Faces
Arise to Conquer: The Real Hurricane Pilot (introduction, commentary and photographs supplied to a new edition of Wing Commander IR Gleed DSO DFC's wartime memoir)
Free French Spitfire Hero: The Diaries of and Search for René Mouchotte (with Jan Leeming)
Battle of Britain: The Finest Hour in Cinema
Battle of Britain: The Movie (contributor to and publisher of the now late Robert Rudhall's original edition (2000), and editor and substantial contributor to 2022 revised edition)
Faces of HMS Royal Oak: The 'Mighty Oak' Disaster at Scapa Flow
Battle of Britain Volume 1: The Gathering Storm: Prelude to the Spitfire Summer of 1940
Battle of Britain Volume 2: The Breaking Storm, 10 July 1940 - 12 August 1940

Index